JOURNAL FOR THE STUDY OF THE OLD TESTAMENT
SUPPLEMENT SERIES
126

Editors
David J.A. Clines
Philip R. Davies

JSOT Press
Sheffield

De Wette 1843

W.M.L. de Wette
Founder of Modern
Biblical Criticism

An Intellectual Biography

John W. Rogerson

Journal for the Study of the Old Testament
Supplement Series 126

Copyright © 1992 Sheffield Academic Press

Published by JSOT Press
JSOT Press is an imprint of
Sheffield Academic Press Ltd
The University of Sheffield
343 Fulwood Road
Sheffield S10 3BP
England

Typeset by Sheffield Academic Press
and
Printed on acid-free paper in Great Britain
by Billing & Sons Ltd
Worcester

British Library Cataloguing in Publication Data

Rogerson, John W., *1935-*
  W.M.L. de Wette, founder of modern Biblical
  criticism: an intellectual biography.
  I. Title
  220.6092

ISBN 1-85075-330-X

CONTENTS

ABBREVIATIONS

AEWK	*Allgemeine Enzyklopädie der Wissenschaften und Künste* (ed. J.S. Ersch and J.G.Gruber, Leipzig 1818–1889)
AKZ	*Allgemeine Kirchen-Zeitung*
ASZ	*Allgemeine Schul-Zeitung* (Darmstadt)
AZ	*Allgemeine Zeitung* (Augsburg)
BMFG	*Baseler Mittheilung zur Förderung des Gemeinwohls*
BZ	*Baseler Zeitung*
HJL	*Heidelbergerische Jahrbücher der Litteratur*
JALZ	*Jenaer Allgemeine Literatur-Zeitung*
JLKLM	*Journal für Literatur, Kunst, Luxus und Mode* (Weimar)
KRS	*Kirchenblatt für die reformierte Schweiz*
NV	*Nouvelliste vaudrois*
NZZ	*Neue Züricher Zeitung*
OJABTUL	*Ostergabe oder Jahrbuch häuslicher Andacht und frommer Betrachtung über Tod, Unsterblichkeit, ewiges Leben und Wiedersehen*
TRE	*Theologische Realenzyklopädie*
TSK	*Theologische Studien und Kritiken*
TZ	*Theologische Zeitschrift* (ed. W.M.L. de Wette, F. Lücke, F. Schleiermacher; Berlin)
WZ	*Wissenschaftliche Zeitschrift* (ed. lecturers in the University of Basel)
ZPW	*Zeitschrift für Predigerwissenschaft* (Karlsruhe)

PREFACE

'He has not yet found a worthy biographer'.[1] It will be for readers to judge whether K.R. Hagenbach's words, written in 1860, are still true once they have finished perusing the work that is now offered. However, they are not quoted in order to be confirmed or denied, but to draw attention to the curious fact that it has taken over 140 years since de Wette's death for someone to try to write a biography. A further curious fact is that the writer is an Englishman, and that there are, and have been, scholars much better equipped than him to undertake this task.

It is surprising that Hagenbach himself did not write a de Wette biography, and it is to be regretted that he did not do so. He was de Wette's colleague in Basel for over twenty-five years, knew de Wette's son and daughter, would have had access to letters that have since been lost, and was a church historian of some distinction.[2] Another scholar who could have written a biography was the Basel church historian Ernst Staehelin. Indeed, Staehelin did a great deal of preparatory work, including obtaining photocopies of all the letters of de Wette that were known to exist in the 1950s. He thus supplemented the rather meagre de Wette archive in Basel immeasurably, and in his *Dewettiana* and 'Kleine Dewettiana' provided an indispensable resource for anyone attempting a biography.[3]

1. K.R. Hagenbach, *Die theologische Schule Basels und ihre Lehrer von Stiftung der Hochschule 1460 bis zu de Wette's Tod 1849* (Basel, 1860), p. 57. (I should point out that the original German spellings have been retained throughout this book.)

2. We do, of course, have two important works by Hagenbach on de Wette: the funeral address (*Rede bei der Beerdigung des Herrn W.M.L. de Wette* [Basel, 1849]) and the academic memorial address (*Wilhelm Martin Leberecht de Wette: eine akademische Gedächtnisrede* [Leipzig, 1850]).

3. E. Staehelin, *Dewettiana: Forschungen und Texte zu Wilhelm Martin Leberecht de Wettes Leben und Werk* (Studien zur Geschichte der Wissenschaften in Basel, 2; Basel: Helbing & Lichtenhahn, 1956); 'Kleine Dewettiana', *TZ* (1957), pp. 33ff.

At this point it should be mentioned that, in 1879, Adelbert Wiegand published a work of just over 100 pages to mark the centenary of de Wette's birth in 1780.[1] Wiegand certainly cannot lay claim to Hagenbach's title of a worthy biographer. Although Wiegand was able to use some 400 letters in the possession of de Wette's daughter together with letters of de Wette to his friend and publisher Georg Reimer, all of which are now lost, he produced an account of de Wette's life which I have called a well-intentioned caricature. Wiegand deliberately misquoted from letters, wilfully used material from later periods in de Wette's life to refer to earlier periods, and produced a portrait of de Wette as a Christian believer that made him more pietist and orthodox than was actually the case. Yet Wiegand is sometimes our only source of information for some of the details of de Wette's life, and to that extent is indispensable.

A third scholar better suited than the present writer to producing a de Wette biography is Rudolf Smend. Indeed, Smend's brilliant and irreplaceable book on de Wette's work as an Old and New Testament scholar created a great impression on me when I read it over twenty years ago, and when I first met Professor Smend he told me that he hoped to write a biography of de Wette, but not until 1999.[2] Following our first meeting, he not only generously encouraged me to write the biography instead of him, but backed this up with gifts of de Wette material without which it would have been impossible for me to write the book in England. Further, he has done me the honour of reading the manuscript and of saving me from making a number of mistakes. I wish to record my deepest gratitude to him and to Frau Smend for the many kindnesses that I have received from them.

Writing the book in England, with various sorties to Germany and Switzerland that I shall mention below, has made me aware of many inadequacies in my preparation. I have not, for example, been able to immerse myself in the German and Swiss press of the period, so as to be better informed of the context of de Wette's life. Together with inadequate preparation I am also aware of inadequate coverage; but

---

1.   A. Wiegand, *W.M.L. de Wette 1780–1849: Eine Säkularschrift* (Erfurt, 1879).
2.   R. Smend, *Wilhelm Martin Leberecht de Wettes Arbeit am Alten und am Neuen Testament* (Basel: Helbing & Lichtenhahn, 1958). If I have not constantly referred to this work in the footnotes it is because this is a work that is an interpretation of de Wette in its own right and not to be regarded simply as secondary literature.

this latter has been by way of strategic choice. It has become clear to me that I could have written three times as much as I have done. A whole book could be written on de Wette's dismissal from Berlin and its aftermath, and another could be written on him as novelist, poet and writer on aesthetics. Yet another could study de Wette in relation to Schleiermacher. Smend has already written the definitive work on de Wette as biblical scholar. My aim has thus been the limited one (in spite of the book's length) of presenting his life and work with particular reference to his theological development. This is not to say, however, that there is nothing about de Wette as a biblical scholar. There is indeed much on this theme, but it is written from a different perspective compared with Smend's book and does not attempt, for example, to deal with de Wette's many reviews. This is therefore not a comprehensively definitive biography, and I would hope that it will stimulate further studies of de Wette rather than suggest that the subject has been exhausted.

I began work in earnest on the biography during a period of study leave in Basel in 1985, and wish to express my gratitude to the University Library for its help on that occasion as well as in 1986. My stay in Basel produced a number of friendships, chief of which was with Frau Erika Wegmann with whom I lodged on several occasions. Frau Wegmann belonged to the Basel Mission, and thus it was good to have a link with that foundation which played a somewhat ambiguous role in de Wette's life during his Basel period. I was also able to become a temporary member of the Christkatholische (Old Catholic) congregation in Basel, and wish to express my gratitude to Pfarrer (now Bishop) Hans Gerny. De Wette was a great traveller in Switzerland and elsewhere, and I wish to record my gratitude to my wife Rosalind for being willing to accompany me on obscure journeys by public transport to such places as Seengen, Gais and the Klausenpass simply because de Wette had at some time visited them.

Other libraries to which I wish to express my gratitude are the Staatsarchiv Basel, the Niedersächsische Landes- und Universitätsbibliothek in Göttingen, the Staatsbibliothek Preussischer Kulturbesitz in (West) Berlin, the Schleswig-Holsteinische Landesbibliothek in Kiel, the Zentralbibliothek Zürich, the Nationale Forschungs- und Gedenkstätten der klassischen deutschen Literatur in Weimar, Goethe- und Schiller-Archiv und das Staatsarchiv Weimar. In addition, the inter-library loan section of the Sheffield University library dealt with obscure requests with great courtesy, and I made a number of visits to the British Library in London. For almost all of the time that I was doing my research and writing, access to libraries in the former East Germany was impossible and there may be scope for de Wette research in the future in the university libraries in Jena and in (East) Berlin, as well as the central archives of the former German Democratic Republic in Merseburg.

Individuals who have helped with providing material include my colleague David Clines, John Hayes of Atlanta and Pfarrer Jürgen Thiede. I am also grateful to Birgit Mänz and her mother, Frau G. Mänz, for help in deciphering some of the de Wette letters. De Wette's handwriting, in old German script, is often quite difficult to read and I have spent more hours than I care to count pouring over many photocopies.

My final thanks must go to de Wette himself. I first came across him over twenty years ago when researching for my book *Myth in Old Testament Interpretation*, and was struck by the originality of his views and his interest in aesthetics. Studying him has taken me into many areas of enquiry that I would not otherwise have pursued. Also, I have done a lot of travelling in his footsteps to delightful parts of Germany and Switzerland. Although I cannot accept many of his views, I have been challenged by his honesty, moved by his personal tragedies and greatly enlightened by his works. I hope that readers will have the same experience, and above all that they will be challenged by de Wette's belief that biblical studies and theology must be related to every aspect of human life.

J.W. Rogerson
Sheffield, January 1991

Chapter 1

THE HIDDEN YEARS

On 31 May 1847 a torchlight procession, the like of which had not been seen for many years, ended the celebrations in Basel which honoured twenty-five years of work as a professor of theology by Wilhelm Martin Leberecht de Wette.[1] Basel owed much to de Wette. His arrival in 1822 had rejuvenated the Theological Faculty and had given it an international reputation. He had reorganized the syllabus and teaching, and had ensured the appointment of young scholars of promise. He had given extra-mural lectures to large audiences. In the troubles of 1831–34, when the civil war between Basel-Land and Basel-Stadt left the city with the sole responsibility for maintaining the university, de Wette issued a noble—and successful—call to the city to put the university at the top of its financial priorities. He had been prominent in church and public affairs in Basel, and was to die in June 1849 as a Swiss citizen and Reformed clergyman.

When de Wette was born on 12 January 1780 in the small village of Ulla on the road between Erfurt and Weimar, it was inconceivable that this son of a German Lutheran pastor would spend the last third of his life as a Swiss citizen and Reformed clergyman. Yet more important than the way in which unforeseen events shaped de Wette's life is the fact that he was an unusual man who brought together a rare combination of gifts, and whose journey from doubt to faith enabled him to make a decisive and lasting contribution to biblical scholarship in the nineteenth and twentieth centuries.

Little is known about de Wette's childhood and adolescence. The main source of information is an article by Wiegand[2] who, although

---

1. Wiegand, *De Wette*, p. 71.
2. A. Wiegand, 'De Wette als Knabe und Jüngling in Ulla, Grosskromsdorf, Buttstädt und Weimar', *Kirchen und Schulblatt* 21 (1872), pp. 20-25.

he had access to family papers that were apparently later destroyed, and lived close to where de Wette grew up, admitted that this period in de Wette's life was largely unknown.[1]

The de Wette family was originally a Dutch family which early embraced Protestantism and moved to Germany in 1523 to escape persecution.[2] De Wette's father, Johann Augustin (1744–1812), had been the Lutheran pastor in Ulla for four years prior to the birth of Wilhelm, who was the second child and first son. There were eventually nine children, all of whom survived to adulthood. Closest in age to Wilhelm were Sophie, sixteen months his elder, and Anna and Amalie, respectively two and four years younger. According to Wiegand,[3] the family life of the de Wettes was close-knit and idyllic— a contrast to Wilhelm's often lonely and unhappy adult family life after the death of his first wife.

When Wilhelm was four, his father moved to Grosskromsdorf, not far from Weimar. Thus began an association with Weimar that was to last for the remainder of de Wette's life. As a small boy he saw Schiller and Goethe walking near the castle, and was told about the great Herder who preached in the parish church.[4] At this stage in his life, Wilhelm was taught by his father, and made considerable progress in the classical languages. From 1792 to 1796 he attended the school in Buttstädt, seven miles north of Weimar, where he lodged with a purse maker.[5] In 1796 he entered the Grammar School in Weimar itself.

One of his fellow students was Gotthilf Heinrich von Schubert, who in later life described the schoolboy de Wette as

> an extremely gifted earnest young man, who lived almost entirely for his studies and only rarely sought or needed social contacts. Through his

---

1.   Wiegand, 'De Wette als Knabe', p. 21: 'Die stille Jugendzeit de Wette's ist im Zusammenhange ob zerstreuter biographischer Notizen im Ganzen wenig bekannt'.

2.   Wiegand, *De Wette,* pp. 1-2; also R. de Wette, *Die Familie de Wette* (Arnstadt, 1869).

3.   Wiegand, *De Wette,* p. 2.

4.   Wiegand, 'De Wette als Knabe', p. 22.

5.   For a brief description of this time see the letter of de Wette's fellow student Peucer to K.R. Hagenbach in Hagenbach, *Wilhelm Martin Leberecht de Wette,* p. 63 n. 2.

sincere and successful industry and his calm and good behaviour he earned the love of his teachers and the respect of his fellow-students.[1]

The only description of de Wette's physical appearance known to me is that given in a letter by the American Theodore Parker, who visited de Wette in Basel in 1844.[2] According to Parker, de Wette was a small, solid man. We can therefore picture him at the age of sixteen as a small, sensitive and shy student, with his small circle of friends, and respected for his dedication to his studies. It is also likely that de Wette, perhaps because of being small, and out of determination to be able to take care of himself, learned to swim as a boy. It is striking that, twice in de Wette's semi-autobiographical novel *Theodor*, there are incidents in which the hero saves others because of his swimming prowess.[3] It may be that de Wette was not only a swimmer, but that he once actually saved someone.

What spare time de Wette had at the Grammar School was spent with a group of students that met in the evenings to read the plays of Goethe and Schiller and the poetry and philosophical writings of Herder and Wieland. Already as a teenager, de Wette had read Herder's *Ideas on the Philosophy of the History of Mankind.*[4]

Herder, as the Lutheran General Superintendent in Weimar, had overall responsibility for the work of the Grammar School and was also its examiner, conducting examinations in his house and publicly. Von Schubert has left a graphic account of such a public examination, in which de Wette is mentioned.

> We stood together in the great examination hall. . .and a servant placed on the table. . .the pile of scripts. There entered the man whom I never saw without feeling awe and respect. He sat down in his examiner's chair. It was always Herder's custom first of all to remind us, in a few words that made a deep impression on us, why we were here, and to

1. G.H. von Schubert, *Der Erwerb aus einem vergangenen und die Erwartungen von einem zukünftigen Leben* (Erlangen, 1854), I, p. 258.
2. J. Weiss, *Life and Correspondence of Theodore Parker* (New York, 1864), I, p. 244: 'At Bâle, of course, I saw De Wette, a compact little man with a rather dry face, a little irritable, I fancy, perhaps something soured by his long disasters'. The letter is in German translation in A. Alther, *Theodor Parker in seinem Leben und Wirken* (St Gallen, 1895), p. 115.
3. *Theodor, oder des Zweiflers Weihe: Bildungsgeschichte eines evangelischen Geistlichen* (Berlin, 2nd edn, 1828), I, p. 16; II, p. 127.
4. Wiegand, 'De Wette als Knabe', p. 23.

warn us about what we ought to do and what he and the whole school
expected of us. The scripts lay in an order which was not exactly the order
of our seniority. The efforts of several of the best and most hard-working
students were considered first. A prose essay by the industrious de Wette
received its due praise.[1]

If Herder recognized the ability of the young de Wette, Wilhelm had a
deep respect for Herder, and never missed an opportunity to hear him
preach. Nearly fifty years later, in 1844, he wrote about the profound
effect that Herder's presence and preaching had made on him:

I still have a vivid impression of how I looked, with youthful admiration,
at Herder's figure—a presence that was both kindly and inspired respect;
how I listened to his sonorous voice and his solemnly formal words as he
opened the public examination at the Grammar School; how I heard his
verdict on my submitted work with beating heart; how, at the examination
of scholars at his house, I diffidently translated from Horace and how I
forgot my fear and myself and hung on his eyes and lips, because of the
warm way in which he encouraged and emboldened the readers and
translators and entered into the heart of this favourite poet through his
observations and questions. His words on that occasion still remain in my
memory; for example, how he stressed to us that each Horace Ode must
be grasped as a unity. I can still see him standing in the pulpit, quiet and
still, his hands one on top of the other, and I can still hear his unique
monotone declaiming and expounding the Lord's Prayer in a reverent and
profound manner.[2]

In 1798 de Wette interrupted his studies in Weimar in order to
accompany to Geneva the son of a French emigré living in the
beautiful Schloss Belvedere.[3] De Wette had become the Greek tutor to
the family's fourteen-year-old son, and was invited to be his travelling
companion as far as Geneva, while the family investigated the possibility of returning to France after the revolution. This was the first of
many journeys made by de Wette, to whom travelling was to become
a first love. It was also a visit to Switzerland, which was later to
become his home.

It is deeply to be regretted that the eight letters which de Wette
wrote to his parents during the journey no longer exist. However, we
have a letter which he wrote from Geneva on 8 December 1798 to the

1.   Von Schubert, *Erwerb*, pp. 272-73.
2.   Staehelin, *Dewettiana*, p. 183.
3.   Wiegand, *De Wette*, pp. 8-10, gives a summary of the journey.

headmaster of the Grammar School in Weimar, Karl August Böttiger.[1] This deals particularly with the number of French soldiers to be found in Schaffhausen, Zürich and Geneva and the threatening military situation in the confrontation between the French and the allied Austrians and Russians. We also detect a note of anxiety in his letter about the length of time that he is likely to be away from Weimar. He had planned to be away for six weeks only, but already a month has passed.

From Wiegand's biography, for which the eight lost letters were available, we learn that the journey, which began on 4 November 1798, took a devious and cultural route via Dresden, Nuremberg, Stuttgart, Schaffhausen and Zürich. The travellers were especially impressed by the artistic treasures of Dresden, and were overwhelmed by the spectacle of the Rhine Fall at Schaffhausen. De Wette spent longer in Geneva than anticipated, while his fourteen-year-old charge waited for clearance to enter France. It was not until mid-February 1799 that he finally got back to Weimar. The planned absence of six weeks had become three-and-a-half months; but the experience of travel, and of seeing outstanding beauty in nature, art and architecture had made a lasting impression on de Wette, one that was to play an important part in his quest for a philosophy and theology that satisfied the demands of his sharply critical mind and his deeply aesthetic sensitivity.

---

1. Staehelin, *Dewettiana*, p. 64. De Wette's Weimar headmaster, Karl August Böttiger (1760–1835), was a considerable classical scholar and man of letters, and in close touch with the leading literary figures of his day. See E.F. Sondermann, *Karl August Böttiger, literarischer Journalist der Goethezeit in Weimar* (Mitteilungen zur Theatergeschichte der Goethezeit, 7; Bonn: Bouvier, 1983).

University of Jena 1799 (artist's impression) Drawing by M. Mallallah

Chapter 2

JENA 1799–1807: DOUBT AND HOPE, SUCCESS AND TRAGEDY

Around Easter 1799, de Wette left Weimar and travelled, with five of his friends, the thirteen miles to Jena, where he enrolled at the university as a law student. In addition to three articles and the biography by Wiegand,[1] and a short essay by de Wette entitled *Eine Idee über das Studium der Theologie* and usually dated to the summer of 1801,[2] an important source for this most crucial period of de Wette's life is the semi-autobiographical novel *Theodor*. Because of this, it is necessary to outline the plot of the novel, and to decide to what degree it can be used as a guide to de Wette's religious and intellectual development.

Theodor is the son of a pious and wealthy widow, whose late husband was the squire of the village of Schönbeck. On one occasion while her husband was alive, she had vowed that, if he recovered from an illness, she would do all in her power to ensure that Theodor became a Lutheran clergyman and succeeded to the pastorate of Schönbeck. The husband recovered, with the result that Theodor is left in no doubt about his family's wishes for his future. He begins theological studies at university, but loses his boyhood faith under the impact of Kantian philosophy and the rationalistic exegesis of his biblical teachers. However, attendance at lectures on ethics by a Kantian philosopher opens up a new world to him, and enables him to translate into philosophical convictions his childhood belief in divine grace, love and regeneration.

On returning home during the vacation, he is told by the elderly

1. A. Wiegand, 'De Wette in Jena, 1799–1807', *Kirchen und Schulblatt* 24 (1875), pp. 311-14, 338-43, 355-59.
2. W.M.L. de Wette, *Eine Idee über das Studium der Theologie* (ed. A. Stieren; Leipzig, 1850).

village clergyman in Schönbeck that, with his current beliefs, he ought not to enter the ministry. Two sermons that Theodor preaches in the village church are generally judged to be technically good but spiritually empty. On returning to university, Theodor keeps a promise made to his village clergyman, that he will attend the lectures of an orthodox professor. These lectures, however, only serve to make him more dissatisfied with orthodox Christian belief, and to doubt more strongly his vocation to the ministry. His future career is further complicated when he falls in love with the sister of a fellow student. Terese is the daughter of a nobleman who is prominent in government, and who makes it clear that marriage with Terese is possible only if Theodor enters government service and reaches a high position. At about this time, Theodor is deeply impressed by Schelling's 'Vorlesungen über die Methode des akademischen Studiums' and by discussions with a fellow student, Seebald, who arouses his interest in art.

Theodor now decides to abandon his vocation to the ministry, and moves to Terese's home town to enter government service. News of his mother's death reaches him shortly after he has taken this step. However, his longing for knowledge of theology and philosophy is still strong, and he begins to attend the lectures of a 'Professor A.' at the local university. These help him to unite what he had found best in Kant and Schelling, and to deepen his faith. Theodor also reads at this time Schleiermacher's *Reden über die Religion*, and this all makes a deep impression on him. His continuing interest in theology and philosophy alienates him from Terese's father, as does his friendship with Härtling, a man of strong democratic views. The warlike threats of a neighbouring power bring further conflict between Theodor and Terese's father. The latter is against the general arming of the people for fear that this will overthrow the old order when war is over. Theodor, on the other hand, favours a new order in society based upon a mutual acceptance by the people of their freedom and responsibility. In discussion with Härtling, Theodor suddenly finds his doubt resolved when Härtling suggests that the life of Christ is a positive occurrence in history of a timeless symbol of what is most beautiful and true in religion.

Theodor decides to enlist in the army with Härtling. He returns to his home village of Schönbeck, and there raises a small militia, which he commands. The break with Terese's family is now final. Theodor serves in the war with distinction, is wounded, and is nursed initially by a beautiful Catholic girl, Hildegard. Although he loses touch with Hildegard, he later discovers that she is the sister of one of his fellow officers. Theodor and Hildegard are reunited by chance on the Rigi, overlooking Lake Luzern in Switzerland. The remainder of the novel deals with Hildegard's decision to become a Protestant and to marry Theodor, who has now decided to become a clergyman as his mother had wished. One important incident remains to be mentioned. On his return from war, Theodor attends 'a famous German university', where he is taught by the author of a book on Christian doctrine, who helps Theodor to understand the nature of the Church as a community of believers, as well as the importance of historical exegesis and the meaning of the traditional statements of Christian belief. These thoughts assist Theodor greatly in the discussions which lead to Hildegard's decision to become a Protestant.

If the plot of Theodor is compared with de Wette's life up to 1822, many differences can be noted: de Wette's father was not a squire but a clergyman, and he lived until de Wette was 32; de Wette did not enter government service, did not enlist during the Napoleonic wars, and did not marry a convert from Catholicism. It could also be added that he did not become a Lutheran clergyman; but this would have to be qualified by the fact that de Wette, having decided to become a clergyman, was unanimously elected to a pastorate in 1821 by the congregation of the St Katherine Church in Braunschweig. He was prevented from taking this up by the veto of the Elector of Hanover, the British King George IV.

Despite these differences, it can be strongly argued that Theodor's intellectual and religious development in the novel closely resembles that of de Wette, and that the novel is therefore an important source, especially for the Jena period.[1] From the contents of de Wette's

---

1. Other scholars who have explored the connection between Theodor and de Wette are R. Otto, *Kantisch- Fries'sche Religionsphilosophie und ihre Anwendung auf die Theologie: Zur Einleitung in die Glaubenslehre für Studenten der Theologie* (Tübingen: Mohr, 1909), pp. 129-56, ET *The Philosophy of Religion* (trans. E.B. Dicker; London: Williams & Norgate, 1931), pp. 151-80, and P. Handschin, *Wilhelm Martin Leberecht de Wette als Prediger und Schriftsteller* (Basel: Helbing & Lichtenhahn, 1958), pp. 95-114. Otto's treatment is mostly at the level of philosophy and theology, and is most valuable. In the present work, I have tried to make some identifications (e.g. in the case of Härtling) that have not previously been suggested.

library,[1] we know that he possessed most of Kant's works together
with expositions of them published shortly before he became a student
in Jena, and it is thus likely that he attended the lectures of a Kantian
philosopher. Further, Schelling's 'Vorlesungen über die Methode des
akademischen Studiums' were delivered in Jena and published in 1802.
We also know that de Wette preached at least two sermons in his
father's church during one of the vacations,[2] and that he did not
preach again until shortly before the writing of the novel.

Assuming that in broad outline and in many details the events of
Theodor's life correspond to those of de Wette's life, the following
correlations can be made. Theodor's first university is Jena. The town
where Theodor entered government service is Heidelberg, where
de Wette was first an untenured and later a full professor from 1807
to 1810. This identification is secured by a remark in Theodor[3] about
mysticism becoming the vogue in the town. This clearly refers to the
presence in Heidelberg of J.J. Görries and F. Creuzer, who combined
an interest in the study of mythology with Christian mysticism.
Professor A. will be J.F. Fries, who was de Wette's colleague in
Heidelberg, having moved there from Jena in 1805.

The third university, attended by Theodor after the war, will be
Berlin, and the teacher who had published a work on Christian doctrine will be Schleiermacher. De Wette was appointed as a foundation
professor when Berlin opened in 1810. Although, as already noted,
de Wette did not enlist during the Napoleonic wars, it was only after
their conclusion in 1815 that he became reconciled with
Schleiermacher, and began to attend his church and to benefit from his
theological position.

Only one correlation does not work. In Theodor, it is while the
hero is in government service, that is, in Heidelberg (according to the
correlations that are being made here) that he comes to see Christ both
as a symbol of perfect religious truth and as an expression of that
truth at a particular time in history. However, we know from an
important letter to Fries, dated 17 December 1817, that this breakthrough in de Wette's thinking was made not in Heidelberg but in

---

1.   Antiquar J. Meyri in Basel. Catalogue No. 40. Auction on 31 July 1850 of
the libraries of de Wette and F. Hitzig.
2.   Wiegand, De Wette, p. 16.
3.   Theodor, I, p. 98.

Berlin.[1] In what follows, it will be assumed that this one lack of correlation is not sufficient to invalidate the general approach of using the novel *Theodor* to reconstruct de Wette's religious and intellectual development.

Before this is done, it is necessary to draw attention to two mistakes made by Wiegand which concern the use of material from the novel. The first is Wiegand's assertion that, while de Wette was in Jena, the teaching of J.F. Fries brought together the fragmented convictions of de Wette's former faith into an ordered whole. Wiegand uses material from *Theodor* as follows:

> 'It was to me', relates de Wette in his *Theodor*. . . 'after hearing the system of Fries, as though the scattered fragments of my former views and convictions were brought together in a well-ordered and beautiful whole as if by magic'.[2]

The actual text of the novel reads as follows:

> To our friend it was as though, through these insights, the scattered fragments of his former views and convictions were brought together in a well-ordered and beautiful whole as if by magic.[3]

Although Wiegand is correct to identify Fries as the cause of Theodor/de Wette's illumination, he wilfully alters the text of *Theodor*, and, more seriously, places the occasion in Jena, whereas it actually relates to de Wette's Heidelberg period.[4]

Wiegand's second mistake is his assertion that de Wette's 1801 essay *Eine Idee über das Studium der Theologie* was influenced by Schleiermacher's *Reden über die Religion* of 1799 and his *Monologe*

---

1.   See E.L.T. Henke, 'Berliner Briefe von de Wette an Fries: Von 1811 bis 1819', *Monatsblätter für innere Zeitgeschichte* 32 (1868), p. 104.

2.   *De Wette*, p. 12.

3.   *Theodor*, I, p. 84. In the German, the two passages are as follows:

Wiegand	Theodor
'Es war mir', berichtet de Wette in seinem 'Theodor', seiner späteren ungenannten Selbstbiographie, 'nach dem Anhören des Systems von Fries, als hätten sich die zerstreuten Bruchstücke meiner bisherigen Erkentnisse und Ueberzeugungen wie durch Zauberruf zu einem wohlgeordneten, schönen Ganzen zusammengefügt'.	Unserem Freunde war es, als wenn durch diese Ansichten die zerstreuten Bruchstücke seiner bisherigen Erkenntnisse und Ueberzeugungen wie durch Zauberruf sich zu einem wohlgeordneten schönen Ganzen zusammenfügten.

4.   See above, p. 22.

(sic) of 1800, and that these works must have been on de Wette's desk[1]. Almost certainly Wiegand is dependent upon what the editor of *Eine Idee*, Adolf Stieren, wrote in the preface. Stieren merely claims that some of the elevated passages in de Wette's essay have ringing tones similar to those in Schleiermacher's *Monologen* and *Reden*.[2] Wiegand seems to have converted Stieren's statement about the similarities between *Eine Idee* and Schleiermacher's pieces into an assertion of dependence.[3] In fact, there are fundamental differences between the works in question. Further, it has already been pointed out above that, on the evidence of *Theodor*, de Wette did not study Schleiermacher's *Reden* until the Heidelberg period.[4]

Before we can proceed any further, a vital matter has to be considered, and one on which I have changed my mind since writing about de Wette in my *Old Testament Criticism in the Nineteenth Century*.[5] This question is, did de Wette know J.F. Fries during his Jena period, did he attend his lectures and did he give to Fries a copy of his essay *Eine Idee über das Studium der Theologie*?

That de Wette knew Fries well is asserted by Wiegand.[6] He states that de Wette attended Fries's lectures and that, after a particular lecture, spoke to his teacher, thus setting in motion a process in which

1.   Wiegand, *De Wette*, pp. 15-16.

2.   *Eine Idee*, p. 7: 'Mir hat es sogar scheinen wollen, als klingen manche der gehobeneren Stellen an den Ton an, der in Schleiermacher's Monologen und Reden über die Religion weht'.

3.   An examination of *De Wette,* p. 15, and *Eine Idee*, pp. 6-7, shows that Wiegand has quoted and altered sentences from Stieren.

4.   Otto shows that when de Wette refers to the *Reden* in *Theodor* it is to the second edition and not the 1799 edition. See Otto, *Kantisch Fries'sche Religionsphilosophie*, p. 138 n. 2. (ET p. 161 n. 2); and p. 81 below.

5.   *Old Testament Criticism in the Nineteenth Century: England and Germany* (London: SPCK, 1984).

6.   *De Wette*, pp. 11-12. Wiegand has almost certainly, as before, deliberately confused the Jena and Heidelberg periods. De Wette, for example, in his 1843 reminiscence of Fries (in E.L.T. Henke, *Jakob Friedrich Fries: Aus seinem handschriftlichen Nachlase dargestellt* [Leipzig, 1867], pp. 277-93), speaks of how he and Fries walked together along the banks of the Neckar. In Wiegand's account, the two friends walked together along the banks of the Saale! A comparison of Wiegand's text with the 1843 reminiscence shows that Wiegand has often quoted de Wette verbatim but has put together sentences from different parts of de Wette's text and has thus given a quite false impression of what happened.

acquaintance became friendship. Wiegand's statement seems to be strengthened by the suggestion made by the editor of de Wette's essay *Eine Idee*, Adolf Stieren. Stieren states that he received the essay from Professor Mirbt but failed to ask where Mirbt had got it from. After the deaths of both de Wette and Mirbt, Stieren remembered the essay and published it with the suggestion that Mirbt had found it in the papers of J.F. Fries.[1] I am now inclined to believe that both Wiegand and Stieren were wrong.

Wiegand is easily disposed of. As has already been shown, he confused the Jena and Heidelberg periods and deliberately misquoted from *Theodor* in order to maintain his position. Further, he drew heavily on de Wette's 1843 reminiscence of Fries, thus arousing suspicion that he had no independent first-hand evidence. However, the main witnesses in ascertaining the facts are de Wette himself and Fries's biographer, Henke.

In his 1843 reminiscence, de Wette says nothing about a Jena acquaintance with Fries. Instead, he writes of the Heidelberg period, when he and Fries discussed the latter's philosophy while walking the banks of the River Neckar. This might be thought to be an argument from silence, were it not for Henke's biography of Fries, based partly upon Fries's autobiography.[2] From this source, we can ascertain the following about Fries's movements in the period 1801–1804.

Fries did not gain his doctorate until 21 February 1801, and was not habilitated (the step needed in order to be able to lecture) until the summer of the same year. However, he began to lecture from Easter 1801, giving a ten-hour course on the art of philosophizing. In the summer he lectured on philosophical anthropology, while his main activity in the winter semester was a private series of lectures on logic and metaphysics. Fries's prowess as a lecturer was severely limited, and from May 1803 to May 1804 he left Jena to travel in France and Switzerland. He does not appear to have lectured on ethics, and there seems to be no reason why de Wette should have written and presented to him an essay on the study of theology in 1801, even assuming that de Wette attended some of Fries's few lectures that year.

Another piece of evidence that seems to tell against de Wette's involvement with Fries is that Henke gives the names of the group of

1. *Eine Idee*, p. 5.
2. Henke, *Fries*.

similar-aged young men whom he gathered round him in Jena from 1800, who shared an interest in philosophy, medicine and natural science, and who were dissatisfied with Schelling's teaching.[1] Fifteen such people are named, but de Wette is not included, and it is unthinkable, given his later friendship with de Wette, that Fries should have deliberately or accidentally omitted de Wette's name. A final point is that Henke agrees with de Wette's reminiscence of Fries in placing their formative contact in the Heidelberg and not the Jena period. It cannot be said that they never met each other in Jena, or that de Wette never heard Fries there. It can be said with confidence that there was no influence of Fries upon de Wette, and probably no friendship at that time.

As I shall argue later, there is no trace of Fries's influence on de Wette's essay *Eine Idee*, and if it *did* come from Fries's papers, it does not follow that de Wette must have given it to him in 1801. Fries could have acquired it subsequently in any number of ways. The obvious solution is that *Eine Idee* is the essay mentioned in de Wette's reminiscence of Fries as having been composed *before* he became acquainted with Fries and which he sent to the Weimar consistorium.[2] In what follows, I shall assume that de Wette did not attend the lectures of Fries while in Jena.

The University of Jena had, in 1799, what today can only be thought of as an astonishing collection of scholars who had greatly influenced, or who were to influence, the disciplines of philosophy and theology. On the philosophical side, Jena was graced by the presence of Fichte, Schelling and Hegel. On the theological side, J.J. Griesbach had laid a foundation for the study of the synoptic Gospels that would endure long into the nineteenth century and even enjoy a revival in the 1970s.[3] H.E.G. Paulus, on the other hand, although he was to be of

---

1.   Henke, *Fries*, pp. 72-77.

2.   In Henke, *Fries*, p. 285: 'Namentlich hatte ich schon [before accepting Fries's system] die beiden Grundgedanken meiner jetzigen theologischen Ansicht, dass unsere Erkenntniss von den ewigen Dingen subjectiv beschränkt sei und die lebendige Wahrheit der Religion im Gefühle liege. Ja, die Verbindung der letztern mit der Kunst war mit so sehr Lieblingsgedanke, dass ich darüber im Jahre 1802 oder 1803 einen Aufsatz an das weimarische Oberconsistorium einsandte.' The main theme of *Eine Idee* is the importance of art (*Kunst*) for the study of theology.

3.   See C. Tuckett, *The Revival of the Griesbach Hypothesis: An Analysis and Appraisal* (Cambridge: Cambridge University Press, 1983).

great assistance to de Wette in some ways, was a man of the past, even though he was still only in his late thirties.[1] He would represent eighteenth-century rationalism until his death in 1851.[2]

However illustrious his Jena teachers were, the greatest initial impact that was made upon de Wette came from the philosophy of Kant. Indeed, for the remainder of his life, de Wette remained, intellectually, a sort of Kantian; and he spent many years of his life trying to reconcile his intellectual acceptance of Kant with his aesthetic and almost mystical instinct for religion. The catalogue of the sale of the libraries of de Wette and F. Hitzig in July 1850[3] lists twenty-four books by Kant and no fewer than fifty-seven books about him, in addition to a series of commentaries on the major texts of Kant by Bendavid, amounting to seven volumes. Of course, the catalogue is a list of books owned by the two scholars, and there is no way of knowing which volumes belonged to which scholar.[4] But Hitzig was born in 1809, and it is not unreasonable to assume that some of the Kant volumes and all the Bendavid volumes (which were published in the 1790s) were purchased by de Wette when he began to engage in philosophical studies in 1799.

The year before de Wette entered Jena, Kant published an essay entitled *Der Streit der Fakultäten*, which included a part dealing with the conflict between the theological and philosophical faculties.[5] This contained a devastating critique of what Kant called biblical theologians from the point of view of Kant's critical philosophy.

Fundamental to Kant's critique were two distinctions: between the necessary truths of reason and the contingent truths of history; and

---

1. This was the view of A. Merx, 'Die morgenländischen Studien und Professoren an der Universität Heidelberg vor und besonders im 19. Jahrhundert', in *Heidelberger Professoren aus dem 19. Jahrhundert* (Heidelberg: C. Winter, 1903), p. 41. Commenting on the appointment of Paulus to succeed de Wette in 1810, Merx writes, 'ein Mann der Vergangenheit trat an die Stelle eines Mannes der Zukunft'.

2. On Paulus, see K.A. Freiherr v. Reichlin-Meldegg, *Heinrich Eberhard Gottlob Paulus und seine Zeit* (Stuttgart, 1853).

3. See p. 23 n. 1 above.

4. Also, some of de Wette's books were looted after the French victory at the Battle of Jena.

5. I. Kant, *Der Streit der Fakultäten in Kants Werke: Akademie Textausgabe* (Berlin: Preussische Akademie der Wissenschaften, 1907 [repr.; Berlin: de Gruyter, 1968]), VII, pp. 1-116.

between the religion of reason and the belief of the church. Because truths derived from reason were the only necessary truths having universal validity, the only type of religion that was necessarily true and of universal validity was religion derived from reason. This religion was principally concerned with morality. It sought to demonstrate that each person could become aware of what ought to be done, and that it lay within the possibility of human freedom to perform this duty in opposition to the tendency to do wrong that was latent in every person. Although Christianity was the most seemly (*schicklichste*) form of religion, this did not mean that philosophy could accept its dogmas based upon the idea of a revelation within the contingency of history.[1]

Some Christian doctrines, such as the Trinity, were either meaningless or made claims about what could not, in any case, be known. Further, they did not assist people to live better lives. The belief that Jesus was God incarnate, as opposed to an expression of what it meant to be fully human, was also meaningless; and it was pernicious in that it implied that it was pointless to follow the example of Jesus if he had the unfair advantage of being God as well as man.[2] Jesus' divinity was to be understood in terms of the moral achievement of his life, as one who had done all that God could expect. Jesus did not expect to survive death in such a way as to appear to his followers. Had he had such an expectation, he would not have founded a memorial meal and would not have cried despairingly from the cross. And he certainly would have prepared his followers to expect his resurrection; yet they clearly did not expect it, to judge from their reactions in the Gospel narratives. Paul's claim 'if Christ is not risen your faith is in vain' was not convincing, and needed to be understood as follows: it is impossible that such a noble life as Christ's should have no continuance beyond death, and we also shall share in immortality. This conviction was given to Paul by reason, but became tied to the historical saga about the resurrection.[3]

Kant's religion of reason required the redefinition of key theological terms. Revelation is not truth contained in a historical document, the Bible, nor is it something handed down by human tradition. If it were, it would not be necessarily true and universally binding, since

---

1. Kant, *Streit*, pp. 36-38.
2. Kant, *Streit*, pp. 38-39.
3. Kant, *Streit*, p. 40.

truths of history are contingent. Revelation is what God discloses through each person's reason. Faith is not the acceptance of claims made in the Bible or in Christian doctrine; it is the putting into practice of what reason discloses. Grace is not an external endowment of power enabling a person to do what could not otherwise be done; it is the recognition that it lies within a person's own freedom to do what is right in opposition to the human tendency to do wrong.[1] Conversion is not a miraculous becoming of a new person, but a transforming realization of the possibility of becoming a better person by following the moral dictates of reason.[2]

There are, not surprisingly, radical implications for biblical interpretation in this position. In the first place, Kant justifies interpreting the Bible on the basis of the religion of reason by pointing out that there is no single certain or agreed interpretation of the Bible. The religion of reason, on the other hand, because it provides necessary truths, can yield a universally valid interpretation of the Bible. Kant also considers the objection that the Bible can only be interpreted in the light of its own testimony.[3] His rejoinder is that the proof that a writing is a revelation cannot come from that writing itself, but only from reason. Biblical interpretation, then, must serve to promote the religion of reason, that is, to convince people of the divine revelation in their own reason and of their duty to act in accordance with it. Kant sees as pointless the type of exposition designed to prove that recorded biblical events, especially miracles, actually happened, since getting people to accept that something happened in the past is not the same as persuading them to act according to their duty.[4] The following quotation encapsulates Kant's position:

> The God who speaks through his own (moral-practical) reason is an infallible, and altogether understandable, interpreter of his own word. There is no other credible interpreter of his word (certainly not of a historical form) since religion is a matter of pure reason.[5]

This, then, was something of the view of religion that made an immediate impact on de Wette in Jena in 1799–1800. In some senses,

1. Kant, *Streit*, pp. 42-47.
2. Kant, *Streit*, pp. 53-57.
3. Kant, *Streit*, p. 46.
4. Kant, *Streit*, p. 41.
5. Kant, *Streit*, p. 67.

of course, what Kant said was not new. In the writings of the English deists we find the idea that, in order to be believed, a thing must be understood; and that if it cannot be understood it cannot be believed.[1] Thus, Christianity can have no mysteries and reason is the ultimate arbiter. Again, the distinction between necessary truths of reason and contingent truths of history is commonplace in the eighteenth century, and the exposition of miracle stories so as to make them conform with the rational scientific assumptions of the age was already being practised before Kant's critical philosophy began to affect theology.[2]

But if Kant's viewpoint was in some senses not new, it was presented with a sincerity and power of conviction that can still be sensed nearly 200 years later. It is not necessary to accept Kant's definition of religion in order to agree with the common sense rightness of some of his views. What *is* the point of trying to make people accept that Jesus changed 120 gallons of water into wine, or fed 5,000 people from five barley loaves and two small fishes? How do we judge the respective claims of the Bible, the Qur'an and the Book of Mormon to be God's revelation other than by introducing an element of reason into the discussion, and by saying that a book cannot be revelation if it cannot stand up to historical-critical investigation? That Kant's philosophy was bound to make an impression on de Wette was a foregone conclusion not only because of the power of Kant's presentation, but because de Wette, if we can appeal to *Theodor*, had already as a schoolboy displayed an enquiring mind that sometimes left his teachers sorely pressed.[3]

During his first year at Jena, de Wette attended, in addition to philosophical lectures, those of Griesbach on the Gospels. These are described in *Theodor*[4] as having presented various scholarly positions, including the rationalizing of miracles, with Griesbach pointing out their strengths and weaknesses rather than advancing any opinions of his own. De Wette seems to have accepted, on philosophical grounds, that miracles were not possible and that accounts of them in the Gospels were not to be accepted, since the evangelists often disagreed

   1.   J. Toland, *Christianity not Mysterious or a Treatise Shewing, that there is Nothing in the Gospel contrary to Reason* (London, 1696).
   2.   See my *Old Testament Criticism*, pp. 151-52.
   3.   *Theodor*, I, p. 17.
   4.   *Theodor*, I, p. 18.

among themselves about the details of the events.[1]

In his second year, 1800–1801, de Wette attended the lectures of the rationalist Paulus, and these made a deep impression on him. In *Theodor*, we are told:

> he followed with pleasure the penetrating and bold solutions in which the miraculous and inexplicable elements in the Gospel narratives were transformed into what was natural and understandable, by being explained in terms of the customs of the times, their historical circumstances and the hidden and unconscious clues which the narratives themselves contained. However, what especially drew him on and gave him satisfaction was the unforced, clear exposition of the sayings of Jesus and their reference to the general truths of reason.[2]

During this year, de Wette also attended the lectures of a Kantian philosopher on ethics, which introduced the religion of reason in a new, and for the moment, satisfying way.[3] He now learned how to translate the key terms of the faith of his youth—conversion, putting on the new man, grace, the love of God and Christ—into Kantian philosophical language. These ideas now seemed to him to be more meaningful, and they made the lectures of Paulus even more exciting:

> he felt himself especially uplifted and satisfied when his biblical teacher presented Christ as a Kantian sage, who taught, in pictures and ideas appropriate to his time, what the present age could deduce clearly and purely from reason.

But together with this intellectual excitement there was much emotional dissatisfaction:

> The Kantian doctrine of God which reason enjoined, namely that the rule of virtue should be established in the world and should be rewarded with good fortune, this fell like a damp squib into his soul, extinguishing the holy fire of devotion and leaving in its place a dismal darkness.[4]

This seemed to deny the idea that God exists, and that we come from him and belong to him. It implied that human reason exists, and that God exists only at reason's behest. De Wette (Theodor) found himself asking:

1. *Theodor*, I, p. 19.
2. *Theodor*, I, p. 20.
3. *Theodor*, I, p. 21.
4. *Theodor*, I, p. 24.

is this a real and living God, and not rather a projection of our own
thoughts? Is this the God who spoke to the patriarchs and prophets, and
who revealed himself in mighty deeds? Is this the Father of Jesus Christ,
of whom Jesus said that he only did what he heard and saw from the
Father?[1]

The answer to these questions appeared to be no, and de Wette
suddenly found himself alone in the world. He might have his self-
sufficient reason which was God's revelation to him; but in practice he
felt like a child who had lost his father, and he discovered that prayer
was now pointless, and at best a conversation with himself. On the
other hand, he was able to compensate partly for this loss of religious
assurance by the stimulus he gained from his intellectual studies, to
which he devoted himself with new vigour.

In his vacations de Wette preached, presumably in his father's
church. We do not know exactly how many sermons he preached. In a
letter to a Frau Trübner dated 2 March 1801,[2] de Wette mentioned
that he was attaching a copy of his last (i.e. most recent) sermon,
which he had delivered on 16 January 1801. This implies at least two
sermons; and in *Theodor* the hero preaches two sermons during his
vacation in his home village. On the reasonable assumption that
Theodor describes the sermons preached by de Wette at this time, we
obtain the following picture of his convictions.[3] The first sermon was
about prayer, and urged that one should not pray for material things
but only for spiritual things such as virtue and wisdom. The rest
should be left in God's hands. The second sermon dealt with a moral
theme, namely, self-control, and its value for producing virtue. These
sermons are what would be expected from someone deeply affected by
Kantian philosophy. In *Theodor* the sermons have a mixed reception,
and, from this point on, the hero does not preach again. As far as we
know, de Wette did not preach again until 1820, by which time he had
established his mature Christian convictions.

The next major happening in de Wette's intellectual development
was his reaction to the philosophy of Schelling. In the summer
semester of 1802, Schelling delivered in Jena his 'Vorlesungen über
die Methode des akademischen Studiums' and he followed these up

1. *Theodor*, I, pp. 24-25.
2. Wiegand, *De Wette*, p. 16.
3. *Theodor*, I, pp. 43ff.

with his 'Philosophie der Kunst' in the winter semester of 1802 and the summer semester of 1803.[1] It is clear from *Theodor* that these lectures made a deep impression upon de Wette.[2] In the novel, Theodor reads the 'Vorlesungen' and although the 'Philosophie der Kunst' is not explicitly mentioned, we can confidently assume that these lectures are intended by the conversations on art and poetry that Theodor has with a Schelling devotee named Seebald.

The 'Vorlesungen' explicitly criticize Kant's *Streit der Fakultäten* as one-sided.[3] Kant, in effect, wanted to make philosophy as he understood it the arbiter of all other disciplines. We have already seen the implications of this for biblical exegesis and theology. Schelling, on the other hand, argues that every discipline includes philosophy, if by the latter is understood a speculation that enables an observer to see a particular thing as a manifestation of the Absolute, and, apprehending the Absolute, to see the particular in the light of the Absolute.[4] Thus, although the natural world can be studied in purely physical ways, the science of nature needs to see the natural world as an expression of the Absolute. Similarly, the purpose of theology is not merely to apply to the biblical text a whole panoply of philological and grammatical learning. The Bible and religious traditions are also an expression of the Absolute, and one needs to understand the nature of the Absolute and its modes of expression in order to carry out exegesis correctly. Schelling is sharply critical of what he calls the watering-down method (*Verwässerungsmethode*) of biblical interpretation, which, using the excuse that the Bible is the product of oriental fantasy, reduces it to a set of moral precepts.[5]

Schelling's lectures struck home at the points where the Kantian system left de Wette emotionally unsatisfied. Instead of being a postulate of reason, God, or the Absolute, was primary, and human reason was itself a part of the Absolute that enabled the individual to perceive the Absolute in the particular. Religion was no longer a set of moral precepts; it was the contemplation of the origin of all being,

---

1.   The two series of lectures are printed in *Schellings Werke* (ed. M. Schröter; Munich: Beck, 1927), III, pp. 229-374, 375-507.
2.   *Theodor*, I, p. 59.
3.   *Schellings Werke*, III, p. 305.
4.   *Schellings Werke*, III, p. 297.
5.   *Schellings Werke*, III, pp. 324-35.

which was manifested in nature, history and art. Christ was no longer simply a unique example of a perfect moral life; he was the eternal, manifesting itself in the real and the temporal in order to reconcile and unite the ideal and the real.[1] Even the Trinity was no longer nonsense if it was seen in terms of an ultimate reality that united within itself the paradoxes of the ideal and the real, the eternal and the temporal, the Absolute and the particular.

In his lectures, Schelling also dealt briefly with something that would be crucial in de Wette's first great work, the *Beiträge zur Einleitung in das Alte Testament*, namely, mythology. Schelling rejected the idea, based partly upon descriptions of 'primitive' peoples, that ancient man was crude and barbaric. Such barbarity was, in Schelling's view, always a deterioration from a once more cultured position.[2] Thus, mythology was not the attempt of crude natives to understand the world of nature; it was a necessary form of religion in which an admittedly incomplete attempt was made to grasp the Absolute. The fault of the Greek myths was that they represented the eternal in temporal forms, whereas to be complete they should have grasped the unity of the eternal. In this sense, Christianity opened up a new and better way to the Absolute. But it was no accident that Greek myths provided the raw material for so much art, poetry and drama, for they were profound apprehensions of the Absolute.[3] These themes were later fully developed by Schelling in the 'Philosophie der Kunst'.[4]

In *Theodor* the hero is presented as being deeply impressed by the lectures, and even shaken (*erschüttert*) by the strictures of Schelling against precisely the kind of biblical interpretation that he was hearing from his professors. He had lost the sense of spiritual assurance partly because of such teaching, and now here it was being described as empty and cold. Further, the hero of *Theodor* is led by Schelling's lectures to a deeper understanding of the nature of religion, as opposed to its reduction to morality as in the Kantian religion of reason:

1.   *Schellings Werke*, III, p. 314.
2.   *Schellings Werke*, III, p. 309.
3.   *Schellings Werke*, III, pp. 310-11.
4.   See especially *Schellings Werke*, III, pp. 433ff.

The mysterious depth of Schelling's lectures attracted him, and he decided to read the other works of this man with attention.[1]

However, we cannot speak of a conversion to Schelling's philosophy. Theodor is puzzled by much in it. He cannot see how it can construct an ethical system, and if human history is an expression of the Absolute of which the individual is part, in what sense are human beings free?[2] Theodor is left in the position in which he is still basically a Kantian intellectually, but spiritually and aesthetically he is attracted by Schelling's views. Nature, poetry and drama are important in his life, and Schelling helps him to see how these can have a religious significance. From now on, his quest is for a philosophy that enables him to have, in effect, the best of both Kant and Schelling.

At this point, it is necessary to consider the earliest writing by de Wette that we possess, *Eine Idee über das Studium der Theologie*, obtained by Adolf Stieren from his colleague Professor Mirbt. We have already considered, and rejected, Stieren's suggestion that Mirbt had obtained it from the papers of Fries.[3] It bears the words 'Wilhelm Wette [his usual self-designation at that time][4] Summer 1801'. Crucial to its composition was an 'unforgettable external occurrence' which de Wette describes in the following words:

> An unforgettable external occurrence brought about the happiest revolution in my inner life, and gave me back my lost peace. The incomplete, dim faith of my childhood was replaced by a better and higher faith; attention to God awoke in my heart with new life, and belief in immortality came back to me in a higher and clearer manner. No longer was Theology a cold and dark judge of morals, nor simply a sister to History. Before my eyes she raised herself more and more to a high, heavenly majesty, to a divine value.[5]

What was this 'unforgettable external occurrence'? The date, summer 1801, rules out the hearing of Schelling's 'Vorlesungen'. According to

---

1. *Theodor*, I, p. 63.
2. *Theodor*, I, p. 66.
3. *Eine Idee*, p. 5: 'Nur als Vermuthung kann ich es deshalb aussprechen, dass das Autographon vielleicht aus dem Nachlasse des seligen Fries an Mirbt gekommen ist'. I am increasingly convinced that Stieren's guess was incorrect.
4. See Smend, *De Wettes Arbeit*, p. 190.
5. *Eine Idee*, p. 11.

Wiegand it was de Wette's attendance at Fries's lectures;[1] but Wiegand misquotes *Theodor*, adds material to the novel, and clearly has no first-hand knowledge. In fact, *Eine Idee* cannot be understood in terms of Fries's philosophical system, and, as I have already argued, it is probably identical with the composition mentioned by de Wette in his reminiscence of Fries, a work that he wrote before Fries began to influence him.[2] There is another possibility, which is that de Wette had read Tieck and Wackenroder's *Phantasien über die Kunst*. We know from a letter dated 14 May 1825 that this book had a profound influence upon de Wette;[3] and it was published shortly before de Wette began his university studies.[4] It regards art and religion as two mirrors which enable the true spirit of all things to be recognized and learnt.[5] The work both breathes a mysticism and shows how this mysticism is expressed in art and religion.

Although what follows can only be a surmise, a solution to the problem of the relationship between *Eine Idee* and the information from *Theodor* is to be worked out along the following lines. It was the reading of the book by Tieck and Wackenroder that changed

1. *De Wette*, p. 13.
2. See Henke, *Fries*, p. 285:

> man wusste nicht, dass ich, noch ehe ich mit ihm [i.e. Fries] und seiner Philosophie bekannt wurde, infolge eigenes Studiums und Nachdenkens ganz denselben Standpunkt wie er einnahm, ohne mir jedoch ein vollständiges System gebildet zu haben, wozu ich weder Geduld noch Gabe hatte, und dass ich bei ihm nur die wissenschaftliche Klarheit dessen fand, was ich mir selbst errungen hatte. Namentlich hatte ich schon die beiden Grundgedanken meiner jetztigen theologischen Ansicht, dass unsere Erkenntniss von den ewigen Dingen subjectiv beschränkt sei und die lebendige Wahrheit der Religion im Gefühle liege. Ja, die Verbindung der letztern mit der Kunst war mir so sehr Lieblingsgedanke, dass ich darüber im Jahre 1802 oder 1803 einen Aufsatz an das weimarische Oberconsistorium einsandte. . . '

I am convinced that this latter work, listed separately by Staehelin (*Dewettiana*, p. 13), is the *Eine Idee*.

3. Excerpts from this letter to Amalie von Voigt are given by Staehelin, *Dewettiana*, pp. 135-36, but not including the reference to *Phantasien über die Kunst*. This occurs on page 3, line 25 of the letter and describes how Frau VanderMühll had been reading the work, had told de Wette, and had re-kindled his youthful enthusiasm for it ('Ich fand meine jugendliche Begeisterung wieder').

4. L. Tieck and J. Wackenroder, *Phantasien über die Kunst für Freunde der Kunst* (Hamburg, 1799).

5. See F. Strich, *Die Mythologie in der deutschen Literatur von Klopstock bis Wagner*, I ([Halle: Niemeyer, 1910], p. 445 [repr. Bern and Munich: Francke, 1970]).

de Wette's outlook between the early part of 1801, when he preached the two Kantian sermons, and the summer of 1801, when he wrote *Eine Idee*. However, although Tieck and Wackenroder brought spiritual relief to de Wette, they did not provide him with a philosophy, so that when he heard Schelling attacking the very citadel of the Kantian position, he was amazed, and encouraged to look further. In fact, he may have forgotten the impact of the Tieck and Wackenroder book when he wrote *Theodor*. He sent the manuscript away, and in the letter of 14 May 1825, he writes as though with surprise at the rediscovery of the influence that the book had once had. Whatever the truth of the matter, it is now necessary to outline *Eine Idee*.

It begins with an attack on the effects of the Kantian philosophy on theology and preaching. The clergy have changed their profession. Instead of faith they preach morality; instead of proclaiming God they teach the importance of recognizing one's duty. At one stage, de Wette writes, he had welcomed this; early doubts had cost him his faith, and admiring the morality of atheists, he had been pleased to see that theology now stressed morality and regarded Jesus primarily as a moral teacher. This opening to *Eine Idee* very closely parallels the account of Theodor's intellectual development in the novel, and substantiates the use of the novel for reconstructing the Jena period. It may also explain why de Wette enrolled initially to study law at Jena. He may have lost his faith while still at school,[1] in spite of his great respect for Herder, and decided to embark on a non-theological career.

De Wette now describes how he was soon disillusioned with the new theology. In words similar to those in *Theodor*, he writes that he began to feel isolated and lonely, with himself and humanity cast into the world for no obvious purpose. His feelings fought against his intellect, and convinced him that his theology was lifeless, indifferent, and without nourishment for his heart or soul. Then there occurred the 'unforgettable external event' that brought an inner revolution, in which his apprehension of God was restored to him with new life. From now on, the study of theology was the highest calling and the only one that could satisfy him.

How is theology to be studied? For de Wette, it is to begin with the contemplation of art (*Kunst*):

1. See *Theodor,* I, p. 17.

> O holy art, you alone can open up to me the sense of the divine, and teach
> of the divine, and teach to the heart better, nobler feelings. In your
> magical creations, as in a clear, beautiful mirror, you present to limited
> vision the beauty and harmony that is not to be perceived in the infinite
> universe. You bring down to us from heaven the divine in earthly form,
> and bringing it into our view you move the cold and narrow heart to
> accept feelings that are divine and mediate harmony.[1]

The noble feelings engendered by art then give the clue to the contemplation of nature. Familiar scenes and objects are now evidence of
the work of a higher spirit, expressing a divine harmony. Everything
becomes a living pointer (*Sinnbild*) to divinity. If de Wette now turns
to history, he finds here also a mirror of God's activities that speaks
of the divine direction of all that happens.

It is only at this point that de Wette turns to theology, reading the
Bible in order to find the same evidence for the divine that he sees in
art, nature and history. In reading the Old Testament his spirit is
greatly lifted by the inspired utterances of the psalmists, and
impressed by the characters of the prophets, the patience of Job and
the simple robust religion of a simple people. In the New Testament
the person of Jesus, and the love and zeal of the disciples, are his
greatest treasures.

After some repetition of earlier sentiments, *Eine Idee* closes with
de Wette acknowledging that, as yet, his apprehensions (*Ahnungen*) of
the divine are weak, but this is why he will strive to his utmost in his
theological studies. His most trusted guide will be art, and he will not
look for God with the help of philosophy—a sentiment that would
hardly have appealed to Fries! He will seek it in nature and experience.

During the early Jena years, de Wette was not only wrestling with
faith and doubt; he was also struggling to maintain himself financially.
In a letter to his former head teacher, Karl August Böttiger, dated
28 March 1800, de Wette explained that he wanted to enter for
the Lynker studentship.[2] This had been founded in 1726 by Baron
von Lynker, and it provided a small stipend for two students for three
years. Holders of the scholarship were required, in turn, to deliver an
annual lecture in the Collegiate Church in Jena in defence of the
Augsburg Confession. De Wette had learned that only students of two

---

1. *Eine Idee*, p. 20.
2. De Wette Nachlass, A2.

years' standing were eligible, and he had been at Jena for only six months! Further, it seems that Paulus was influential in the award of the scholarships, and at the time of writing to Böttiger, de Wette had not attended any of Paulus's lectures. Also, he was not as well known to Griesbach as were the students in the year above him. Whether Böttiger wrote to Paulus, as requested by de Wette, we do not know. It appears, however, that de Wette did not at that time gain the scholarship.

Some of the money that he earned to support himself came from three students from Latvia, to whom he taught Latin;[1] but from a letter dated 28 June 1801,[2] we learn that de Wette was now so well known to Paulus that he was translating a book for the professor, and was hoping to visit Herder in order to show him the translation. This was almost certainly one of the volumes of Schiller's *General Collection of Historical Memoires*, the editorship of which had been taken over by Paulus. In the same letter, de Wette adds that he is now only attending the lectures of Paulus, although we do not know whether this was before or after the 'unforgettable external occurrence' that occasioned the writing of *Eine Idee* in the summer of 1801.

De Wette's initial studies seem to have ended in the summer of 1803, at which point he decided not to take the state examinations that would have set him on the road to becoming a Lutheran pastor. One reason for this may have been that, having now been successful in obtaining the Lynker studentship, de Wette wished to continue his studies with a view to an academic career. De Wette's nephew, Gustav Thöllden, in an obituary,[3] suggests either that de Wette disliked the officials in the Landeskirche, or that he had been discouraged by the failure of his sermons. At any rate, de Wette's decision caused a breach with his father. From the winter of 1803, he worked on his doctoral dissertation. This was submitted in September 1804, and on 11 March 1805 de Wette was awarded the degree of Doctor of Philosophy.[4]

De Wette's dissertation has become famous in the history of Old Testament scholarship, because it is supposed to have established that

1. Wiegand, 'De Wette in Jena', p. 355.
2. Wiegand, 'De Wette in Jena', p. 354.
3. *Neuer Nekrolog der Deutschen* 27, Jahrgang 1849 (Weimar, 1851), pp. 427-55.
4. Wiegand, 'De Wette in Jena', p. 355.

Deuteronomy was the law book discovered in the temple in the reign
of Josiah in 622 BCE, and that Deuteronomy must have been written in
the seventh century. In fact, the reference to Deuteronomy and
Josiah's law book comes only in a footnote, and then only as a not-
improbable deduction. If the dissertation deserves an honoured
position, it must be for different reasons.

The main aim of the *Dissertatio critica qua a prioribus
Deuteronomium pentateuchi libris diversum, alius cuiusdam recentioris auctoris opus esse monstratur*—a work of only sixteen pages
in its 1830 format—is to show that Deuteronomy was written later
than the other four books of the Pentateuch.[1] It is full of shrewd and
penetrating insights, and it clearly prefigures the major work
which would appear in 1806–1807, the *Beiträge zur Einleitung in das
Alte Testament*.

The argument is divided into six parts, following a brief introduction which asserts that Moses was not the author of the Pentateuch,
that Genesis is based upon two sources, and that Exodus–Numbers is
the work of more than one author. The first part of the dissertation
points out that the history of Moses is complete by the end of
Numbers. Moses has given the law, has left instructions as to how the
land of Canaan is to be divided (Num. 26.52-56) and has appointed
Joshua as his successor (Num. 27.12-23). Deuteronomy suddenly provides a Moses redivivus, promulgating a new set of laws, reappointing
Joshua as his successor, and repeating in ch. 28 what has already been
said in Leviticus 26 (the text says Lev. 27 [XXVII], but Lev. 26 is
clearly entailed by what then follows).

Part Two is very brief. It points out that the opening verses of
Deuteronomy paraphrase what has been fully related in Numbers.
Part Three is by far the longest, and is a detailed examination of the
distinctive style of Deuteronomy. Initially, de Wette argues that what
is said briefly in the earlier books is stated elaborately in Deuteronomy.
For example, Exod. 20.18 is expanded in Deuteronomy 5 to six verses,
22-27, while Lev. 26.29 becomes five verses in Deut. 28.53-57. There
are ten such examples. Next, de Wette turns his attention to the words
and phrases that are peculiar to Deuteronomy, such as 'that you may
live in the land which the LORD gives you', and lists over thirty

---

1.   Reference is made to the version in *Opuscula theologica* (Berlin, 1830),
pp. 149-68.

instances. Particularly interesting is the use that is made of the comparison between Leviticus 26 and Deuteronomy 28. By showing that the distinctive Deuteronomy phrases occur in Deuteronomy 28, de Wette is able to refute the argument that Deuteronomy differs from the style of the earlier books because it is a speech. De Wette points out that Leviticus 26 is also a speech, similar to Deuteronomy 28 and lacking its peculiar style.

Part Four turns from the style to the religious spirit of Deuteronomy. De Wette detects in the book a movement away from the simplicity of the earlier books towards the religion of later Judaism. Deuteronomy is more mystical, superstitious und subtle, and miracles such as the gift of the manna are given a theological interpretation. This tendency towards sophisticated theologizing is confirmed in Part Five by an examination of the cultic ordinances. The idea of a single sanctuary, the place which the Lord will choose, as the sole legitimate sanctuary, is an innovation in Deuteronomy, and requires new regulations, for instance, about the Passover, which can now only be celebrated at the divinely-appointed single sanctuary.

At this point there is a lengthy footnote which not only contains the suggestion that Deuteronomy might be the law book discovered in the temple in 622 BCE, but which sets out in summary the argument of de Wette's epoch-making *Beiträge* of 1806–1807.[1] The point at issue is that the command to sacrifice at a single sanctuary is unique to Deuteronomy. The nearest that the earlier books of the Pentateuch get to this is in Leviticus 17, where all sacrifices, wherever they are killed, must be brought to the door of the Tent of Meeting to be properly offered to God. De Wette argues that the Leviticus passage is earlier than Deuteronomy; but it is also post-Mosaic because it contradicts Exod. 20.24-25, where a multiplicity of altars for sacrifice is envisaged. It also contradicts the behaviour of Samuel, Saul, David and Solomon, who sacrificed wherever necessary without incurring divine disfavour. This continued after the building of the temple by Solomon until the time of Josiah when the law book, not unlikely to be Deuteronomy, was found in the temple: *illum enim codicem legum ab Hilkia sacerdote inventum (2 Reg. XXII) Deuteronomium nostrum fuisse haud improbabile coniectura assequi licet.*[2]

---

1. *Dissertatio*, p. 164 n. 5.
2. *Dissertatio*, p. 165 n. 5 (cont.).

In this footnote, we see already the theory of the history of Israelite religion and sacrifice that would be developed in the *Beiträge*, and would receive classical formulation in the hands of Wellhausen. We also see de Wette committed to the view that priestly material in Leviticus is earlier than Deuteronomy. For the remainder of his life he would disagree with attempts to date this priestly material later than Deuteronomy.

Part Five deals with the Levites and the prominent place that they occupy in Deuteronomy, together with the law of the king (17.14-20), of prophets (18.9-22) and of divorce (24.1-4), showing that these are all later laws. The dissertation concludes by pointing out that the opening of Deuteronomy, in paraphrasing the events recorded in Numbers, at some points contradicts the earlier account. Deuteronomy is designed to supplement and correct the earlier books in the light of a new understanding of religion based upon the centrality of the Jerusalem temple, in an age where the simplicity of earlier Israelite religion had been lost.

De Wette was not the first scholar to link Deuteronomy with Josiah's law book, nor was he the first to argue that there had been a development of Israelite law after the time of Moses.[1] Further, his *Beiträge* of 1806–1807 presented his position with much greater power and precision. Nonetheless, we find present in the dissertation a portrait of the history of Israelite religion that varies radically from that of the Old Testament itself, and which formed the basis for the development of critical scholarship in the nineteenth and twentieth centuries. It is for this that the dissertation ought to be famous!

From where did de Wette get this new conception of Israelite religion? In the first place, it came from the text of the Old Testament itself, and from a readiness to read it in a way that was not constricted by theories of unity of authorship. But underlying this reading is a view of religion that sees it as a simple phenomenon that becomes more complex in the course of time. Where did this come from?

A possible answer is that it came from Schelling's 'Philosophie der Kunst', the lectures of which de Wette almost certainly heard in Jena in 1802–1803.[2] These lectures contain an important section on mythology, in which it is argued that the myths of the Greeks were a

---

1. See my *Old Testament Criticism*, p. 29.
2. *Schellings Werke*, III, pp. 408ff.

spontaneous poetic grasping of the Absolute, and the basis for later religion and philosophy. This idea was not, of course, peculiar to Schelling, but was to be found in the distinction made by Herder, Heyne and Wieland between spontaneous and poetic mythology (*Urmythologie* and *Dichtermythologie*).[1]

Soon after the award of his doctorate in March 1805, de Wette married Eberhardine Boye, the daughter of the Stadtdirektor in Bayreuth. She was five years older than de Wette, and she was living in Jena with her elder sister, who was married to a distinguished physicist, Thomas Johann Seebeck (1770–1831). The Seebecks had been living in Jena since 1802, and numbered among their acquaintances Hegel, Schelling, and de Wette's teacher Griesbach.[2] It is most likely that Griesbach played a part in bringing Eberhardine and de Wette together from the way in which Eberhardine wrote about Griesbach's almost fatherly concern for the couple.[3] In 1811 the Seebecks moved back from Jena to Bayreuth, and lived for some months in the same house as the poet and writer Jean Paul Richter. The link between the Boyes/Seebecks and Jean Paul opens up an intriguing possibility.

In 1835, de Wette visited Bayreuth and was warmly received by Jean Paul's widow. In a letter about his visit dated 11 October 1835,[4] he reminisced about the days when he had visited Bayreuth during the lifetime of Jean Paul and his father-in-law. When did these visits take place? They could have occurred any time up to Jean Paul's death in 1826;[5] but de Wette's marriage to Eberhardine lasted for only ten months, when Eberhardine died in childbirth. It is therefore most likely that de Wette's acquaintance with Jean Paul was at its most intense during his courtship and during his brief marriage, when he will have visited Eberhardine's family. The link between de Wette, Eberhardine and Jean Paul makes it highly likely that Eberhardine appears in de Wette's second novel, *Heinrich Melchthal*.[6]

In this novel, the central female figure is Euphrosyne, and she has a

1. See Strich, *Mythologie* I, pp. 106ff.
2. *Allgemeine Deutsche Biographie* 33 (Leipzig, 1891), pp. 564-65.
3. Wiegand, 'De Wette in Jena', p. 355.
4. Staehelin, *Dewettiana*, p. 166.
5. We know that there was a visit in 1818; see below p. 50.
6. *Heinrich Melchthal, oder Bildung und Gemeingeist: Eine belehrende Geschichte* (Berlin, 1829).

close relationship with Heinrich. The parallels between her and Eberhardine are hardly accidental. She is older than Heinrich, as Eberhardine was older than de Wette. She had lost her first child; Eberhardine's fatal pregnancy produced a stillborn child. Most striking, Euphrosyne's favourite poet was Jean Paul, and in the novel, she introduces Heinrich to his work. Although in the novel Euphrosyne is married to a merchant with whom she has only a very formal relationship, this hardly outweighs the striking parallels between Eberhardine and Euphrosyne.

On the assumption that Eberhardine is represented in the novel by Euphrosyne, the following can be learned about her. Euphrosyne is described as follows:

> a tall, slim figure, almost too slim; a dainty head with the most beautiful chestnut-brown hair, the contours of the face regular and intelligent, but rather sharply formed; blue eyes beneath the slenderest eyebrows.[1]

From this description we get an idea of an almost gaunt woman, possibly taller than de Wette, with slightly angular features. This would agree with Wiegand's comment:

> neither rich nor beautiful, but with a rich spirit [*reich an Geist*], a noble character, and loving and loveable.[2]

We also learn of Euphrosyne that she lacked a deep religious sense and had no conviction of the truth of the Christian faith, having suffered in her youth at the hands of a rationalist preacher who had reduced religion to morality. However, what she lacked in religious conviction she made up for in aesthetic sensitivity, finding in Jean Paul's poetry an ability to put into words the wistful longings of the human heart and a degree of reassurance for such longings. If this was true of Eberhardine, this would explain the opposition of de Wette's father to the marriage, an opposition that Eberhardine sought to break down by writing regularly to her father-in-law during her all-too-brief married life. A union with a woman without any strong religious convictions would indicate a further step away from the ministry, which de Wette's father still hoped his son would enter.

It is to some of the letters written by Eberhardine to her estranged father-in-law that we owe our information about the next stage of

1. *Melchthal*, p. 56.
2. Wiegand, 'De Wette in Jena', p. 355.

de Wette's life. On 2 May 1805 she indicates that de Wette hopes to begin lecturing at Michaelmas.[1] On 29 June she writes to say that a book that her husband has been working on is finished, that in fourteen days or three weeks he will have his disputation, and that his dissertation is complete.[2] All this indicates that he will soon become a *Privatdozent* and begin lectures in the winter semester of 1805. The book referred to must undoubtedly be the *Auffoderung zum Studium der hebräischen Sprache und Litteratur*, which was published in 1805 to coincide with the beginning of his work as a lecturer. It is another important witness to de Wette's intellectual position in this early and vital period of his life.[3]

The *Auffoderung* begins with a complaint that might have been written in the 1990s not 1805, namely, that the study of theology in general, and of Hebrew language and literature in particular, was not being taken sufficiently seriously. De Wette ascribes this situation to the low esteem in which historical studies are held among aspiring theologians. What was the value, it was being asked, of studying the past when time could be better spent on trying to understand the nature of human personality and how it can be built up upon spiritual values? De Wette accepts the force of this argument. Theology should not be a narrow but an all-embracing study, and no one should undertake it who does not aspire to the widest understanding of truth. Thus, certain preparatory studies are necessary for theologians, principal among them being philosophy, art and poetry. These are the avenues that lead to an understanding of what religion essentially is; but they also open the way to the proper study of the history of religions.[4]

Why is the history of religions important? In the first place it enables students to learn to appreciate the many forms that religious experience and conviction take. Secondly, it makes possible a process of discrimination between religious phenomena by means of which the wheat can be separated from the chaff. Although religious phenomena are many and varied, they are not all equally adequate expressions of the essence of religion, and the work of a teacher of religion is not

1. Wiegand, 'De Wette in Jena', p. 355.
2. Wiegand, 'De Wette in Jena', p. 355.
3. Staehelin, *Dewettiana*, p. 11.
4. *Auffoderung zum Studium der Hebräischen Sprache und Litteratur Zur Eröffnung seiner Vorlesungen* (Jena and Leipzig, 1805), pp. 3-9.

merely to sow seeds, but to educate students in terms of clearly-perceived goals, just as a sculptor produces a finished work from a slab of marble. This does not mean, however, that the teacher of religion tries to impose one form of religion upon students; each has to discover personally what is authentically true.[1]

Granted, then, that the history of religion makes possible an appreciation of the variety of forms of religion and provides the means for discriminating between them, de Wette commends what he calls Judaism as offering an unrivalled storehouse for study. It contains many forms of religious expression: myths, philosophy, ceremonies, symbols, prophecies, poetry, folk-religion, mysticism. But it presents these in the context of a growth from chaos to order, from diversity to unity, culminating in the highest achievement of Judaism, namely, monotheism.[2]

At this point, de Wette breaks off his argument to comment on the relation between Judaism and Christianity, and especially the question of continuity and discontinuity. He accepts that Christianity has developed from Judaism, but denies that to say this is to say that Christianity is a 'natural' phenomenon. On the other hand, it is undeniable that, in its language and thought forms, Christianity is deeply indebted to Judaism; and this assertion is the bridge that enables de Wette to comment on the study of Hebrew language. In terms strongly reminiscent of Herder's *Vom Geist der hebräischen Poesie* de Wette speaks of the almost inseparable connection between Hebrew language and ideas. He demands that Hebrew poetry should not be translated, but heard in the original language:

> There is no law here, no fixed form, no metre; the stream of language
> rises and falls like feelings in the breast.[3]

A language gives expression to the distinctive spirit of a people, and is the only means of entry into such a spirit.

Having justified the study of Hebrew, de Wette returns to the point at which he is arguing that the study of Judaism enables forms of religion to be discerned, and discrimination between them to be made. He now describes how this is to be achieved—by a religious rather

1. *Auffoderung*, pp. 10-14.
2. *Auffoderung*, p. 16.
3. *Auffoderung*, p. 24.

than by a historical criticism. To make this clear, he launches a
devastating attack upon the historical criticism of the Old Testament.[1]
It is quite impossible, he maintains, to write a history of the Hebrew
nation. The Old Testament documents are myths or traditions without
historical value, for the simple reason that their authors were not
interested in history in the modern sense. When they looked back and
described their past, they were trying to awake in their readers a
religious response, by drawing attention to how God's plans and
judgments had shown themselves in the pattern of events. But even if
it were possible for a modern scholar to reconstruct a history of the
Hebrews, this would not enable the scholar to find in this history the
revelation of God. The Hebrews had not achieved that synthesis of the
temporal and the eternal which would result in their history being, at
every step, an expression of the eternal in the temporal. Rather, the
history of the Hebrews is a disconnected collection of individual
sequences in which God is revealed, but in no unified way. The
history of the Hebrews has no universal significance; only their religion has this significance, and the study of it requires not a historical
criticism, but a criticism that begins from an understanding of religion, based upon reflection. Only such a criticism can distinguish the
early from the late documents and make possible a history of Old
Testament religion.

The most striking feature of the *Auffoderung* is its attack on the
possibility of recovering very much history from the Old Testament.
Although this has been summarized above, a direct quotation will
indicate the force of de Wette's position:

> a complete and thoroughgoing criticism will show that not one of the his-
> torical books of the Old Testament has any historical value, and that they
> all more or less contain myths and traditions; and that we do not have
> from among any of the books of the Old Testament any real historical wit-
> nesses, except for several prophetic books, which, however, yield little
> historical information.[2]

The same outlook will be found in the *Beiträge*, where de Wette
argues that much of the Pentateuch is mythical, by which he means,
among other things, of no historical value.

Viewed in the light of the history of Old Testament interpretation,

1. *Auffoderung*, pp. 27ff.
2. *Auffoderung*, p. 23.

this is a very radical position. Even the rationalists and neologists held that it was possible to get history out of the Old Testament once it had been suitably decontaminated from crude supernatural and pre-scientific elements. De Wette was going much further and denying the historical value of the Old Testament altogether.

However, looked at in the light of what was happening in literary and philosophical circles, de Wette's position, while remaining radical, is quite understandable. Mythology was one of the major preoccupations of the literary world in Germany from the last third of the eighteenth century, a preoccupation described in massive detail in Fritz Strich's *Die Mythologie in der deutschen Literatur*.[1] Studies of the epic poems of Homer, and the publication of texts relating to Nordic and Celtic mythology had raised many questions. One was whether it was possible for there to be a Christian mythology in the sense of a poetic and dramatic movement inspired by Christian themes rather than by themes drawn from Greek mythology. One attempt to answer this question was Klopstock's monumental poem *Der Messias*, published between 1748 and 1773.[2] But on the whole, literary writers took a different approach, which was to see in Greek mythology in particular an important stage in the philosophical and religious development of mankind, a development which had culminated in Christianity but which could still be of inestimable value to the modern world.

The work from this period which comes closest to what we find later in de Wette's *Auffoderung* and *Beiträge* is Karl Philipp Moritz's *Die Götterlehre*, of 1791.[3] Moritz maintained that myths were neither history nor allegory, but poetry, and to be treated as such. As poetry they were the product of fantasy, the fantasy of a dream-like existence in which the lifeless world of nature was incarnated in gods and heroes. Yet myths also contained sublime ideas and were expressed in noble artistic form.

If de Wette had not read Moritz, he must have known of his work

1. See p. 36 n. 5 above.
2. See K.A. Schleiden (ed.), *Friedrich Gottlieb Klopstock: Ausgewählte Werke* (Munich: Karl Hanser, 1962), pp. 195-770.
3. This work was unobtainable in Britain, but is fully described by Strich, *Mythologie*, pp. 290ff.

from references to it in Schelling's 'Philosophie der Kunst';[1] and it is noteworthy that, shortly after a reference to Moritz, Schelling expressly disassociates himself from the historical-rationalizing interpretation of myths.[2] It is also interesting that de Wette frequently uses the notion of poetic fantasy in the *Beiträge*, as in the sentence:

> here [the writer's] poetic fantasy gave him a suitable opportunity to introduce the Sabbath law, and, untroubled by the need for historical accuracy, he used this opportunity.[3]

Looked at, then, from the perspective of the literary and philosophical world of his day, de Wette was not a rationalizing critic who summarily dismissed the historical value of the Old Testament. It was widely accepted among biblical scholars that the Bible contained myths. De Wette simply applied to their interpretation a view derived from literary and philosophical interpretation: that they were to be seen as instances of fantasy-inspired poetry, expressing the ideas of the people. From this standpoint, it is now possible to turn to the *Beiträge*.

The first part of the *Beiträge* to be written was the second volume, which was published in 1807. This was the re-working of de Wette's dissertation, which he undertook during the early summer of 1805. For this reason, and because it has much in common with the *Auffoderung*, it will be considered first, after an account of its history of composition.

In a letter to Paulus dated 25 April 1805, de Wette wrote:

> this summer I am working on another publication—'On the authenticity of the books of Moses'—in which I hope to settle this old question and shed light on the discussion from all sides.[4]

---

1. *Schellings Werke*, III, p. 432.
2. *Schellings Werke*, III, p. 433:

> Die wunderbare Verflechtung, die in diesen göttlichen Ganzen stattfindet, lässt uns allerdings erwarten, dass auch Züge aus der Geschichte darein spielen. Aber wer kann in diesem lebendigen Ganzen das Einzelne sondern, ohne den Zusammenhang des Ganzen zu zerstören? . . . Sie werden sich nun ferner auch nicht wundern, wenn ich von jenen beliebten historisch-psychologischen Erklärungen der Mythologie keinen Gebrauch gemacht habe, nach welchen der Ursprung der Mythologie in der Bestrebungen roher Natursähne gesucht wird, alles zu personificieren und zu beleben, ungefähr wie es der amerikanische Wilde auch thut. . .

3. *Beiträge*, II, p. 55.
4. Reichlin-Meldegg, *Paulus*, p. 230.

This book was completed early in July, and Griesbach undertook the task of finding a publisher for it.[1] In the meantime the third volume of J.S. Vater's commentary on the Pentateuch appeared, and in some respects it anticipated and duplicated what de Wette had written.[2] The effect of the discovery was shattering. De Wette had been beaten to the post, and, as if this was not bad enough, the financial consequences of not getting his book published were serious for the de Wette family. 'We have lost 80 to 100 Talers!'[3] wrote Eberhardine to de Wette's father on 9 September.

The similarities between de Wette's work and that of Vater were that both adopted a fragmentary hypothesis of the origin of the Pentateuchal traditions, and then used the fragmentary theory to argue for the late composition of the Pentateuch in the form in which we have it. The strategy behind this procedure was the following. Critical defenders of the Mosaic authorship of the Pentateuch, such as Eichhorn, appealed to a documentary hypothesis of the origin of the traditions based, in the first place, upon the fact that the different divine names were used in different chapters of Genesis. On the basis of a documentary theory it could be claimed that the documents had had authors, and that these authors, in the case of the Genesis traditions, had provided the sources used by Moses in his compilation of the Pentateuch.

The strategy used by Vater and de Wette was quite different. They asserted that Genesis to Numbers was a collection of *fragments* which had little or no connection with each other, and which had been gathered together by a collector many hundreds of years after the time of Moses. If each fragment was examined independently, it could be seen to belong to times far later than those of Moses. This view not only had implications for the date and manner of the composition of the Pentateuch, but also for its interpretation. Eichhorn and his followers, especially Gabler and G.L. Bauer, held that the traditions about Abraham and the other patriarchs, about the exodus from Egypt and the wanderings in the wilderness contained authentic historical information about the events which they related, once the supernatural and miraculous trimmings which had embellished them had been

1.   Wiegand, 'De Wette in Jena', p. 356.
2.   Rogerson, *Old Testament Criticism*, pp. 35-36.
3.   Wiegand, 'De Wette in Jena', p. 357.

stripped away. Vater and de Wette did not accept that the narratives contained authentic historical material; rather, the narratives had to be seen as the product of much later times, and interpreted accordingly.[1]

De Wette's 1805 book, then, resembled part of Volume III of Vater's commentary, by being a discussion of the individual fragments which were held to be the basic ingredients of the Pentateuch, with a view to demonstrating their late and thus non-Mosaic origin. We can well understand how shaken and disappointed de Wette was to discover that he had been beaten to the post. But there were also significant differences between the two works, in content and in underlying theory. From Griesbach's foreword to the first volume of de Wette's *Beiträge*, we learn that the 1805 book contained not only the detailed critical handling of the fragments of the Pentateuch, but a section on the unreliability of the books of Chronicles, which argued that these books wrongly projected levitical institutions back to the time of David.[2] Also, Vater's handling of the fragments is not dominated by the overriding concern of de Wette to show that practically everything in the Pentateuch is 'mythical'.

Griesbach explains in his foreword that he advised de Wette to re-work his material, concentrating upon what was original, and down-grading what he had in common with Vater.[3] This de Wette did in what can only have been a matter of about six hectic weeks in August and September 1805. He enlarged the section on Chronicles, using this as a basis for a new theory of the history of Israelite religion, and he postponed to a second volume his treatment of the fragments that made up the Pentateuch. By advising de Wette thus, Griesbach played a vital role in the production of an epoch-making work of scholarship; for of the two volumes of the *Beiträge*, the first is by far the more significant.

However, I propose to deal with the second volume before dealing with the first, because, as stated above, it represents the bulk of what de Wette wrote in the first half of 1805, and is closely connected with the *Auffoderung*. Its main aim is to demonstrate that the Pentateuch, as a whole and in its parts, is 'mythical', the background to which

---

1. J.W. Rogerson, *Myth in Old Testament Interpretation* (Berlin: de Gruyter, 1974), Ch. 1.
2. *Beiträge*, I, p. iv.
3. *Beiträge*, I, pp. vi-vii.

position has already been outlined.[1] De Wette was certain that nothing could be known about the historical Abraham, Isaac, Jacob or Moses, the exodus, the lawgiving or the wilderness wanderings. The reasons were simple. Only with the time of David were the cultural conditions present which made possible the writing down of traditions. That oral traditions had existed prior to the time of David was not in doubt[2] but their unreliability was proved by three accounts of a wife of a patriarch being in danger (Gen. 12.10-19; 20.1-18; 26.1-11) where the same basic event was now related in three quite different ways.[3] But it was an examination of the fragments themselves that more clearly indicated their mythical and thus their non-historical character. Stories which contained miraculous elements, or in which God spoke directly or through an angel, were mythical because such happenings contradicted both general experience and the laws of nature. Stories in which names or customs were explained in terms of etymology were myths, as were those where, without necessary mention of the supernatural, the facts were simply illogical or self-contradictory. Under the latter heading, de Wette wryly remarked that the extermination policy of Pharaoh could not have been particularly successful if 600,000 Israelite males took part in the exodus![4] He also noted that, whereas Solomon had to hire specialists from Sidon to help build the temple, Moses in the wilderness was able to find all the craftsmen and special materials he needed from among the Israelites who were with him when he constructed the tabernacle.[5]

De Wette did not deny the existence of Abraham and Moses, and did not claim that the Israelites had not experienced the exodus from Egypt. His point was that the historical evidence that would enable scholars to know anything about these persons and the circumstances in which they lived was entirely lacking.[6] The fragmentary stories about them were not composed in order to satisfy modern historical curiosity; they served as a vehicle for expressing the religious hopes and identity of much later times. Instead of Abraham the sheikh as

1. See pp. 47-48.
2. *Beiträge*, II, p. 23.
3. *Beiträge*, II, p. 112.
4. *Beiträge*, II, p. 173.
5. *Beiträge*, II, pp. 260-61.
6. *Beiträge*, II, pp. 201ff.

constructed by Eichhorn,[1] the fragments presented Abraham as the ancestor of the Hebrew nation and an example of Hebrew piety.[2] Instead of the historical Moses, the traditions presented the founder of the Israelite theocracy. These figures were valueless for the historian, but of immense value to the theologian who wished to discover the religious beliefs of the Israelite people after the time of David.

In the case of Moses, one or two scraps of information could be gleaned. He had most likely promulgated the Ten Commandments, albeit in a shorter form than that known to us in Exodus 20 and Deuteronomy 5,[3] and had constructed a simple form of tent shrine.[4] On the other hand, he had not established a priesthood, nor given the laws and ceremonies attributed to him.[5]

Volume II of the *Beiträge* does not deal in any systematic manner with the date and composition of the Pentateuch, although the following points can be gleaned from the text. Although de Wette adopted a fragmentary approach,[6] he also accepted the documentary theory in two respects. First he accepted Ilgen's view that the story of Joseph (Gen. 37, 39–47) could be divided into two sources, which could be seen to be self-contained narratives with important differences of detail.[7] Here, de Wette disagreed with Vater, who defended the unity of the passage. Second, and more important, de Wette believed that the Pentateuch had a basic framework, into which other fragments had been incorporated. This framework, which de Wette felt he could sketch only vaguely,[8] coincided, where it could be identified, with Eichhorn's 'Elohim' document. It began with Genesis 1.1–2.4, continued to Genesis 5, contained a flood narrative (6.9-22; 7.11-24; 8.1-5, 13-19; 9.1-17), a genealogy including Abraham from 11.10ff., and then moved to Genesis 17. Thereafter, it was difficult to trace but was detected by de Wette in Genesis 23, 35.9-15, Exodus 1–2, 11–12 (where its traces have all but vanished), 13, 19.17-19, 20.1-17 (fragments).

---

1. Rogerson, *Myth*, p. 17.
2. *Beiträge*, II, p. 103.
3. *Beiträge*, II, p. 274.
4. *Beiträge*, II, p. 268.
5. *Beiträge*, II, p. 267.
6. *Beiträge*, II, p. 311.
7. *Beiträge*, II, pp. 143-57. On Ilgen, see Rogerson, *Old Testament Criticism*, pp. 20-21.
8. *Beiträge*, II, p. 29.

De Wette recognized the presence of this framework, not on the formal grounds of the use of the divine name (this was an unreliable criterion) but on 'inner' grounds of the character of the material, e.g. its simplicity.[1] This framework had been the basis of an epic composition which expressed the rationale of the Israelite theocracy, helping Israel to identify itself as God's chosen people. It described God's promises to the Hebrew forebears that a land would be given and a state founded, and it laid stress on God's covenant with Abraham. The epic, which was the national epic of the Hebrew nation, was written during the monarchy, and inspired imitation (*Nachahmung*). For example, the account of the covenant-making between God and Abraham in Genesis 15 was an imitation of the earlier account in Genesis 17.[2]

De Wette also detected ideological differences between the 'Elohim' epic and the later 'Jehovistic' fragments. The latter make their heroes offer sacrifices, whereas the former knows nothing of sacrifice.[3] Also, although the divine name is not the prime criterion for distinguishing the epic from the later fragments, Jehovah is a later name for God among the Hebrews than Elohim.[4] The epic as a whole is not a historical account:

> It is an epic poem, and the poet wishes to be nothing other than a poet, and certainly not a historian.[5]

De Wette believed that the conclusion to Exodus showed that this book was a complete work. Leviticus, the work of later priests, appended ceremonial law.[6] Numbers was also later than Exodus; it imitated fragments in Exodus and displayed the sort of heightened mythology typical of a later composition. Deuteronomy was pure myth, in the sense that it was a re-presentation of material contained in the previous books.[7] It was the mythical keystone to a mythical Pentateuch, achieving this position by ascribing both historical accounts and legal enactments to a speech delivered by Moses to the Israelites.

---

1. *Beiträge*, II, pp. 29-30.
2. *Beiträge*, II, pp. 79-80.
3. *Beiträge*, II, p. 84.
4. *Beiträge*, II, p. 90.
5. *Beiträge*, II, p. 52.
6. *Beiträge*, II, p. 279.
7. *Beiträge*, II, p. 385ff.

The conclusions of Volume II of the *Beiträge* echo what we have heard in the *Auffoderung*:the value of the Pentateuch lies not in its witness to history but in its witness to religion.

> It is a product of the religious poetry of the Israelite people, which reflects their spirit [*Geist*], way of thought, love of the nation, philosophy of religion.[1]

Thus, as already emphasized, it is not a hard rationalism that is at the heart of de Wette's attempt to show that hardly anything in the Pentateuch is authentic at the level of history. The main motivation is the aesthetic artistic desire to save the Pentateuch from the rationalizing historian so that its poetic beauty will be available to theologians.

There is another interesting connection between Volume II of the *Beiträge* and the *Auffoderung* which sheds light on an otherwise strange passage in the latter. In the *Auffoderung*, de Wette states that history is God's revelation, and that a historian should write as seer, prophet and interpreter of that revelation. But in the case of the Hebrews, he argues, there is no history in the sense of a connected set of events which reveal God at work. Rather, there are only separated glimpses of God's revelation. This puzzling observation becomes clear in its meaning when we remember that, according to Volume II of the *Beiträge*, the Pentateuch is not a connected narrative. It is a series of fragments integrated into a framework of a Hebrew epic, but distorting and obscuring its order. Further, because we cannot know Israel's history, it is clear that we cannot therefore see it as God's revelation, for all that we *can* grasp the spirit of Hebrew religion in the period of the monarchy.

If de Wette had been able to publish his 1805 book in its original form, it is doubtful whether it would have been an epoch-making work. Its observations on many parts of Genesis to Numbers are shrewd and penetrating; yet it presents no overall synthesis except the view that, in order to understand the Pentateuch, its historical authenticity must be completely denied and it must be regarded as a collection of fragments. The first volume of the *Beiträge*, on which de Wette worked feverishly in August and September 1805, is quite a different matter, and it is to this that we must now turn.

Volume I of the *Beiträge* falls into two main sections, the first

---

1. *Beiträge*, II, pp. 359.

dealing with the books of Chronicles, the second with the history of books of Moses and the law-giving. The second section can be subdivided into an examination of the books of Joshua, Psalms and Ezra and Nehemiah, a discussion of the date of the Samaritan Pentateuch, a section on the history of the Israelite cult, and a concluding discussion of the date of Deuteronomy. It is not difficult to guess that the sections that de Wette wrote by way of enlargement of the original work were those on Chronicles and on the history of the Israelite cult; and these are by far the most significant sections, for it is here that new ground is broken. The remainder had been anticipated in Vater's commentary, while the section on Deuteronomy was substantially a re-working of the doctoral dissertation.

The section on Chronicles amounts to two-fifths of the first volume of the *Beiträge*. It opens by claiming that the history of Israelite religion and worship must be the main concern of anyone interested in the history of Israel. This history, from the time of David, is contained in two works, the books of Samuel and Kings, and the books of Chronicles. However, these two accounts are in fact contradictory, although de Wette claims to be the first to have recognized this:

This contradiction, so far as I know, has not been recognized by anyone.[1]

It is thus necessary to discover which is the true and which is the false account. The results obtained will be important both for the history of Israelite religion and for dating the books of Moses.

The first part of de Wette's attempt to demonstrate the unreliability of Chronicles is directed at the then standard critical view that where Samuel and Kings on the one hand, and Chronicles on the other, have material in common, it is because they have drawn on a common source, which included lives of David and Solomon.[2] De Wette argues that Chronicles had in fact used Samuel and Kings as a source, leaving out anything that was detrimental to David, such as his adultery with Bath-sheba and its aftermath as described in 2 Samuel 10–20. The story of David as presented especially in 2 Samuel gives the impression of being an original work whose parts follow on logically from each other. This would not be possible if the author of Samuel had

---

1.   *Beiträge*, I, p. 5.
2.   This was the view of Eichhorn. See Rogerson, *Old Testament Criticism*, p. 22.

been taking excerpts from a source. At certain points, the Chronicler's account contradicts that in Samuel and Kings. These cases can be best explained by supposing that Chronicles had deliberately altered the material in Samuel and Kings to conform to a particular standpoint.

De Wette's next point is that Chronicles is a much later work than Samuel and Kings, possibly dating from the time of Alexander the Great (c. 330 BCE), whereas Samuel and Kings were probably written during the exile (c. 550 BCE);[1] but he returns quickly to the first point, bringing more evidence that Chronicles is a compilation, using Samuel and Kings as a source. Among very many examples adduced is the account of the bringing of the Ark of the Covenant to Jerusalem, which in 2 Samuel 6 gives every indication of being a literary unity, but which appears only in sections, and not in its entirety, in 1 Chronicles 13–15, interspersed with much other material.[2]

The argument is finally completed by indicating tendencies that are present in Chronicles but lacking in Samuel and Kings, which indicate the later and derivative nature of Chronicles. These are, first, a tendency to heighten crude, supernatural details of narratives;[3] second, a preoccupation with the tribe of Levi (in 1 Chron. 15.25 the Ark is carried by Levites when it is brought to Jerusalem; in 2 Sam. 6.13 Levites are not mentioned);[4] third, a deliberate attempt to remove any hints that the cult in Judah or Jerusalem may from time to time have been heterodox (2 Kgs 16.10 says that Ahaz ordered a copy of a Damascus altar to be placed in the Jerusalem temple; 2 Chron. 28.23 says that Ahaz worshipped the gods of Damascus);[5] and fourth, a deliberate bias against Israel and in favour of Judah, which amounts to Chronicles omitting practically everything in Samuel and Kings that has to do with Israel.[6] Such is the power of de Wette's detailed advocacy that the position advanced in this first part of the *Beiträge* has become the generally accepted view of modern scholarship, even if it took over fifty years for this view to gain wide acceptance in the nineteenth century.

---

1. *Beiträge*, I, p. 45.
2. *Beiträge*, I, pp. 85-91.
3. *Beiträge*, I, pp. 78ff.
4. *Beiträge*, I, pp. 80ff.
5. *Beiträge*, I, pp. 102ff.
6. *Beiträge*, I, pp. 126ff.

The next part of the *Beiträge* deals with Joshua, and the purpose of the discussion is to argue that Joshua is a very late book, and that references in it to the Mosaic law cannot be taken as evidence of the Pentateuch in early times. It is worth noting that de Wette recognizes the Deuteronomic nature of Joshua,[1] a view that is another commonplace of modern scholarship. Brief discussions of Samuel, Psalms and Kings prove that there is no evidence for the existence of a Mosaic law before the time of Josiah in the seventh century BCE.[2] In connection with the Psalms, it is interesting to observe that de Wette regards the book as an exilic compilation. The ascription of many Psalms to David is unhistorical. David probably composed the lament over Saul and Jonathan (2 Sam. 1.19-27), and this is sufficient evidence of his style to show that he did not write the psalms ascribed to him in the Psalter.[3]

De Wette now examines closely the account of the discovery of the book of the law in the temple in 622 BCE (2 Kgs 22.8-10).[4] He observes that it is nowhere called the law of Moses, that it seems to be innovatory in character, and that it probably was a version of Deuteronomy:

> we do not maintain that the book that was found was our Deuteronomy in its present form and extent since, as Vater has shown, it has been put together from a number of pieces.[5]

As to its mode of entrance into the temple, one can only speculate, and de Wette does not rule out the possibility that it had been introduced and then 'found' in the temple by Hilkiah the high priest. An examination of books such as Ezra and Nehemiah enables the following conclusion to be drawn:

> until the time of Josiah there is no trace of the existence of the Pentateuch. After that time, especially after the exile, there are the most frequent and evident indications [of its existence].[6]

In the section beginning with his examination of Joshua, de Wette had

---

1. *Beiträge*, I, p. 137 n. 2.
2. *Beiträge*, I, pp. 136-51.
3. *Beiträge*, I, pp. 156-57.
4. *Beiträge*, I, pp. 168-79.
5. *Beiträge*, I, p. 177.
6. *Beiträge*, I, p. 182.

been anticipated by Vater in his commentary, and was also working out what was hinted at in his dissertation. The next part of his argument had also been anticipated by Vater, and concerned the date of the Samaritan Pentateuch.[1] One of the standard arguments in favour of the antiquity of the Pentateuch was that because the Samaritans, thought to be the descendants of the ten northern tribes, possessed the Pentateuch substantially in its canonical form, the Pentateuch must have been complete before the division of the kingdom at the death of Solomon in the tenth century. De Wette points to the abundant evidence for good relations between Judah and Israel after the division of the kingdom, and suggests that the Jewish Pentateuch was most likely introduced to the Samaritans in the fourth century, when a deposed Jerusalem priest set up the Samaritan temple on Mount Gerizim.[2]

With the next section, we come to material most probably written specially for the re-working of the *Beiträge*.[3] It is not duplicated in Vater's commentary, and together with the section on Chronicles it represents an epoch-making contribution to Old Testament study. Here, de Wette sets out to show that the picture of the Israelite cult contained in Exodus to Deuteronomy, with its stress on worship at the sanctuary chosen by God at the hands of duly appointed ministers, contradicts the state of affairs described in parts of Joshua, and in Judges, Samuel and Kings. De Wette identifies the many places where sacrifice was offered to God, and where Israel gathered—Bethel, Shiloh, Shechem, Mizpah, Gilgal, Gibeon, Nob. He points out that there seem to have been temples at Shiloh and Nob. He also stresses the priestly role played by David when the Ark was brought up to Jerusalem. Only under Josiah was a serious attempt first made to centralize the worship and to stamp out the other shrines.

The results of his investigation are summarized as follows:[4]

1. There was no single national sanctuary in Israel until the time of David and Solomon. God was worshipped at many holy places.

---

1. *Beiträge*, I, pp. 188ff.
2. *Beiträge*, I, p. 216.
3. *Beiträge*, I, pp. 226-58.
4. *Beiträge*, I, pp. 254-57.

2. Until the time of David there was complete freedom as to
    how, where and by whom sacrifice should be offered.[1]
3. Only with David were any regular priestly arrangements
    introduced, but probably only for the royal court.
4. After the building of the temple, freedom of worship for
    ordinary Israelites continued. Even pious kings did not try to
    close down the local sanctuaries.
5. The struggle waged, especially by the prophets, against the
    idolatry of the people indicated that the priests had no power
    or influence over the people at large.
6. Only with the reign of Josiah was the first attack made upon
    the freedom of religious worship.

With these observations, de Wette had not quite reached the end of
volume one of the *Beiträge*. There remained some observations about
the Mosaic Tent of Meeting, and a re-presentation, based upon the
doctoral dissertation, of the arguments for Deuteronomy being later
than the others books of the Pentateuch.[2] The volume concludes with a
reassertion of its main thesis: only under Josiah and Hilkiah was a
serious attempt first made to centralize the cult, and the reason was the
'discovery' of Deuteronomy and the enforcing of its prescriptions.

The originality of the *Beiträge* lies in those parts which Griesbach
urged de Wette to expand—the demonstration of the unreliability of
Chronicles and the outlining of a history of Israelite religion radically
at variance with the surface-level account contained in the Old
Testament itself. By showing that Chronicles was an entirely tenden-
tious account of Israelite religion that falsely presented David as the
founder of the postexilic Levitical-Mosaic ceremonial religion, de
Wette unlocked the door that allowed access to a critical scholarly
reconstruction of the history of Israelite religion. Vater had knocked
loudly upon that door, as had J.C.K. Nachtigall at the end of the
eighteenth century.[3] Only de Wette had found the key, and with it, not
only the possibility of critically reconstructing the history of Israelite

---

1. As with the patriarchs and the Homeric Greeks, God's open heaven was his
temple, every meal was a sacrifice, every festive or special occasion was a feast, and
each prophet, king or head of family was without any further ado a priest (*Beiträge*,
I, p. 255).
2. *Beiträge*, I, pp. 258ff.
3. Rogerson, *Old Testament Criticism*, p. 29.

religion but also of dating the books of the Pentateuch and of perceiving the deuteronomic influence upon Joshua and Kings. De Wette himself did not work out all the implications of his discovery; and in some respects, for example in his insistence that Deuteronomy was later than all other parts of the Pentateuch, he was not only wrong but later led himself into inconsistencies. But it was a remarkable achievement for a young man, worked out in a few agonizing weeks in the late summer of 1805.

De Wette could not, of course, have realized the importance for future scholarship of his discoveries. His immediate concern was how to make a living to support his wife, and an expected first child. In 1805 he had finally obtained a Lynker studentship, which yielded 264 thalers for three years. He also became an editorial assistant for the *Jena Literary Magazine*, which yielded 180 thalers annually. There was also the translating from French to German on behalf of Paulus, for the final volume of Schiller's series of translations of historical chronicles from the twelfth century onwards. However, those monies and his earnings from the lectures that he gave from October 1805 were not sufficient to support him.

On 5 January 1806, he wrote to his old head teacher Böttiger:

> the times are bad, and the situation of the book-trade and of the university here is also bad. I have the desire and the courage to work, and I have no work. Can you perhaps get me some translation work? You know my acquaintance with French and English, and I have worked as a translator with the first of these. The last volumes of the Schiller memoirs are mostly my work.[1]

The background to this pessimistic letter was, of course, the Napoleonic attempt to unite Europe under French hegemony, which had a paralysing effect upon central Germany, and which would cost de Wette dearly some months later. Hope seems to glimmer soon after he had written to Böttiger because, in a letter dated 26 January, de Wette says that he has been offered a post in Heidelberg, which he

---

1. Staehelin, *Dewettiana*, pp. 64-65. After Schiller's death in 1805, Paulus had taken over the editorship of the *Allgemeine Sammlung historischer Memoirs vom zwölften Jahrhundert bis auf die neuesten Zeiten*. The 29th volume of Section 2 (Jena, 1806) is the first to carry Paulus's name, and de Wette is presumably referring to this volume.

has accepted.[1] In fact, this is a difficult piece of information to evaluate. De Wette did move to Heidelberg, but not until the spring of 1807, to replace the departing Dereser.

For the remainder of 1806 de Wette stayed in Jena, presumably preparing Volume II of the *Beiträge* for publication, giving his lectures, and on 16 August delivering an address in Latin in defence of the Augsburg Confession as part of his duty as a holder of the Lynker scholarship.[2] However, 1806 proved to be the saddest year of his life. After the victorious French troops entered Jena on 13 October 1806, de Wette's possessions were plundered, and his impecunious situation was made even worse. But the greatest loss, and one which he never forgot, was the death of Eberhardine on 18 February in childbirth. The child had been stillborn. De Wette was never again to achieve the domestic bliss which he had enjoyed for barely ten months, and if the conjecture is correct, that Eberhardine appears in the novel *Heinrich Melchthal* as Euphrosyne, she was still in his thoughts twenty-five years later. The intensity of de Wette's grief can be more readily understood from a letter he wrote to Eberhardine's mother after the stillbirth and shortly before his wife's death:

> I am informing you about my dear wife's delivery. It is a sad story, and it is with painful feeling that I write these first lines. At 3 a.m. this morning the terrible struggle ended through an operation carried out by Hofrat Stark; the child was dead. Spare me the description of the suffering which my poor wife endured. Apart from extreme exhaustion, my poor wife is well, and her good nature vouches for her recovery. It is a difficult fate; the loss which I have suffered is irreparable. But as I was composed in the awful struggle, so I am now composed. My love for Eberhardine, which stands before God, gives me comfort. Oh, what a mother she would have been! O good God, why have you not permitted the offspring [reading *Erbe* for *Erde*] of this beautiful example to live? My Eberhardine has suffered unspeakably and in vain; but I will reward her. Even if

---

1.   De Wette Nachlass, A4.
2.   'Vindiciae auctoritatis qua Augustana Confessio praedita est symbolicae. Oratio solemnis quam ex instituto Lynkeriano habuit Guil. Mart. Leber. de Wette', *Zeitschrift für die historische Theologie* 17 n.s. (1853), pp. 644-51. In view of de Wette's 'discovery' in Berlin in 1817 (see below pp. 136-38) the following passage is of interest: 'Christus summum boni exemplar est, quod nobis ad imitandum proponamus; primus est veritatis fons, ex quo hauriamus; nemo enim Deum vidit nisi filius, qui e coelis descendit eumque nobis revelavit, Jesus Christus.'

previously I have lived in her and for her, so from now on, every drop of blood will be dedicated to her. I will summon up my complete supply of love. O God, preserve her for me.[1]

De Wette's hopes and prayers were not answered. Eberhardine died in his arms, an event no doubt described in *Heinrich Melchthal* where the hero's wife Gertrud dies in his arms, and there is a noble reflection upon the process of the death of a loved one.[2] That reflection was, of course, written over twenty years later. For the moment, de Wette was absolutely shattered; and he never really recovered from this loss.

When the time came to leave Jena, de Wette wrote to Böttiger:

Here I was awoken and developed manhood, here I have loved and suffered, here I have friends whose like I shall not find again.

He looks forward to the opportunities that Heidelberg will offer and concludes, significantly for his future development:

As soon as I can, I shall go over the Church History, to the goal of my theological striving.[3]

---

1. Wiegand, 'De Wette in Jena', pp. 357-58.
2. *Melchthal*, I, pp. 216-20.
3. Staehelin, *Dewettiana*, p. 65.

Chapter 3

HEIDELBERG

Between the end of March, when he wrote to Böttiger from Jena, and the beginning of the summer semester in May 1807, de Wette moved to Heidelberg. Some confusion exists as to the exact nature of his appointment. Wiegand says that he was appointed to a position in philosophy,[1] others say, that it was to a post in theology. The matter is explained by the fact that, in Heidelberg at that time, teachers in the theological faculty were also given nominal positions in the philosophical faculty so that they could receive a full salary.[2] De Wette's starting salary is given as 500 guilders. The reason for de Wette's appointment was the break-up in 1807 of the united Catholic–Lutheran–Reformed Faculty, when the Catholics withdrew to Freiburg. De Wette succeeded the Catholic Dereser.[3]

During his time in Heidelberg, de Wette lectured on Hebrew, Syriac and Aramaic, on hermeneutics and introduction to the Bible, and on the Pentateuch, Job, Psalms and Isaiah.[4] We learn from a letter

1. Wiegand, 'De Wette in Heidelberg', *Kirchen und Schulblatt* 23 (1874), p. 82: 'Mit Freuden nimmt er diesen Ruf an, obgleich die Stelle als ausserordentlicher Professor der Philosophie nur mit 500 Gulden dotirt war'.
2. Reichlin-Meldegg, *Paulus*, p. 425.
3. On the reorganization, see H. Bornkamm, 'Die theologische Fakultät Heidelberg', in *Ruperto-Carola: Aus der Geschichte der Universität Heildelberg und ihrer Fakultäten* (Heidelberg, 1961), pp. 144ff. On de Wette's appointment, Merx ('Morgenländische Studien', p. 29 n. 1) says that the archives of the Baden government give no information as to who invited de Wette to Heidelberg. R.A. Keller (*Geschichte der Universität Heidelberg im ersten Jahrzehnt nach der Reorganisation durch Karl Friedrich 1803–1813* [Heidelberger Abhandlungen zur mittleren und neueren Geschichte, 40; Heidelberg: C. Winter, 1913], pp. 175-76) credits S. von Reitzenstein with the invitation.
4. Merx, 'Morgenländische Studien', p. 41.

written to Schleiermacher on 24 July 1810[1] that he had been lecturing on New Testament literature and on biblical theology. The same letter says that an air of dissatisfaction is prevalant in Heidelberg. Two years earlier he had written to Böttiger that things were going well, and that he was well satisfied with his situation.[2] In a letter dated 10 February 1817 to the publisher Johann Georg Zimmer, de Wette reminisced about the lovely time when they had enjoyed together the blossoming university in Heidelberg, although he admits that he has done better in Berlin, freed from the pressures of Heidelberg.[3] In 1809 he was promoted to a full professorship in theology, with a salary of 1,000 guilders. In September of the same year he married Henrietta Beck, a widow with a son of eleven. The marriage was to bring the very opposite of the satisfaction of his relationship with Eberhardine.

Generally speaking we know very little about de Wette's time in Heidelberg. Few letters have survived, and Wiegand's accounts are sparse. Keller lifts the veil slightly when he lists de Wette as one of thirty-one professors who signed a document opposing the attempt of a professor Klüber to reorganize the university police and discipline on 21 December 1808.[4] The occasion for this reorganization was alleged immorality and bad behaviour among the students. Once again, however, it will be necessary to turn to the novel *Theodor*, for this provides much information about the discussions that de Wette had while in Heidelberg with his friend Fries. First, however, his main published work written while he was in Heidelberg will be considered, namely, the *Beytrag zur Charakteristik des Hebräismus* of 1807, the translation of parts of the Old Testament of 1809–11 and the Psalms commentary, which, although published after he had arrived in Berlin, was the fruit of his time in Heidelberg.[5]

The *Beytrag* was published in the Heidelberg series of *Studien* edited by Daub and Creuzer in 1807. In it, we find an apparently totally different de Wette from the de Wette of the *Beiträge*. Whereas the latter is sharply and brilliantly critical, the *Beytrag* is mystical and

1. Staehelin, *Dewettiana*, p. 68.
2. Staehelin, *Dewettiana*, p. 67.
3. H.W.B. Zimmer (ed.), *Johann Georg Zimmer und die Romantiker: Ein Beitrag zur Geschichte der Romantik* (Frankfurt, 1888), pp. 335-36.
4. Keller, *Geschichte*, pp. 140-41.
5. *Beytrag zur Charakteristik des Hebräismus* (ed. C. Daub and F. Creuzer; Studien, III. 2; Heidelberg, 1807), pp. 241-312.

meditative. Yet this must not be attributed to the influence of Heidelberg upon de Wette, as though he suddenly fell under the spell of men such as Görries and Creuzer, who were interested in the mystical interpretation of myths.[1] De Wette was described by the American Theodore Parker as a rationalist and a mystic at the same time, without, however, quite succeeding in reconciling these contrasting aspects of his character.[2] In the *Beytrag* we see the mystical side of de Wette. Indeed, there is perhaps no work which so deeply expresses his mysticism; and it is also one of his most remarkable works on the Old Testament.

From one point of view, it is an enlargement of one of the themes of the *Auffoderung*. There, he had spoken of the relationship between Judaism and Christianity, and of the importance of tracing the development of the latter out of the former. Here, he seems to undertake that task; but, true to his position in the *Beiträge* he does not attempt to do it historically, but in an aesthetic, 'inner' way. The bulk of the piece is devoted to an examination of the Psalms, Job, and Ecclesiastes from the standpoint of the question: how do these writings grapple with the problem of contradiction (*Zweckwiedrigkeit*), that is, the contradictions involved in the suffering of the innocent individual, and of the nation that is called to be God's people? Or, to put it in different words, the contradiction between the inner and the outer, between the (inner) conviction of individuals that they are free, and the (outer) constraints and conditions in life which seem to coerce a person.

This is a problem that was fully discussed by Fries, both in his *Wissen, Glaube und Ahndung* of 1805 and his *Neue oder anthropologische Kritik der Vernunft*, which began to appear in 1807, the year of publication of the *Beytrag*.[3] Fries held that the age-old problem of theodicy, that of justifying the ways of a good God in an apparently imperfect and evil world, did not belong to the realm of reason but to *Ahndung*, that human capacity that sensed eternal realities and

1. Thus, wrongly, Keller, *Geschichte*, pp. 175-76.
2. See Weiss, *Parker*, p. 245: 'He is both critical and mystical, so seems sometimes to waver, and does lean as one or the other element gets the upper hand' (German trans. in Alther, *Parker*, p. 116).
3. J.F. Fries, *Wissen, Glaube und Ahndung* (Jena, 1805). New edition L. Nelson (ed.) (Göttingen: Vandenhoeck & Ruprecht, 1905), with exactly the same pagination; *Neue oder anthropologische Kritik der Vernunft* (Heidelberg, 1807). A reprint of the second edition (1828) can be found in *Sämmtliche Werke* (Aalen, 1967).

expressed these intuitions in myths, poetry, art, and so forth. At the level of reason there was simply no explanation for injustice and innocent suffering. In art and religion, however, these problems were explored, and the person involved was able to learn to accept the paradox.[1]

It is most likely that de Wette's acquaintance with Fries in Heidelberg, and the fact that Fries had been lecturing on this theme in Heidelberg in 1805–1806 and was preparing his lectures for publication in the *Neue Kritik* was the immediate source of de Wette's standpoint on the *Beytrag*. The question, then, was how did the Old Testament deal with the contradictions of life? In answering this on behalf of the Psalms, de Wette identified the categories that, over one hundred years later, would come to be known as individual and communal psalms of lament.[2] De Wette called them *Unglückspsalmen*: psalms of ill fortune. *Unglück* was almost a technical term in Fries's philosophy for the contradiction between the ideal and the real, between the innocence of the just, and the injustice of their suffering.[3] More than half of the 150 psalms were, de Wette pointed out, concerned with misfortune, suffering, toil, and the like. The Hebrews, then, clearly perceived the contradictions of life, and struggled with them in the lyrical collection of the Psalter.[4]

The book of Job also perceived the difficulty of belief in order and justice, but solved the problem in a manner unsurpassed in the Old Testament.[5] This was achieved in the divine speeches, and in Job's submissive response in 42.5-6. De Wette's conclusion deserves to be quoted in full:

> The knot is not untied but cut. Peace is not concluded between the temporal and the eternal; the temporal achieves complete submission, giving up all claim to its own existence, freedom and insight. God (Eloah) is not justified but removed above the need for justification. Instead of the sought-for answer, there comes blind faith; and it is not the faith of love, but that of the feeling of weakness and nothingness that reconciles Job with God.[6]

1. Fries, *Wissen*, pp. 149ff.; *Neue Kritik*, III, p. 364.
2. *Beytrag*, pp. 253-67.
3. Fries, *Wissen*, pp. 150ff.
4. Cf. Fries, *Neue Kritik*, III, p. 364.
5. *Beytrag*, pp. 278-86.
6. *Beytrag*, p. 286.

In Ecclesiastes, de Wette found a product of Hebrew philosophy that combined scepticism and belief in a remarkable manner. Its author resembled a man who, coming to the end of his life and looking back over it, saw that nothing that he had hoped or worked for had been achieved. So overwhelmed was he by what he saw as the purposelessness and futility of human living, that he found value only in enjoying the present moment. But he did not abandon belief in God, and herein lies the supreme religious value of Ecclesiastes—that its author held on to belief in spite of his feelings of the pointlessness of the world.[1]

The characteristic feature of Hebrew religion, then, as illustrated by Psalms, Job and Ecclesiastes, was an inwardness based upon attempts to grapple with the contradictory nature of human existence. De Wette likened the Hebrew nation to a child that had never been young, and that spent its time thinking about its inner life. Granted this, it was no surprise that both the prophetic and the historical traditions of the Old Testament devoted so much space to the self-criticism of the nation.[2] Yet it was precisely this feature of Hebrew religion that provided the matrix for the emergence of Christianity. Along with and because of the attempts to cope with the perceptions of the contradictions of human existence, there were in the Old Testament intuitions of a future order of existence from which these contradictions were absent. These were the so-called messianic prophecies, although it was wrong to see them simply as searching for what ought to be.

The longings for a new order were fulfilled in Christianity, and in the work of Christ. Judaism was a religion of misfortune (*Unglück*) and Christianity was the consolation for it.[3] Yet this consolation was a spiritual, not a material consolation.[4] Christ, in the Sermon on the Mount, offered consolation to the poor and sad in spirit, to those whose experience was expressed in the psalms of lament. But Christ offered no new philosophy or solution to the problem of the contradictions of life. Rather, he showed in the way he lived how the problem was to be overcome, through love and obedience.

The *Beytrag* is not only a highly original interpretation of the Old Testament; it is also an important clue to de Wette's own belief at this

---

1. *Beytrag*, pp. 288ff.
2. *Beytrag*, p. 251.
3. *Beytrag*, p. 245.
4. *Beytrag*, p. 312.

time, a belief no doubt deeply affected by the death of his wife. It was a belief which, if it did not deny the ultimate reality of evil, at least held that our experience of evil and misfortune was not the only clue to ultimate reality. Account had also to be taken of our inner moral and aesthetic experience, on the grounds of which we could believe that we were morally free, and that ultimate reality was in fact a harmony of the highest values of truth, beauty and goodness. Evil and misfortune were to be overcome by seeing them in the light of the total experience of reality, a total experience in which the moral and the aesthetic played the primary role. The Old Testament had not been able to appreciate the totality of reality. Only with the coming of Christ was an indication given on how the vicissitudes of life could be put in their proper place in the light of a mission dedicated to eternal spiritual values.

De Wette's next project was a new translation of the Bible, which began to appear in 1809 as a joint venture between de Wette and the Jena professor of Oriental Languages, J.C.W. Augusti. As the senior partner, Augusti provided the preface for the first volume. However, according to the preface to the second edition, for which de Wette was wholly responsible when it was published in 1831, it was de Wette who was the moving force behind the original undertaking.[1] For the Old Testament, which was published in four parts in 1809–10, de Wette was responsible for the Pentateuch, Samuel, Kings, Chronicles, Job, Psalms, Jeremiah, Lamentations, Daniel and the twelve minor prophets. The translation project was part of an ambitious scheme to provide not only a new translation but also a complete set of commentaries on the Bible.[2] De Wette's Psalms commentary

---

1. *Die heilige Schrift des Alten und Neuen Testaments* (trans. W.M.L. de Wette; Heidelberg, 1831), II, p. iii:

> Da nun die erste Auflage vergriffen war, so machte ich, von dem die erste Anregung zum Unternehmen ausgegangen, auch die meisten Bücher übersetzt worden waren, meinem verehrten Freunde und Mitarbeiter den Vorschlag, ob er mir nicht die Umarbeitung des Ganzen überlassen wollte.

2. *Die Schriften des Alten Testaments: Neu übersetzt von J.C.W. Augusti und W.M.L. de Wette* (Heidelberg, 1809–11). See, in vol. IV (1810):

> eine Ankündigung eines Commentars über alle biblischen Bücher. . . Von diesem Commentar über das A.T. wird schon zu Weihnachten d.J. des III Bandes 2 Abth. oder der Commentar über die Psalmen erscheinen.

was the first (and last) contribution to the commentary series, although in his later years he wrote commentaries on all the books of the New Testament.

Bible translation was nothing new in Germany in 1809, and among recent versions that were mentioned in Augusti's preface were those by W.F. Hezel (1780–91), J.D. Michaelis (1769–83) and the Roman Catholic Dominic von Brentano (1797–1800). De Wette's aims and assumptions were set out in the preface to the second edition.[1] He was not trying to translate the Bible into the German of the nineteenth century, because he believed it was difficult to separate the form of a language and the ideas that were expressed in it. Hebrew had a child-like and naive way of expressing its ideas, as witnessed by the frequent use of 'and' which could be found today in the speech of children and of ordinary people. Fortunately, Luther's translation of the Bible had introduced many Hebraisms into the German language, and de Wette felt sure that, in any case, German could be receptive to the simplicity of Hebrew, and to its concrete images. The translation was intended for students, preachers or general readers who desired the best possible acccess to the original text, via a translation.

What follows now can only be an impression based upon sampling of the translation. In the first place it is a bold translation in the sense that it is prepared to depart from the traditional Hebrew text, following the evidence of the ancient versions and, in some cases, conjectural emendations. Thus in Gen. 4.8 the words 'let us go into the field' are added with the ancient versions, while in 2 Sam. 4.6, 'and Uzzah went' are added by conjecture before 'with the Ark'. In places where it seemed that something was lost, dots were put in, as in 2 Sam. 5.8, 'whoever smites the Jebusites and reaches the water channel, and the lame and the blind who are hated by David in (his) heart. . .'. In cases where there were possible radical and important differences in translation, these were indicated. Gen. 49.10 is a famous messianic passage, with several textual and translation difficulties. De Wette translated it:

> Until he comes, to whom honour is due
> And to him the nations are obedient;

---

1. *Heilige Schrift*, pp. iiiff.

but he gave as possible alternatives:

> Until one comes to Shiloh
> [or] Until rest comes
> [or] As long as posterity comes.

There were also critical and philological notes to explain these and similar difficulties. Another feature was a series of explanatory footnotes, for example at 1 Sam. 10.5, where 'to prophesy' is explained as 'to sing prophetic (inspired religious) songs or to recite speeches'. Proper names whose sense is thought to be important are explained; for example, in Gen. 32.2 we find 'Mahanaim' (double camp).

In the translation of the poetic books, de Wette attempted to provide a version that reproduced something of the rhythm of the Hebrew, something that he revised out of the second and third editions. The result is striking, as the following example from Job 9 indicates:

> 2. Fürwahr! ich weiss es, also ists.
>   Welcher Mensch ist gerecht vor Gott?
> 3. Wenn er auch möchte mit ihm rechten
>   Nicht antwortet' er ihm eins von tausend.
> 4. Ihm, dem Weisen, dem Gewaltigen
>   Wer widersetzt sich ihm ungestraft?
> 5. Er reisst Berge aus unversehens,
>   Und kehret sie um in Zorn;
> 6. Er rüttelt die Erde von ihrer Stelle,
>   Dass ihre Säulen erbeben;
> 7. Er befiehlt der Sonne, dass sie nicht aufgeht,
>   Und schliesst die Sterne unter Siegel.
> 8. Er senket den Himmel, er allein,
>   und wandelt über die Wogen des Meeres.

> [Truly! I know it, therefore it is.
> What man is just before God?
> If he would dispute with him,
> not one in a thousand could answer him.
> Against him, the wise, the mighty,
> who could oppose him unscathed?
> He rips out mountains unawares,
> and overturns them in anger.
> He shakes the earth from its place
> so that its pillars shudder;
> he commands the sun not to rise

and shuts the stars under a seal.
He bends the heaven, he alone,
and walks on the waves of the sea.]

De Wette's part in the translation combined the two sides of his nature, the critical and the poetic. On the one hand, the translation was to be as true as possible by way of indicating the sense, and the nosense of the original; yet it was to be a work of art, especially in its translation of poetry. The *Beytrag* had concentrated upon the poetic books of Psalms and Job, and it is therefore natural that, as the first contribution of the projected commentary series, de Wette should have turned to the Psalms.

The main approaches to the interpretation of the Psalms in 1811 were historical and cultic. The historical interpretation had very deep roots, going back to the titles of the psalms, which, while not authentic, dated from the first century BCE. In some cases, the titles related psalms to incidents in the life of David thus indicating a historical interpretation. The titles had then exerted great infuence upon Jewish and Christian interpreters. With the rise of critical scholarship in the seventeenth and eighteenth centuries, the authenticity of the titles was challenged, but commentators had not abandoned the historical interpretation. They merely looked for different, usually later, situations than those of David's life for the original setting of the psalms. Already in the eighteenth century could be found the suggestion that many of the psalms were as late as the second century BCE, i.e. that they were Maccabaean. A commentary often cited by de Wette that urged this viewpoint was that of Herrmann Venema, published in 1762–67. The cultic interpretation, which in many ways was a type of historical interpretation, linked certain psalms to cultic occasions, for example the dedication of the temple, or the bringing of the Ark to Jerusalem by David. It, too, can be found in mediaeval Jewish interpretations but was stressed in the eighteenth century, for example, by Othmar (Nachtigall).[1]

De Wette set out to oppose as strongly as possible both the historical and the cultic approaches for reasons that combined both the critical and the aesthetic sides of his personality. On the critical side, his objection to suggested historical and cultic original settings for many of the psalms was the simple fact that the details of the psalms did not

---

1.   Rogerson, *Old Testament Criticism*, p. 160.

fit the proposed settings. On the aesthetic side, de Wette wanted to argue that a good number of psalms were composed by individual pious Israelites who were giving lyrical poetic expression to their feelings of pain, trouble, hope, joy and thankfulness. As such, they were evidence not only for the great deal of poetry that the Hebrews must once have possessed, they were also an indication of the nature of Hebrew religion. They were certainly not, except in a few cases, the work of cultic officials, which, by definition, would be non-poetic set prayers, temple hymns and collections of proverbs.[1]

De Wette's desire to locate the heart of the Psalter in the poetic outpourings of individual Israelites was reinforced by his view of the nature of Hebrew poetry. In what was by far the longest section of the introduction to the commentary, he set out carefully the history of interpretation of Hebrew poetry, noting three types of view: those who had tried to discover metre in Hebrew poetry, those who denied that there was any metre, and those who accepted that there had been metre but doubted whether it could be rediscovered. De Wette sided with those who denied that metre was a feature of Hebrew poetry.[2] He appreciated the point of those who said that it was not known how biblical Hebrew had been spoken, but preferred the view that the Massoretic punctuation was a reliable guide to how Hebrew had been pronounced and held that this displayed no trace of poetic metre.[3]

His own view of poetry in general was that it did not require metre, as indicated not only by ancient German poetry, but even by some of the poems of Goethe. In the particular case of Hebrew poetry, it was characterized by a 'rhythm of ideas' (*Gedanken-Rhythmus*) which resulted from a particular way of thinking and speaking on the part of someone who was deeply moved. Very short sentences were used, and because words were not adequate to express the feelings, the short sentences dealt with the same subject matter several times over, using different expressions, or looking at the main point from different angles. Thus arose the phenomenon of parallelism, in which the same idea was expressed in more than one way.[4]

De Wette did not discuss parallelism in detail, but referred readers

---

1. *Commentar über die Psalmen* (Heidelberg, 1811), p. 2.
2. *Commentar*, pp. 55-59.
3. *Commentar*, p. 59.
4. *Commentar*, pp. 68ff.

to Lowth's famous *Praelectiones*.[1] He was more interested in following up how the attempt to express ideas affected the number of words used. He pointed out, first, that 'equality of ideas' (*Gedankengleichheit*) could result in 'equality of words' (*Wortgleichheit*) in two parallel sentences, giving as an example the Song of Lamech in Gen. 4.23.[2] Opposed to instances of 'equality of words' were those where there was obvious imbalance, which was clearly a poetic device. This could take a number of forms. For example, not only could a long line be followed by a shorter one, or vice versa, but one line could also be balanced by two lines.[3]

Hebrew poetry, then, was essentially 'inner', in that inner feelings determined the mode of expression of ideas, and whether this would entail equal or unequal numbers of words in each line. Opposed to 'inner' poetry was 'outer' poetry, which had imitated the outward form of the 'inner' poetry, in particular the formal equality of numbers of words in each line. This poetry could be distinguished from the 'inner' poetry, because the parallelism was one of words not ideas, as, for example, in Psalm 19.12:

> Through them your servant will be instructed,
> In keeping them there is great reward.[4]

De Wette considered that the book of Lamentations was an instance of this 'outer' poetry of parallelism of words, as were all of the acrostic psalms in the Old Testament, which he regarded as evidence of a late devalued type of poetry.

In his introduction to the commentary, de Wette classified the Psalms

1. R. Lowth, *Praelectiones de sacra poesie hebraeorum* (trans. R. Gregory, London, 1787).

2. *Commentar*, p. 70:

> Ada und Zilla höret meine Stimme!
> Weiber Lamechs, vernehmet meine Rede!
> Wenn einen Mann ich schlug mit Wunden.
> Und einen Jüngling—mit Beulen:
> Wenn siebenmal gerochen ward Kain,
> So Lamech—sieben und siebenzig Mal.

3. E.g. Ps. 68.33 (*Commentar*, p. 71):

> Ihr Könige der Erde, singet Gott;
> Spielet dem Herrn!

4. *Commentar*, p. 77.

into six main categories: Hymns, National Psalms, Zion and Temple Psalms, Royal Psalms, Laments, and Religious and Moral Psalms;[1] yet this division does not do justice to what appears in the commentary proper, and indeed is sometimes contradicted in what follows. For example, Psalm 15 is given in the introduction as a Zion and Temple Psalm, in accordance with the general opinion that it was used when David brought the Ark to Jerusalem. In the commentary, however, de Wette warned against building too much on this hypothesis, and pointed out that Psalm 15 was similar in many respects to Psalm 1, a commendation of moral teaching. It is unsafe to rely on de Wette's introduction if one wants to know how he classified the Psalms, not only because he was not completely consistent, but because much information in the commentary proper is not to be found in the introduction. At the same time, de Wette is not always as clear as one would wish in the commentary proper, partly because he sometimes feels that certainty is not attainable. For example, it is not always clear whether he thinks that a psalm is an individual or a national lament. Bearing these difficulties in mind, the following is the result of an analysis of de Wette's view of the content, function and date of the Psalms.

Date of the Psalms
Only eight psalms—10, 18, 48, 68, 83, 89, 132 and 141—are definitely pre-exilic, with a further five—24, 25, 32, 87 and 133—possibly pre-exilic. Of these, Psalm 18 is Davidic, 132 was used for the dedication of the temple, and 133 composed possibly for David's coronation. Psalm 10 is one of the oldest, and is a model for other laments. The idea that, with Psalm 9, it was once an acrostic psalm, is rejected.

Psalms dating from the exile or early postexilic period are: (13), 14, 22, (24), 33-35, 37, 51, 56–58, 61, 63, 77, 78, 82, 85, 86, 88, 96, 98, 99, 102-107, 115, 120–22, (123), 126–27, 135–36, 145, 147.

There are no fewer than twenty-nine certain and five possible psalms from the Maccabaean period, namely, (5), (9), 44, 60, 66, 74–76, 79, (87), (92), 94–95, 97, (109), 110–114, 116, 118–19, 124–25, 129–30, 135–39, 144, 148–50. It is interesting that most of these come from the second half of the Psalter.

1. *Commentar*, pp. 4-5.

Types of Psalm

Although it is not always clear whether a psalm is an individual or national lament, the largest class seems to be the national lament, comprising thirty-two psalms: (5), 6, 11, 12, 14, 17, 25, (26), (28), 30–31, (34), 35–36, 44, (54), 59, 62, 65, 69–70, 74, 77, 86, 90, 94, 115–16, 123, 130, 140, 142. There are twenty-six individual laments: 3, (4), 7, 10, 13, 16, 19, 22, 27, 38–41, 52, 55–58, 64, 69, 88, 120, 141, 143, 145. Psalms which are moral-teaching psalms include 1, 5, 15, 37, 49, 50, 73, 80, 91; while to the category of hymns belong 8, 29, 33, 46–47, 146. Among psalms to which de Wette believes a historical or cultic interpretation can be given are 20–21 (prayer for a royal expedition); 24 (dedication of Solomon's or Zerubbabel's temple); 32 (an atonement festival); 45 (ode to a Persian king); 61 (prayer for ending of exile); 68 (return of the Ark after a battle); 72 (a coronation); 81 (used at Passover); 93, 99–100 (temple Psalms); 118 (inauguration of Simon Maccabeus); 132 (dedication of Solomon's temple); 133 (coronation of David).

On individual psalms the following comments are noteworthy. Psalm 1 is seen as a psalm of reassurance, deliberately placed at the head of a collection of many laments in which the difficulties of the faithful will be rehearsed. Psalm 32 concerns an inner experience of forgiveness that brings it close to Christianity. Psalm 51, on the other hand, receives short shrift. It is one of the latest and worst of the psalms, because the psalmist believes that God would want him to offer a sacrifice if this were physically possible (which it is not). The messianic interpretation of the Psalms is largely rejected on two grounds. First, it involves reading into the text alien ideas: second, it does scant justice to what the Christian conception of the messiah ought to be, in the light of Jesus, who is not a warmonger. Psalm 22 is almost messianic in a Christian sense, in that it envisages the conversion of the nations (vv. 27-28). In Ps. 17.15 there is a reference to immortality, which suggests that this belief was present in Israel from early times.

The Psalms commentary, then, is fully representative of de Wette's thinking during the Jena and Heidelberg periods. It displays scepticism and indifference to matters historical. It is not impossible, and in any case of little value, to determine the original historical setting of many psalms. What matters most is religion, seen as an expression in lyrical aesthetic forms of experiences of doubt, uncertainty, joy and hope.

The lament psalms, which comprise well over a third of the whole collection, are at the heart of the Psalter, expressing at individual and corporate levels the religious struggles of the nation and its pious members. It is a way in to the inner sanctuary of Old Testament religion.

If the Psalms commentary is representative of de Wette's Heidelberg views, it must also be recognized that, while in Heidelberg, de Wette spent much time in conversation with his colleague Fries. In his reminiscence, written in September 1843 following Fries's death, de Wette recalled that he and Fries had had many conversations while walking along the banks of the River Neckar.[1] In *Theodor*, the hero has four long dialogues with Professor A., who is undoubtedly Fries. In what follows, I shall assume that this section of *Theodor* recalls de Wette's conversations with Fries, and that this chronicles his theological development at this time. Four matters were of central concern: the relation between reason and revelation, the status of miracles, the relation between religion and morality, and the function of traditional Christian dogmatic formularies.

It will be recalled that de Wette was acutely aware of the problem of the relation between reason and revelation, in the sense that reason could articulate necessary truths whereas revelation was always in a historical, that is, contingent form. De Wette accepted that reason must be the final arbiter of whether something was revelation or not, but he was unhappy that human reason thereby seemed to take the place of God in the scheme of things. Fries distinguished between reason (*Vernunft*) and understanding (*Verstand*), and held that there were two types of revelation, one of which was necessarily true, the other of which was contingent.

Understanding (*Verstand*) was the facility whereby a person organized sense-perceptions into an ordered whole. It was concerned with the world of empirical experience. Reason (*Vernunft*) was the facility connected with moral and aesthetic experience, and had as its source a revelation that was necessarily true. This revelation, possessed by all human beings, was a reflection of the ultimate and ideal values of goodness, truth and beauty. The clash between reason and revelation, which had exercized so many minds from the seventeenth century onwards, was really a clash between understanding (*Verstand*) and

---

1.   Staehelin, *Dewettiana*, pp. 179-80; cf. Henke, *Fries*, p. 284.

revelation understood in terms of historical events and their records. It was natural that if a record related miraculous events that contradicted scientific experience of the world, then a tension between understanding and revelation would be felt. However, there was no clash between reason (*Vernunft*) and the revelation, that is, the reflection of ideal values, that was its source. The origin of the commonly-understood clash between reason and revelation resulted from an insufficiently sophisticated understanding of the nature of human knowledge. Empirical understanding was not placed in its proper relationship with reason and with moral and aesthetic values. Further, it was necessary to accept that reason needed faith in order to realize that its intimations of goodness and truth were reflections of eternal values.

These distinctions made by Fries had a powerful effect on de Wette. In *Theodor* we read:

> To our friend [Theodor] it was as though by magic that these insights ordered into a beautiful system the scattered fragments of his previous insights and convictions. The gap which he had seen between the systems of Kant and Schelling seemed to him to be bridged. The idealistic or inner view of the world was upheld, but not as the highest or only view. The dependency and limitation of human knowledge was recognized, and the point was identified where it connected with the nature of things and with eternal truth. The teaching of Schelling about the Absolute, about the involvement of the individual thing in the whole, was also to some extent upheld; but the point of view of individual experience was not abandoned, and the [individual] human soul did not lose itself in the whole. For the human soul possessed faith as supernatural awareness, and was raised up above limited, transient knowledge and the whole world of empirical experience, and could not be troubled by the transience of empirical experience.[1]

One outcome of this view of things was that de Wette obtained a new way of considering the relation between revelation in historical terms and reason. Revelation in historical terms was no longer to be judged by its correspondence with the empirical understanding of reality; rather, it was to be judged by its correspondence with the understanding of eternal values mediated by reason (*Vernunft*) reflecting upon moral and aesthetic experience. Christianity, in spite of the problem of the contradiction between the miracles related in the Gospels and the modern empirical understanding of reality, was the truest religion because it

1. *Theodor*, I, pp. 84-85.

was most in accord with the eternal values which reason was able to perceive. This latter point was to become of great importance for de Wette.

In the novel *Theodor*, de Wette's first encounter with Professor A. is followed by an incident in which Theodor discusses Schiller's play *Die Jungfrau von Orleans* at the house of his fiancée Therese, the assembled company having returned from seeing the play.[1] Theodor finds himself in opposition to a rationalist clergyman who opines that Joan of Arc is an unsuitable subject for a play given her belief that she had been spoken to by the Virgin Mary. This is superstitious nonsense, which cannot be taken seriously. Theodor agrees that, from the point of view of empirical understanding, Joan was mistaken; but he argues passionately that if she was inspired by an intuition of what was good and right, then her actions can be justified, even if the ignorant Joan wrongly understood the source of her convictions as the voice of the Virgin Mary. The rationalist clergyman retorts that, from this point of view, any superstition can be justified, but he does not understand Theodor when the latter replies that reason (*Vernunft*) is to be the arbiter of whether actions are good or not.

The incident helps to clarify de Wette's understanding of the relation between reason (*Vernunft*) and revelation in historical terms, and shows how he was beginning to understand miracles. Revelation in historical terms was not a reliable source of knowledge because it was the product of an inadequate empirical understanding of the world, even if it was prompted by the revelation which was the source of reason (*Vernunft*). The founder of a religion could be responsible for expressing his insights in ways that were based upon a false (to modern ideas) empirical understanding of the world. Further, the followers of a founder, for example, the disciples of Jesus, could be misled by the moral and spiritual power of their leader into thinking that he had performed deeds that contradicted what modern empirical knowledge of the world knew to be possible. De Wette had reached the point where, although he still rejected the claims of the miracle stories in the New Testament that the laws of nature had been violated,

---

1. *Theodor*, I, pp. 92-101. Schiller's *Die Jungfrau von Orleans* was first staged in Weimar in 1801. De Wette, together with some fellow students, had walked from Jena to Weimar to see the first performance of Schiller's *Maria Stuart* in 1800 (see Wiegand, *De Wette*, p. 7) and had almost certainly seen *Die Jungfrau von Orleans*, probably in the same way.

he did not seek for a rationalizing or moralizing interpretation of the stories. He now recognized that behind the stories lay the disciples' experience of the unique moral and spiritual power of Jesus, even if the Gospels recorded this experience by means of stories that, scientifically speaking, could not be true.[1]

In *Theodor*, the hero's next discovery led him to distinguish between philosophy and theology, and to understand the role of the church in the matter of faith. His starting-point was the view that the life of Jesus was the highest embodiment of the eternal values that constituted the revelation that was the source of reason (*Vernunft*). The church was the fellowship of those who held to the values proclaimed by Jesus. The church functioned not only as a witness to these values; insofar as it sought to educate people into these values, it provided the means by which they would discover for themselves the revelation that they each possessed as the source of their reason. The church was like a parent, bringing up a child in such a way as to enable it to follow for itself the right and good path. In this sense, it had a constraining effect upon its members and it was the existence of the church and its constraining, educative role that marked the difference between theology and philosophy. According to Professor A. in *Theodor*, the difference between theology and philosophy was that

> the former starts out from a particular experience [*Gefühl*] and a firm assumption [of its meaning] in its investigation of the truth, whereas philosophy follows without constraints the path of investigation, following it wherever it leads. Our present-day theologians have all too often mistakenly adopted the standpoint of philosophy, and have thus introduced doubt into the realm of theology.[2]

This discovery also had a powerful effect upon Theodor:

> Our friend was greatly delighted with these insights that he had gained, and his whole being seemed to have received a new impetus. It seemed as though he had been divided from the world, and that he was now reconciled with it.[3]

---

1. *Theodor*, I, pp. 107-108. Professor A. (Fries) adds that, when considering such a personality as Jesus, it may be the case that his relation to the laws of nature was not that of other people, i.e. that the possibility of a miracle breaking the laws of nature cannot be ruled out.
2. *Theodor*, I, p. 119.
3. *Theodor*, I, p. 119.

One can well imagine, although this point is not made in this incident in *Theodor*, that de Wette had now almost struggled free from Kant. The latter unashamedly subordinated religion to philosophy, as we have seen. De Wette's new-found position enabled him to take philosophy seriously, but within the context of the guiding tradition of the church. However, he still had to take another step away from Kant, and this he did in considering the relation between religion and morality. It was also in this connection that he had to come to terms with Schleiermacher's *Reden über die Religion*.

It will be recalled that Wiegand claimed that Schleiermacher's *Reden* were the inspiration behind de Wette's 1801 piece *Eine Idee*.[1] It is true that, in an obituary dated 20 February 1834, after Schleiermacher's death, de Wette wrote,

> Anyone who, in 1799 when the Addresses on Religion to its Cultured Despisers appeared, was studying theology in a Semler-Kantian school, will remember how wonderfully attractive this publication was, the morning star of a new sun in the theological heavens.[2]

But the evidence of *Theodor* suggests strongly that Schleiermacher's *Reden* were first read seriously by de Wette in the Heidelberg period, while Fries was helping him to reconcile the elements of his thinking that derived from Kant and Schelling. The passage from *Theodor* is as follows:

> At that time Schleiermacher's *Addresses on Religion* came into his hands, whose basic aim was to describe religion as something distinct and independent, yet having much in common with other areas of spiritual life. No book had ever had such an impression on our friend as this, and he read it through many times in order to grasp the many ideas that it suggested to him.[3]

The passage in *Theodor* goes on to suggest that the *Reden* did not introduce him to any new ideas, but rather clarified and deepened what he was already thinking. *Theodor* also indicates that he was puzzled by the *Reden* on one point. This concerned the relationship between feeling that was the basis of religion and feeling that stirred

1. See above p. 23-24.
2. Staehelin, *Dewettiana*, p. 163.
3. *Theodor*, I, p. 167. See Otto, *Religionsphilosophie*, p. 151 (ET p. 174), for the important observation that, in *Theodor*, the discussion is *not* of the 1799 edition, but of a later edition of the *Reden*.

the will into action for ethical behaviour. Were they one and the same feeling, or different feelings?[1]

In the novel, Theodor takes this puzzle to Professor A., who explains the difference between his position and that of Schleiermacher. He agrees with Schleiermacher that religion is a feeling (*Gefühl*) based upon harmony between the individual and the universe; but he tries to be more specific about what this harmony consists of. It consists of two elements: an intuition of unity and an intuition of the purpose of things. From the intuition of unity derives the desire to order the objects of the external world into a coherent system, and from the intuition of the purpose of things derives the system of values which is the basis of morality. These factors, corresponding respectively to theoretical and practical philosophy, are the way in which intimations of the eternal in the human experience relate themselves to the external world of science and morals. Religion is the relating of these intimations to an unseen and eternal world, which can be summed up in the words 'the eternal unity and purposefulness of things'. Religion thus provides an eternal perspective that unites and explains the scientific and moral experience of humanity. Schleiermacher's view, on the other hand, leaves unexplained what is meant by the universe, the eternal and the world spirit. Schleiermacher is also criticized by Professor A. for saying too little about the subject of art (*Kunst*), a subject that had deeply concerned de Wette from his Jena student days. It is to Professor A.'s lectures on aesthetics and their effect upon Theodor that we must turn in order to conclude the chapter.[2]

The Professor connected morality, religion and aesthetics together in the following way. Human intuition of goodness worked itself out in the area of morality in good behaviour, although such behaviour was always in conflict with sin and error. Religion saw in the intuition of goodness a realm in which all struggle had ceased, and where goodness alone was paramount. Where goodness was able to express itself fully in the visible world it was beautiful. Not every good action was necessarily beautiful; those actions which were performed merely for a sense of obligation or duty were neither fully good nor fully beautiful. Actions that were both fully good and fully beautiful were

1.   See also below p. 128-29.
2.   *Theodor*, I, pp. 223ff.

those that sprang from love and were a spontaneous expression of the desire to do good. Such actions were recognized to be beautiful by an instinctive judgment by those who saw them.

Such beauty was moral beauty. Corresponding to it was natural or physical beauty. In the world of objects, this beauty was recognized by the harmony and symmetry of its form. A vessel for pouring water, for example, could be judged for its usefulness; but it could also be judged for the beauty of its form. In the world of human characters, people could be judged as to whether they were useful to us, or from the point of view of whether their lives had an intrinsic harmony and beauty.

The way of judging things that appreciated them on the basis of their beauty was called, by Professor A., the free aesthetic viewpoint. Moral beauty and natural or physical beauty were united when an artist or an architect produced works of art which were perceived to be beautiful. However, these were not mere imitations of what existed in the natural world. Using symbols drawn from the natural world they were actually expressions of the intimations of ultimate beauty that were felt in inner experience; and this brought the discussion close to the subject of religion.

If religion was an intuition of the harmony and purposefulness of all that exists, it could be given approximate expression only in poetry and art. It was much less adequately expressed in moral behaviour, and even less adequately expressed in concepts and ideas. This was because, of all the activities of the human personality, art and poetry came nearest to achieving a harmony between inner feelings and outward expression.

In the history of religions, two aesthetic forms of religious expression had developed. The one was mythology, which used supernatural and sometimes fantastic symbols of stories to express the apprehension of the eternal in human experience. The other was religious customs and symbols that helped worshippers to focus their attention on the eternal. In the opinion of Professor A., although empirical knowledge was necessary to prevent expressions of religion from becoming pure superstition, Christianity had gone too far in the direction of giving absolute priority to empirical knowledge. It needed to recover a proper aesthetic understanding of religion in order to become a dynamic factor in everyday life.

Theodor indicates that de Wette accepted all these viewpoints, and that he began to apply them to Christianity in its historical and dogmatic form, to the detriment of the latter.[1] He began to blame Judaism, with its ban on images and its emphasis on the law, for having virtually destroyed the aesthetic dimension of religion. In this regard, Judaism compared badly with Greek religion. Jesus had set things right by teaching that God must be worshipped in spirit and in truth, but the early church had then become obsessed with defining in concepts the nature and work of Jesus. The Reformation had destroyed the superstitious and inferior symbolism of the western church, but had opened the door to the danger of being tied to the letter of the Bible. If it was true that Christianity had laid too much emphasis on ideas and concepts to the detriment of the aesthetic viewpoint, then it would be necessary to undertake a thorough-going reappraisal of traditional Christian doctrine. The section in *Theodor* ends with the following significant words:

> Thus our friend [Theodor] was pointed to a new false way, just at the moment when he had recognized his earlier mistakes, and had once again begun to take the road towards the truth.[2]

This was how matters stood for de Wette at the end of the Heidelberg period. It would be another seven years before he finally made the 'discovery' that signalled his arrival at a mature and lasting theological position.

In July 1810 de Wette received a letter from the department of education in the Prussian administration offering him a chair in theology at the newly-founded university of Berlin.[3] The salary would be 1,500 thalers, with 300 thalers for the cost of removal. The appointment would be in the Michaelmas term of 1810. The decision to leave Heidelberg for Berlin does not seem to have been a difficult one to make. In a letter to Schleiermacher dated 24 July 1810, de Wette complained that in Heidelberg he had been teaching from fifteen to seventeen hours a week, and had, unaided, covered the Old and New Testaments. He also complained that his hearers had been half barbarians, and cheats. Berlin would afford a more worthy scene for his labours![4] Thus, on 12 October, after a journey that included a visit

1. *Theodor*, I, pp. 234ff.
2. *Theodor*, I, p. 238.
3. Staehelin, *Dewettiana*, p. 67.
4. Staehelin, *Dewettiana*, p. 68. For another, much abbreviated, printed form

to his parents in Mannstedt, de Wette arrived in Berlin.[1] The next nine years would see him rise to the pinnacle of his career, and then crash in ruins.

---

of the letter, see W. Dilthey, *Aus Schleiermacher's Leben: In Briefen* (Berlin, 1863; repr. Berlin: de Gruyter, 1974]), IV, p. 179.

1. Wiegand, 'De Wette in Heidelberg', pp. 86-87.

De Wette in Berlin

Chapter 4

BERLIN I: TOWARDS CERTAINTY

De Wette's time in Berlin can be divided into two periods, from 1810 to 1815 and from 1815 to 1819. In the first period he experienced initial success. His lectures attracted more students than those of Schleiermacher, he felt that he had now mastered Fries's philosophical system, and he thus saw himself as poised to resolve once and for all the contradictions between rationalism and orthodoxy. To this first period belong important works such as the *Lehrbuch der christlichen Dogmatik* (1813), the *Lehrbuch der hebräisch-jüdischen Archäologie* (1814), *Über Religion und Theologie* (1815), and anonymously published, but very important, *Die neue Kirche* (1815).

The second period saw a distinct change in his fortunes. With the growth of pietist and orthodox influence in Berlin, de Wette was increasingly regarded as dangerous theologically. The support of the students moved towards the seemingly more orthodox Schleiermacher and the pietist Neander. In addition, de Wette, along with Schleiermacher, became increasingly suspect because of his democratic political opinions. As will be explained later, the Prussian court and cabinet looked with anxiety on the movement among students for the creation of a democratic Germany. Professors were held to be responsible for this tendency, and any professors known to have democratic sympathies became marked men. This suspicion under which de Wette and Schleiermacher stood drew them closer together, a process further assisted by the presence in Berlin from 1816 of Friedrich Lücke. De Wette began to attend Schleiermacher's church, and began to attach a much greater importance to the church as an institution mediating Christian values. When, in 1821, he published the second edition of that part of his *Christian Dogmatics* dealing with Christian doctrine, there were significant changes resulting from his more positive view of the church. Thus Schleiermacher had an important effect upon de Wette's outlook, and one which lasted for the remainder of his life. It was Fries, however, whose work made the most significant impact on de Wette during his Berlin period. In a letter to Fries dated 17 December 1817, de Wette described how Fries's practical philosophy had given him the intellectual tools to express his theology, especially in the light of his 'discovery' in 1817 that Christ's life was the aesthetic expression of the ideal within the contingency of history. De Wette believed that he could now write a treatise on ethics from a christological standpoint. The search that had begun nearly twenty years earlier, in 1799, had come to an end. He had seen how to reconcile philosophy with positive religion. But as a new era opened up for him in Berlin, in which he could build on his newly-found convictions, the tragedy of his dismissal, described in the next chapter, shut him off from exercizing the great influence that he might have hoped to have if he had stayed in Berlin for another thirty years.

When he arrived in Berlin on 12 October 1810, de Wette must have been filled with high hopes for his future. It was true that Prussia still lived under what many regarded as the 'shame' of its defeat at the hands of Napoleon in 1807; but new, spiritual energies were at work in Prussia, of which the founding of the university was an instance. Here was an opportunity to help build a new future.[1]

The choice of theology professors for the new university seems to have been governed by a desire to foster a type of reconciliation theology that would supercede rationalism. Thus it was no surprise that Schleiermacher was not only one of the foundation professors, but that he also played an important part in establishing the new university. His *Reden* of 1799 had enabled many students to overcome rationalism, and had also argued persuasively that religion should be taken seriously by the general thinking public. The other theological foundation professor was K.P. Marheineke who, like de Wette, moved to Berlin from Heidelberg. He was primarily a church historian, but philosophically he was attracted increasingly to Hegel. He was thus an idealist and an opponent of rationalism.

Exactly why de Wette was chosen as a foundation professor is hard

---

1.   De Wette was also delighted with the university buildings in Berlin. 'What a splendid building, and what splendid buildings surround it', he wrote to Fries on arrival. See M. Lenz, *Geschichte der Königlichen Friedrich-Wilhems-Universität zu Berlin*, (Halle: Buchhandlung des Waisenhauses, 1910–1918), I, p. 291.

to say. It is true that he already had some substantial publications to his credit, but anyone reading his *Beiträge* of 1806–1807 might have found them excessively negative, and not much improvement on the work of the rationalists. On the other hand, his *Auffoderung* and *Beytrag* exhibited a spirit far removed from rationalism, and perhaps indicated that here was a man who could help to further a theology that mediated between rationalism and orthodoxy.[1]

De Wette's work in Berlin began uneventfully. For the winter semester of the new university, which began at the end of October 1810, there were few students. De Wette had six at his lectures on Old Testament Introduction, eight for his lectures on Psalms, and none for Hebrew Archaeology, which course was postponed to the summer semester. Private classes on Hebrew language were also poorly supported.[2] With the summer semester, the scene had begun to alter. De Wette had thirty-two for his lectures on the Gospels, eighteen for Isaiah, nineteen for Hebrew Archaeology, and no fewer than twenty-five for Hebrew. There were also seven for private classes in Arabic.[3] On 19 April 1811, we find de Wette boasting to Fries that student numbers in Berlin are already higher than in Heidelberg; this mood, however, was not to last.[4]

On 2 August 1811, de Wette wrote to Fries regretting that he had left Heidelberg for Berlin.

> It is mainly on account of my wife, who cannot get used to Berlin. My public was not as good at Heidelberg [as in Berlin] but not much worse. From the point of view of Hebrew I am less satisfied here than I was there.[5]

De Wette went on to complain about the excessive amount of teaching that he had to do—'four hours a day, and a Collegium to prepare that takes four hours a day'. He also mentioned that he was writing a work on the atonement, the book later published as the Latin work *Commentatio de morte Jesu Christi expiatoria.*

A month later, de Wette submitted a memorandum to the Education

---

1. See Lenz, *Universität Berlin*, I, p. 224.
2. Lenz, *Universität Berlin*, I, p. 356.
3. Lenz, *Universität Berlin*, I, p. 357.
4. Staehelin, *Dewettiana*, p. 69.
5. Henke, 'Berliner Briefe von de Wette an Fries von 1811 bis 1819', *Monatsblätter für innere Zeitgeschichte* 32 (1868), pp. 90-91.

Ministry respectfully drawing attention to a gap in the staffing of the university—the lack of an orientalist. He pointed out that he had not been appointed to Berlin as an orientalist, and was not one in the strict sense of the word, although he used oriental studies in biblical interpretation. Although he was prepared to meet the initial and urgent needs of the university in providing Hebrew classes, he did not have the time to lecture in the field of theology and to provide a Hebrew course every six months. He drew the attention of the Ministry to a young *Privatdozent* in Jena, Dr Bernstein, and suggested that, if it was impossible to appoint an accomplished orientalist such as Wilken (a Heidelberg colleague), the appointment of a young man such as Bernstein would be the next best step.[1]

Whatever the outcome of this attempt to reduce his teaching load, we find de Wette boasting to Fries, in a letter dated 11 November 1811, that numbers in the university had increased to 600 in all, with 130 theological students among them. In New Testament Exegesis, he has over fifty at his lectures and, what is at this period important, more than his rivals Schleiermacher and Marheineke. The latter's lectures are being attended by fewer students than in the previous semester, and there are complaints that Schleiermacher and Marheineke are difficult to understand.[2]

The heart of the rivalry with Schleiermacher was spelled out in a long letter to Fries, written on 26 September 1811. Whether or not de Wette was fairly representing Schleiermacher's position, he took Schleiermacher to be saying that

> Christianity is something that develops with time, a unity that is amenable to development, namely. . .a basic disposition [*Grundbestimmung*] of the religious mind which is made conscious to the understanding only in various forms and according to the influence of various periods [*nur verschieden nach verschiedener Zeitbildung zur Selbstverständigung gebracht wird*]. This awareness is then the temporary; the disposition is the permanent. We are Christians to the extent that we possess only the disposition. We can therefore dispense with what belongs to the understanding of the various past periods of time including those of the pre-Christian period. Thus is untied the knot at which our theologians labour

1.   De Wette to the Ministry for Culture and Public Education, 25 Oct. 1811, Staatsbibliothek Preussischer Kulturbesitz, (West)-Berlin, MS Darmstaedter, 2 b 1840 (13) M.L. de Wette.
2.   Staehelin, *Dewettiana*, pp. 71-72.

so pitifully. They see that the biblical and other Christian dogmas are no longer valid for us, because our knowledge [*Verstand*] is much more developed. They try to up-date them, or, to put it another way, to substitute appropriate ideas [*Begriffe*] for the inappropriate ones. Schleiermacher would say 'Let go of the dogmas and hold on to the ideas that lie behind them', that is, that we should free the ideas from the body which has died, so that, God willing, they form another [body]. This latter cannot be done so easily, but is achieved most readily when they are grasped purely and re-presented purely. This is done scientifically in dogmatics and also—and this is difficult and requires an aesthetic presentation—in preaching and catechism. I want to indicate the religious ideas in the Bible and in that way present the basic idea of Christianity; however, I want to show, by means of philosophical criticism, that the dogmas are nothing [*nichtig*].[1]

A number of interesting points emerge from this criticism of Schleiermacher. The first is that Schleiermacher's position had negative implications for the Old Testament, which de Wette was teaching in Berlin. It belonged with the understandings of religion of pre-Christian times, which were to be discarded. Second, we may fairly assume that de Wette perceived a similarity between what Schleiermacher was advocating and what the historical critics of the mythical school had advocated. Just as these latter writers had discarded the form of many narratives in the Bible in order to discover the true historical kernel that they contained, so Schleiermacher seemed to be suggesting that the form of Christian doctrines could be discarded in favour of their underlying idea. But this procedure not only raised the question of how this was to be done in a way open to control, but begged the question of the nature of religion and of the kind of judgments that were appropriate to its subject matter.

There was also the question of the nature of the church, a subject which de Wette addressed in the final section of the letter to Fries of 26 September 1811. Schleiermacher, according to de Wette, assumed that religion contained in itself a drive (*Trieb*) towards establishing a community, something which de Wette could not understand, probably because he could not understand the sense in which the word 'religion' was being used in this context. De Wette seems to have sided with Fries in wanting to see the church not as a specifically religious community with its own dogmas, but as part of the life of the state, expressing and mediating through its cultic practices some of the basic human intuitions

1. Henke, 'Berliner Briefe', pp. 97-98.

of reality. In this religion, the state would play its part in enabling the nation to attain the highest ideals and values in its common life.

De Wette's opposition to Schleiermacher, then, was based upon a fundamental difference of understanding of the nature of religion and theology. De Wette believed that, with the help of Fries's philosophy, he could show the church the true path that it should follow, while Schleiermacher was leading people along a false path; hence de Wette's pleasure that, at this stage, he was attracting more hearers to his lectures than Schleiermacher.

The letter of 26 September 1811 is also important in another respect. It charts de Wette's progress in his study of Fries's philosophy, indicating that this was not an easy path, and that de Wette did not always find it easy to accommodate his views to Fries's system.

The letter begins with the words:

> for some days I have been up to my ears in your philosophy. Apart from many details, I have been able to understand your *Kritik*, although I feel a great lack in myself, which is probably because I am not good at abstraction. What I want to get out of philosophy for the purposes of this history of religion is the correct identification of what is characteristic, and the organization of what remains in relation to it.[1]

From the references to Fries's *Neue Kritik der Vernunft* in the letter, it is clear that de Wette had concentrated on Book 3 of Volume III, on aesthetics, nature and religion;[2] but it is noticeable that the discussion in this long letter of some 5,000 words lacks the assurance and polish of the *Über Religion und Theologie* of 1815, which is de Wette's most authoritative statement of his position of the 1810–15 period. He is very much feeling his way.

It seems that de Wette had to wait a long time for Fries to answer the letter of September 1811; and we do not possess that reply. But before the arrival of Fries's letter, de Wette had obtained a new work by Fries which seems to have helped him substantially in his appropriation of Fries's philosophy. This was *Von deutscher Philosophie Art und Kunst, ein Votum für F.H. Jacobi gegen F.W.J. Schelling*,

---

1.   Henke, 'Berliner Briefe', p. 91.
2.   De Wette refers to the first edition of Fries's *Neue oder anthropologische Kritik der Vernunft*, which was unavailable to me. I have used the second edition, produced in Heidelberg in 1831, and reprinted Aalen, 1967. For the pages used by de Wette see vol. III, pp. 203ff., 363, 369.

which was published in Heidelberg in the first part of 1812.[1]

In a letter to Fries dated 15 June 1812, de Wette was almost ecstatic about this work of 102 pages, which, it must be said, is probably the best introduction to Fries's thought for any reader wishing to become familiar with it.

> On Sunday evening I had a group of students at home to whom I read it [*Von deutscher Philosophie*...] and gave my views... In great simplicity you have said something splendid splendidly [*Herrliches herrlich*]. May God grant success [*Eingang*] to this good cause. Your philosophy is beginning to warm me and to fill me with zeal to support you and to advocate you. My Biblical Dogmatics will do this. You have no idea how useful your philosophy is in this connection. I find its ideas on religion to be useful in every sphere and they cast light everywhere. I am often amazed at my good fortune. Often, I cannot see more than a few steps ahead but I always press on confidently, and when I arrive, I find the light again.[2]

De Wette adds that leaving Fries in Heidelberg at least had the advantage that he could no longer depend upon his friend's tuition, and had to master the Friesian philosophy for himself. He also adds something that has implications for the future:

> I would not have been able to speak so freely in Heidelberg as here without being called a heretic.

Fries's *Von deutscher Philosophie* is largely devoted to exposition and criticism of the religious philosophies of Kant, Schelling and Jacobi, but ends with an irenic section entitled 'Purity of the religious doctrine' (*Lauterkeit der Religionslehre*), whose ideas must have been meat and drink to de Wette.

Fries denies the distinction between God's general revelation in nature, his *inner* revelation in individual conscience and the positive revelation in historical Christianity:

> In truth there is for human beings only one religious revelation, that of faith, which lives in them. As Asmus says 'the human is in itself richer than heaven and earth and has what these cannot give. The wisdom and order that humans find in visible nature, are more what they place there, than what they find there. This truth, that all knowledge of the Spirit and

---

1. *Von deutscher Philosophie Art und Kunst: Ein Votum für Friedrich Heinrich Jacobi gegen F.W. Schelling* (Heidelberg, 1812), reprinted in *Sämtliche Schriften*, XXIV (Aalen, 1978), pp. 623-728.

2. Henke, 'Berliner Briefe', pp. 100-101.

of the life of mankind comes only through self-knowledge was not sufficiently clear to dogmatics (although Scripture says that the kingdom of
God is within you, and God is a spirit and those who worship him must
worship him in spirit and in truth). This is why dogmatics needed to distinguish inner and outer revelation, whose light flowed only in fact from
the inner source.[1]

Fries goes on to criticize the view that humanity was unfit to know the
good, and needed the miracles of the Incarnation of God and the
inspiration of the prophets and apostles as a basis for faith. The problem with this is that it puts forward as the basis for belief a tradition
(*Erzählung*) that contradicts what humans know to be true. The same
can be said of belief in the atoning death of Christ:

This teaching is derived from the Jewish symbol of the sin offering and
has meaning only for those whose ethical understanding is not sufficiently
developed; for in God's sight a person is worth only what he is in
himself. . .[2]

Fries is critical of any appeal to miracles and, with some justification,
points out that, when contemporary exegetes either remove the miraculous from biblical stories or explain them in terms of natural laws,
they are destroying the miracle.

On the other hand, Fries defends his view of Christianity, by
appealing to the beliefs of the Moravian Brothers among whom he
grew up.

Their old, pure teaching was that religious dogmas were human precepts,
in respect of which all had to follow their own opinions. Only Scripture is
valid for all, and each had to understand Scripture as the Spirit made it
clear to him. Where else shall I ask the Spirit for meaning than in the spirit
of true love of truth in myself?[3]

Fries denies that this is simply a rehash of the old discredited natural
religion. For Fries this latter was based upon false metaphysical distinctions and upon a childish teleology

that sought a proof for the existence of God from every blade of grass and
every bee, but not from the living spirit within oneself.[4]

1. *Von deutscher Philosophie*, pp. 90-91 (repr. pp. 714-15).
2. *Von deutscher Philosophie*, p. 92 (repr. p. 716).
3. *Von deutscher Philosophie*, pp. 96-97 (repr. pp. 720-21).
4. *Von deutscher Philosophie*, p. 98 (repr. p. 722).

Thus Fries moves to a ringing conclusion to his book. What he wants to do in the name of the truth of science is to effect the establishment of religious teaching without dogmatics. This means that we need to become aware of the limits of our knowledge so that we can grasp religious convictions to see

> how faith comes alive only in feeling and, to say with Paul, only through love.[1]

The point that religion consists not primarily of dogma or speculative knowledge about God and eternity, but of virtuous action inspired and warmed by feeling, and informed by self-knowledge of all that is most noble and beautiful, is a message that Fries wishes to promote as earnestly as a missionary. He wishes it to become the guiding light of the people and of the young. It is a noble ideal passionately expressed.

This, then, was the piece by Fries which de Wette read with such enthusiasm, around the middle of 1812; and although it was in some ways more radical than de Wette's own position we can immediately see its influence upon two of de Wette's works: on the *Commentatio de morte Jesu Christi*, in which de Wette denied that Jesus taught his atoning death, and the *Lehrbuch der christlichen Dogmatik*, which dealt with biblical and Christian dogmatics.

The first volume of the *Lehrbuch der christlichen Dogmatik*, dealing with the religious teaching of Hebrew religion, Judaism and early Christianity was published in 1813 with its foreword dated March 1813, that is, ten months after de Wette's letter to Fries about the latter's *Von deutscher Philosophie*.[2] It is subtitled 'for use in academic lectures' and it represents de Wette's own lectures on this subject. It is typical of a well-known genre of the times. Its many sections are brief, sometimes to the point of obscurity, and there are unconnected sentences at the end of sections, which look like reminders to de Wette that he must deal with a particular related matter. De Wette clearly felt this unsatisfactoriness himself, for, in 1815, he published a book subtitled 'Explanations of his Handbook of Christian Dogmatics' under the main title of *Über Religion und Theologie*.[3] In the foreword to this he recognized that his 1813

---

1. *Von deutscher Philosophie*, p. 100 (repr. p. 724).
2. *Lehrbuch der christlichen Dogmatik in ihrer historischen Entwickelung*. I. *Die biblische Dogmatik* (Berlin, 1813).
3. *Über Religion und Theologie: Erläuterungen zu seinem Lehrbuche der*

handbook on dogmatics had proved to be abortive, and that the very cryptic presentation of the material to be found there had led to misunderstanding on the part of those who had been unable to attend his lectures and to hear his oral amplifications.

It has already been remarked that the *Über Religion und Theologie* represents the best statement of de Wette's theological outlook of this period, for which reason considerable space will shortly be devoted to an exposition of its contents. Before this is done, however, a summary will be given of the important foreword to the *Lehrbuch der christlichen Dogmatik*.

It is written in a combative tone, with the self-confidence of one who feels that he has something to convey which will transform scholarship, provided that not too many swine are around to trample on his pearls. He states that what is distinctive about the work is, first, its mode of historical investigation and, second, the philosophical foundation which it presupposes. With regard to the latter, he expects that only those few who have bothered to try to master recent philosophy will be able to appreciate his aims and offer constructive criticism. Fries is mentioned as one whose reactions he will be keen to know, and de Wette adds that the philosophy that he has embraced holds out the prospect of initiating a great philosophical revolution.[1]

He next recognizes that some readers will find his mythical approach to Old and New Testament narratives off-putting, and he refers them to his *Kritik der israelitischen Geschichte* where, he says, he has sufficiently outlined the hermeneutical and critical basis of this approach. Whether this is a fair observation is certainly a matter for dispute. However, he claims that, in the *Lehrbuch* he has proved what is assumed in the *Beiträge*, that the mythical approach is much more suited to the study of religion and human development than the historical approach.

According to the latter, the Hebrews entertained notions appropriate to semi-civilized nations, and at odds with their pure and sublime religion. One could detect the deceit of priests and soothsayers or the blatant desire for the miraculous. De Wette's mythical approach, on the other hand, put all this in a different light, showing that Old Testament narratives were poetic expressions of sacred ideas, and

Dogmatik (Berlin, 1815).
1. *Lehrbuch der christlichen Dogmatik*, p. iv.

indicating how all ancient peoples should be studied. Indeed, the need to establish universal criteria for understanding religion on the basis of analogies and comparisons between ancient peoples was indicated by actual examples. If it was hard enough to be sure of what Paul was saying even when there existed authentic writings by him, how much harder was it to understand what Moses and Jesus meant, given that our information about them rested on second-hand, and in some cases distorted, narratives.[1]

De Wette's next task is to stress the importance of a philosophical understanding of the nature of religion. Agreement on this issue will bring about great changes in theology as well as being of importance for the historical and dogmatic treatment of religion. History indicates both that religion is essentially feeling which cannot be adequately described, and that peoples try to describe the feeling in quite divergent ways. This shows that scholarship must achieve an understanding of what the heart of religion is in order truly to appreciate the various forms of its expression. In saying this, de Wette is opposing two approaches: that of the old literalists and that of the new rationalists, both of whom fail to understand the true nature of religion. He urges his readers to consider how a proper use of philosophy can deliver theology from misleading mysticism on the one hand and from unbelieving criticism on the other. He expects his *Dogmatik* to achieve the following goals:

> Through my presentation the young theologian will be in a position not only to make an unbiased judgment about the origin of Christianity and its original spirit, as well as to follow with a critical eye its development, degeneration and re-birth in the course of the history of the church, but at the same time to foresee how it will develop in the future. The second part will follow, hopefully, at Easter 1814.[2]

In the event, at least two hopes were not to be realized. First, the second part of the *Dogmatik*, entitled *Dogmatik der evangelisch-lutherischen Kirche nach den symbolischen Büchern und den älteren Dogmatikern*, did not appear until 1816. Second, the first volume was so cryptic that, as we have seen, de Wette needed to explain it by publishing, in 1815, his *Über Religion und Theologie*. To the exposition of this accomplished work we must now turn.

---

1. *Lehrbuch der christlichen Dogmatik*, p. vi.
2. *Lehrbuch der christlichen Dogmatik*, pp. ix-x.

The book follows the plan of the *Dogmatik* with its first
chapter, 'The different types of human certainty', corresponding to
paragraphs 4-14 of the *Dogmatik*. It deals with three types of human
certainty, which are *Wissen* (knowledge), *Glaube* (faith) and *Ahnung*
(intimation). These categories are, of course, the title of the book by
Fries published in 1805.[1]

Most space is devoted to *Wissen*, the faculty that deals with empirical knowledge, whether that is of the senses or to do with knowledge
of the past based upon human testimony. De Wette points out that the
causes of things and the laws that are formed from the observation of
regularities are not given in the sense impressions of the natural world
or the happenings of history. It is we, the perceiving subjects, who
classify and order reality and who formulate the rules of logic
designed to understand reality and unity. It is we who perceive the
whole as a *world*.

But when we have done all that we can in measuring the world and
describing its functioning in terms of laws, we have not explained why
it exists, or what its purpose is, or how we are to relate to it. In order
to do this we need the second way of gaining certainty, that of *Glaube*.
Here, without mentioning them as such, de Wette bases his argument
upon the so-called Kantian antinomies, that is, the contradictions
between our experience viewed from the perspective of knowledge
derived from sense or historical data on the one hand, and from
reflection upon our inner convictions on the other hand. Thus, from
the first perspective, human beings, as part of nature, are subject to
the laws of nature and are thus not free agents; yet, humans are
convinced that they are free agents and that they do not behave
according to pre-determined laws. Again, human beings are convinced
that there are such things as values and that these endure in spite of the
continual flux and change of the natural world. Thus *Glaube* makes us
certain that we have an immortal soul and free will, and that our lives
have eternal value. As de Wette writes:

> Over everything, we perceive with the spiritual eye of *Glaube* the source
> of all being, the law-giver and ruler of the world on whose almighty
> power everything depends, and whose holy will leads everything to the

---

1. *Religion und Theologie*, pp. 1-19.

best end. In this highest idea of human reason we find the firm foothold which does not let us slip; the sacred peace of mind which we can gain from nowhere else.[1]

De Wette rejects the view that we should call this type of human conviction *Wissen* as well as that pertaining to empirical knowledge. This only causes confusion; and in any case, *Wissen* has to do with classifying, unifying and so forth. It has nothing to do with grasping the eternal. But even *Glaube* has its limitations, and needs *Ahnung* (intimation) and its closely-associated *Gefühl* (feeling) to give it life and warmth.

Without *Ahnung* and *Gefühl* it becomes difficult to accept, on the basis of *Glaube*, that everything is being led to its best possible end when life is so full of disappointments, frustration and tragedy. (We must never forget that de Wette himself grieved the death of Eberhardine for the rest of his life.) But *Ahnung* allows us to experience the realities that *Glaube* posits, and thus to know that they exist:

> In the beauty and sublimity of nature and the spiritual lives of humans, the religious *Ahnung* comes across a manifestation of true being and of the eternal purpose of things. From the lovely flower to the sublime view of a glacier, from the laughing infant to the great soul of a Cato or a Socrates, nature and spirit proclaim to us the truth and reality of the eternal ideas; that something higher lives in things than can be grasped by measurement or definition. Indeed, there are sacred moments in which we glimpse in the world a reflection of the divine glory itself, the traces of the eternal power and goodness, whether in the great spectacles of nature or the mighty processes of destiny.[2]

In employing the faculty of *Ahnung* we make judgments about the relation of parts to the whole, but in a very different way from the exercise of *Wissen*. De Wette concludes the chapter by rebutting the view that, of the three ways of certainty, the first (*Wissen*), which deals with empirical knowledge, should take precedence. All three must be exercized in proper relation to each other if reality is to be apprehended in its fullness.

Chapter 2, covering paragraphs 15-27 of the *Dogmatik*, deals with the 'Idea of Religion'. It represents the clearest statement of de Wette's philosophical theology, and serves as an important marker

---

1. *Religion und Theologie*, p. 9.
2. *Religion und Theologie*, p. 12.

against which his later thought can be evaluated. Basically, it deals with the religious aspects to which religion belongs, and it does it under three categories: the ideal or speculative, the practical or ethical, and feeling (*Gefühl*). At the same time it attacks what de Wette regards as popular and serious misunderstandings of the nature of religion, and that in a way which is often instructive for present-day readers.

The chapter begins with a definition of the firm building of religion, on which all else rests:

> the recognition of the temporality, transience and incompleteness of the world of the senses, and belief in the eternity and completeness of what lies beyond [the senses].[1]

This can be summed up in the words of the Bible 'our business [*Wandel*] is in heaven'. (Phil. 3.20 [Greek]—*Wandel* in de Wette's version.) This view corresponds to the Kantian teaching concerning the subjectivity of the forms of time and space.

The importance of this is as follows. Only when the perceiving individual considers the world in terms of the subjective forms of time and space does it become a world as opposed to a chaotic mass of impressions. The next stage is for the perceiving subject to reflect beyond the limits of time and space to eternity, and to consider the world from that standpoint. Only the perceiving subject accords form and purpose to the otherwise dead world; and here, de Wette criticizes Schelling without naming him.[2] He may here be dependent upon Fries's 1807 piece, *Fichte's und Schelling's neueste Lehren von Gott und der Welt*.

There now follow treatments of theological topics, designed to show the mistakes that are made when they are considered from the point of view of *Wissen* or *Verstand* as opposed to *Glaube* or the ideal point of view. Thus, the idea of the soul is misunderstood when we want to know (*wissen*) about its nature. Granted that our spiritual life can be affected by illness or similar factors, our 'soul' is an ideal and not a material thing. The immortality of a *material* soul is nonsense; and although it is understandable that people think in terms of a

---

1. *Religion und Theologie*, p. 19.
2. *Religion und Theologie*, p. 31: 'Dies thun diejenigen, welche Gott als das Ganze, als das All und Eins der Welt denken, und die Idee Gottes für nichts weiter als die unter der Form der Identität gedachte Welt erklären'.

continuation of our life into eternity, we are, in fact, talking about something for which we have no adequate ideas or language at the level of knowing (*Wissen*). On the other hand, de Wette has no time for the view that fastens all hopes upon eternity and that despises the present world. Belief in immortality is the foundation for the religious raising of the mind above the changes and misfortunes (*Unglück*) of this life so that we live each moment here in the context of eternity.

The next section deals with the philosophy of nature, and contains an unnamed attack on Schelling, who, we remember, had been criticized in Fries's *Von deutscher Philosophie*, the 1812 piece which excited de Wette's admiration.[1] The starting point is the statement that, from an ideal point of view, nature can be seen as a living and organic whole. The mistake occurs when this ordered life is considered from the viewpoint of *Wissen*, and it is forgotten that it is the perceiving subject who has attributed ordered life to the world. Further, the statements that the world is created and thus its creator is God, are statements that belong to the ideal judgment, and are not deduced from the material world itself. To talk about the beginning of the created order is to confuse the ideal and the material:

> There was never a time when the world came into existence through God, but it exists through God. I cannot explain its existence on the basis of God, for I would simply be explaining how things have been synthesized from simple elements. . . If we want explanation, we have to remain with material things, from which we can only free ourselves by means of the ideal leap to freedom and eternity.[2]

It is at this point that de Wette criticizes a view that Spinoza had advocated in the seventeeth century, and that had recently been given new expression by Schelling. This was to think of God and the world as related ideas, to regard God as that which encompassed the whole of reality in its diversity and unity. It will be remembered from de Wette's account of his student days in *Theodor*, how Schelling's *Vorlesungen* had started from the idea of the Absolute, and had regarded all that existed, including perceiving subjects as part of that absolute.[3] Now, de Wette argued that this position completely misunderstood the nature and being of God:

1. See p. 93 n. 1.
2. *Religion und Theologie*, p. 29.
3. See pp. 32-34.

> Such a God consists of parts, and since this synthesis must continue unendingly, we cannot really say that God is but only that he *will be*.[1]

At this point, there is an important paragraph which indicates the importance of the Bible in de Wette's position, and which helps us to understand his opposition to what he took to be Schleiermacher's view. He insists that we should prefer to use the terms God, Lord and Father, because these words express the ideas of unity and aliveness (*Lebendigkeit*):

> We think of God most correctly when we think of him as the ultimate origin of the existence of things and as the absolute ground of the eternal world order, and thus place him above the world. This is also what is being done in the biblical and popular ideas of the creator and law-giver of the world, and speculation needs to do no more than add philosophical clarity. . . The anthropomorphisms of the Old Testament are more suitable to speculation than any philosophical refinements.[2]

If we are to think of God in relation to nature as revealing himself in nature, we do not achieve this by assuming that God is identical to nature, or is the absolute substance. We do this by seeing God ideally as the basic cause of all substance, powers and world order, and at the same time as quite different from the world and standing above it.

De Wette now turns to answer a question that, according to his account of his student days in *Theodor*, had once troubled him greatly. If the eternal truths of religion are grounded in our human reason (*Vernunft*), how can they be objective? How can we deny that eternity and God are simply the products of human thought, and lacking any objective existence of their own? De Wette answers this in two ways. First, he asks believers in a divine revelation in Christianity how they would defend their belief, and assumes that they would appeal to agreement between that revelation and human reason (*Vernunft*). To put it another way, an objective revelation has to be received (subjectively) by humans, and thus its teaching about eternity depends ultimately on subjectivity.

The second reply to the objection points out that it is more apparent than real. It is because philosophical reflection upon experience works from the material to the ideal that it *seems* that the idea of God is dependent on human thinking. In actual experience, as opposed to

1. *Religion und Theologie*, p. 31.
2. *Religion und Theologie*, p. 33.

human reflection upon it, the distinction between the material and the ideal disappears. Experience is of reality in its fullness, whether material or ideal:

> in the mind itself, all is given simultaneously in one stroke, without a sequence. Indeed, if one finds it objectionable that we arrive finally at the idea of God, which depends upon everything else, we can insist on the opposite: that this idea [of God] stands supreme in the mind, and that everything else depends upon it. The analysis goes in the opposite direction, from living faith [*Glaube*]. Ultimately the subjective demonstration of the ideas does not rob them of their objective validity. They carry this [objective validity] in themselves, and reason [*Vernunft*] cannot doubt this without being self-contradictory. What more can we want?[1]

With these words de Wette ends this section, and now moves to discuss more specifically ethical and religious matters.

He begins by distinguishing between judgments of value made at the material level, and those made at the ideal level. Regarding the former, we judge things to be good or bad in relation to their use to us; or we judge people to be educated or uneducated, to be developed or barbarian. Our ideal judgments of value, on the other hand, are concerned with things as good and valuable in themselves. Thus, from this standpoint, uneducated or uncivilized people have value in themselves and are thus entitled to our respect. We also acknowledge that our duty, or what we *ought* to do, has an unconditional claim upon us regardless of the circumstances. It is the province of ethics, or practical reason, to work out the implications of the ideal perception of things as good, valuable and purposive in their own right. Brought into harmony with speculative belief (*Glaube*), practical reason becomes philosophical theology (*Religionslehre*). For this reason, de Wette next deals with three topics in philosophical theology: good and evil, teleology and providence.

The treatment of teleology is brief and straightforward.[2] From the standpoint of reflection upon the material world, it is not possible to deduce an overriding purpose that will explain and justify every facet of the material world. We do not know that the innumerable species of insects were created in order to be food for animals, nor do we know that the animals were created for the benefit of humans. We

---

1. *Religion und Theologie*, p. 37.
2. *Religion und Theologie*, pp. 46-47.

simply cannot explain the enormous diversity of life-forms in the material world by means of a simple theory. In order to contemplate nature we need to begin from the idea of beauty (*Schönheit*). De Wette stresses that it is fatal to try to base a religious interpretation of nature upon our experience of it through our senses. That he was undoubtedly right was proved to me long before I had even heard of de Wette, when I heard an Air Force chaplain trying, with disastrous results, to explain to a group of airmen how lice fitted into God's providential ordering of nature.

The section on good and evil, by contrast, is longer, complicated and difficult.[1] The notions of good and evil appear to come from reflection upon our moral experience and performance. The ideal notion of freedom is our conviction that we are not subject to the laws of necessity as perceived in nature. The idea of duty is a moral imperative given independently of circumstances. But we know that we do not always do what we ought to do. If we excuse these lapses by blaming our circumstances, then we are saying that we are not free; and our consciences do not support our excuses. It follows from this that we have an inclination to evil that is part of our ideal nature, and that is not the result of a struggle between our animal and our reasoning instincts. If it seems contradictory to say that we have an inclination to evil as part of our ideal nature, that contradiction disappears when we contemplate God, whose kingdom is our ultimate destiny. In God there is no conflict between good and evil, and his kingdom is one of perfect harmony of all ultimate values. Thus our experience of good and evil serves to reinforce our determination to do what is good, while lifting our thoughts to that realm where the conflict does not exist.

But de Wette's section on good and evil also criticizes various positions that, in his view, fail to separate the material from the ideal standpoint; and embedded in the discussion is his treatment of providence. His first warning is against expressing the idea of the human inclination to evil in terms of religious speculation such as the fall of souls, and their becoming entombed in material bodies. Such explanations are mythological dreams that can have the bad effect of excusing us from moral striving.

Another mistake is to maintain that evil is something external to

1. *Religion und Theologie*, pp. 47ff.

humans; but in human dealings with each other, there is no such thing as absolute evil, but only evil which is relatively determined by circumstances. In illustration of this point, there comes a passage whose importance cannot be over-estimated in view of what was to happen to de Wette in 1819. Discussing the difficulty of deciding the value of an act when it is judged outwardly, and taking a hated despot as an example, de Wette writes:

> It is indeed possible that his moral convictions differ so much from our own, that we do him an injustice when we condemn him. Anyone who did not believe in Rome's freedom and who was Caesar's friend must have regarded his murder as a crime, while republicans could admire it as a noble [*erhabener*] deed. . . an act that seems to us to be evil can be morally good if it also comes from ethical motives.[1]

As a comment on what must have been the case in Rome of the first century BCE this cannot be faulted. It was quite a different matter when, in 1819, he made a not dissimilar comment on a political murder that had just taken place. Unfortunately for de Wette, those in power in Berlin did not believe in its freedom, and de Wette's comment would lead to his dismissal.

Another mistake in this area arises in the discussion of theodicy—the attempt to justify the existence of evil in the world. When it is the argument that evil is a necessary part of existence, because without it there can be no good, and no achievement of what is good, this is a confusion of the material and ideal standpoints. God is not responsible for evil and he does not will it, neither is the highest form of human nature that which comes from victory over evil. As a free agent, a human freely chooses to do what is unconditionally right, regardless of the fact that there is also an inclination towards evil. Another mistake is that which tries to see the hand of God at work in our material lives, and which inspires the false hope that God will grant us luck and happiness. The proper course is to rise above the material to the ideal, whence we gain the confidence to cope with the uncertainties of the material world, using our setbacks as opportunities for sacrifice, and in the knowledge that, from the viewpoint of eternity, God provides only what is best. Our watchword must always be 'our thoughts are not God's thoughts, our ways are not his ways'.[2]

1. *Religion und Theologie*, p. 51.
2. *Religion und Theologie*, p. 58.

De Wette now passes to his third section in this chapter, that dealing with the specifically religious matter of feeling (*Gefühl*). The importance of feeling is that, without it, religion is dead and abstract. Feeling brings it to life, and reflection upon feeling indicates that it can be analysed into three aesthetic ideas. The first is inspiration (*Begeisterung*), according to which we apprehend (*ahnen*) the eternal in the noble deeds and achievements of men and women as well as in the beauty of nature:

> Inspiration enlivens the heroes, the leaders of the people, the artists and the wise, and helps them to grasp the eternal in the ideals that they follow.[1]

Whereas it is forbidden to understanding (*Verstand*) to find subjective (ideal) principles in what is material, feeling (*Gefühl*) is permitted to do this.

> Inspiration is the satisfying, exalting participation, with which we observe the manifestations of beautiful, sublime spiritual life in the stories of antiquity and the deeds of the present day; with which we see the life of the nations and the exploits and character of great heroes and saints, in their pure, spiritual significance and apart from lower circumstances and aims. Inspiration is the pleasure in beautiful nature, the warm feeeling that flows into us from a view of a beautiful spring, and the loveliness, charm and complex harmony of a landscape.[2]

The second aesthetic idea corresponds to the practical ideas of good and evil, and is the feeling of resignation (*Ergebung*). While acknowledging our guilt we submit to the holy all-powerful (*der heiligen Allmacht*) and receive the feeling of inner peace and the feeling that we are of infinite value. Religiously, this is the feeling of forgiveness and of reconciliation with God. In turn, this enables us to interpret history correctly. We perceive the contradiction between good and evil when we contemplate the destruction of civilizations or the triumph of barbarism; but when we see this in the spirit of resignation, faith grants the vision of a spiritual kingdom of reality which shines over the ruins of time with eternal, untroubled beauty.

The third aesthetic idea is that of worship (*Andacht*), which is, again, a form of contemplation of the sublime in life and nature, in which we intuit the eternal goodness that directs everything to what is best.

---

1. *Religion und Theologie*, p. 59.
2. *Religion und Theologie*, p. 60.

Here, de Wette uses words that remind us of part of his first writing, *Eine Idee*:

> through religious feeling the world, as well as our inwardness, will be-
> come a temple of God. The hieroglyphs of nature and history develop, for
> pious beholders, into living, clear pictures of the eternal. Just as the
> cherub in the Old Testament, made up of lion, bull, eagle and man indi-
> cated the presence of the divine majesty, so will the whole of nature, but
> especially humanity and its history, become a symbol and witness to God
> and his creative and life-giving spirit.[1]

We can almost say that the quest begun in *Eine Idee* has here reached its goal—although de Wette's theology was still not complete.

Two small points are to be noted in the final pages of this chapter. The first is a reference to Herder, who pointed out to his contemporaries the need to look at human history and culture as an expression of the religious spirit of humanity.[2] We may detect here something of de Wette's own indebtedness to Herder, and see once again a link between his student days and this 1815 writing. The second is a reference to the author of the *Reden über die Religion* (Schleiermacher is not explicitly named), who is praised for having shown that the poetic way of regarding history was, in fact, religion.[3] Since relations between de Wette and Schleiermacher were not at their most cordial in 1815, we can only speculate on the reason for de Wette's oblique reference to his colleague.

The remainder of the first part of *Über Religion und Theologie*, that dealing with religion in general, is devoted to two main topics: the expression of religion in literary forms and the history of religion as a phenomenon, or more exactly, the history of Egyptian, Greek and Hebrew religion and Christianity.

In close reliance upon Fries, de Wette matches types of literature to the three aesthetic ideas of inspiration (*Begeisterung*), submission (*Resignation*) and worship (*Andacht*). To inspiration belongs epic-idyllic poetry, which speaks of the successful exploits of heroes or which depicts the tranquillity of a pastoral world. Such literature therefore reflects the ideas respectively of the free, individual achievement of a purpose, and the harmonious unity of all existence. The first

---

1. *Religion und Theologie*, p. 63.
2. *Religion und Theologie*, p. 64.
3. *Religion und Theologie*, p. 65.

idea is also reflected in the artistic or sculptured portrayal of Greek heroes and gods.

Resignation is connected with tragic, comic and elegaic literature. Tragedy explores the seeming contradictions of life, which tragic heroes overcome in their response to their circumstances. Elegy overcomes the contradictions by expresssing intuitions of a beautiful future, while comedy simply laughs at the contradictions. Yet comedy is deeply religious in that it intuits a higher reality and purposefulness, by mocking at life's contradictions.[1]

Worship corresponds to the lyrical in literature and especially in music. Music is especially appropriate for the aesthetic idea of worship, since it is abstract and cannot represent or portray reality. It can, however, lift the listener to the highest contemplation.

These classifications lead de Wette to comment on the importance of *mythology* in religion. Myths are spontaneous and poetic creations which give expression to intimations of freedom, harmony and purpose. They are indispensable to religion; but they are double-edged because they can begin to be taken literally and be believed to be expressing explanations at the level of knowing (*Wissen*):

> a healthy, tasteful, living mythology can only develop where faith [*Glaube*] has broken free from the fetters of a knowledge that wishes to put everything into definitions [*ein begriffsmässiges Wissen*].[2]

De Wette's account of the history of religion is important because it sets his view of Hebrew religion in context. He begins by describing Egyptian fetishism, which is an intimation of the divine in nature without the achievement of any idea of transcendence.[3] However, the Egyptian priests achieved a degree of reflection upon reality in their astronomy; and the story of Osiris as well as belief in immortality are evidence of intuition of religious ideas. The Greeks are praised for having risen above their nature religion (still evident in Bachic rites) to an ethical and spiritual view of the world mediated by their myths, which symbolized ethical ideals.[4] Further, their achievements in art and in drama showed how they had intuited the aesthetic ideas of

---

1. *Religion und Theologie*, p. 71.
2. *Religion und Theologie*, p. 76.
3. *Religion und Theologie*, p. 79.
4. *Religion und Theologie*, pp. 82-83. See also Strich, *Mythologie*, I, pp. 262ff.

inspiration and resignation. On the other hand, they did not achieve a national form of religion, as a result of which their gods became the subject of amusement and abuse, and the mystery religions provided a haven for superstition. Against this background, de Wette turns to the religion of Moses.[1]

In a letter to Fries dated 15 June 1812 de Wette had remarked how useful he had found Fries's idea that the religion of Moses had abolished mythology.[2] This was now the great virtue that de Wette attributed to Moses. Hebrew religion, by eschewing mythology such as was found in Greece, concentrated upon truth and morality rather than upon beauty. The glance was turned away from nature and lifted up to the God who had created heaven and earth, and the whole was consolidated by the covenant, which bound God and the people in justice and morality. In the religion of Moses lay the seeds of monotheism, which permitted Hebrew religion to develop a universal outlook. Further, this monotheism was in itself ethical, and rested upon human awareness (*Gefühl*) of a pure ethical ideal. The whole Mosaic system was held together by its sense of history. It was not an arbitrary religion, but based upon the history of God's dealings with his people.

Understandably, the Hebrews had no possibility of distinguishing knowledge from faith by means of philosophical reflection, and thus knowledge (*Wissen*) led them astray, as in supposing that the world was created at the beginning of time. Fortunately, Hebrew religion had little or no dogmatics to confuse the Israelites, and in their belief in history as the sphere of divine activity they sensed the ideas of ultimate purpose and harmony.

On the other hand, de Wette had some hard things to say about the coarseness of Hebrew ethics and their idea of God. It was a religion of compulsion rather than of free choice, of a God who hated non-Hebrews rather than the loving father of all peoples, of conformity rather than pure moral ideals. The Hebrew theocracy was only a distorted reflection of the kingship of God. Yet this religion was open to development in positive directions, especially in the hands of the prophets, who preached a religion of the heart. It was only after the Babylonian exile that Hebrew religion declined, through the introduc-

1. *Religion und Theologie*, pp. 84-87.
2. Henke, 'Berliner Briefe', pp. 100-101.

tion of foreign metaphysical mythology, theological speculation and the exalting of the Bible and the law to the status of literal truth.

De Wette's treatment of Christianity, which now follows, can be quickly dealt with. Christ restored what was best in Hebrew religion and gave it a universal character, in spirit and in truth. The developing Catholic Church made Christianity into a type of Judaism until the Reformation restored its original aims. Even so, Protestantism could not preserve these gains intact, and had to await the rise of historical criticism to restore to Christianity the free spirit of enquiry in the service of living faith. God said that the spirit would lead people into all truth, and that spirit was in the mind (*Gemüth*) of believers, and came to expression in the quest for truth. Thus ends the section of the book dealing with religion.

Part 2, dealing with theology, can be outlined more briefly. Its most important section deals with biblical criticism of the Gospels in particular. It addresses problems which are still acutely felt by believers today, and makes important distinctions that still have validity, even if it is difficult for us today to accept the philosophical framework into which the distinctions are cast.

Basic to the discussion is de Wette's distinction between knowledge (*Wissen*) and faith (*Glaube*) and his insistence that religion belongs properly to faith and intuition (*Ahnung*). De Wette was faced, as are biblical scholars in Britain today, with a widespread refusal of believers to admit the validity of the historical criticism of the Bible. For such believers, the authority of the Bible was inextricably bound up with traditional views about the authorship of its books, together with the presupposition that the historical content of the Bible was accurate because inspired.

De Wette attacked this position from two sides. The first was to point out that the historical study of the Bible was fundamental to the Reformation, and was what made Protestantism distinctive. Far from undermining faith, historical criticism served faith by distinguishing what in the Bible was inaccurate from what was correct. What the conservatives were doing was defending a presupposition about the historical accuracy of the Bible rather than defending the content of the Bible itself; and they were content to base their faith upon what was partly inaccurate. De Wette insisted, rightly we must say, that questions about the authorship and accurate history of the Bible were matters for historical investigation, and that the Bible's historical content could only be defended by historical criticism.

The second line of attack was to insist that, since faith was not a matter of knowledge (*Wissen*) or understanding (*Verstand*), the religious truth of the Bible had nothing to do with its historicity, and was perceived by faith and intuition. Faith perceived that the teaching of Jesus as recorded in the New Testament was true, regardless of whether Jesus actually delivered it. Further, if Jesus taught the unity and holiness of God, this did not make these beliefs more true. Had Jesus denied them, we would not believe him.

De Wette now addressed himself to two opposing views, that which feared the critical investigation of the Gospels, and that which took criticism of the Gospels to the point of scepticism. To the first group, de Wette pointed out the difficulties inherent in the Gospel narratives: their disagreements, their lack of completeness such that it was not possible to know how long the ministry of Jesus lasted, their appeal to miracle which modern people could not accept. Against the sceptics de Wette urged that the Gospels were not mythical. They rested upon historical tradition, and patient research could establish some, if not all, details of the origins of Christianity. An important historical point was that it was the portrayal of early Christianity by Paul which provided a clue for the historical search for that which had brought Christianity into being.[1]

But, as de Wette had insisted all along, the historical treatment of religious narratives is not the route to their proper interpretation as *religious* traditions, and thus he now turned to this question. Since all history is in one sense symbolic, that is, an expression of the human spirit and its activity, then it demands appropriate interpretation. In the case of the Gospels it is necessary to concentrate upon the eternal ideas implied in the narratives rather than upon temporal details of the story. Thus, the narrative of the Virgin Birth expresses the idea of the divine origin of religion and of the divine value of the life of Jesus, although as a historical narrative, it causes difficulties for understanding (*Verstand*) because it relates a fact (the conception of Jesus by the power of the Holy Spirit) that lies beyond historical investigation.

The miracles of Jesus are similarly to be seen as symbolic expressions of the triumph of the divine spirit in Jesus over nature, and what is material and contradictory in the world. The lack of correspon-

1. *Religion und Theologie*, pp. 155ff.

dence between the miracles and what is possible is less important than their articulation of the idea of the self-sufficient power of the human spirit and the sublime doctrine of spiritual self-reliance. The Resurrection in particular is, for the disciples, the greatest demonstration of the triumph of the mission of Jesus over the power of evil; and we today can agree with this in the sense that it expresses the visible actualization and realization of the divine government of the world as well as the triumph of the truth. These ideas are validly expressed in the narrative, whether or not we believe in the Resurrection as a historical fact.[1] This last matter is one of understanding (*Verstand*). The miracle remains at the level of the ideal even if we hold that Jesus revived naturally. The ascension is a symbol that the path to the eternal kingdom is via death, and also expresses Jesus' passage to eternal glory. This is in spite of the fact that the story of the ascension itself is hardly acceptable, with its claim that Jesus has physically entered a heaven above the clouds. De Wette notes, interestingly, that the stories of the Virgin Birth and ascension do not come from the apostles themselves, but belong to the Gospel tradition (*Sage*) and are absent from Paul and John, and, we could add, Mark.

De Wette concludes this discussion by linking the Gospel tradition with the aesthetic ideas of religion. Thus the life of Jesus is epic, that is, an example of the inspiration (*Begeisterung*) of a heroic figure. But his death is an expression of resignation:

> Christ on the cross is a picture of humanity purified by self-sacrifice.[2]

Finally, the simple trust of Jesus in God, his perfect obedience and his willingness to drink the cup of suffering are an inspiration for worship (*Andacht*). Handled in a historical and symbolic-aesthetic manner, the Gospels will be properly understood, avoiding on the one hand the negative use of historical criticism, and on the other hand the conservative criticism that distorts miracles in order to defend them.

The other matter in Part 2 of *Über Religion und Theologie* that will be outlined is de Wette's view of the nature of dogmatics and its historical study, including the place of the Old Testament in Christian

---

1. *Religion und Theologie*, p. 161: 'das Wunder [the Resurrection] bleibt, wenn wir auch eine natürliche Wiederbelebung annehmen'.
2. *Religion und Theologie*, pp. 163-64.

dogmatics.[1] De Wette begins by pointing out the subjective element in all history writing, that it is the historian who describes the manifold of history from a standpoint of unity. Thus, one can write the history of agriculture or the history of philosophy, and in each case the chosen subject will determine the treatment. In the case of the history of dogmatics, the subject matter (dogmatics) belongs to the realm of the ideal and of feeling (*Gefühl*), for all that dogmas are expressions of the ideal and the aesthetic in terms that belong to understanding (*Verstand*). The first task of a history of dogmatics is to identify the ideal and the aesthetic which dogmas are expressing. A proper understanding of the nature of dogma and its relation to explanation at the level of *Verstand* would avoid absurdities such as the division between Lutherans and Calvinists over the doctrine of the Eucharist.

There next comes a historical task, in that religions vary in the way that they grasp and express the ideal and the aesthetic. Christianity is characterized by worship (*Andacht*) in harmony with inspiration (*Begeisterung*) and resignation (*Ergebung*). Judaism, on the other hand, is characterized by a one-sided concentration upon worship (*Andacht*) while paganism has a similar unbalanced preoccupation with inspiration (*Begeisterung*). A recognition of the characteristic feature of a religion will enable the historian of dogmatics to write a history using the characteristic features as a standard against which to measure the Christianity of any given period. In this way, the falling away of Catholicism from essential Christianity can be demonstrated, as can its rediscovery in Protestantism. De Wette criticizes the way in which dogmatics has previously been treated as a series of teachings logically arranged.

There now follows the important and delicately argued section about the Old Testament as the starting-point of a Christian dogmatics. As usual, de Wette is mediating betweeen two extremes. On the one hand is the traditional view that the Old Testament is indissolubly bound to the New Testament by its prophecies of a future, atoning messiah. Against this is the modern view that the religion of Jesus is so new that it makes all other religions irrelevant. There is also the view that the New Testament completes the Old, an opinion which, de Wette argues, entails that only those should read the Old Testament who have antiquarian interests.

1. *Religion und Theologie*, pp. 171-91.

De Wette's defence of the Old Testament is again on the two fronts of the historical and the ideal. While he allows that Christianity is superior to the religion of the Old Testament, he insists that, historically speaking, Christianity arose on the foundation of the Old Testament and Judaism, and that the language and ideas of the New Testament cannot be understood without reference to the Old Testament. His ideal argument is that, in its own right, Old Testament religion has much of abiding value:

> The Old Testament itself offers an instance of religion from which we can learn, be strengthened and gain pleasure. Above all it contains many expressions of religious faith which affirm their value apart from Christianity, and which cannot be superseded. Here belong many Psalms which present the sublime feelings of worship (*Andacht*) in true poetic form. Indeed, given that religion ought especially to appear in poetic form we can allow the Old Testament an advantage over the New Testament on account of its sacred poetry.[1]

De Wette further exalts the Old Testament over the New by saying that the former's search and longing for truth without finding it is preferable to the latter's conviction that the truth is known. Also he praises the way in which the religion of Moses so firmly and nobly opposed the paganism of his day.

With this section, *Über Religion und Theologie* is by no means complete. There comes a section in which de Wette discusses Christian doctrines from the viewpoint of the aesthetic ideas; but this topic will not be treated here. The purpose of this long account of *Über Religion und Theologie* has been to show how, by 1815, de Wette had turned the philosophy of Fries into a confident, lucid and consistent vehicle for his own position. We can understand how and why he felt that the theological world lay at his feet and that he could deliver what was needed to free theology from excessive conservatism and excessive scepticism.

In the light of this exposition of de Wette's position, we can return to the *Dogmatik* which *Über Religion und Theologie* was written to elucidate. The material in the *Dogmatik* can be divided into three types: (a) philosophical explanation; (b) the history of Hebrew religion, Judaism and Christianity; and (c) the discussion of the content of the Bible from de Wette's dogmatic perspective. Of this

---

1.   *Religion und Theologie*, p. 190.

material, the first will not be discussed, given that it is more fully dealt with in *Über Religion und Theologie*. The other two types need our attention, beginning with the third type. This can best be explained by setting it out in a chart as Figure 1.

The first striking feature revealed by the chart is that the symbolic particularism or theocracy belongs only to Hebrew religion, so that the messiah becomes, for Judaism, part of the general doctrine of ideas. This is in accordance with de Wette's view that, after the return from exile, there was a break with what had preceded, and that Jewish ideas of the messiah (as so much else) had been affected by the adoption of mythologies from surrounding peoples. It is also striking that, in Hebrew religion, angels are intimations of God whereas for Judaism and Christianity they have assumed a separate existence. Within the New Testament, the distinctions between Jewish and Pauline Christianity, for example, are noteworthy. The whole scheme illustrates de Wette's view of dogmatics: that each instance of religion or Christianity must be described in terms of its characteristics and evaluated according to the adequacy of its articulation of the essence of religion.

On the other hand, the chart of the *Dogmatik* may give the impression that the work promises more than it in fact delivers. In some ways, it is disappointing to read, consisting as it does of extremely short sections which cite the relevant biblical or other passages, followed by bibliographies. Nowhere does de Wette synthesize his results in the way that the chart attempts to do, so that the reader is left to note the interesting points that arise from the sections, such as that John's Gospel is entirely free of reference to angels. Of greatest interest are the two historical sections which introduce, respectively, Hebrew religion and Judaism, and Christianity.

Some of what is said about Hebrew religion and Judaism is already familiar. Although we have no actual historical material about Moses, and much of what is said about him is later projection back to his time as well as historical myth, de Wette still asserts the importance of Moses in giving to Israel a religion stripped of pagan mythology,[1]

---

1. *Lehrbuch der christlichen Dogmatik*, p. 41: 'Wir haben von der mosaischen Geschichte kein ächt geschichtliches Denkmal. Der Pentateuch ist traditionelles, mythisches Document, in welchem die Geschichte im wunderbaren Lichte dargestellt, und Moses Einrichtungen mit späteren vermischt sind. . .Ihm gehört die Grundlage der theokratischen Verfassung. . .'

	Allgemeine Ideenlehre	*Symbolische Particularismus von der Theokratie*
Hebräismus	*God and Angels*: Idea of God; God's relationship to world; God's relationship to nature; *Man*: Immortality and pre-existence; spiritual value	Idea and institutions of Theocracy; Theocratic world-view; Ideal Theocracy, or the Messiah
Judenthum (a) Apocrypha (b) Philo	*God*: Idea of God; God's relationship to world; God's relationship to nature	
(c) Josephus	God's being and nature; providence and rewards/punishments	
OT exilic books Apocrypha, Philo Josephus, Sadducees	*Angels and demons* *Man*: Origin, pre-existence, immortality spiritual value, ethical view	
Daniel, Apocrypha Philo, Josephus *4 Ezra*, Judaism of time of Jesus	*Messiah*	
Dogmatik Jesu	*God*: Idea of God; God's relationship to world; God's relationship to nature; the Trinity *Angels and Demons* *Man*: immortality; spiritual value, ethical view *World-view*: state of mankind; God's mediation; Jesus' call; Kingdom of God; spirit of God;	

Apostel	**God's relation to nature; the Trinity** *Angels and Demons* *Man*: immortality; spiritual value; ethical view
John	*God's mediation*: Divine attestation of Jesus His high value, double *Zustand*, redeeming work mercy and grace, spirit of God, kingdom of God
Jewish Christianity	World view: Jesus the prophesied messiah His divine confirmation, high status double *Zustand*, redemptive work, battle with Satan, reconciliation of men to God, conditions and means of grace, spirit of God, kingdom of God
Epistle to the Hebrews	Messianic world plan and God's mediation Christ's high value, double *Zustand* etc.
Pauline Christianity	Condition of mankind; messianic world plan and God's mediation. Christ's high value: his double *Zustand*, redemptive work, teaching, death, resurrection, the Christian community, conditions and means of grace, spirit of God kingdom of God

Figure 1

based upon a single, exalted God and made actual in the theocracy. The natural tendency of the people to polytheism appeared in the time of the Judges, manifesting itself in the worship of nature, and it was Samuel who re-founded the theocracy in association with prophetic groups. The establishment of a national sanctuary by David and Solomon did not affect the worship at local sanctuaries, but did at least introduce music to the cultus together with its aesthetic value.

The division of the kingdom after Solomon's death resulted in the introduction of an image into Israel's religion, when Jeroboam set up the calves. The prophets fought in vain against this illegal cult. The precarious political existence of Judah and Israel after the division engendered an anxious and longing character among the people from which the messianic hope sprang. The Psalms and prophetic writings offer the best evidence for the ideal development of Mosaic religion as well as some postexilic compositions, including Isaiah 40–66, Job and Ecclesiastes.

The exile and the return produce a quite new state of affairs, with dependence upon the letter of the Mosaic law. Preoccupation with the causes of the exile turned attention away from the true spirit of Mosaic religion and an unwelcome arrival was the mythology of surrounding nations, especially Zoroastrianism. Here, de Wette provides a long exposition of Zoroastrianism, and criticizes the part it played in providing Judaism with mythical ideas received as metaphysical explanations of reality.[1] Thus Judaism developed its angelology and demonology, its doctrine of the messiah and of the Resurrection. The Hellenistic era added elements of Greek philosophy, especially that of Plato and Pythagoras, and sects such as the Essenes and Therapeutae came into existence. Philo is seen as the culmination of the combination of Judaism and Greek philosophy.

De Wette's account of the history of Christianity begins with the appearance of John the Baptist and with Jesus' baptism by John, except that de Wette doubts, on internal grounds (e.g. John's later uncertainty), that John recognized and testified to who Jesus was. De Wette's bibliography here cites with apparent approval the radical work of Reimarus and Bahrdt on this subject.[2]

In the Sermon on the Mount, Jesus proclaimed a spiritual programme,

1. *Lehrbuch der christlichen Dogmatik*, pp. 49-56.
2. *Lehrbuch der christlichen Dogmatik*, pp. 196-97.

and in so doing he was true to the spirit of Mosaic religion, rejecting the belief in authorities typical of Judaism, and proclaiming no new dogmas. He was inspired by a newly-born spirit of prophecy, and opposed the formal religion of the Pharisees. De Wette emphasizes the uniqueness of Jesus' religion. While not denying that it had something in common with movements of his day such as the Essenes and the Sadducees, he affirms that Jesus, as an uneducated man reared in Nazareth, had an unusually gifted nature, and that the only necessary part of his formation was his reading of the Old Testament.

Jesus taught a *spiritual* form of messianic hope, but as he gathered around him a group of uneducated men, he found himself unwillingly conforming to their material hopes of a messiah. Only his death could achieve his aim, and help the disciples to understand his message. De Wette appears to regard as inauthentic those teachings of Jesus about the kingdom of God that see it as a wonderful realm to be established on earth in the near future. If Jesus did utter these sayings, he did not take them seriously. Another possibility is that his followers misunderstood and distorted the teaching of Jesus about the spiritual nature of the kingdom of God.

The death of Jesus was foretold by him—but not his resurrection. Mt. 16.21 and parallels are later explanations, and the disciples certainly did not expect the resurrection. His death was certainly not seen by Jesus as an atoning death.[1] This is an understanding developed by the apostles.

The teaching of Jesus was not methodical and systematic. Its purpose was not to instruct but to arouse, and it was directed towards experience (*Gefühl*). Although he performed healings, something which was not unusual at the time, Jesus did not regard these as a ground for faith in the way that the apostles did later. Before his death, Jesus instituted a ceremony which, according to the Synoptic Gospels, symbolized his death, but which according to John was an example of humility. However, to his and his disciples' surprise, he survived the crucifixion and saw his disciples again, giving them new courage to continue his mission.[2] They were emboldened to trust in

---

1. *Lehrbuch der christlichen Dogmatik*, p. 212: 'Die Versöhnungslehre lässt sich aus Jesu Aussprüchen nicht beweisen. Der Tod Jesu ist erst den Aposteln in so wichtiger Bedeutung erschienen.'
2. *Lehrbuch der christlichen Dogmatik*, p. 219: 'Unerwartet für seine Jünger

their own spiritual strength and to proclaim the gospel. However, they could not break out of their Judaistic particularism, and only Paul was able to make the Gospel a message for all humanity. Even so, Paul bound the free teaching of Jesus in dogmatic fetters. The books of the New Testament have therefore to be classified under three headings: (1) Jewish Christian (the Synoptics, Acts, Peter, James, Jude, Revelation); (2) Alexandrian or Hellenistic (John, Epistles of John, Hebrews); and (3) Pauline. It is necessary to separate the teaching of Jesus from that of the apostles, and to identify the characteristic features of his teaching as well as that of the three types of early Christianity.

It will be seen from this outline that de Wette's historical understanding of the origins of Christianity was a radical one, and this radicalism was reinforced by his Latin work *Commentatio de morte Jesu Christi expiatoria* (1813), in which he argued that neither the Old Testament, nor Judaism nor Jesus knew of or taught that the messiah would die an atoning death. This was a doctrine formulated by the early church, and not to be taken literally, since it was, at best, a symbol of that aspect of the aesthetic idea of resignation whereby the individual experienced the feeling of reconciliation with God.[1]

De Wette's other work from this period was an anonymous, quasi-political book that appeared in the first half of 1815. It foreshadows a growing crisis, and one which would lead to disaster for de Wette's career and work. During de Wette's early years in Berlin, continental Europe was living uneasily under the domination or forbearance of Napoleon. Prussia had been defeated by Napoleon at Jena in 1806, on the occasion when de Wette's belongings had been pillaged, and it gradually began to come to terms with its humiliation. Reforms that would otherwise have been impossible became necessary, and included reorganization of taxation, the removal of restrictions on the social and economic activities of Jews and the nationalization of lands belonging to Catholic and Protestant churches.[2]

An important part of the policy of regeneration was to create a

---

und für ihn selbst war das Kreuz für ihn nicht tödtlich gewesen, und er zeigte sich wieder den staunenden Jüngern'.

1.   Reference is to the version in de Wette's *Opuscula Theologica* (Berlin, 1830), pp. 3-148.

2.   J.J. Sheehan, *German History 1770–1886* (Oxford: Clarendon Press, 1989), p. 308.

citizenry consisting of 'free, independent, prosperous and patriotic men, ready and able to die for their state'. The architect of this new army, Scharnhorst, wrote in 1807 that

> We must interject a feeling of independence, to destroy the old forms, to dissolve the bonds of privilege, to lead and nurture and unfetter the free development of regeneration—there can be no higher purpose.[1]

However, such an idea was unwelcome to Friedrich Wilhelm III of Prussia. He did not share Scharnhorst's faith in an armed citizenry, nor favour the political implications of its preconditions. This point is of importance in relation to de Wette's stance.

Napoleon's invasion of Russia in June 1812 was the beginning of his undoing, abetted by the fact that a Prussian army of 20,000 went over to the Russian side at a crucial moment against the knowledge and will of Friedrich Wilhelm. On 25 March 1813, a proclamation to the German peoples and princes issued in the name of Tsar Alexander and Friedrich Wilhelm urged all Germans to rise in pursuit of German freedom. When, in August 1813, Austria declared war on Napoleon, the forces against Napoleon were stacked so strongly that defeat for him was inevitable even though his opponents paid a high price for it in new killed or wounded. Napoleon was defeated at Leipzig in October 1813 and then pursued into France where he surrendered and abdicated in April 1814. His last fling consisted of his escape from imprisonment from Elba in February 1815, his rallying of the French nation and his final defeat in Belgium at Waterloo on 18 June 1815.

The defeat of Napoleon at Leipzig in October 1813 had set in train discussions about the future condition of Europe in general and of the German peoples in particular. Eventually, two main options were advocated, first, that there should be a German nation under the leadership of Prussia, second, that there should be a federation (*Bund*) including Prussia, Austria and the Napoleonic federation of Rhineland German states. In the event, it was the *Bund* that came into being in June 1815 before Napoleon's final defeat. It was a confederation of free, independent states, and it determined the political set-up in Central Europe for the next fifty years.[2]

We do not know exactly when de Wette wrote *Die neue Kirche oder*

---

1. Sheehan, *German History*, p. 309.
2. Sheehan, *German History*, pp. 402-403.

Verstand und Glaube im Bunde.[1] A letter to Fries, dated 12 July 1815, indicates that Fries had received and commentated favourably on the work, so it must have been completed early in 1815, or possibly at the end of 1814.[2] Being anonymous it contained no foreword. The anonymity, however, was compromised by the publisher associating de Wette's name with the book in an advanced publicity notice.

At the political level the work is a passionate plea for the first of the two political options mentioned above, namely, for a German nation under the leadership of Prussia. De Wette describes how men, especially young men, had rallied to fight for Prussia when given the chance, and he sees in the free and independent allegiance of citizens to the German cause the surest guarantee of the order and stability of a German state.[3]

But although this is a writing addressing a burning political issue, it is primarily a theological work which defines Protestantism and maintains that a Protestant-led (and thus, Prussian) Germany alone can achieve its destiny. This latter point not only addresses a suggestion that had been made about the organization of the church within the new *Bund*, but indicates that battle-lines were beginning to be drawn up in Berlin between more radical theologians such as de Wette and Schleiermacher on the one hand, and an alliance of orthodox and pietist believers, represented in the nobility and gaining in influence in the court of Friedrich Wilhelm, on the other hand. Thus the events of de Wette's dismissal in 1819 were beginning to cast their shadow, although at this stage, de Wette could not be aware of this.

De Wette had the following objections to the proposed *Bund* and its ecclesiastical ramifications. First, although a federation of states, it would include Catholic states such as Austria. This would increase the danger that people would minimize the difference between Protestantism and Catholicism. This was a real danger because the Romantic interest in mythology and mysticism had brought about conversions to Catholicism, for example, of Friedrich Schlegel.[4]

1. *Die neue Kirche, oder Verstand und Glaube im Bunde* (Berlin, 1815).
2. Henke, 'Berliner Briefe', p. 101. Henke wrongly suggests that de Wette is referring to *Über Religion und Theologie*.
3. It must be made clear that de Wette was echoing what others such as F.J. Jahn, E.M. Arndt, Schleiermacher and Fries himself were advocating.
4. T. Nipperdey, *Deutsche Geschichte 1800–1866: Bürgerwelt und starker Staat* (Munich: Beck, 1987), p. 405.

Further, there was a tendency within Protestantism, led by the orthodox-pietist alliance, that de Wette regarded as an incipient catholicizing. This tendency wanted to lay stress upon subscription to articles of belief, and had even suggested that there should be a chief bishop (*Oberbischof*) for Protestant churches.[1]

In reply de Wette drew upon the position that he had so elegantly worked out in *Über Religion und Theologie*. He emphasized that the true sources of Protestantism were the Bible, historical criticism and reason (*Vernunft*), and that this was why Protestantism could not be confused with Catholicism. The latter rejected historical criticism and was a religion of the coercion of reason. Protestantism could not mimic the hierarchy of Catholicism precisely because it was based upon the freedom of the individual Christian. Nor could it insist on subscription to articles of belief because religion was a matter of *Glaube* not *Verstand* and because no articles of belief were ever adequate or valid for all times.

De Wette was particularly concerned with the relation between art and religion, especially between art and Protestantism. He maintained that it was Protestant freedom that lay behind the work of Goethe and Schiller, and that the spirit of Catholicism was inimical to the production of great art. At the same time de Wette made his customary observations about Catholicisim having a better artistic tradition than Protestantism.

What, then, should the Church be like in a German nation under the leadership of Protestant Prussia? De Wette notes the tendency within Protestantism to schism, a tendency which is the price of its commitment to freedom. On the other hand, he is not unduly worried about this, and points out the things that Protestants have in common: the Bible, hymns (important for de Wette because of the part played by music in the aesthetic idea of worship [*Andacht*]), the sacraments of baptism and communion. De Wette's remarks on the latter are instructive. He recommends that communion should stress its original purpose, to be a fellowship meal binding together the participants in love. He says that this purpose cannot be achieved in large groups

1. *Die neue Kirche*, p. 44: 'man soll die Kirche wieder an Symbole binden, ihr wieder durch Excommunication und strenge Zucht aufhelfen, ja man hat sogar zur Aufrechthaltung der Einheit im Glauben einen protestantischen Oberbischof oder Pabst vorgeschlagen'.

where people do not know each other, and he seems to recommend that small, perhaps more informal, groups should hold the fellowship meal, with celebrations of communion for larger numbers on particular occasions, such as Good Friday.[1]

This brings us to de Wette's view of the relation between church and state. As I understand him, de Wette advocates an enabling role for the state. The state will provide the unity and focus in terms of which German Christians will practise their religion in Protestant freedom. In turn, this freedom will produce a sincere commitment to the state, a patriotism based upon the desire to uphold the primary Christian values of truth, love of neighbour, justice and hard work. De Wette also envisages that the state will provide opportunities for Christians, including Catholics, to express their unity as Germans and their faith as Christians through national festivals. He pleads for the building in each large city or provincial capital of a gothic cathedral-type building, where such festivals could culminate in festal worship.[2]

De Wette comes over, in this work, as a passionate advocate of at least two things that, from 1815, were increasingly viewed with suspicion in Berlin: a critical theology building on the best insights of the Enlightenment and the Romantic period, and a commitment to democracy that would sweep away that old social order that had led to Prussia's defeat, and would fulfil the aspirations of a hoped-for new order in response to which the young men had fought for Prussia's freedom.

The last observation in this chapter is that, as far as I know, de Wette did not attend public worship during these years (1810–15). This was to change shortly, when he began to attend Schleiermacher's church, and to draw closer to Schleiermacher without embracing his theology. No doubt the political events of 1815 onwards brought them closer together, for both were to fall under suspicion, even if it was de Wette who was to be the scapegoat.

---

1. *Die neue Kirche*, pp. 92ff.

2. *Die neue Kirche*, p. 116: 'Man schaffe Symbole und Feste für die Begeisterung der Vaterlandsliebe, woran alle Confessionen ohne Unterschied, und selbst die katholische, Thiel nehmen'.

Chapter 5

BERLIN II: BREAKTHROUGH AND DISASTER

On 14 May 1816 a man in his mid-twenties arrived in Berlin to begin work for the Licentiate and *Habilitation* which would qualify him as a *Privatdozent*.[1] On 23 May he was interviewed by de Wette who, as dean of the faculty, informed him about the regulations for becoming a *Privatdozent*.[2] This was not the first time that Friedrich Lücke had met de Wette. They had seen each other in the university library in Göttingen the previous year, and that encounter seems to have made a negative impression upon Lücke.[3] According to Lücke's own account, de Wette was, at first acquaintance, a rather stiff, dry and curt man with a certain cold earnestness.[4]

If Lücke had met de Wette previously, he had also read some of de Wette's writings, and had even experienced a period of enthusiasm for his work.[5] However, acquaintance with Schleiermacher's writings had won him over to the latter's position; and in a prize essay written in Göttingen in 1812 he had attacked de Wette as a rationalist critic.[6]

Lücke soon discovered that de Wette's outward manner concealed a

1. F. Sander, *D. Friedrich Lücke: Abt zu Bursfelde und Professor der Theologie in Göttingen (1791–1855)* (Hannover-Linden, 1891), p. 70.

2. Sander, *Lücke*, p. 82.

3. F. Lücke, 'Zur freundschaftlichen Erinnerung an D. Wilhelm Martin Leberecht de Wette', *TSK* (1850), p. 502: 'Seine äussere Erscheinung war nicht von der Art, um bei der ersten flüchtigen Berührung auf einen Fremden einen besonderen, anziehenden Eindruck zu machen'.

4. Sander, *Lücke*, p. 99: 'Das Steife, Trockene, Kurze des Mannes stiess auch hier anfangs mehr zürück'. Lücke, 'Erinnerung', p. 504: 'De Wette hatte in seiner Erscheinung auf den ersten Anblick etwas äusserlich Steifes, auch Trockenes, Kurzes, einen gewissen kalten Ernst'.

5. Lücke, 'Erinnerung', p. 502.

6. Sander, *Lücke*, p. 99.

warm personality, and one which was particularly attractive to students. Lücke gradually became a close friend and confidant of de Wette in the years 1817–18, after which he moved to a professorship in Bonn.

Lücke has given us the only intimate picture that we possess of de Wette's life at university in any of the periods of his activity. In Berlin, it was a life of academic solitude, broken only by teaching and administration at the university, and by gatherings of small groups of students at his home.[1] On Sundays, there were walks to the Charlottenburg with students such as Lücke, at which the discussion centred on theological topics.

There was no contact between de Wette and his colleagues Schleiermacher and Neander (Lücke does not even mention Marheinecke). Partly, this was because Berlin was too large a city to make social visits to colleagues easy, and partly because there were no formal or informal arrangements for colleagues to meet regularly for academic discussions. It also seems to be the case that de Wette and his colleagues were the sort of people who accepted rather than initiated invitations of a social nature. To this must be added the fact that de Wette's own domestic arrangements were not ideal.

Shortly before moving from Heidelberg to Berlin, de Wette had married Henriette Beck. She was the widow of a Mannheim trader, whose death had left her in desperate financial circumstances, and with a dependent eleven-year-old son Karl. Apparently, de Wette married Henriette more out of pity than love, and the marriage was far from harmonious. According to Wiegand, de Wette's second wife had no understanding of de Wette's commitment to scholarship and the demands that this made upon him, and she was erratic, self-willed, jealous and prodigal.[2] In Berlin, Henriette bore two children, Anna, born on de Wette's birthday, 12 January 1811, and Ludwig, born on 9 November 1812. Wiegand writes of how de Wette loved to play with his children in the garden of the Berlin house; but it is clear that Henriette would not have been an ideal hostess if her husband had wished to invite colleagues, and it is, perhaps, significant that Lücke makes no mention of her in his account of his close friendship with de Wette.[3]

---

1. Lücke, 'Erinnerung', p. 515.
2. Wiegand, *De Wette*, pp. 21 n. 3, 29.
3. According to Sander (*Lücke*, p. 100), de Wette succeeded in concealing from

As Lücke and de Wette drew closer together, the younger man began to appreciate de Wette's position without abandoning his preference for Schleiermacher. De Wette never succeeded in persuading Lücke to read Fries's philosophy.[1] On the other hand, Lücke expressed his admiration for the clarity of de Wette's position over against the obscurities of Schleiermacher, and he regarded de Wette as the better exegete. For his part, de Wette expressed his misgivings over Schleiermacher's role as preacher at the Holy Trinity Church. In de Wette's view, the roles of university lecturer and church preacher were incompatible, and the result could only be that the preacher would have to compromise the truth, something that deeply offended de Wette's absolute commitment to the truth.[2]

For his part, Lücke denied that for Schleiermacher there was any such conflict of roles or compromising of the truth, and he prevailed upon de Wette to accompany him to hear Schleiermacher preach. Apparently, de Wette had once attended Schleiermacher's church, but had long since given up because of his deep reservations about Schleiermacher's position. Lücke describes how, on a beautiful summer morning, he succeeded in getting de Wette to accompany him to the Holy Trinity Church, and how de Wette was so impressed that, from then on, he attended Schleiermacher's sermons regularly.[3] Unfortunately, Lücke does not give us a date.

Of the three years that Lücke spent in Berlin, only 1816 and 1817 are possibilities for the dating of the 'beautiful summer morning'. 1816 will be too early, given that Lücke had arrived in Berlin only in May 1816. There is also the remark of Lücke's biographer, on the basis of Lücke's letters to his wife and friends, that Lücke's friendship with de Wette did not ripen immediately, but that the two men began to draw closer together in the autumn of 1816 and especially from the beginning of 1817.[4] This is confirmed by a letter of de Wette to Fries, dated 10 November 1816, in which he mentions the arrival of Lücke in Berlin, and their acquaintance notwithstanding their differences and

his friends the strains of his marriage.

1. Lücke, 'Erinnerung', p. 529.
2. Lücke, 'Erinnerung', p. 516.
3. Lücke, 'Erinnerung', p. 517.
4. Sander, *Lücke*, p. 99.

Lücke's 'inclination to mysticism'.[1] We can be certain, therefore, that
de Wette's visit to Schleiermacher's church took place in the summer
of 1817 and that, from this time onwards, there was not only a
warming of relationships between the two men, but a positive
influence upon de Wette through the worship and preaching of the
institutional church. Prior to this, it would seem that Schleiermacher
had had a higher opinion of de Wette than the latter of the former, to
judge from remarks of de Wette to Fries in letters dated 31 December
1814 and 12 July 1815, as well as Lücke's testimony.[2]

In the previous chapter, the differences between de Wette and
Schleiermacher as perceived by the former were mentioned.[3] The
matter can usefully be examined more closely in the present context
based upon material from *Theodor*.

De Wette understood Schleiermacher to hold that religion consists
of the mind being grasped by the spirit of the universe, which incho-
ate and immediate experience must be distinguished from knowledge
of it and from the expression of it in a system of meanings. The task
of critical reflection is to understand the nature of religion in its
purest form by ridding religious expressions and formulations of fake
or misleading ideas.[4]

De Wette next understood Schleiermacher to distinguish religion
from investigation (*Wissenschaft*) and moral practice (*Sittlichkeit*) in
the following way. Knowledge and action were attempts to achieve
harmony with the universe by dealing with particular aspects of it.
Thus knowledge and action were concerned with particular aspects of
the world, whereas religion was an apprehension of the world as a
whole. De Wette's problem with this was that he believed that religious
experience (*Gefühl*) was an important motivating factor to the will in
moral practice, and he could not see how this motivating religious
experience was related to religion in the sense of an apprehension
of the universe as a whole. To put it another way, he found
Schleiermacher's idea of the mind being grasped by the spirit of the

1. Staehelin, *Dewettiana*, p. 78. See also the letter to Fries of 15 March 1817
(*Dewettiana*, p. 78): 'Schleiermacher ist schon viel offener gegen mich, und auch
das muss mich sehr freuen'.
2. Staehelin, *Dewettiana*, pp. 73-74, and Henke, 'Berliner Briefe', p. 101.
3. Pp. 81-82.
4. *Theodor*, I, p. 167.

universe too vague, and lacking a clear application to moral practice.[1]

At the point where Schleiermacher was vague, Fries was, for de Wette, clear and practical. Fries defined the reality which was sensed by religious experience in terms of two moments: the law of the unity of everything and the law of the purpose of everything. In human life, the law of unity provided the impulse for the intellectual investigation of reality, while the law of purpose was the impulse for moral action. The experience, or feeling, that was essential to religion was at one and the same time something passive, giving satisfaction to the heart and stilling all striving and longing, and yet also the source of all human activity, challenging humans to achieve in life that satisfaction that was experienced in religion. From de Wette's point of view, we can well understand why the Friesian position was preferable to that of Schleiermacher.[2]

Another difficulty for de Wette was that he understood Schleiermacher to say that religion was concerned with reflection (*Betrachtung*); but reflection belonged to the area of knowledge (*Verstand*), and this contradicted the view that religion belonged to the sphere of feeling (*Gefühl*). The answer of Professor A. in *Theodor* is that the reflection meant by Schleiermacher is a different type of reflection from that which belongs to knowledge, but the implication of the discussion is that Schleiermacher's terms are ambiguous and confusing. This is also true of Schleiermacher's use of the word 'notion' (*Begriff*) to describe how religious experiences are presented to consciousness. For de Wette, who believed that religion could only be consciously grasped by aesthetic symbols, the idea that it could be grasped in terms of notions (*Begriffe*) again implied that religion belonged to the sphere of knowledge. Once more, Professor A. has to explain that Schleiermacher is using the term 'notion' (*Begriff*) in a special sense that relates it to religion as defined by Schleiermacher, and not to knowledge as in a Kantian scheme.[3]

For de Wette, then, Schleiermacher's position was unsatisfactory in the following ways. It began from a definition whose meaning was far from clear (being grasped by the spirit of the universe), did not convincingly relate moral practice to religious experience, and required

1. *Theodor*, I, pp. 168-69.
2. *Theodor*, I, p. 169.
3. *Theodor*, I, pp. 172-73.

terms such as reflection (*Betrachtung*) and notion (*Begriff*) to be understood in relation to the unclear definition of the nature of religion. That, in some ways, the position of the two men was close only compounded the difficulties. They both agreed that religion was grounded in experience of ultimate reality, and that religion was distinct from knowledge and from moral practice, while at the same time providing the clue to the meaning of knowledge and morality. Yet their respective working out of these positions was quite different. That of de Wette was an elegant and philosophical solution which neatly distinguished the differing types of knowledge, but which in effect reduced religion to philosophy, morality and aesthetics with little room for the institutional church. Schleiermacher, in de Wette's view, advocated a position that was vague and sometimes confusing, and which laid positive stress upon the place, in religion, of the church and its fellowship of pious believers. If, for this latter reason, Schleiermacher drew more followers than de Wette, this only increased de Wette's frustration that the vaguer, more religious position was preferred to the clearer, philosophical one. There was also annoyance on de Wette's part that, precisely because of his clarity, it was easy for him to be branded as a free-thinker. Schleiermacher's 'lax mysticism', as de Wette called it, probably made him more acceptable to the growing orthodox party.[1]

De Wette's differences with Schleiermacher were not confined to matters theological, but came into the open in the discussions that took place early in 1816 over the filling of a chair of philosophy.[2] The university senate, meeting on 13 March 1816, decided to petition the government for the establishment of two chairs, one in speculative philosophy, the other in practical (i.e. moral) philosophy. The senate proposed as candidates for the former chair G.W.F. Hegel, F.W.J. Schelling and G.H. von Schubert.[3] De Wette saw the occasion

1. See de Wette's letter to Fries dated 31 December 1814 (Staehelin, *Dewettiana*, pp. 73-74).
2. In fact, there were three chairs of philosophy vacant, those of Fichte (who had died on 29 January 1814), von Hoffmann and Klaproth. See Lenz, *Universität Berlin*, I, p. 570.
3. Schleiermacher, as rector and thus the chairman of the senate, had earlier succeeded in getting the matter referred to the individual faculties so that they could propose candidates for the one chair that the senate had been instructed to consider. On 13 March 1816, Schleiermacher now persuaded the senate to nominate candidates for

as an opportunity to bring Fries from Heidelberg to Berlin, and proposed Fries as the main candidate for both chairs. Although Fries was not nominated for the chair of speculative philosophy, he narrowly gained first place for the chair of practical philosophy. But the government had authorized the filling of only one chair, and thus de Wette addressed a memorandum to the ministry protesting against the nomination of Hegel and the others to the first chair, and urging the claims of Fries.[1]

De Wette's argument against Hegel and Schelling was that they were philosophers of nature, advocating positions which were not helpful to theology. In de Wette's opinion, the kind of philosopher that was needed was one who would support from the philosophical side the fundamental ideas of God, immortality and reconciliation (*Versöhnung*). Against von Schubert, de Wette's complaint was that he was almost a philosopher of the occult, having written on the symbolism of dreams, and letters on astrology. If the university was filling a chair of mystical physics, complained de Wette, von Schubert would be a worthy candidate. But he could only be taken seriously for a philosophical chair if one understood by philosophy something completely different from de Wette.

The memorandum concluded with the information that, when a vote had been taken in the senate on whether von Schubert or Fries should be the third person proposed for the first chair, there had been a tie. What de Wette did not say in the memorandum is that Schleiermacher, as rector, had given his casting vote to von Schubert.[2] It is difficult not to see this either as a deliberate snub to de Wette, or as a determined attempt to keep Fries away from Berlin, which would amount to almost the same thing. It could well be that Schleiermacher feared an alliance in Berlin between Fries and de Wette and what this might do to his own position, and that he was therefore prepared to decide for a man who he must have realized did not have the stature of Fries when it came to philosophy. This incident explains why, when

two chairs. De Wette opposed Schleiermacher on both matters. The debates in the Faculty of Theology, where de Wette was dean, were acrimonious. See further Lenz, *Universität Berlin*, I, pp. 573-74, and de Wette's long account to Fries in Henke, *Fries*, pp. 354-57.

1. The memorandum is printed in Staehelin, *Dewettiana*, pp. 75-76.
2. Henke, *Fries*, p. 356.

de Wette and Schleiermacher began to draw closer together, de Wette was very careful to justify this to Fries, and to assert that this in no way affected his friendship with Fries.[1]

In 1816 de Wette published the second volume of his *Lehrbuch der christlichen Dogmatik*, dealing with the dogmatics of the Lutheran church. This added nothing to what had been written in *Über Religion und Theologie* but was further evidence of de Wette's radical attitude towards dogmatic formulations of Christian belief.[2] In accordance with the *Lehrbuch* formula, the book consisted of short, pithy sections, accompanied by bibliographies, and would have made most sense to those who heard him elaborate his views in lectures, or who were familiar with his position from, for example, the *Über Religion und Theologie*.

In the preface, de Wette claimed (disingenuously, his opponents would have said) that, on the basis of his philosophy, there was no main teaching of the Lutheran church that he could not unreservedly accept in its true spiritual sense.[3] The rub, of course, lay in the words 'true spiritual sense' for, in the course of the work, de Wette rejected the traditional understandings of the Trinity, Christology and the Atonement. For him, dogmatics involved philosophical reflection upon the historical development of Christian doctrine and upon its systematic presentation from the point of view of the universal laws of human nature. This led to the now familiar historical sketch of Catholicism and Protestantism, culminating in the Enlightenment and

---

1. Over a year later, when the theological faculty was asked to nominate three candidates for the award of honorary degrees in honour of the 300th anniversary of the Reformation, de Wette and Schleiermacher seem to have been on the same side, in opposition to Neander and Marheinecke. See Lenz, *Universität Berlin*, I, p. 642 and n. 1. The outcome of the attempt to fill the chair of philosophy was that Hegel was made an offer, but declined because he had accepted a chair at Heidelberg. Two years later, Hegel did move to Berlin. Fries moved from Heidelberg to Jena in 1816.

2. *Lehrbuch der christlichen Dogmatik. Theil 2: Dogmatik der evangelisch-lutherischen Kirche nach den symbolischen Bücher und den älteren Dogmatikern* (Berlin, 1816).

3. *Dogmatik der evangelisch-lutherischen Kirche*, p. xii 'es gibt kein Haupt-dogma, das ich nicht, dessen wahren geistigen Sinne nach, mit voller Überzeugung unterschreiben könnte'.

Kant, and what de Wette believed to be the post-Kantian recovery of the true spirit of Christianity.[1]

Among observations that can be made are that, first, de Wette rejected the understanding of revelation in an objective or positive sense. Revelation was the apprehension (*Ahnung*) of the divine rule of the world in the history of religious development. It was an aesthetic idea which required the abandonment of belief in revelation as belonging to the sphere of knowledge, whether that knowledge was mediated through nature or history.[2] De Wette also rejected the views that belief in revelation entailed the acceptance of miracles, or that revelation was something before which human reason must bow in submission.

On Christology, de Wette maintained that belief in the divinity of Christ was an aesthetic judgment, and one which could not be explained at the level of empirical knowledge (*Verstand*). As a perfect human being, Christ lived an ordinary, natural and historical life. Faith, however, could perceive (*ahnen*) something divine about his life. The relationship between the human and the divine could not be expressed in any theory that used empirical notions (*Begriffe*).[3]

De Wette also dealt with the Atonement in a radical fashion. He declared that the view that Christ had borne the guilt of human sin in order to fulfil the demands of the law was a view of which the Bible knew nothing. The truth was that Christ had indeed suffered, that he had been blameless, and that he had exhibited in his death a sublime example of virtue and submission (*Resignation*). What was false was that attempts to explain Christ's death at the level of *Verstand* had drawn upon legal ideas and had formulated the theory of Christ bearing the guilt of others.[4]

As if these ideas would not have been alarming enough to representatives of the orthodox party in Berlin, de Wette also indicated that he was a universalist. On the doctrine of eternal damnation, he maintained that it should only be used to warn oneself, and should never be used to condemn others. No one, however evil, was unfit for God's grace, evil would be finally destroyed, and no human soul would be

---

1. *Dogmatik der evangelisch-lutherischen Kirche*, pp. 1-24.
2. *Dogmatik der evangelisch-lutherischen Kirche*, p. 53.
3. *Dogmatik der evangelisch-lutherischen Kirche*, p. 148.
4. *Dogmatik der evangelisch-lutherischen Kirche*, p. 157.

eternally lost, given that it was created by God.[1] In this volume, then, dealing with the central doctrines of the Lutheran church, de Wette provided further evidence, to those who needed it, of his free-thinking heterodoxy.

De Wette's next important work to appear was his *Lehrbuch der historisch-kritischen Einleitung in die kanonischen und apokryphischen Bücher des Alten Testaments*, whose preface is dated June 1817, and which can be considered with his *Lehrbuch der hebräisch-jüdischen Archäologie*, which had appeared in 1814.[2] Both books follow the *Lehrbuch* format, with very short sections illuminated by bibliographies. The purpose of the latter book, in dealing with the society, institutions, practices, political and geographical context of the people of the Old Testament, is to indicate the permanent features of their life that underpinned their historical development. To illustrate this, the discussion of the institutions is preceded by a sketch of 'Hebrew-Jewish' history which does not, however, amount to even a historical outline. Although the history is divided into three periods —(1) the legendary (*sagenhafte*) period from Abraham to Saul, (2) from Saul to the Babylonian exile, and (3) from the exile to the Roman destruction of Jerusalem (70 CE)—these periods are broken down into brief sections with the usual terse comments and bibliography. Typical is the comment on Solomon:

> Solomon enjoyed, but also misused, the fruits of David's efforts during a long and peaceful reign. He introduced art and luxury, made himself rich through trade and seafaring, embellished the worship of God, but oppressed the people and allowed foreign wives to incline him to foreign customs. His luck seems eventually to have been broken by disturbances (1 Kgs 11.14-25).[3]

On the earlier history we find such observations as the following on the exodus:

> No part of history is more adorned with miracles or influenced by legend [*Sagendichtung*] than this. Consequently, the careful historian will prefer

---

1. *Dogmatik der evangelisch-lutherischen Kirche*, p. 214.

2. *Lehrbuch der historisch-kritischen Einleitung in die kanonischen und apokryphischen Bücher des Alten Testaments* (Berlin, 1817); *Lehrbuch der hebräisch-jüdischen Archäologie* (Leipzig, 1814).

3. *Archäologie* (2nd edn), p. 35.

to tell these stories [*Sagen*] as such rather than to turn them arbitrarily into history.[1]

The historical-critical introduction deals with the canon of the Old and New Testaments, and then turns to the language, versions and text of the Old Testament before discussing the individual books of the Old Testament and Apocrypha. The tone of this discussion is critical, in that de Wette, drawing upon the work of his predecessors, identified authentic passages in prophetic books (i.e. verses that cannot be ascribed to the prophet), denied traditional views of authorship (e.g. of Daniel, Ecclesiastes, Proverbs) and denied the unity of Isaiah, Job (where the Elihu speeches are a later insertion) and Zechariah. De Wette's views on the Pentateuch and Chronicles are as set out in the epoch-making *Beiträge* of 1806–1807. The work is thus representative of the critical achievements of the late eighteenth and early nineteenth centuries, and places de Wette clearly among those who fully accepted the right of criticism to reject traditional views of the authorship, authenticity and unity of the Old Testament. The historical-critical introduction was, in a sense, de Wette's last work on the Old Testament. It is true that, in later years, he revised his Psalms commentary and the *Einleitung* and the *Archäologie*, and that he continued to lecture on the Old Testament; but by the time that the critical introduction appeared in 1817 he had long since been primarily interested in other areas of theology and philosophy, as has been made clear in the previous chapter.

Another writing to appear in 1817 was a substantial article of over seventy pages in the *Reformations-Almanach* entitled 'Über den Verfall der protestantischen Kirche in Deutschland und die Mittel, ihr wieder aufzuhelfen'.[2] This added nothing to what de Wette had written in *Über Religion und Theologie*. It gave the familiar account of the Reformation and its aftermath, emphasizing that, to be true to itself, it needed help from two directions: from critical investigation and from the application of philosophy to religion. De Wette credited Semler and Kant with having initiated these things, albeit in a manner which had led to doubt. Fries and Jacobi are praised as having discovered the truth that faith is an unmediated grasp of truth in the

1. *Archäologie* (2nd edn), p. 27.
2. See F. Keyser (ed.), *Reformations-Almanach für Luthers Verehrer auf das evangelische Jubeljahr 1817* (Erfurt, 1817), pp. 296-371.

human mind, which cannot be reached by empirical knowledge (*Wissen*), and de Wette warns of the consequences of ignoring the inner revelation that God has placed in each human mind. We also find de Wette's familiar anxiety that people, especially young people, should be repelled by rationalism and should turn, in reaction, to the new pietism because of the latter's warmth and light. It is not the right warmth, warns de Wette. Finally, we hear de Wette's familiar complaint about the state dealing from above with a clergy-controlled church, instead of there being cooperation between the state and the ordinary people.

While de Wette was penning these variations on *Über Religion und Theologie*, he was closely studying Fries's moral philosophy with a view to writing a Christian Ethics. He was certainly working on the first section of Volume III of Fries's *Neue Kritik*, in which 250 pages are devoted to practical (i.e. moral) philosophy, and it may be that he had an advanced copy of material relating to Fries's *Handbuch der praktischen Philosophie*, which appeared in 1818. In a letter at the end of March 1816 he was requesting a copy and promising not to steal his friend's work.[1]

At the same time that he was studying Fries's morals, a significant change was happening, or was about to happen, in de Wette's whole view of the nature of revelation, a change that would bring him a greater certainty of faith, that would entail important revisions to works such as the *Über Religion und Theologie* and the *Handbuch der christlichen Dogmatik*, and that would make him much more sympathetic to the institutional church. The first intimation of this change is in a letter to Fries, dated 17 December 1817 that is of sufficient importance to warrant a long excerpt:

> Regarding your practical philosophy, as far as I have read it, I have enjoyed the completion and filling out [*Rundung*] of the speculation as well as the presentation. But you get the greatest praise from me because you have given me the key to the treatment of a Christian Ethics which, as I hope, will astonish the world. Perhaps it will also astonish you initially, because at last I have been able to find and hold fast the standpoint of revelation, albeit in agreement with your teaching. To use a phrase that you used in conversation with me, Christ is for me the anticipation of the educated reason [*Verstandesbildung*] that has brought about the whole modern period; he is the first free point from which our free life has

1. Henke, 'Berliner Briefe' pp. 102-103.

developed. I work out Christian morality from the unmediated aesthetic view of Christ, just as you do so from the unmediated ideal [*Urbild*] that mankind carries in itself. Thus my ethics is thoroughly theological as well as being thoroughly philosophical, in that the outer coincides with the inner. The work will appear, God willing, in the summer. Ahead of it will appear the second edition of my Biblical Dogmatics, which I shall revise in many respects.[1]

If de Wette's language about the role of Christ is not immediately clear from this letter, it becomes clear in the first volume of the *Christliche Sittenlehre*, which appeared in 1819 with a dedication to Fries, dated 3 December 1818.

It is to *Theodor* that we must now turn our attention, because, towards the end of Volume I, the hero makes a discovery that appears to be identical with that mentioned in the letter to Fries.[2] Theodor is in discussion with Walther and Härtling, whose identity will be discussed shortly. The following exchange takes place.

> *Theodor*:   The Faith [*Glaube*] and the community of Christianity are, according to my view, aesthetic, that is, based upon feeling [*Gefühl*]; but this beautiful, living basis is not as developed as might be wished. Understanding [*Verstand*], [that is] empirical reflection, has been a hindrance to the creative, poetic forces, so that no true symbolism of religion has come into being.

> *Härtling*:   But I hold the life and death of Christ himself to be the most beautiful symbolism, which surpasses everything else of this sort in the history of religion.

> [*Theodor*] Theodor looked at him in amazement and said: You have just said something of the greatest importance by which, as I believe, you have dispelled all my doubt.

> *Walther*:   Perhaps he has only conformed himself to your opinion by making into symbolism what is historical and moral truth. I believe that I have already read this idea somewhere, that Christian history and teaching must be taken symbolically. If I am not mistaken, it comes from Schelling's school.

> *Theodor*:   Quite right. Schelling himself wants Christianity to be expressed symbolically, something that I was earlier reluctant to accept, since it seems to run contrary to the truth. Schelling

1. Henke, 'Berliner Briefe', p. 104.
2. *Theodor*, I, pp. 241-42, for what follows.

> himself has certainly not been completely master of this idea,
> because he expressed himself so unclearly about it. But now
> everything is clear to me, and I know that I can bring historical
> and moral truth into complete harmony with symbolic meaning,
> so that the one is not destroyed by the other, but rather con-
> firmed and completed by it.

There can be little doubt that the letter to Fries and the passage in
Theodor are describing the same discovery, and it is not difficult to
see what it meant to de Wette. Up to now he had embraced a philosophical theology that lacked a real centre. It was true that he could
sense the eternal realities such as the purposefulness of everything and
the divine ordering of everything into a realm of value and unity. It
was also true that he believed that the possibility of knowing this was a
divine gift and not merely a human deduction. But there was an
emptiness at the centre in the sense that one could only catch glimpses
of something whose true form was beyond all types of human apprehension, in this world at any rate.[1] One had to be content with aesthetic expressions or intuitions of a reality which must always remain
essentially mysterious and unknown.[2]

De Wette's 'discovery' changed all this. Whereas previously the life
of Christ had been a means through which intuitions of the mysterious
reality found expression—and found expression in most noble and
sublime ways—he now saw that the life of Christ was itself a symbolic
representation of the mysterious reality, within the particularities of
human history. He was able to accept the life of Christ as a positive
revelation, as something which, without losing its aesthetic nature, had
entered fully into the historical process. The separate moments of
knowledge, faith and intuition were thus brought into harmony.[3] The
life of Christ, which belonged essentially to the sphere of intuition
(*Ahnung*), was presented to knowledge through its historical particu-
larity, and became the basis for the Christian's moral life. How this
was worked out in practice will be of concern later on. For the
moment we have to ask whether we can discover any more about the

---

1. Note Otto's analogy, *Kantisch-Fries'sche Religionsphilosophie*, p. 50 (ET
p. 67): 'He who sees a landscape through a mist does not perceive an utter nothing;
he is not dreaming, and it is no *fata morgana* that he beholds: he perceives the
landscape itself, and his knowledge is valid, but valid with limitations'.
2. Cf. *Theodor*, I, pp. 232-33.
3. *Theodor*, I, p. 243.

identity of Härtling, who, in *Theodor*, helps to dispel Theodor's doubts. The simplest solution would be to say that Härtling is Fries, in view of the statement in de Wette's letter to him that Fries 'has given him the key' to writing a Christian Ethics that will astonish the world. However, in *Theodor*, Härtling is clearly distinct from Professor A., and hears his lectures along with Theodor. The letter of 17 December 1817 does not credit Fries with having given de Wette a new understanding of the nature of revelation, but only with a clue to writing a Christian Ethics; and we may detect a certain defensiveness in de Wette's letter, especially in his stress that what he is doing is in accordance with Fries's teaching. Certainly in later years, Fries found de Wette's more positive attitudes to the notion of revelation difficult to understand.[1]

Another candidate would be Lücke, whose conversations with de Wette had become an important part of the latter's life from the autumn of 1816 onwards. However, Härtling is described in a way that seems to rule out Lücke. When he first appears in *Theodor*, Härtling is described as having a long beard and wearing clothing cut in the old German manner.[2] He had studied various subjects at university, especially history, but was now interested in education and was taken with Pestalozzi's ideas. For the education of the young, he was taken with the Spartan model, and recommended fitness in body and soul, the practice of combat exercises (*Turnkunst*), and the banishment of unnecessary luxuries. Above all, Härtling's love of his country is emphasized; Härtling opposes the treaty of his country with another land, enlists in the fight against this enemy, and is unremittingly hostile to the ruling group in his country that is unwilling to rally the people as a whole to the cause of liberation. His views correspond with those expressed by de Wette in *Die neue Kirche*. In the novel, Härtling criticizes Theodor for abandoning the calling of a preacher in favour of that of a bureaucrat, and plays a part in Theodor's decision to go to war and to sever his connections with the bureaucratic family into which he was hoping to marry.

In fact, this detailed description of Härtling accords so closely with someone who was in Berlin at the same time as de Wette, that the

---

1. *Theodor*, I, p. 110.
2. *Theodor*, I, pp. 109-110.

identification can be established with complete certainty. Härtling is Friedrich Ludwig Jahn.[1]

Jahn was born in 1778, was brought up to have a prodigious knowledge of the Bible, and studied history at Halle (1796–1800)[2] and Nordic languages at Greifswald.[3] In Halle, Jena and Greifswald he was active in student political affairs. From 1803–1805 he was private tutor to the family of a glassmaker in Mecklenburg, before moving to Berlin in 1809 via Göttingen, during which time he was caught up in the flights of people from the Napoleonic campaigns in Germany. In Berlin he became a teacher at the so-called *grauen Kloster*, and soon after was engaged to teach also at a Pestalozzi school in Berlin founded in 1805 by Dr Plamann.[4] Jahn played a prominent part in directing this Pestalozzi institute into activities suited to the circumstances of the times. From 1810 he regularly taught *Turnkunst* and in 1811 opened the first *Turnplatz*.

Too many things fit the description of Härtling to be a coincidence. Pictures of Jahn show him to be bearded and dressed in the old German fashion, just as de Wette describes Härtling's appearance. Both Härtling and Jahn studied history, were educators of the young, had connections with Pestalozzi's ideas, fought against Napoleon, initiated *Turnkunst* and possessed a passionate love of the fatherland.

This close correspondence between Härtling and Jahn is all the more important, since there is no other evidence known to me to connect de Wette and Jahn; but this is probably the result of the loss of sources such as letters. There can be no doubt that, either in conversation or through his writings, Jahn uttered a few words which brought de Wette a new certainty in belief that remained with him for the rest of his life. The immediate fruit was born in the first volume of the *Christliche Sittenlehre*, which de Wette completed in 1818 and which appeared in 1819.[5] This must now receive our attention.

The *Christliche Sittenlehre* appeared in four volumes between 1818 and 1823 and thus overlapped with de Wette's *Vorlesungen über die*

1. See Carl Euler, *Friedrich Ludwig Jahn: Sein Leben und Wirken* (Stuttgart, 1881).
2. Euler, *Jahn*, pp. 19-34.
3. Euler, *Jahn*, pp. 47ff.
4. Euler, *Jahn*, pp. 155-57.
5. *Christliche Sittenlehre*. I. *Die allgemeine Sittenlehre* (Berlin, 1819).

Sittenlehre, which appeared in four volumes from 1823 to 1824. The fact that the former work contains the word 'Christian' is not without significance. Although the latter work is in no sense unchristian, it is much more a work of philosophy than its earlier counterpart, with detailed sections on human 'psychology' in strong dependence upon Fries's *Handbuch der praktischen Philosophie* of 1818.

The *Christliche Sittenlehre,* especially its first volume, is more than anything an exposition and defence of de Wette's newly-established position. The centrality of the life of Christ for faith and morals is repeatedly stressed, the relationship between revelation and philosophy is expounded, and no opportunity is lost to interpret philosophical ideas in terms of the New Testament.

For all this, the *Christliche Sittenlehre* remains an unorthodox work from the standpoint of traditional Christian theology, and this fact is of importance if we are to understand how de Wette's 'discovery' had affected his theology as a whole. The best place to begin is with Fries's exposition of the nature of evil in the third volume of the *Neue Kritik*.[1] De Wette accepted this view of evil, and consequently continued to maintain a radical view of the work of Christ in spite of his 'discovery'. Also, his understanding of the nature of evil was now expressed with greater clarity and confidence than in *Über Religion und Theologie.*

Fries's starting-point was Kant's discussion of 'radical evil' in *Die Religion innerhalb der Grenzen der blossen Vernunft*.[2] In Fries's opinion, Kant made the mistake of locating evil in the nature of humanity, and accounted for it in terms of a disordering of the values and duties that a person ought to put into practice. Fries denied that humanity was in any sense naturally evil, and rejected Kant's theory of a disorder of values. The view that there was such a thing as evil was an *ideal* judgment, and came about in the following way.

Given that humanity is a part of nature and possesses instincts such as self-preservation which impel the will to act; and granted also that reflection upon moral experience discloses that humans have duties and values that are higher than instincts such as that for self-preservation, reflection discloses a conflict of contradiction between the two

1. Fries, *Neue Kritik*, III para. 219, and cf. paras. 114-15, 170, 189, 204 for what follows.
2. *Kants Werke*, VI, pp. 1-202.

types of willing: between willing in response to instinct and willing in response to the demands of duties and values. Further, philosophical reflection discloses that mankind is essentially free; but this freedom is denied by that part of human activity that is willed in response to instinct. According to Fries, evil is the name for the perceived contradiction between instinctive willing and reflective willing or between a human considered as governed by instinct and a human conceived as possessing freedom. It is not, therefore, something inherent in human nature. It is not, for example, to be identified with the instinctive side of humanity. It is, rather, something that arises from the conviction of belief (*Glaube*) that we are free. It is therefore ideal. The implication of this for traditional Christian theology is that humanity is not sinful or fallen in the sense of being 'damaged' or corrupted in relation to an ideal humanity that once existed. It also follows that 'redemption' from evil must ultimately be a human achievement whereby a person achieves the kind of character in which the highest duties and values are performed spontaneously, lovingly and altruistically.

De Wette accepts this understanding of evil and the analysis of human 'psychology' that undergirds it, and in the process identifies aspects of the analysis with ideas in the New Testament. Thus, the critical reflection that discloses the highest duties is identified with the 'inner light' spoken of in Mt. 6.22.[1] The conflict between instinct-led and duty-led action is part (but not all) of the dichotomy between flesh and spirit as expounded in Gal. 5.16-24.[2] Paul's anguished cry in Rom. 7.15a, that he does not know what he is doing, is understood in the context of the need for critical reflection to enable a person to activate the ethical impulses that come from reason (*Vernunft*) above those that are instinctual, limited in outlook and dependent.[3] The task of building a Christian character is a matter of trying to root out the instinct-led behaviour. This leads to zeal without insight and to Pharisaism.[4] The task is to overcome the instinct-led behaviour by critical reflection and Christian love.

On the question of evil, de Wette agrees entirely with Fries. 'Evil

---

1. *Christliche Sittenlehre*, I, p. 60.
2. *Christliche Sittenlehre*, I, p. 50.
3. *Christliche Sittenlehre*, I, p. 44.
4. *Christliche Sittenlehre*, I, p. 67.

lies in the sensual [*sinnliche*] weakness of the 'will',[1] a statement which can easily be misunderstood. De Wette is not saying that the will as such has a weakness. The key words are 'sensual' (*sinnliche*) and 'will'. The will, as driven by basic instincts, or the sensual will, is not bad. It is only when its instinctual behaviour is seen in the light of the duties disclosed by critical reflection that it appears to be weak, and that we use the word evil to describe the contradiction that has become apparent. Evil, in an absolute sense, does not exist, since it is an ideal judgment made to describe our perception of the human make-up. We can, and do, however, *think* of evil in an absolute sense, with the result that we postulate the existence of the devil.[2] This idea is, of course, mythological in the sense of being an attempt to account for the origin of evil at the level of explanation (*Verstand*), whereas it is an ideal notion. But de Wette allows that the idea of the devil has been valuable as a means of awakening moral consciousness among people lacking the possibility of philosophical reflection. It was a feature of the time of Jesus, and it has been held by all of Christendom until now. It has prevented moral laxity and opposed the idea that evil is simply a lack of good.

It will be remembered that, for Fries, the notion of evil was also related to that of freedom. That we are free to act as we wish is an ideal belief in opposition to the fact of our instinctual behaviour. The ideas of freedom and evil belong together because it is the judgment that we are free that brings to light the contradiction we call evil. This view, which de Wette accepts, has implications for the interpretation of Genesis 3.

The biblical account (at any rate in Christian interpretation) ascribes the entry of evil into the world as the disobedience of the first humans. This understanding of the passage had been contested by Kant and Schiller, to name two of de Wette's heroes, in their respective writings *Über den muthmasslichen Anfang des Menschengeschlechts* and *Etwas über die erste Menschengesellschaft*.[3] In effect, they had interpreted the story as a vital moment in the progress of the human race, as a 'fall upwards' as it has been called. Their claim was that an important point in the development of humanity came with the

1. *Christliche Sittenlehre*, I, p. 120.
2. *Christliche Sittenlehre*, I, p. 124.
3. *Christliche Sittenlehre*, I, p. 132

decision to disobey a command and to exercise human freedom.

De Wette accepted some of this. Of course, Genesis 3 could not be a story about the origin of evil, since evil was an ideal notion and could not have a historical origin. The story was also about development, in that it described the first human ancestors as exercising their freedom. However, it was not entirely a matter of human progress. There had been a fall in the sense that the exercise of freedom had made apparent the contradiction that critical reflection called evil; and that contradiction was apparent in the form of guilt, and of the loss of a feeling of purity and blessedness.[1]

This led to the Christian belief in the necessity of salvation, and it was here that de Wette was able to capitalize on his 'discovery' of the centrality of Christ. Basically, Christ brought salvation in the sense that his life was the perfect example of a human whose character was formed out of love for all the highest duties and values. Like us, he was born with weakness (i.e. the contradiction between instinct-led and duty-led action), was tempted (to deny the claims of duty), but was never defeated. His virtue was always active and victorious, as ours is not but ought to be.[2] That this victory was the result of a character based on love for the highest duties was shown in his death, which was the most unselfish act of self-sacrifice. It purified and transfigured his humanity and so completed the divine revelation.[3]

This revelation consisted above all in the moral life of Jesus. It revealed a humanity of such immeasurable greatness that, although it was manifested in history, it achieved absolute significance.[4] He demonstrated a love for others that was so free from self-interest, that he bequeathed to posterity an example that had the power to awaken the desire for freedom even in unpromising situations.[5] Thus he revealed within the constraints of history that perfection of humanity that was otherwise disclosed to human reason through critical reflection. In this way, theology and philosophy were brought together, a place was found for revelation, and salvation was shown to come from God, in that the example of Jesus and the fellowship of the

1. *Christliche Sittenlehre*, I, pp. 129-35.
2. *Christliche Sittenlehre*, I, p. 186.
3. *Christliche Sittenlehre*, I, p. 178.
4. *Christliche Sittenlehre*, I, p. 187.
5. *Christliche Sittenlehre*, I, p. 158.

church were positive influences to enable a person to become truly human, and therefore to have gained salvation.

The *Christliche Sittenlehre* was not simply theological exposition. Volume I treated the history of Christian ethics within the New Testament, while Volume II, whose first part also appeared in 1819, dealt with the history of ethics prior to the Reformation. A later volume would discuss many specific practical issues. For the moment, the purpose is to show how de Wette's discovery affected his general theological position; and one can say that it committed him in advance to a fairly traditional acceptance of the main outline of the life of Jesus, that it enabled him to be more positive about theological notions such as revelation and salvation as well as of the importance of the church. At the same time, it remained firmly embedded within the philosophy of Fries (even though it puzzled Fries), and was a radical theology in that it denied the traditional interpretation of the Fall, sin, and atoning death of Christ, all of which were pillars of faith for the orthodox party in Berlin. He also continued to reject traditional Christology. Christ's divinity was made apparent in his perfect (moral) humanity, and could not be described in dogmatic terms. Similar points could be made of the second edition of the *Biblische Dogmatik*, which appeared in 1819 with a dedication to Schleiermacher.

The point has now been reached where the events of de Wette's dismissal must be described and discussed. In the previous chapter reference was made to de Wette's 'anonymous' work *Die neue Kirche*, and to its opposition both to the German Confederation of 1815 and to the suppression of democratic hopes aroused by participation in the defeat of Napoleon. References have also been made to the orthodox or pietist circle in Berlin. These matters must be spelled out in greater detail.

The reforms in Prussia, especially those from 1807 to 1819 have been described as the substitution of 'bureaucratic absolutism for monarchical authority'.[1] This move to create an administrative elite in Prussia gave an opportunity to the landed aristocracy to exercise influence and control over the affairs of Prussia; and this circle was strongly identified with the Pietist movements in the German church. What is important for our concern is that pietism laid particular stress

1. R.M. Bigler, *The Politics of German Protestantism: The Rise of the Protestant Church Elite in Prussia 1815–1848* (Berkeley, University of California Press, 1972), p. 22.

upon the personal experience of salvation through Christ, through whom alone came the forgiveness of sins. The stress upon human sinfulness, and on the atoning death of Christ as the only means of salvation was totally different from de Wette's view of evil as something ideal (i.e. a postulate of critical reflection) and of Christ's death as a noble example of unselfish love.

In the second half of the eighteenth century, under the 'enlightened' Friedrich II, rationalism had been allowed to flourish in Prussian universities. In the first decades of the nineteenth century, influential pietists saw it as their God-given mission to destroy rationalism by appointing pietists to influential positions, including positions in the university theological faculties where protestant clergy were trained. One such man was Georg Heinrich Ludwig Nicolovius (1767–1839), who, from 1810, directed a new section within the Ministry of the Interior whose task was to oversee the provincial boards for ecclesiastical affairs and education, which had been established in 1808 to replace all previous similar organs of the Lutheran and Reformed churches in Prussia.[1] Another influential man was the Baron Hans Ernst von Kottwitz (1757–1831), a Silesian nobleman and landowner who had settled in Berlin in 1807 and who was the centre of the most influential pietist circle there.[2] Something of the determination of men such as Nicolovius and the Baron to fight against rationalism can be seen in their success in persuading the government in 1817 to reconstitute the University of Wittenberg as a seminary for the training of clergy, under the leadership of pietist teachers.[3]

In connection with this development, it is not without significance that a memorandum was sent from the Berlin theological faculty protesting against the founding of the seminary. The writer of the memorandum was de Wette, and although it was also signed by Schleiermacher, it put de Wette more obviously in the vanguard of the opposition. The memorandum contained the view that if one large seminary at Wittenberg was established, however carefully its teachers were chosen,

1. Bigler, *Politics*, pp. 22-23.
2. Bigler, *Politics*, p. 64.
3. Bigler, *Politics*, pp. 63-68. See also O. Dibelius, *Das königliche Predigerseminar zu Wittenberg 1817-1917* (Berlin–Lichterfeld: Verlag von Edwin Runge, n.d. [presumably 1917]).

sooner or later the institution will turn into a stronghold of one-sidedness and narrowness of outlook, hardly worthy to be established as a memorial to the noble and great Luther in the very place where he lived and taught.[1]

This was direct confrontation with an influential group that could persuade the government to part with a good sum of money.

Another incident of relevance to de Wette's eventual dismissal is noted by Foerster.[2] On 3 December 1816 Count Christian Friedrich von Stolberg-Wernigerode complained to the responsible Minister about the 'blasphemous utterances of several theologians' and requested that they be made to retract or to resign from their posts. Among those complained of were Schleiermacher, on account of his lectures on Luke 1–3; Gesenius, because of his *Geschichte der hebräischen Sprache und Schrift*; Augusti, whose introduction to the Old Testament caused offence; and de Wette. In de Wette's case, the objectionable works were his *Dogmatik*, the treatment of the Pentateuch (presumably in the *Beiträge*) and the Latin work *Commentatio de morte Jesu Christi expiatoria*. The reply on behalf of the king expressed his majesty's resolve not to interfere with intellectual enquiry, and pointed out that synods were being set up which would best enable the church to put its house in order in regard to the Count's complaint. Not satisfied, the Count made a personal complaint to the king on 17 May 1817, without, however, gaining any satisfaction.

With this background in mind, we can turn to Schleiermacher's dedication of his *Kritischer Versuch über das Evangelium des Lukas* to de Wette on 5 April 1817.[3] We know from Lücke's information that Schleiermacher dedicated the work to de Wette in order to give his colleague a public vote of confidence in face of growing distrust of de Wette among the pietists of the royal court.[4] Schleiermacher discussed the content of the dedication with Lücke so as to be certain that de Wette would not in any way be offended. The date of the

---

1. Dibelius, *Predigerseminar*, pp. 30-31.

2. E. Foester, *Die Entstehung der preussischen Landeskirche unter der Regierung König Friedrich Wilhelms des Dritten* (Tübingen: Mohr, 1905), I, pp. 265ff.

3. The dedication is reprinted in Lücke, 'Erinnerung', pp. 521-23 (without the final paragraph), and Staehelin, *Dewettiana*, pp. 78-80, where other publication details are given.

4. Lücke, 'Erinnerung', pp. 520-21.

dedication indicates that this was shortly before de Wette began to attend Schleiermacher's sermons.

It is a strange dedication, the greater part of it intended not for de Wette but for others ('forgive me for this effusion [*Erguss*] which is more for others than for you'). It was intended to make it clear that, despite his respect for de Wette, Schleiermacher was in no sense his man. It has an opening paragraph which expresses Schleiermacher's respect:

> a respect that is concerned not only with your basic and acquired learning, nor your exemplary zeal as a teacher, but above all on your marvellous sense of truth and your earnest and strong theological character. This respect is far from allowing the slightest breach between us to come about, on account of the differences between us, recognized by ourselves and others, on the most important matter of our discipline and our calling.

There then follows a long and involved paragraph about the many-sidedness of truth and about the dangers of people failing to recognize in those who disagree with them their sincere desire for that truth. There is also a passage on how Schleiermacher reacts to those whom he believes to be mistaken, and how he imagines an opponent would react to what Schleiermacher considers to be wrong if only the opponent then saw the truth! He hopes that all sincere attempts to discover the truth about Christian faith will succeed. He does not expect de Wette to accept everything in the dedicated work, and promises that any disagreements that may arise will be taken by him in the spirit of understanding that the dedication is intended to signal.

It is difficult not to feel that the dedication is clumsy and even patronizing. Schleiermacher was also at pains to justify it to various correspondents, and to say that

> whoever misunderstands it and takes me to be a partisan of de Wette must be very prejudiced.[1]

On the other hand, and what is more important, de Wette himself was not offended by the dedication. 'You will have heard', he wrote to Fries on 19 July 1817, 'of my reconciliation (*Frieden*) with Schleiermacher and of his dedication'.[2] There can also be no doubt of Schleiermacher's sincerity in the attempted defence of his colleague,

---

1. Staehelin, *Dewettiana*, p. 82.
2. Staehelin, *Dewettiana*, p. 82.

even though Schleiermacher was as disturbed by the strength of the reactionary group at court as he was at the attacks on de Wette. In one of his letters justifying the dedication of his book to de Wette, he mentions a 'cabinet order' of which he has heard whose content is that

> the king has learned with regret that at this and other universities false teachings are widely propagated, and the Minister should remove the false teachers forthwith [*Fördersamt*].[1]

This letter is dated 11 May 1817 and, taken together with the complaints made by Count von Stolberg-Wernigerode mentioned previously, it indicates the pressure that was building up against de Wette on theological grounds.

When de Wette's dismissal came, it was on political grounds, but he was already a marked man, and the dismissal was not unrelated to the view that he was a dangerous theologian.

With the approach of the 300th anniversary of the Reformation on 31 October 1817, the government of Prussia found itself in difficulty about the official celebrations to be held. These difficulties arose from the Lutheran and Reformed churches themselves, and concerned matters such as the liturgy to be used, the mode of administration of the Lord's Supper, and whether it was right to participate in a united service when outstanding differences had not been resolved in view of the impending union of the churches that had been decreed in Prussia.[2] To these irritations was added the fact that the student unions (*Burschenschaften*) planned to hold a rally at the Wartburg in Sachsen-Weimar in order to demand, in the name of the Reformation, the democratization and union of Germany. The demonstration was held on 18 October, and among the few professors present was Fries.[3] There were also present some students from Berlin who would later be in the front line of suspicion.

In the autumn of 1818 de Wette accompanied his step-son Karl Beck on a journey to collect his family, who were staying with relatives (presumably in the Heidelberg area), and went via Jena. Here, he met

---

1. Staehelin, *Dewettiana*, p. 81.
2. Foerster, *Enstehung*, pp. 267-79. In the event, the difficulties seem to have been overcome, and Lutheran and Reformed congregations joined in celebrating the anniversary.
3. R. and R. Keil, *Die burschenschaftlichen Wartburgfeste von 1817 und 1867* (Jena, 1868).

Fries and the theology student Karl Ludwig Sand, and at the latter's request visited the Sand family in Wunsiedel.[1] An attraction of such a visit for de Wette would have been that Wunsiedel was the birth-place of the writer Jean Paul, whom de Wette had come to know through the family of his first wife.

On 23 March 1819, Sand assassinated the popular playwright Kotzebue in Mannheim. Kotzebue was regarded by the student unions as a Russian agent and traitor, and his murder was seen as an expression of loyalty to the fatherland. Sand's attempt to commit suicide following the murder failed. He was subsequently tried, and on 20 May was executed. The immediate fear of the German Confederation was that the murder would be a signal for political uprising. At the same time, the widespread revulsion provoked by the murder was a benefit to be exploited, and on 1 August the Austrian leader Metternich met with the Prussian king at Teplitz, and secured his cooperation in summoning a meeting of representatives of the Confederation to respond to the murder. This took place in Karlsbad (now Karlovy Varn in Czechoslovakia) from 6 to 31 August, and resulted in the so-called Karlsbad decrees.[2] The first of these called for close supervision of the universities in the Confederation. An overall commission of investigation was established in Mainz, and each university appointed a commissioner with power to investigate political dissidents. In Prussia a proclamation of 1819 stated:

> The federated government oblige themselves to remove from universities those teachers who have obviously demonstrated their incapacity to fill their office by demonstrable deviation from their duty, or transgressing against the limits of their profession, or misusing their proper influence on the young, or spreading harmful theories inimical to the public order and peace or destructive to existing political institutions.[3]

Sheehan has written,[4] 'Everyone whose life had touched his was hurt by Sand's deed'. De Wette had certainly touched Sand's life, as a result of meeting Sand and his family. Also, de Wette was a close friend of Fries, who had attended the Wartburg demonstration by the student

---

1. Wiegand, *De Wette*, pp. 32-33.
2. Sheehan, *German History*, p. 408.
3. C.E. McClelland, *State, Society and University in Germany 1700–1914* (Cambridge: Cambridge University Press, 1980), pp. 218-19.
4. Sheehan, *German History*, p. 407.

unions, to which Sand belonged. Further, Sand was a pupil of Fries. It was to be expected, therefore, that de Wette would be investigated by the commission. The evidence is that, in Prussia, action was already being taken *before* the Karlsbad meeting, and that de Wette was under investigation in the July of 1819. A full account of the background has been provided by Lenz.[1]

On 24 June 1819, Wilhelm Ludwig Georg Wittgenstein, Minister of Police, proposed to the king that a commission should be a set up to investigate 'demagogic intrigues'.[2] The Chancellor, Carl August von Hardenberg, added his weight to the proposal on 30 June, and on 7 July the first arrests were made, and papers were seized. Two of the arrested were former students of Fries, while others had been at the Wartburg demonstration. On 12 July, de Wette's publisher Reimer had his house searched in his absence, and on 13 July, de Wette was summoned to the commission to explain why he had attended a meeting of a group convened by Hans Rudolph von Plehwe.[3] De Wette

---

1. M. Lenz, 'Zur Entlassung de Wettes', in *Philotesia: Paul Kleinert zum LXX Geburtstag dargebracht* (ed. A. Harnack *et al.*; Berlin: Trowitzsch & Son, 1907), pp. 337-88, and *Geschichte der Königliche Wilhems-Universität Berlin* (Berlin, 1910), II, 1, pp. 34-83.

2. 'Entlassung', p. 342; *Geschichte*, II, pp. 55-61.

3. De Wette to Fries on 20 July in Henke, *Fries*, p. 361, and *Dewettiana*, p. 87. Schleiermacher's letters at this time also mention the investigations (but not of de Wette). See Dilthey, *Aus Schleiermachers Leben*, IV, pp. 257-59. On Plehwe, a guards officer, see Lenz, *Geschichte*, II.1, p. 46; and H. Münebeck, 'Siegmund Peter Martin und Hans Rudolf v. Plehwe, zwei Vertreter des deutschen Einheitsgedankens von 1806–1820', in *Quellen und Darstellungen zur Geschichte der Burschenschaft und der deutschen Einheitsbewegung* (Heidelberg: C. Winter, 1911), II, pp. 151-94. Plehwe's life (1794–1835) shows that the links between Sand, de Wette and Reimer's circle (including Schleiermacher) were complex and deserve a more thorough investigation than is possible here. From 1816, Plehwe often visited de Wette to seek his advice on difficult passages of the Bible. He also visited Schleiermacher. He met Sand in July 1817, and, although he did not agree with Sand, wrote an article praising him in the *Bremer Zeitung* after his execution. His group, attendance at which brought about one of de Wette's interrogations, was known as the 'blue pleasure' (*blaue Vergnügen*) and had no identifiable political programme. However, it was suspected by the authorities of having the aim 'die gegenwärtige öffentliche Verfassung sowohl des gesamten Deutschlands als der einzelnen Bundesstaaten teils durch Verbreitung demagogischer Grundsätze und religiösen Fanatismus unter die Jugend und das Volk, teils durch Gewalt zu verändern und auf Einheit, Volksthümlichkeit und Freiheit eine neue Verfassung einzuführen'.

replied that he had attended this harmless gathering once during the winter, and no more.

On 8 August, a Sunday, de Wette was summoned to appear before the commission the following day to explain some matters mentioned in a student's letter. De Wette replied that he did not have the time to attend and complained to Wittgenstein about the interference. This produced no result. A renewed summons was received by de Wette on Monday 9 August, to which he did not respond. On the following day as he left the lecture auditorium he was served with a notice requiring him to attend the commission between 9 a.m. and 2 p.m. that same day. De Wette penned a strong letter of protest to Altenstein, the Minister responsible for universities.[1] He had been asked whether he had spoken publicly about the Sand assassination in a manner such as to justify the deed. That he had done so was alleged in a letter by a Swiss student David Ulrich. De Wette replied that he had indeed commented, from a scholarly point of view, on the Sand action, but that his alleged comments misrepresented him. The Minister marked in red pencil de Wette's admission that he had discussed the Sand case in lectures.[2]

While these interrogations were in progress, the police were investigating the matter of a letter which de Wette had written to Sand's mother—the letter that would result in his dismissal. Lenz has pieced together the slender threads that led to de Wette's downfall.[3] On 7 July the police had discovered in the confiscated papers of the student leader Karl von Wangenheim a letter to de Wette from Sand's brother-in-law, Dürrschmidt. This established a link between de Wette and Sand's family. Further, Dürrschmidt's letter to de Wette mentioned the receipt of two letters, one of which, it could be worked out, had been written by de Wette to Sand's parents. On 9 July, the Prussian representative at the Bavarian court in Munich formally requested that the letters be requisitioned. Apparently, the Bavarian authorities were reluctant to comply. At any rate, no action was taken until 5 August, when two officials questioned the Sand family in Wunsiedel, establishing that de Wette had visited the family in 1818.

1. Lenz, 'Entlassung', pp. 351-53.
2. Lenz, 'Entlassung', p. 353 n. 15. Lenz, *Geschichte*, II.1, p. 65, reports the interrogation of the student concerned, David Ulrich, who said that he had not attended de Wette's lectures, but had heard the alleged views in a small private gathering.
3. Lenz, *Geschichte*, II.1, pp. 69ff.

The most damaging part of the investigation was the seizure of a letter of de Wette to Dürrschmidt, dated 31 March, in which de Wette stated that he had written to Frau Sand and not to her husband, in case a letter to the husband was opened by the authorities. Clearly de Wette had something to hide. Although Herr Sand dismissed the letter to his wife as having no importance, Frau Sand herself eventually disclosed that she had copied it in a letter to her second son, who lived in Kemnath. The original had, it was thought, been sent to the eldest son in St Gallen in Switzerland. An order to requisition the letter to the son in Kemnath was now made, and it was obtained on 7 August.

From de Wette's point of view, the train of events was bad luck of the highest order. Had Dürrschmidt's letter to de Wette not been in Wangenheim's possession, or had it not mentioned the receipt of de Wette's two letters; had de Wette's letter to Dürrschmidt not been seized or had it not mentioned that he had written to Frau rather than Herr Sand; had a copy of the fateful letter not been sent to the second son. . . if any of these links in the chain had been missing de Wette might well have escaped. In the event, his whole career was changed by the tracking down not of the *original* letter to Frau Sand, but of a *copy* made in a letter to a son, minus a passage from Jean Paul's essay on Charlotte Corday. It is now given in full as discovered on 7 August:[1]

> You have, as a mother, received such a hard blow that I feel duty bound to write a word of comfort to you because of the friendship that you evinced towards me. If you had only the simple loss of your fine son to mourn, I would remain silent and leave the healing of your pain to your pious heart and to time. But since, with an element of justice, the opinion of the great majority [*Haufen*] brands your son as a criminal, this urges me, who has an opinion in the matter, to defend his case before you and at any rate in his family to protect his memory from dishonour.
>
> The action that he carried out is indeed not only illegal and culpable

---

1. *Dewettiana* 85-87, based upon de Wette's version in *Aktensammlung über die Entlassung des Professors D. de Wette vom theologischen Lehramt zu Berlin, Zur Berichtigung des öffentlichen Urtheil von ihm selbst herausgegeben* (Leipzig, 1820), pp. 2-6. According to J. Rohls (in *Profile des neuzeitlichen Protestantismus* [ed. F.W. Graf; Gütersloh: Gerd Mohn, 1990], I, p. 249) the original is in the Boie-Voss literary remains in the Landesbibliothek Kiel; but, in fact, the Kiel holding is also a copy, with various small, insignificant, variations from the version in the *Aktensammlung*.

before a worldly judge, but also, generally considered, immoral and contrary to legal, moral decrees. Justice cannot be established by injustice, trickery and force, and a good end cannot justify unlawful means. As a teacher of morals I can never urge or advise anyone to do such things. Evil cannot be overcome by any evil but only by good.

But if we are talking about the assessment of an action that has already taken place, it is not the general law that is to be used as a criterion, but the conviction and motivation of the actor. Only on the basis of faith [*Glaube*] will each be judged.

Now, I am in any case of the opinion that the decision of your son was based upon an error, and was not entirely free from passion.

But who can boast that they are free from any error and passion? Only one was ever so.

The error can be excused and to some extent mitigated [*aufgehoben*] by the firmness and integrity of conviction; and passion can be sanctified by the good source from which it flows. That this was the case with your pious and virtuous son I have no doubt. He was certain about his cause, he believed that it was right for him to do what he did, and thus he did what was right.

Each has to act according to his best conviction, and thus do what is best.

When I say that his decision was not entirely free from passion I do not mean thereby a blind passion [*trüber Rausch*] or a foaming exuberance [*schaumende Aufwallung*]. It was the purest inspiration that filled him, which came from the best source, and which borrowed from youthful strength a power which raised it above the limitations of life. No great human action can be completed without participating in this type of passion. The light of inspiration will always burst into flames.

I assure you, with complete sincerity, that I cannot take away from the memory of your son that love that he called forth from me at first sight; I must add it in greater measure.

Thus, this deed, in the way it was carried out by this pure, pious youth, with this faith and with this confidence, is a beautiful sign of the times. Whatever the fate of your son may be, he has had sufficient life, since he decided to die for the highest impulse of his heart. Whoever dares life has the true highest feeling for it; and the value of life is to be assessed not according to its length but according to its fullness and beauty. Unfortunately, the prevailing opinion is that a life of cowardice or indolence is to be preferred to a beautiful death. Do not say that it is to be regretted that so many will not recognize what is noble about this death! At the very least it is surely a sign of a better outlook on life through which many will be awakened. A youth devotes his life to eradicating a man whom so many worshipped as an idol. Will this remain without effect? But then [*doch*] no action is to be judged by its success, and not by the brilliance [*Glanz*] that it casts, a life. The most noble often sinks unrecognized in the dust.

Honoured friend! May you find these remarks true and hold firm to this view of the matter against all contradiction! You have borne and brought up this exceptional son, and thus will you be able to understand him and treasure him; and bear with his chosen fate with courage and acceptance [*Ergebung*]. May God add his blessing to this end, who is also mighty in weakness!

With inner regard and sincere friendship,
            Your faithful servant
                        de Wette.

P.S. After I had written this, Jean Paul's beautiful essay on Charlotte Corday in D. Katzenberger's *Badereise ZB* came into my possession, from which I have copied for you the following passage p. 222.[1]

This letter was in the hands of the Prussian authorities from 7 August, i.e. while de Wette was being interrogated on other matters, and it made its way through the bureaucracy, reaching the Ministry of Education on 20 August. When the Minister, von Altenstein, returned from holiday on 26 August he was faced with a cabinet order requiring him to ascertain from de Wette whether he had written the letter to Frau Sand. This latest interrogation took place on 28 August.

At the interrogation de Wette maintained that he could only verify that he was the author of the letter if he was shown the original. He could not verify that he was the author of a copy of a letter that he had written five months previously, especially when the copy appeared to contain mistakes. On the same day, in response to a royal order to the senate and rector of the university to investigate the matter, de Wette repeated his statement in a written submission. He did not deny that he had written a letter to Sand's mother, but was not willing to accept responsibility for a copy whose accuracy he could not check.

In an appendix to the written submission dated the following day,

---

1. The passage from Jean Paul's essay on Charlotte Corday, who carried out a political murder during the aftermath of the French revolution is on p. 319 of Jean Paul's *Sämmtliche Werke*, I, p. 13. It compares Corday's act to that of Brutus in murdering Caesar and describes her as a warrior killing an enemy of the state in a civil war. De Wette evidently thought of Sand in this way. In a footnote to the passage after de Wette's dismissal, Jean Paul criticized 'Ein höchst achtbarer Gelehrter voll Geist und Herz' for using the passage. Kotzebue's crime was his opinions not his deeds, and his opinions were to be defeated by the pen and not a dagger.

29 August, de Wette described his visit to the Sand family and then justified his action in writing a letter in the following words:

> neither as a human being nor as a Christian could I be so hard as to condemn the actor [Sand] unreservedly because he had acted against the law. For Christ commanded: judge not that you be not judged; and also the worst sinner can hope to find mercy from God.[1]

Over a month was to pass before, on Monday 30 September, a cabinet order dismissing de Wette was issued, which order de Wette and the university received on 2 October. Altenstein wrote to the king on 30 August explaining that he had compared the copy of the letter shown to de Wette with the copy obtained from Frau Sand, and that it was identical save for a writing error and the omission of the quotation from Jean Paul. However, he emphasized that the original had not been obtained, and expressed the view that either the original, or a copy that could be accepted as legal evidence (*eine gerichtlich beglaubigte Abschrift*), ought to be procured. He added that de Wette had earlier been investigated because of allegations made in a letter from a student concerning de Wette's comment on the Sand case.[2] For his part, de Wette urged Altenstein in a letter of 30 August to convey to the king the view that he ought to be judged on the basis of his public statements and not his private correspondence.

It would appear that Friedrich Wilhelm was reluctant to act. Lenz suggests that this was partly because of the influence of distinguished judges who would be unhappy with what, in effect, was a secret trial. In fact, one judge, Reinhold Focke, committed suicide, depressed at what he regarded as the injustice and danger of the reprisals that followed Kotzebue's assassination.[3] De Wette had made an effective point

---

1. *Aktensammlung*, p. 9.
2. Lenz, 'Entlassung', p. 362.
3. Lenz, 'Entlassung', p. 363. For Focke's suicide, see H. J. Schoeps, *Aus den Jahren preussischer Not und Erneuerung: Tagebücher und Briefe der Gebrüder Gerlach und ihres Kreises 1805–20* (Berlin: Haude & Spenersche Verlagsbuchhandlung, 1963). Ludwig von Gerlach relates (p. 312):

> Der Kammergerichtsrat (Reinhold) Focke, älterer Bruder meines Freundes Fritz, fasste dies und überhaupt die seit Kotzebues Ermordung in ganz gekommene Reaktion als Unrecht und als Gefahr einer dunklen Zukunft auf. Er war zur Melancholie geneigt; ich erinnere mich seiner trüben Äusserungen, als wir zusammen aus dem Kammergericht nach Hause gingen. Einige Tage darauf wurde seine Leiche in der Spree gefunden. Dies war Oktober 1819.

in his submission to Altenstein of 30 August. If he was to be dismissed from a public position it ought to be on the basis of evidence which could be confirmed or denied by those who heard his public statements. Although de Wette did not say this, his argument implied that it was unseemly for a private tribunal to ruin a man's career on the basis of a private communication.

Lenz has argued that the balance was tipped against de Wette by Wittgenstein and Hardenberg. They had little to show for the establishment of their investigating commission, whereas de Wette's dismissal would justify the operation.[1] Although Wittgenstein had by now resigned as Police Minister,[2] he was sufficiently involved in the de Wette affair to obtain from Bishop Eylert an opinion on the Sand letter, and to transmit it to the king.[3] After the assassination of Kotzebue, Eylert had preached a sermon in the garrison church in Potsdam denouncing all opposition to the government.[4] His position was, therefore, hardly that of a neutral. His reflections on the Sand letter concluded with dire warnings about the need for immediate action to overcome the evil which threatened the state, the universities and the church. Without such action, God's blessing would be withheld.[5] The king could not resist such a view. Thus, although de Wette was dismissed on political grounds, his enemies in the church played a decisive role, and achieved their long-term aim of getting rid of him.

Vain attempts were made by de Wette and his colleagues to reverse the decision. On 16 October, de Wette addressed a long appeal to the king which amounted to a commentary upon his letter, and an appeal to the king to consider how the dismissal would impose great hardship.[6] De Wette could not expect to get further work as a teacher easily (the Karlsbad decrees contained an agreement that no member of the Confederation would re-employ a teacher dismissed by another member) and at the age of forty and with two children and a step-son to support he had only gloomy prospects. Memoranda of support for de Wette were also submitted by the senate and the Faculty of

1. Lenz, 'Entlassung', p. 364.
2. Nipperdey (*Deutsche Geschichte*, p. 275) wrongly gives the year of Wittgenstein's resignation as 1818.
3. Lenz, 'Entlassung', p. 367.
4. Bigler, *Politics*, p. 43.
5. Lenz, 'Entlassung', p. 367.
6. *Aktensammlung*, pp. 16-20.

Theology. But by the end of October, de Wette had left Berlin for Weimar, having received financial support from his colleagues and various gifts from the students.

Was the dismissal unfair? This is a difficult matter to decide. De Wette was dismissed on the basis of a copy of a quite private letter that was intended only for the eyes of the recipient, a grieving and shocked mother. If a copy had been made for circulation within Sand's family, this was not de Wette's fault. On the other hand, there can be no doubt that de Wette justified and excused, and even glorified, the political murder that Sand had carried out.

In support of de Wette, it could be urged that he made a clear distinction between what he would advise people to do, and how an action once done was to be evaluated. Thus he had stated unequivocally that he would never counsel anyone to perform an illegal act. But against this, he had now clearly stated that the error and passion on which Sand's act rested could be excused and mitigated, and in language whose meaning could not be in doubt he had compared Sand with those who carry out great and noble deeds. He had described the action and its manner of execution as a beautiful sign of the times, and he had expressed the hope that it would affect the way in which others thought about life and about death. Whatever our views may be on the morality of requisitioning private documents, there can be no doubt that, once the letter had been seen by the king, the latter was likely to yield to pressure to take the action he did, quite apart from the fact that de Wette had been under suspicion for some time and that his enemies were looking for grounds for dismissal.[1]

What would have happened if de Wette had not written the letter or if its existence had not been tracked down by the police? The likelihood is that, at the worst, de Wette would have shared a fate similiar to that of his friend Fries in Jena. Fries was dismissed from his chair of philosophy and forbidden to teach it, but was then given a chair of physics and astronomy, remaining in Jena until his death.[2] Exactly how de Wette would, at the worst, have been treated we can only speculate. A way would need to have been found to prevent him from teaching theology and ethics, perhaps by confining him to oriental languages. In the event, his hopes for the future in Berlin were dashed

1. See above, p. 147.
2. Henke, *Fries*, pp. 209ff.

just at the point where so much seemed to be going well. His 'discovery' had given him a new certainty, and a more positive attitude towards the church and its dogmas. He had drawn closer to Schleiermacher and, together with Lücke, had announced the launch of a new theological journal. Ironically enough, the preface which de Wette wrote for the first number of the *Theologische Zeitschrift* was dated 2 October 1819, the day of the publication of the order dismissing de Wette![1] And since de Wette was the driving force of the project it did not long survive his departure from Berlin. Another joint project that had been announced by Lücke but which it would fall to de Wette to execute was the preparation of a complete edition of the letters of Luther.

Had de Wette remained in Berlin, it does not follow that he would have reaped the fruits of the new sphere of work that seemed to be opening up. Even if he had not been restricted in what he could teach, the 1820s and 1830s witnessed the emergence in Berlin of a strident neo-orthodoxy that would dominate the theological life of Prussia for another forty years or so. De Wette's eventual arrival in Basel in 1821 would give him for the remainder of his life a place where he could enjoy much more freedom than Berlin would have been able to offer. But between Berlin and Basel lay the readjustments and the frustrations of the Weimar period.

---

1. The preface is reprinted in Staehelin, *Dewettiana*, pp. 88-89.

Stadtkirche Weimar, interior (artist's impression)
Drawing by M. Mallallah

Chapter 6

WEIMAR

On 2 November 1819 de Wette arrived in Weimar. The following day his wife and their two children Anna and Ludwig departed for Heidelberg.[1] These arrangements made sense. De Wette had been born in the Duchy of Sachsen-Weimar, had attended school in Weimar and had been a student at the Duchy's university of Jena. Weimar, then, was a place he knew, it was outside Prussia (though within the German Confederation), and it was not the seat of a university. The Prussian government could not object to his presence in Weimar. His wife, on the other hand, had no connections with Weimar, and had never reconciled herself to leaving Heidelberg for Berlin. It made sense for her to return to where her family lived and away from a husband who had gained such notoriety. Naturally, the separation increased de Wette's sense of isolation and it also caused the additional headache of having to maintain two sets of domestic arrangements instead of one. On the other hand, it gave him a freedom of action and movement that would help to heal his wounds more quickly than if he had had to cope with his wife in Weimar.

Although de Wette arrived in Weimar as an unemployed, and in his eyes unemployable, man of thirty-nine, his immediate financial circumstances were not pressing. He had refused an ex-gratia payment from the Prussian government of a quarter of his salary,[2] but had received small gifts from well-wishers. His colleagues in Berlin had begun to organize a subscription list which would guarantee his full

---

1. Wiegand, *De Wette*, p. 39.
2. De Wette, *Aktensammlung*, pp. 44-46; cf. Lenz, 'Entlassung', p. 377 n. 33, who records that the former Police Minister Wittgenstein urged Altenstein and the king to remember de Wette's financial needs.

salary at least for the first year after his dismissal,[1] so that his only financial problem would be the profligacy of his wife. But his long-term employment and financial prospects remained a large cloud on his horizon.

His first days in Weimar were busy. On 4 November, Fries arrived from Jena and persuaded de Wette to make a short visit to Jena before Fries departed on enforced leave.[2] Wiegand states that the two-day visit remained a pleasant memory;[3] but Jena had unhappy associations for de Wette, and it would be surprising if he had not visited the grave of Eberhardine and had not contrasted his short-lived happiness with her with his present misery.

What little we know about de Wette's life for the next five months, that is, until the end of March 1820, comes from Wiegand, who had at his disposal some letters of de Wette to his publisher Reimer, which have not otherwise survived, and information based upon reminiscences of those in Weimar at the time. De Wette's deep sense of shock and bewilderment was expressed in a letter to Reimer whose date is not given by Wiegand:

> I see my loss clearly and feel that it cannot be made good. I am filled by an endless yearning which pulls me from one direction to another. I do not know what I want or ought to do. Where can I find such friends again as you were, and where can I find such a good opportunity for work? And what can be a substitute for the separation from you, my dear friend? Correspondence is a poor substitute. I am a bad, slow correspondent and the uncertainty of letters makes my pen diffident. Will you love me as strongly as you once loved me when you have little from me to read; when you have no living or complete picture of my life? Will I not lose you? That is the greatest anxiety, that I might be forgotten by you all. First, my place at the university will be filled in some way and the gap that I have left will be filled. Then no student will think any more about me in the way that many miss me at present. The memory of me will remain with you all a little longer, but time will do its work. The bond of friendship is maintained by giving and receiving; but what can I give you in the future? I shall never forget the last evening that I spent with you all. There was so much affection in happiness and sadness, there was such

1. Lenz, 'Entlassung', p. 377 n. 34, and Wiegand, *De Wette*, p. 42.
2. Wiegand, *De Wette*, p. 42, and Henke, *Fries*, pp. 209ff.
3. Wiegand, *De Wette*, p. 42.

conversation, such love and intimacy and—with such richness such emptiness and desolation.[1]

In this state of despair, de Wette found solace in two ways. First, he regularly attended the parish church, where, as an adolescent, he had heard Herder preach. The chaplain (*Stiftsprediger*) Carl Friedrich Horn had been instituted by Herder in 1801, and was a great admirer of Herder. Thus de Wette had much in common with Horn, spent much time at his house, and received a good deal of help from him.[2] It was presumably Horn who would later arrange for de Wette to be invited to preach in the parish church.

The second source of solace for de Wette was a circle that met regularly for literary, poetic and musical conversations.[3] As a result of this participation, de Wette wrote an opera libretto in the latter part of 1820 entitled *Der Graf von Gleichen*, and the following year a play entitled *Die Entsagung*.[4] Although he was well received in Weimar, a letter to Schleiermacher, dated 3 December 1819, indicates that Goethe had been unwilling to receive him.[5] He was also distressed by the fact that the police in Heidelberg had made frequent enquiries as to whether de Wette was in Heidelberg with his family. This made de Wette gloomy about the possibility of visiting his family in Heidelberg in the new year. So far as his theological work was concerned, de Wette seems to have spent the months up to March 1820 working on the letters of Luther and preparing an answer to Schleiermacher's article on 'Election' which had appeared in the first volume of the *Theologische Zeitschrift*.[6] De Wette's 'reply' indicated that, in spite of the friendship that had formed between the two men, especially since de Wette's dismissal, de Wette still felt strongly about the theological differences between them. He had also worked on the *Aktensammlung*, a publication of the documents pertinent to his

1.   Wiegand, *De Wette*, p. 40.

2.   Wiegand, *De Wette*, p. 41.

3.   Wiegand, *De Wette*, p. 41.

4.   The text of *Der Graf von Gleichen* is given in Handschin, *De Wette als Prediger und Schriftsteller*, pp. 299-321. Handschin summarizes *Die Entsagung* (pp. 79-85). I was not able to obtain this work.

5.   Staehelin, *Dewettiana*, p. 92.

6.   De Wette to Schleiermacher on 18 Feb. 1820 (Staehelin, *Dewettiana*, pp. 93-94) and on 23 May 1820 (Staehelin, *Dewettiana*, pp. 95-96).

dismissal from Berlin, whose preface was dated 10 January 1820.[1]

An important new phase in the Weimar period began in April 1820. Indeed, for most of the period from early April to the end of August, de Wette was travelling through Germany, Switzerland and Austria (which then included what is now Czechoslovakia). This enabled de Wette to meet and travel with old friends such as Reimer, and to make new friends with men such as Hirzel. The whole period gave him new hope, even though it was shot through with despair, and on his return he began his theological writing with renewed vigour.

De Wette left Weimar on 7 April 1820, arriving two days later in Frankfurt, where he stayed until the 15th. On that day he departed for Heidelberg, met his family in Weinheim and then travelled on with them to Heidelberg. Wiegand's account is, at this point, quite misleading.[2] He has de Wette meeting the family in Mannheim, and makes no mention of a visit to Heidelberg. This may be because he believed, rightly or wrongly, that de Wette had been refused permission to enter the Grand Duchy of Baden, and that he could not, therefore, have visited Heidelberg from 16–18 April 1820.[3] The evidence for the Heidelberg visit is indisputable in a letter to Amalie von Voigt dated from Frankfurt on 20 April 1820.[4] Wiegand, who quotes from this letter, has not only altered the place of the meeting between de Wette and his family, but has omitted and altered other material without any indication of this. The meeting was a success. Anna (9) and Ludwig (7) seemed like two angels who had come down from heaven. Anna

1.   For the *Aktensammlung*, de Wette seems to have had the cooperation of Altenstein's Ministry in making available to him certain official documents. On this question and the apparent difficulty that, at one time, the king's view was that de Wette's defence should be submitted to the censor, see Lenz, 'Entlassung', pp. 339-42. This cooperation may indicate a certain sympathy for de Wette on the part of Altenstein. The publication of the *Aktensammlung* provoked a counter-piece: an anonymous *Gegen die Aktensammlung welche der Professor D. de Wette, über seine Entlassung. . . herausgegeben hat* (Berlin, 1820). According to Lenz ('Entlassung', p. 380 n. 39), its author was a certain Beckedorff. This work claims that Frau Sand had sent copies of de Wette's letter to distant relatives. Its position is that de Wette has misused notions such as freedom, which, for Christians, must be exercised so as to yield obedience to God's revealed laws.

2.   Wiegand, *De Wette*, p. 43.

3.   Cf. Wiegand, *De Wette*, p. 45.

4.   The letter is partly printed in Staehelin, *Dewettiana*, p. 95, but without the disputed passage. The photocopy reads 'Heidelberg'.

hung on to her father's arm, and got him to pluck and name flowers. Even his wife was more agreeable—a plant which thrived in the Rhine-Neckar region but which sickened if transplanted. Even though the parting from his family and especially from Anna was hard, de Wette accepted that this was the best possible arrangement, and one which gave him freedom to write and travel.[1]

De Wette returned to Weimar around 22 April 1820, and a few days later set off to visit Reimer in Leipzig. This visit was to some extent interrupted, although de Wette does not say why.[2] He then travelled to Giebichenstein, 4 km north of Halle, to stay with Raumer and his family. Karl Georg Raumer was a long-standing friend of Schleiermacher's, and had married into the Reichardt family, which lived in a fine house at the foot of the mound crowned by the ruins of a tenth-century castle.[3] Here, de Wette met a number of friends of Schleiermacher including the preacher L.G. Blanc and the Weimar Minister of State Professor Schweizer. The latter accompanied him to Jena on 20 May, but the visit did him little good. 'Everything reminded me of destruction and the past, and filled me with sad memories', he wrote to Reimer.[4] On 22 May he returned to Weimar, accompanied by the widow of his old professor J.J. Griesbach.[5] His travels had given him the urge for new explorations, and thus he planned to journey to Switzerland beginning in June.

Of his Swiss journey, de Wette wrote a full account which was available to Wiegand, but which has not survived. Wiegand makes only scant reference to it; but we know that de Wette drew extensively upon it in writing Volume II of *Theodor*, and we can get a clear idea of his travels with the help of the novel. On his journey to Switzerland de Wette travelled to Frankfurt via Gotha and Eisenach, and then met his family in Mannheim because the government of Baden had refused

1. Staehelin, *Dewettiana*, p. 95.

2. De Wette to Schleiermacher, 23 May 1820, in Dilthey, *Aus Schleiermachers Leben*, IV, pp. 264ff.

3. See further W. Dilthey, *Leben Schleiermachers* (Göttingen, 1870, [repr. Berlin; de Gruyter, 1970]), I, pp. 2, 117ff.

4. Wiegand, *De Wette*, p. 44.

5. Griesbach had died in 1812; we possess a letter of comfort from de Wette to Frau Griesbach of 7 June 1812. The original is in the Staatsbibliothek preussischer Kulturbesitz, (West-)Berlin, M141 (Adam).

him permission to visit Heidelberg.[1] From Mannheim he travelled via Stuttgart and Karlsruhe to Strasbourg. He was so impressed with Strasbourg Cathedral that he climbed the tower twice, and wrote a description of the cathedral. This was published in 1822 and included in the second edition of *Theodor* in 1828.[2]

From Strasbourg, de Wette travelled to Zürich via the Rhinefall at Schaffhausen. He had first seen this in November 1798. It now made the following impression on him:

> Because I have seen it before, the impression was not so great, but it was beneficial. It is not a manifestation of great sublimity, but belongs to the category of the beautiful. An intuition of eternity seized me. Here the Rhine has been falling over the rocks for thousands of years, changing itself into mist and spray and then reappearing as blue-green water. There is neither standing still nor change, but endless repetition.[3]

De Wette arrived in Zürich on 16 June 1820, and between that date and 10 July undertook two journeys into the mountains. The first is described from ch. 11 onwards in Volume II of *Theodor*. De Wette went by boat from Zürich as far as Bocken, and then up onto the mountains between Schwyz and Glarus before making his way to Kulm on the Rigi. It is here, in *Theodor*, that the hero is reunited with Hildegard, after their first and fleeting encounter during the war against the French. From Weggis he crossed the Vierwaldstättersee to Küssnacht and Tell's Chapel, and thence to Luzern. Several days later they set out from Luzern to the Rütli and then by boat to Altdorf at the very far end of the lake. On the way back, they were overtaken by a storm. It is difficult, of course, to know how far this event is fiction. In the novel, it is Theodor's prowess as a swimmer which saves the day for his group, and they arrive thankfully at Brunnen where they stay overnight. From Brunnen they return to Luzern.[4]

The other journey, in the Bernese Oberland, is related from ch. 17. In the novel, Theodor's journey follows one earlier undertaken by Hildegard and her father, and recorded in a diary which Hildegard presents to Theodor. A boat trip from Luzern to Alpnach is followed by a journey along the Melchthal via Kerns. This eventually brings the

1. Wiegand, *De Wette*, p. 45.
2. *Theodor*, II, pp. 163-81.
3. Wiegand, *De Wette*, p. 45.
4. *Theodor*, II, p. 127.

party to Meiringen and the Reichenbach Falls, famous in later fiction
for the fight there between Sherlock Holmes and Professor Moriarty.
In *Theodor*, Hildegard's diary notes that these falls are smaller in
mass than at the Rhinefall, but that they make a greater impression.
They are a picture of virtue achieved by struggle and suffering. There
can be little doubt that these are de Wette's impressions at the time.[1]

The next part of the journey took the group to Grindelwald and
Lauterbrun, before returning to the lakes at Interlaken. The return to
Luzern was via Brienz, Brunig, Lungern and Samen. As the Swiss visit
began to come to an end, de Wette travelled to St Gallen where, on 10
July, he made a visit that would be of an importance that could not be
foreseen. The person visited was the pietist writer Anna Schlatter,
who was an acquaintance of Reimer. The purpose of the visit was to
use de Wette as a postman, since he intended to meet up with Reimer
in Munich for the journey back to Weimar; but in the two hours that
he spent with Anna Schlatter he made a very favourable impression.

Her opinion before she met de Wette was that he was unlikely to be
'a true disciple and worshipper of Jesus Christ, our Lord given to us
by God'. In a letter to Reimer, she thanks 'our royal Friend' (i.e.
Jesus) that she had been freed from this supposition, and prayerfully
accepted his answer 'come, and see' to her question 'can any good
come out of Nazareth?'[2] For his part, de Wette was also impressed
with the encounter and, on his return to Weimar, wrote to Anna
Schlatter on 4 October, in reply to a letter of hers. He was delighted
with the harmony that they had experienced in spite of their
difference in ideas and language. It demonstrated to de Wette the
strength of faith and love when it came to essentials, namely,

> belief in the exalted majesty of our saviour, in the redemptive power of his
> life and death, in the grasping and holding on to fellowship with him,
> who is the head of his body the church, whose living and true members
> we are only when we have died to the flesh, selfishness and sin, and
> begun a new, purified and spiritual life in him and through him.[3]

Such pious language did not indicate any real shift in de Wette's position following his discovery of 1817; but it showed his readiness to be

1. *Theodor*, II, p. 150.
2. Staehelin, *Dewettiana*, pp. 97-98, for Anna Schlatter's letter of 10 July
1820.
3. Staehelin, *Dewettiana*, pp. 99-100.

open to viewpoints that he would probably earlier have dismissed.

On 13 July, de Wette arrived in Munich and stayed until the 30th.[1] The party made an abortive journey as far as Wolfratshausen before returning to Munich, apparently on account of some letters, and set off again on 1 August as far as Rosenheim. The next day the party travelled east to the Chiemsee, where they crossed to an island where they spent the night. On 3 August they came to Bad Reichenhall, and on the following day they went over the Hallthurm pass and into the valley in which lies Berchtesgaden. De Wette was delighted with Berchtesgaden with its many famous landmarks, and the Königssee. When the journey resumed on 6 August, the party climbed up to Hirschbichl and thence down into the valley of the River Saalach and along to Saalfelden. The next day took them through the narrow valley of Saalach to the Zeller See and then eastwards along the valley of the Salzach to Taxenbach. On 8 August, a detour was made down the Gasteiner valley to Badgastein, and the Nassfelder valley. On 9 August the party re-traced its steps as far as Lend, and the following day continued along the valley of the Salzach as far as Golling. On 11 August, de Wette visited the waterfalls near Golling, and Salzburg was reached on the following day via Hallein.

From Salzburg the party began to travel northwards back to Germany. Leaving Salzburg on 13 August, they reached Linz the following day, where, after a half-day for sight-seeing, they departed for Prague as the next main goal. Prague was reached on the afternoon of 17 August. Prague made a deep impression upon de Wette with its buildings, squares and general views. He described it as the most beautiful city he had seen, and was sorry to have to depart the following day for Dresden, which they reached on 20 August. The party stayed in Dresden for some days until the members began to go their various ways. Reimer and his wife left on 25 August, but de Wette and a companion from Berlin remained in Dresden until 28 August, and then journeyed to Leipzig, visiting the cathedral in Meissen on the way. The last lap of the journey, from Leipzig to Weimar, was undertaken on 31 August, and thus ended five months of travelling, a period which did much to fill de Wette with new hope

---

1. For what follows see the long letter of de Wette to Heinrich Hirzel of 29 September/2 October 1820, photocopy; De Wette Nachlass, F3. Staehelin, *Dewettiana*, p. 98, gives a short extract from this seven-page letter.

and determination in spite of the uncertain future. In the letter to Heinrich Hirzel in Zürich, to which we are indebted for our knowledge of the journey from Munich, de Wette wrote that the journey had made him younger, and given him the incentive to work harder.

For the remainder of the year, de Wette worked on the next volumes of his *Christliche Sittenlehre*, as well as the edition of the letters of Luther. He also wrote essays on Christian tragic poetry and the cathedral at Strasbourg, and began to write the novel *Theodor*. It is also possible that he completed the libretto of the opera *Der Graf von Gleichen*. In a letter to Schleiermacher, dated 30 December 1820, he says:

> I have lived and researched in the Middle Ages. I have been much absorbed with the scholastics and I have studied them with admiration.[1]

The obvious reference here is, of course, to the *Christliche Sittenlehre* whose second volume is a history of Christian ethics; but it may be that de Wette also studied the mediaeval legend of the Count of Gleichen for the purposes of his libretto.[2] The plot is very simple: the count is captured during the Crusades but enabled to escape by the daughter of his Moslem captor. He returns home with this daughter, whom he has married with the help of a dispensation from the Pope allowing him to have two wives: the wife at home and the woman who helped him to escape. On his return, the three live happily ever after.

Three points are of interest in de Wette's choice and handling of this story. The first is the fact that Kotzebue, the playwright murdered by Karl Ludwig Sand, had composed a version for use with marionettes in 1808.[3] In Kotzebue's version the hero and his two wives do not live together in harmony. The wives quarrel and, as the husband tries to mediate, all three stab each other. The two wives enter convents and the husband warns of the fickleness of love. This was undoubtedly regarded by de Wette as an instance of Kotzebue's complete lack of taste—a theme that we meet again in *Theodor*.[4]

This leads to the second point, that de Wette's own treatment has a much higher moral tone. The Count's wife at home in Germany resists the advances of a rival to the Count, and enters a convent. When the

1. Staehelin, *Dewettiana*, p. 100.
2. The text is given by Handschin, *De Wette als Prediger*, pp. 299-321.
3. Handschin, *De Wette als Prediger*, p. 88.
4. *Theodor*, I, p. 150.

Count returns, and has defeated the rival in battle, the problem of how his wife will get on with the second wife is solved by the death of the first wife. In this way, de Wette demonstrates his rejection of the idea that a Pope can give dispensations that run counter to moral sentiment, and enables the Count and his new wife to enjoy a proper marriage.

The third point is that the name of the first wife of the Count is Hildegard, the same name as that of the young woman with whom Theodor falls in love and marries in the novel. While we may never know why de Wette chose this name Hildegard for the heroine of his novel, his use of the same name in *Der Graf von Gleichen* suggests that de Wette composed the libretto before he wrote the novel. He was more likely to give life to the character of Hildegard in the novel having had her only as a shadowy figure in the opera than to kill her off, so to speak, in the opera when she had been so prominent in the novel.[1] The libretto is in verse, with strongly contrasted metres for the varying characters and groups such as Moslem soldiers and crusaders. Wiegand records that, when Goethe was shown the manuscript, he said 'I have never come across anything as delightful recently, and I have read it twice. The work is elegantly versified and has content [*Gehalt*].'[2] For our purposes, the libretto is valuable in showing that ideas to be worked out fully in *Theodor* were already occupying de Wette's mind.

An event of great importance, also not unconnected with *Theodor*, occurred on 26 December 1820 when de Wette preached in the parish church in Weimar. This was the first time that he had preached since his earliest days as a student in Jena, and it has a twofold interest. First, in the novel *Theodor*, the hero begins by rejecting his family's wish that he should become a minister of religion, but eventually returns to this calling. Härtling, in particular, praises the importance of the office of preacher. Although, in the event, de Wette remained an academic, he would have become a preacher if the government of Hanover had not blocked his appointment to the St Katherine Church in Braunschweig in 1821–22. Given that he had probably completed

---

1.   Did de Wette choose the name of Hildegard after Hildegard of Bingen (1098–1171), a German Catholic saint who wrote about nature and music, and who was critical of aspects of the church of her day? For a recent biography see S. Flanagan, *Hildegard of Bingen: A Visionary Life* (London: SPCK, 1989).

2.   Wiegand, *De Wette*, p. 41 n. 3.

Theodor by the end of 1821, when he still hoped for the preaching post in Braunschweig, we have another indication of how de Wette's mind was working at this time, as well as another clue to the purpose of *Theodor*. He had set his mind in the direction of becoming a minister of religion, and intended *Theodor* to justify this decision, among other things.

The second point of interest is in the content of the sermon. What was de Wette the preacher likely to be like? The Gospel for the second day of the Christmas festival was Lk. 2.15-20, the story of the shepherds going to Bethlehem and finding there Joseph, Mary and Jesus. Yet it must be said that de Wette made little or no attempt to expound the passage as such.[1] The sermon owes more to Hebrews 11 than to the prescribed readings for the day; and we must not forget that Hebrews 11 was one of Fries's favourite texts! Heb. 11.1 asserts that faith (*Glaube*) is the assurance for what one hopes and is the evidence of things not seen. De Wette takes as the two key words faith and seeing (*Schauen*), and argues that without faith there is no true understanding of reality. The rainbow would have meant nothing to Noah without faith, and the burning bush would have been similarly meaningless to Moses. Thus the shepherds also had faith—an inner illumination given by God. If they had not had faith they would not have seen or heard the angels that brought the tidings of the baby at Bethlehem.

Seeing (*Schauen*) is important because it enables us to see the things of God at work in our lives; but faith precedes seeing as life in the spirit precedes life in the body. The sermon is summarized as follows:

> Christ appeared so that we might see in faith and in seeing believe; so that we might live spiritually in the body.[2]

It is clear that de Wette the preacher is the de Wette of the *Christliche Sittenlehre*, the de Wette whose Friesian philosophy had been given a centre by belief in Christ as a manifestation of the aesthetic in a historical life. The relation of faith to seeing is that of faith to knowledge, and it is the Incarnation that both nourishes and gives hope to faith. To say all this is not to attack de Wette's integrity. On the contrary, the sermon shows that de Wette's 'discovery' of late 1817

---

1. *Drey Predigten von Dr W.M.L. de Wette* (Berlin, 1821), pp. 1-28.
2. *Drey Predigten*, p. 27.

had given him the confidence to enter a pulpit and to proclaim his newly-found certainty together with its Friesian undergirding. What his hearers would have made of the sermon we cannot say. 'Faith' is a highly ambiguous word even today, and we can imagine that anyone unfamiliar with de Wette's highly sophisticated understanding of the word would feel that the sermon was more orthodox than was actually the case. Nonetheless, the event marked a turning point. Even if he was not to become the occupant of a preaching post, de Wette would now preach occasionally for the rest of his life.

For the first three months of 1821, in addition to work on *Theodor* and the letters of Luther, de Wette prepared a second edition of *Über Religion und Theologie*, with a foreword dated March 1821. The new edition included a new section on the religious community (*Gemeinschaft*) and additions to the two chapters on Christian dogmatics and practical theology. These alterations and additions were in line with de Wette's 'discovery' of late 1817. In the preface, de Wette wrote that the new edition displayed a milder and more circumspect spirit in relation to dogmatics, and the author expressed the hope that it would be taken more notice of by the 'critical institutes' than had been the case with the first edition.[1]

On Sunday 11 March, Invocavit (First Sunday in Lent), de Wette preached again in the Stadtkirche in Weimar. The Gospel was the Matthaean account of the temptations of Jesus (Mt. 4.1-11), a passage that can be expounded temptation by temptation. De Wette fitted the passage into his philosophical theology.[2] The temptations experienced by Christ are also experienced by us, and we have the same means of resisting them that he had. Thus the story is interpreted by de Wette in an exemplarist, individualist manner, and not in terms of Jesus choosing to go along a particular path that would bring redemption for the world. As our example, Jesus rejected using his powers to satisfy his own needs, declined to put God to the test and rejected earthly riches in favour of an eternal kingdom.

De Wette was in the pulpit again on Easter Monday, 23 April 1821, delivering a sermon that had already been published the previous month, together with his Christmas and Lenten sermons.[3] Their

1. *Über Religion und Theologie* (2nd edn, 1821), pp. xiii–xiv.
2. *Drey Predigten*, pp. 30-42.
3. *Drey Predigten*, pp. 43ff.

publication was no doubt meant as a signal that de Wette would be available for appointment to a preaching post in the future. The third sermon is skilful, in that de Wette was uncertain about the Resurrection in a historical sense. The Gospel for the day, the walk of Jesus and two disciples from Jerusalem to Emmaus (Lk. 24.13-35), enabled de Wette to avoid historical questions and to concentrate upon three matters. The first was the sentiment that Christ had to suffer in order to enter into glory (Lk. 24.26). Whatever his views on the empty tomb, de Wette believed strongly that the death of Christ, in its purity of selfless offering, had achieved something that could enlighten and encourage others. Such an achievement could only have come through suffering, which both was a prime instance of resignation and purified the humanity of Jesus. Thus de Wette could confidently assert this theme, and contrast it with worldly outlooks which wanted glory without suffering. The second point was that the two disciples on the Emmaus road had failed to understand the significance of the death of Jesus precisely because they saw it in this-worldy terms. In the narrative, it was Jesus himself who pointed the way to a true understanding of his death. The final point was that, as Christ suffered, so must we if we are to obtain a glory greater than that of the world. Thus de Wette was able to concentrate upon favourite themes: the need for inner understanding and resignation, and the significance of Christ's example.

De Wette next preached four months later, on 5 August (Trinity 8) and 19 August (Trinity 10),[1] but these sermons have not survived. It was after preaching the first of these two sermons that de Wette received an invitation to preach what was in effect a trial sermon at the St Katherine Church in Braunschweig on 16 September in connection with filling a vacant post. The previous month he had received a tentative enquiry as to whether he would be willing to accept a chair in Basel.[2] These two matters, so vital to his future, would occupy him greatly for the next seven months until a decision was reached. The events will be discussed later in the chapter. For the moment, it is necessary to return to *Theodor*, which had occupied him so much in 1821, and which indicated his willingness to accept a preaching position.

---

1. Wiegand, *De Wette*, pp. 54-55.
2. Wiegand, *De Wette*, p. 62; Staehelin, *Dewettiana*, p. 102.

The plot and the importance of *Theodor* for understanding de Wette's development up to the 'discovery' of late 1817 have been referred to already. What is necessary now is to indicate the import-ance of *Theodor* for understanding de Wette during the Weimar period; in particular, his attitude to his dismissal, and his view of the role of the church and of the office of preacher.

In connection with de Wette's dismissal, there is an important sec-tion in Volume II in which Theodor meets up with Walther, someone he first knew in his student days, and then knew later when Theodor was engaged to Therese and working in government administration. When Theodor knew Walther previously, the latter was a rationalist. Indeed, in the incident in which Härtling resolves Theodor's doubts, Walther tries to play down the significance of Härtling's words. In Volume II, Theodor meets Walther again, and discovers that this friend has had a conversion experience that has changed him from rationalism to a supernaturalist pietism. Although, in the story, the friends meet up in Zürich, we are told that Walther owed his conver-sion to an unnamed place: where the old system was beginning to be received again.[1] There can be little doubt that Berlin is meant, with its growth of the influence of orthodoxy and pietism; and the matter is confirmed in the discussions between Walther and Theodor, in which the former defends the sort of teaching typical of the Berlin pietist circles. We may well hear echoes of discussions that de Wette may have had with pietist students in Berlin.

Walther's basic position is that of the irredeemable sinfulness of humankind and of the world. Human pride and reason must bow in submission to God's revelation in the Bible and must accept Christ's redeeming work. Theodor, on the other hand, defends the importance of the use of reason as a God-given faculty, and denies that humanity is evil *per se*. A lively discussion develops around the nature of evil, with Walther maintaining that, because Christ and the apostles believed in the devil, human reason must then accept that the devil is

---

1. *Theodor*, II, p. 63. According to A. Lindt ('C.F. Spittler und W.M.L. de Wette: Zur Begegnung von Erweckungsfrömmigkeit und Universitätstheologie im Basel des 19. Jahrhunderts', in *Gottesreich und Menschenreich: Ernst Staehelin zum 80 Geburtstag* [Basel: Helbing & Lichtenhahn, 1969], p. 366). Basel is meant, and its 'Deutsche Christentumsgesellschaft'. This seems to me to be highly unlikely. At the time of writing *Theodor*, de Wette had no connections with Basel and no need to criticize it. It was quite a different matter when it came to Berlin pietism.

the author of evil. Theodor defends the view that evil is an ideal judgment and not something that exists absolutely. Thus, for all his 'discovery' of late 1817, de Wette is far from being orthodox and pietist, and he is sad at the narrowness of Walther, and at his slavish devotion to the letter of the Bible. Later on, when Theodor and Walther are exploring the beautiful Swiss countryside, Walther is unable to appreciate it because of his belief that nature is fallen and thus not susceptible to disclosing the truth about God. Before it was cursed, the serpent propelled itself upright, and the earth has received the curse of being unfruitful.[1] For Theodor, conversing with Walther is like breathing the foul air of a prison.

The next passage of importance comes when Theodor and Walther have met with Hildegard and her brother Otto, and are visiting Tell's Chapel near Küssnacht. Walther refuses to enter the chapel to pray, on the grounds that Tell's deed (the murder of the tyrant Gessler) was unchristian, and that to think of his memory was not compatible with Christian devotion.[2] Theodor now speaks, and the reader cannot but think here of Sand's murder of Kotzebue. He accepts that private revenge disturbs the moral order, and that Tell's deed should neither be regarded as a noble hero's act nor be held up as an example of Christian virtue. But Tell's action can be understood as a deed that was so driven by the arrogance of the tyrant, the suffering of a father and the desire for freedom and for the fatherland that it bursts the boundaries of the moral world. Tell executed the judgment of God upon a tyrant. His deed was not Tell's deed, it was a happening of history and from that standpoint had a sacred character. Walther interrupts to say that, if Austria still ruled in those Swiss valleys, Tell would be regarded simply as a criminal. Theodor answers that, in that case, the deed would have remained Tell's and would not have become part of history. The fact was that Tell's deed had the effect of setting the Swiss free, and, in this way, Tell's presumption in taking the office of judge was vindicated.

In this incident, de Wette, via Theodor, was justifying Sand's murder of Kotzebue. The victim was cast in the role of tyrant, and the deed was excused on the grounds that its purpose was to bring freedom to Germany just as Tell had inspired the freedom of the Swiss.

---

1. *Theodor*, II, p. 77.
2. *Theodor*, II, p. 103.

Further, readers in 1821 could hardly have missed the fact that Schiller had published his play *Wilhelm Tell* in 1804 and in it had vindicated Tell's murder of Gessler. When Tell returns home after the deed to face not only his wife and son but a Friar who is none other than John of Swabia who has murdered the emperor, Schiller tellingly contrasts the furtive John with the confident Tell, a Tell who says:

> [This hand] has defended you both and has rescued the
> land. I may lift it freely to heaven (Act V scene 2, lines 3144-45).

The whole play ends with the Swiss leaders and people assembled near Tell's house. As Tell emerges, they cry:

> Long live Tell, the protector and the liberator (Act V scene 3, line 3282).

This incident, then, shows us an unrepentant de Wette over the matter of Sand, and Walther, who refuses to pray at Tell's Chapel and who maintains that Tell's act was immoral and unchristian, is a representation of those who had dismissed de Wette. They had looked at the deed only from the point of view of the outside, and had been unable to see nobler motives and higher aims at work. Perhaps de Wette believed that one day in the future Sand's act would be seen to have the significance that Tell's act had assumed. If he did believe this, subsequent history has declared against him.

A second important matter that is discussed in *Theodor* is the nature of the church and its relationship to the state.[1] This helps us to see how de Wette saw himself fitting into the ecclesiastical and political spheres in his willingness to enter the ministry. Basically, the church was, for de Wette, a free association of people who had found Christ to be the truth and the way. The very act of association together then provided the occasion for the expression of Christian love, and in the fellowship of the church individuals were encouraged and enabled to live lives worthy of the example of Christ. De Wette was critical of ecclesiastical hierarchies and of doctrinal compulsion, both of which militated against the freedom that was for him at the heart of Christianity; and thus he was particularly critical of the Catholic Church.

De Wette believed that vital to the life of the church were scholarship and art. Scholarship, in the sense of the unfettered search for

---

1.   *Theodor*, II, pp. 383ff.

truth, was a vital part of Protestantism, and a guarantor of freedom. Art was important for nourishing the aesthetic life of a people, and for enabling them to develop sensitivity to beauty and form. In the church, art needed to play its part in the architecture of church buildings, in the furnishings and paintings in churches, and in the ordering of worship, especially music.

True Christian life could not be confined to the church, but had to express itself in the political life of the people. Thus withdrawalist sects such as Quakers and Mennonites were expressing a one-sided view of Christianity. The relationship of church to state was summed up in the word 'midwife'. The state, without interfering in the life of the church, should nonetheless try to provide the conditions that would enable it to prosper. In any case, the state would be led, ideally, by the most able of its citizens, who could be expected to be Protestants for whom the love of truth and the upholding of freedom would be priorities. De Wette allowed that it would be necessary for the state to proceed against any church whose activities were harmful to the state; and he felt strongly that German Catholics should insist on choosing and consecrating their own bishops, as opposed to this being under the control of Rome. It would be the task of the state to encourage the Germanness of German Catholicism.

De Wette's views on Jews and on women may be offensive to modern readers, who live in a different age from him.[1] He believed that Jews should not be granted citizenship, that they presented the danger of being a state within the state, that their numbers should be restricted (but not by force), and that their children should be encouraged to convert to Christianity. Women were not to have democratic rights, but were to participate in democracy through their partnership with their husbands. The ideal of the relation between church and state was that the church exercized no earthly power but nurtured the powers of the human spirit, while the state allowed itself to be influenced by that same spirit. The work of a clergyman lay in educating and assisting his people in the development of the things of the spirit and of their expression alike in the Christian and political communities.

Although all this sounded innocent enough, it constituted a profound criticism of the state of affairs in Prussia. There, there was no

---

1. *Theodor*, II, p. 348.

democracy, and the universities were subject to a control which would get worse in the years immediately after the dismissal of de Wette. Far from allowing freedom to the churches, the Prussian government had instituted a programme of increased control through regional boards and synods, and was pressing the Lutheran and Reformed denominations to become a united institution. It would be interesting to know whether de Wette would have accepted a post as parish minister in Prussia in the unlikely event of being offered one!

Another matter of importance in *Theodor* to the hero's decision to become a minister of religion is his feeling that he can with good conscience accept the doctrine of Justification, albeit on his own terms. The section dealing with this[1] begins by reminding the reader that it was a devotional talk by Theodor's minister when he was young that had set him on the path to doubt. This is quite probably an autobiographical piece of information.

In the novel, Theodor now accepts that it is impossible for humans to fulfil the law and thus to be justified by so doing; but he means by this the conflict between instinctive and reflective-driven behaviour in the sense that he expounded this in his interpretation of evil. In this context, justification becomes something essentially subjective. It is not a way of removing wrongness or guilt; it is a way of reassuring the conscience that a person is accepted by God in spite of being unable always to behave according to the imperatives of reflective reason.

To be justified before God was to have the unshakeable conviction that Christ achieved a sinless life of human virtue, and that he overcame sin in his death and reconciled humanity with God. This reconciliation comes about because Christ demonstrated that a human life of perfect obedience and virtue is possible, thus encouraging others to the same achievement. It was possible for believers today to trust in Christ so that they received in their turn confidence in the possibility that they could imitate him, a confidence that continued even in the face of failure to do so.

Theodor contrasted this confidence and assurance which came from Christ with the Judaism of Paul's time, and with the Kantian moralism of his own days. These were both instances of work's holiness, of human endeavour without the encouragement and assurance that were afforded by the life and death of Christ. In a moment of ecstacy,

---

1.   *Theodor*, II, pp. 200ff.

Theodor is able to thank God for enabling him to break free from the old forms and expressions of Christianity and to discover the freedom of the spirit:

> You have guided me correctly; you have brought me through the night to the light, just as you have led the whole human race.[1]

Before we leave *Theodor*, one final section must be mentioned. Following Hildegard's decision to marry Theodor and to become a Protestant, she spends part of Holy Week in a Catholic convent at Theodor's suggestion in order to test her decision. Reunited with Theodor and Otto on Good Friday, she asks Theodor to speak about the meaning of the death of Christ, and there follows one of the finest, if not the finest of all the passages in the whole novel. It is far too long to give here in full and one wonders whether it was ever a sermon that de Wette actually preached. The following is an extract:[2]

> The death of Jesus, just like the story of Jesus, has to be considered in the first place from a human and historical standpoint. Impelled by the necessity that spiritual help must be brought to his people and the whole of mankind, and deeply aware that he possessed the truth and was called to bring it into the world, Jesus undertook the great work of bringing about a spiritual change in both his own and all peoples of the world. Experience teaches that whoever undertakes a great task, and comes up against the prejudices and selfishness of mankind, seldom reaches the goal without a great struggle that lies on the road to the goal. The great spiritual movements that have occurred in human history overwhelm those who initiate and carry them out; their ideas are plants that must be watered with blood. Thus it was in the nature of things that Jesus fell victim to his mission; but with him it was uniquely the case that, without falling victim, he would not have achieved his aim, and that had he been victorious he would not have been denied the victory. His kingdom was not of this world, that is to say, he did not live and work for his own time alone, but for all times. He could not with skilled strength set up a work, as lawgivers and founders are accustomed to do, nor could he try to succeed by making use of the time and circumstances. Jesus had to reach out beyond his time and ignore the usual methods of skill, and had to avoid building and completing something. He could only cast the seeds which would spring up in the future, could only cast the spiritual leaven into the dough, and leave everything to time, to the strength of human nature and the blessing of God. If he had wished, Christ could perhaps have been a second Moses,

---

1. *Theodor*, II, p. 207.
2. *Theodor*, II, pp. 332ff.

founder of a new and better national life: and this is what his people expected of him. Even his own followers entertained such hopes. However, in that case his work would have been so one-sidedly national and temporary, like that of Moses himself.

Christ wanted and needed to be a spiritual creator, the founder of a spiritual movement that would continue into eternity. Whoever presents themselves to the rawness of humanity without weapons or the protection accorded by cunning; whoever wants to improve mankind by means of words of truth, bringing their faults to the light of day and placing before them a picture of completeness without compelling them or frightening them into compliance—such a one must necessarily fall victim.

But to the extent that Christ lost, he triumphed, and the spirit stood triumphantly over the broken body. The idea of that which he embodied appeared in his death, and in his death mankind first recognized what he really was. The highest ideas are those which cannot be expressed in life and whose working out remained after his death, ideas which can only be believed, not seen. Faith, however, cannot be proved by a deed, because a deed never approximates to the idea, and conveys only an incomplete representation. Faith is proved through suffering, in which a mortal body is given up for the immortal spirit, limited actuality for eternal idea, the joy and pleasure of present achievement for the sublime happiness of a glimpse of the fully achieved.

The eternal and immortal can only be grasped in the self-destruction of the temporal. Only when the mortal, in recognition of its mortality offers this mortality in sacrifice can it surmount its limitations and achieve the vow of total accomplishment.

The de Wette who wrote these exquisite words and who was sincerely desirous to enter the ministry was now to be caught up in a political intrigue fuelled by the events of his dismissal from Berlin. In June 1821, the second preacher at the St Katherine Church in Braunschweig, Pastor Alers, died, and the Stadtdirektor issued the necessary letters to expedite the filling of the vacancy.[1] De Wette heard about the vacancy from a friend, and applied for the post, agreeing to preach a trial sermon in Braunschweig without travelling expenses. The journey was one of about fifty hours.

At the time of his application, de Wette was known in Braunschweig only as the man who had been dismissed for condoning the Sand

---

1.   For what follows, see K. Venturini, *Beiträge zur neuesten Geschichte des Protestantismus in Deutschland. I. Des Doctor W.M.L. de Wette einstimmige und doch verworfene Wahl zum Prediger an der St Katherinen Kirche in Braunschweig* (Leipzig, 1822).

murder. Moreover, these events were known not from de Wette's *Aktensammlung* but from the rather less reliable source, the newspaper the *Weimarer Oppositionsblatt*. Before de Wette was included among the ten candidates invited to preach a trial sermon, references were sought from scholars and preachers in Braunschweig, Leipzig and elsewhere. Following his inclusion on the short list, an attempt to dissuade him from coming to Braunschweig was made, by the device of writing letters to friends of de Wette which asserted the virtual impossibility that he would succeed. The sequel is therefore remarkable in the light of these gloomy prognostications; and de Wette himself, on arrival in Braunschweig, told the Church Council (*Kirchen-Collegium*) that he entertained no hope of success.

But at the very time that references were bring sought in Braunschweig regarding de Wette, references were being taken up in connection with a possible call to Basel. The theological faculty in Basel had been reorganized in 1813, as a result of which one of the three chairs was filled and the work of the other two was covered by part-time help.[1] A second chair was filled in 1816 but the third, in practical theology, remained unfilled. It was for this chair that de Wette was now sought. The initial suggestion was made by Alexander Stein, who was a pastor in Sachsenhausen, near Frankfurt-am-Main. He had been a student of de Wette in Heidelberg and also had a copy of the letter written by de Wette to the pietist Anna Schlatter.[2] Stein wrote to Karl Rudolf Wolleb, pastor of the St Elisabeth Church in Basel who, after speaking to the Bürgermeister, was able to encourage Stein to write to de Wette in order to sound him out about a call to Basel. The salary would be poor (100 Carolines). Stein wrote to de Wette at the end of June 1821, and on 31 July was able to convey de Wette's reply to Wolleb.[3] The reply from the man regarded by Stein as 'the most learned of living German theologians' contained the following words:

1.   A. Staehelin, *Geschichte der Universität Basel 1818–1835* (Studien zur Geschichte der Wissenschaft in Basel, 7; Basel: Helbing & Lichtenhahn, 1959), p. 29.
2.   E. Staehelin, *Dewettiana*, pp. 102 n. 138, 104. See also E. Jenny, 'Wie de Wette nach Basel kam', *Basler Jahrbuch* (1941), pp. 51ff.
3.   Staehelin, *Dewettiana*, p. 102.

Any position in teaching would be invaluable to me, so that I could disregard the poor salary. I feel the loss of my activity as a teacher most painfully. I shall gladly accept the post in Basel if it is offered to me, and would travel there if there was a wish to get to know me personally.[1]

In the meantime, references had been sought from de Wette's former colleagues in Heidelberg, Professors Creuzer, Daub and Schwarz. These colleagues responded most warmly. In Creuzer's view de Wette had given and continued to give

the best example of a teacher of divinity through his very religious and Christian way of thinking.[2]

Daub wrote of de Wette's learning and exceptional talent while Schwarz described de Wette's removal to Berlin as a great loss to Heidelberg.[3] On 28 July 1821, the curators of the university requested the Education Committee of Basel to appoint de Wette.[4] At this point, the opposition organized itself.

On 8 August the theological faculty directed a protest against the appointment to the Education Committee. Those concerned, Professors Buxtorf, Merian, Falkeisen and La Roche based their objections on passages from *De morte Jesu Christi*, the *Christliche Sittenlehre*, the *Lehrbücher der christlichen Dogmatik*, and his Old and New Testament Introductions.[5] These objections were now referred to three referees, Wolleb, J.J. Fäsch of the St Theodor Church and Rudolf Hanhart who was rector of the Pädagogium. Here the matter rested for the remainder of the summer and winter of 1821.

Whether de Wette was aware of what was going on in Basel we do not know. That he was hedging his bets by declaring his willingness to go to Basel when he was also applying for the preaching post in Braunschweig is understandable. He was desperate for some kind of certainty for the future, and, as we have seen above, he had been warned not to entertain high hopes of the post in Braunschweig. At the same time, there is no doubt that he preferred the Braunschweig

1. The words of de Wette are quoted by Alexander Stein to K.R. Wolleb on 31 July 1821, in Staehelin, *Dewettiana*, p. 104.
2. Staehelin, *Dewettiana*, p. 103.
3. Staehelin, *Dewettiana*, pp. 103-104.
4. A. Staehelin, *Universität Basel*, p. 34.
5. A. Staehelin, *Universität Basel*, p. 34. See Staatsarchiv Basel, Erziehungsakten, section Y8, for a collection of excerpts.

post to that in Basel. It was much better paid (and this did matter to de Wette as a letter recorded by Wiegand shows[1]), and the emotional effort that he had put into writing *Theodor* indicated his commitment to an ecclesiastical position. His sights, then, were set on Braunschweig, whatever may have been going on in Basel.

De Wette arrived in Braunschweig at 5 a.m. on 7 September 1821. His trial sermon would be preached on 16 September (Trinity 13). He was greeted most warmly, and quickly made a good impression upon those he met, whether they belonged to the higher circles or were ordinary members of the congregation. Instead of a pedantic man showing off his learning and insisting that he was always right, his hosts found an unpretentious man whose unpretentiousness

> bordered on modesty; and one gained from his face, which was pale but enlivened by a pair of fiery eyes, the impression of an inner experience of suffering which had not yet been fully overcome by his strong faith, and his pious acceptance of the inscrutible decrees of providence.[2]

On 11 September, de Wette began to memorize his sermon so that, according to custom, he could deliver it without notes. On the same day he wrote to Amalie von Voigt in Weimar, telling a little of the people he had met in Weimar, and asking her to think of him at 9 a.m. on the 16th when he preached his sermon.[3]

On the great day itself, a congregation of 5,000 was already assembled by 8 a.m., including many who were not members of the St Katherine congregation but who were anxious to see and hear the infamous dismissed professor.[4] The Gospel for the day was the Parable of the Good Samaritan (Lk. 10.23-37), and de Wette's treatment of it was unusual and original.[5] He ignored the details of the story itself and thus made nothing, for example, of the two men who passed by on the other side. Also, he did not commend the example of the Good Samaritan. Rather, he concerned himself with the tension

1. Wiegand, *De Wette*, p. 56: 'Die Gegend ist wunderbar fruchtbar, Stadt und Land sehr wohlhabend und Landpfarrien von 1000 Thlrn. sind gar nicht selten'.

2. Venturini, *Beiträge*, p. 31.

3. De Wette to Amalie von Voigt, 11 Sept. 1821, photocopy; De Wette Nachlass S(a)4.

4. Wiegand, *De Wette*, p. 57.

5. *Predigt am XIII Sonntage nach Trinitatis in der St Katherinen Kirche zu Braunschweig gehalten* (Braunschweig, 1821).

between two attitudes, tenderness and rigour, and his main theme was that both sprang from pure love, and that rigour should not lead to intolerance, nor tenderness to indifference.

The behaviour of the Good Samaritan was an instance of tenderness springing from pure love—pure love because the man that he helped was his enemy, a Jew. This enabled de Wette to stress the unity of the human race and to urge his hearers to be generous in their judgment of others:

> In our opponert, whose error we opposed, we must never forget the man, the brother. . .
> The man is always better than his intentions and actions, and the image of God in him can never be obscured. Thus we love him also in his errors and in quarrels with him.[1]

On the other hand, our love needed to gain strength in the first instance from loving those closest to us:

> whoever loves all equally loves nobody.[2]

Thus de Wette was able to commend the love of family, congregation, country and church.

The climax of the sermon was reached as de Wette cited the example of Christ as the supreme example of love, an example that we must follow:

> Let us be true living branches belonging to him, the vine, so that the spirit of love that goes out from him may stream through us, and we bring forth worthy fruits of love.[3]

Looked at from the perspective of 170 years, the sermon strikes one as odd. It ignores the story set for the Gospel, and even undermines it in the sense that de Wette commends the love of those nearest to us, whereas the Good Samaritan loved a stranger and enemy. Further, it is all at the level of abstraction, with no concrete examples or amplification. In the sentence about a man never being as bad as his actions and intentions we may hear an echo of de Wette's justification for writing as he had done to Frau Sand.

But if the sermon looks odd to us today, it made a considerable

1. *Predigt*, p. 17.
2. *Predigt*, p. 20.
3. *Predigt*, p. 23.

impression on the vast congregation in the St Katherine Church. A contemporary reaction states the following:

> Because external impressions are not entirely unimportant regarding a preacher, it must be said for the sake of the truth that the speaker's posture and monologue reminded one unintentionally of an academic lecture. At the same time, his prime tenor voice which was accustomed to the slow and accentuated delivery suited to the taking down of lectures had the good effect that, in the large and full church, practically every single word was understood, the diction was pure and beautiful, and the whole sermon was excellently memorized.[1]

De Wette was elated with the success of the sermon and the visit to Braunschweig. 'You can have no idea', he wrote to Amalie von Voigt the day after the sermon, 'of the enthusiasm of them all for me. Such a triumph is too great; it overwhelms me. Pray for me so that misfortune does not follow.'[2] These were, unfortunately, prophetic words.

When the Church Council met to elect a preacher, de Wette received all twenty-seven votes![3] It was necessary for three names to be presented by the Stadtdirektor to the government (at that time mandated to the Elector of Hanover, George IV of Great Britain). Thus two other names were presented together with that of de Wette, Pastor Damköhler and Pastor Bernhard, and these two candidates were deemed to have received seven and six votes respectively. The names were forwarded to the government on 31 October, together with a statement that emphasized the overwhelming support for de Wette and which expressed the opinion that his dismissal from Berlin should not be a hindrance to his appointment. 'I cannot think,' wrote the Stadtdirektor Wilmerding, 'that the intention to make a talented man for ever unusable...can lie in the sublime character of the Prussian monarch'.[4] However, there was a feeling that not all would go well, such that a letter signed by eleven out of every twelve members of the congregation in support of de Wette was submitted in his support. Meanwhile, de Wette had returned to Weimar via Wolfenbüttel and Nordhausen, in which latter town there was a reunion between de Wette, Lücke, Schleiermacher and his wife and

1.   Venturini, *Beiträge*, p. 37.
2.   Staehelin, *Dewettiana*, p. 105.
3.   Venturini, *Beiträge*, p. 38.
4.   Wiegand, *De Wette*, p. 60.

Gesenius.[1] Although he returned to his writing with considerable enthusiasm, his future was still on his mind, and his equanimity was probably not helped by a newspaper report that he had been offered the post in Basel.[2] This, of course, was premature, but it made de Wette express his preference for the Braunschweig post, although he saw possibilities in the Basel chair.

The Braunschweig matter was resolved on 3 December 1821, when the government announced the appointment of Damköhler, who had been second on the list and who had received a notional seven votes.[3] From now until 7 June 1822, when George IV issued his final refusal to appoint de Wette (by which time de Wette had actually arrived in Basel), the congregation of the St Katherine Church fought a brave but unavailing battle to have as preacher the man whom they had elected. Thus, on 11 December 1821 the Church Council wrote to Damköhler informing him that de Wette had been unanimously elected and that if Damköhler accepted the post, his salary would depend on the good will of the congregation. On 12 December a letter was addressed to the Füstliche Geheimraths-Collegium asking for de Wette to be appointed, this being followed up by a further letter on 26 December.

Meanwhile, Damköhler wrote on 17 December declining the appointment, whether for honourable or financial motives is not known. The letter from the congregation to Damköhler had already angered the authorities, and presumably Damköhler had informed them about it, for on 17 December, the same date on which Damköhler's refusal was written, the Church Council was replying to a letter from the Stadtdirektor asking them to withdraw the letter. De Wette presumably had some news of what was happening, since he wrote rather bitterly to Schleiermacher at the end of 1821 complaining that the election at Braunschweig was a great disappointment.[4]

The correspondence that now went back and forth between the St Katherine Church and the authorities is too copious to follow in

---

1. See de Wette's letter to Ludwig Lucius, 1 Oct. 1821. Staatsbibliothek Preussischer Kulturbesitz, (West-) Berlin, Auto I/1158.
2. Wiegand, *De Wette*, p. 67.
3. Venturini, *Beiträge*, p. 42.
4. Wiegand, *De Wette*, p. 61.

detail.[1] Two matters were in dispute: first, the long-established right of the congregation to elect its preachers, and second, the reluctance of the congregation to hold another election from which de Wette was barred. In vain the congregation obtained references from several theological faculties. George IV refused to alter his decision. Meanwhile, in Basel, the Education Committee voted by eight votes to six on 17 January 1822 to appoint de Wette, and this decision was confirmed by the City Council (Kleiner Rat) two days later.[2]

De Wette now wrote to Braunschweig to say that he had been nominated to the chair in Basel and that, if he accepted, he would have to begin his duties in May. He deeply regretted the possibility of having to turn his back on Braunschweig, and made the remarkable statement that, if he had the financial means, he would run the risk of declining Basel while waiting for the final decision concerning Braunschweig. However, obligation to his family meant that he had to accept what was certain against what was uncertain.[3]

The response of the St Katherine congregation was amazingly generous. They promised to pay de Wette 800 Thalers for two years in case the Basel appointment fell through or the government decided to appoint him to Braunschweig. De Wette's reply, on 20 February, indicates how overwhelmed he was at the support that he had been given. It was 'one of the most beautiful experiences' of his life and a remarkable sign to any impartial observer. It seems to have moved him to the position in which he would have been prepared to accept and then decline the call to Basel, or to return from there to Braunschweig, if this is the sense of the following words:

> if it comes about that you can at last move the government to confirm my election, then I shall follow the call of love, and I shall *then* be yours.[4]

On 7 March, de Wette wrote two letters, one to the Bürgermeister of Basel accepting the call thence, the other to Braunschweig indicating that the lot was now cast against the St Katherine position. The first letter, in spite of its formal language, was not without warmth:

1.   Venturini, *Beiträge*, pp. 48ff.
2.   A. Staehelin, *Universität Basel*, p. 34.
3.   De Wette to the St Katherine Church, 29 Dec. 1821, in Venturini, *Beiträge*, pp. 138-39.
4.   De Wette to the St Katherine Church, 20 Feb. 1822, in Venturini, *Beiträge*, p. 140.

> May God bless this step which I now gladly make following mature
> reflection, and use it for the well-being of the University of Basel and my
> family. I look forward eagerly to the future, which will bring me into the
> midst of a well-favoured free state.[1]

Underneath, however, de Wette had regrets and anxieties. To the
Braunschweig congregation he wrote as follows:

> I must turn my back on dear Braunschweig. I am accustomed in every-
> thing to dispose myself to and follow the promptings of providence; but
> here I do it with an unwilling heart. Whatever the future brings, I remain
> indebted to the good St Katherine congregation and I shall never forget the
> days that I spent in its midst.[2]

At least three things worried de Wette about going to Basel. The
first was that he knew he would be going to work in a faculty which
opposed his appointment, and to a country and town whose opposition
to him on theological grounds was already being organized.

The second problem was that he would have to agree to teach in
accordance with the Basel Reformed confession of faith. In the event,
this would be the least of his worries. He was assured by correspondents that the signing of the confession committed him only to
teaching in accordance with the basic assumptions on which the
confession rested. His old Jena teacher Johann Philipp Gabler assured
him that 'you have nothing to fear from the Basel Confession'.[3]

The third and most pressing worry was that he would, in Basel,
have a poor outlet for his work and would be separated from his
friends. He would also have a poor salary and considerable expenses
in setting up a new home:

> I must drink the cup to the dregs and must part from my friends in order
> to embark on a new, and only partially suitable career.[4]

Thus de Wette prepared to make the long journey to Basel, leaving
Weimar, the town that had happy childhood and student memories,
and that had become his home. He could justifiably feel that he had
been cheated from entering in to a new sphere of activity to which his

---

1.   Staehelin, *Dewettiana*, p. 116.
2.   De Wette to the St Katherine Church, 7 March 1822, in Venturini, *Beiträge*,
p. 141.
3.   Staehelin, *Dewettiana*, p. 115.
4.   De Wette to Reimer, 31 January 1822, in Wiegand, *De Wette*, p. 63.

theological development had brought him and for which, to judge from the response of the St Katherine congregation, he was well suited. Basel was a last resort, and one from which he hoped soon to return to Germany. It was to become his home for the remainder of his life.

Old University Buildings, Basel (artist's impression)
Drawing by M. Mallallah

Chapter 7

BASEL

De Wette arrived with his family in Basel on Friday 3 May 1822, to be met by the Bürgermeister and by representatives of the city and university.[1] The official address book lists him as residing in 1823 in the Schwarzer Pfahlgasse, and we may assume that he lived there from his arrival until 1824 or 1825 when he is listed as dwelling in the Lottergasse in the St Johann quarter.[2] Given his difficult financial situation he could not afford to live in any but one of the poorer neighbourhoods. In spite of this, he had an informal meeting at his house two days later at which 22 students were gathered, and on Tuesday 13 May he began his lectures.[3] For the summer semester of 1822 he lectured on Romans and Galatians, and on the Pentateuch and ethics. The attendance was twenty-one for the two Pauline letters, fifteen for ethics and eleven for the Pentateuch—a far cry from his Berlin audiences. In the following six years, his hearers varied between nineteen and forty.[4]

Among the few original papers in the de Wette archive in Basel is the address that he delivered to his first audience.[5] In it, he thanked God and the city of Basel for the opportunity to begin his work anew, and he left his hearers in no doubt about the high standards of scholarship that would be expected. He emphasized that the historical and the theological were intertwined, just as Christ, the true revelation of God, had lived a historical life. There were the same two sides to the

1. Wiegand, *De Wette*, p. 64.
2. These books are in the Staatsarchiv, Basel.
3. Wiegand, *De Wette*, pp. 64-65.
4. The lecture lists from 1822–49 are in the Universitäts-Archiv, Staatsarchiv, Basel.
5. De Wette Nachlass, Universitätsbibliothek Basel. Full text in Handschin, *De Wette als Prediger*, pp. 322-26, partial text in Staehelin, *Dewettiana*, pp. 117-19.

Bible, which had therefore to be approached with a combination of critical investigation and confidence in the truth.

One person who attended de Wette's lectures on Romans and Galatians during that first semester was the professor of French literature at Basel, Alexandre Vinet. He was one of those who had looked forward to de Wette's arrival with profound misgivings. In a letter dated 18 January 1822 he had written:

> one of my colleagues who has been following M. de Wette's career for several years assures me that he treats in a cavalier fashion what we respect. At the beginning of a course on Isaiah he began by proposing as a certain fact that the prophet had not prophesied. After that I do not know at all what aspect of interpretation he dealt with; but in concluding, he smilingly thanked his audience for the patience with which they had listened to his exposition of this book. It is said that he has since changed, but it is not said that this is a complete change.[1]

On 13 February, Vinet wrote that de Wette was regarded by some as the Antichrist.[2]

Vinet's decision, then, to attend some of de Wette's lectures at least did de Wette the credit of being judged at first hand rather than at second hand, and Vinet's first reaction was favourable. 'I have seen M. de Wette', he wrote on 24 May, 'who pleased me greatly by his frank cordiality and his agreeable manners. I am following one of his courses with great interest, and I understand it without difficulty.'[3]

Two days later, on Sunday 26 May, which was Whit Sunday, de Wette preached in the St Elisabeth Church in Basel, and impressed not only Vinet, but the majority of his hearers. It was Pastor Wolleb of the St Elisabeth Church who had first approached the Bürgermeister about appointing de Wette, and who had supported him against the opposition. The invitation to preach was not only a kindness, but a chance for Wolleb to be vindicated in his support for de Wette.

The sermon was entitled 'Concerning the Testing of the Spirits', and was based upon 1 Jn 4.1-3.[4] It expressed de Wette's mature theology,

1. Alexandre Vinet, *Oeuvres Ve serie—Lettres* (ed. Pierre Bovet; Lausanne: Payot, 1947-49), I, p. 136.
2. Vinet, *Lettres*, p. 139. Staehelin, *Dewettiana*, wrongly gives the date as 1 February.
3. Vinet, *Lettres*, p. 148.
4. *Von der Prüfung der Geister: Predigt am heil. Pfingsfest in der St Elisabeth-*

and is in no way a concession to orthodoxy or pietism. Beginning from the story of the first Whit Sunday in Acts 2, it states that the spirit of Christ remained in the first community of believers and was passed on to its successors. The sentiments are reminiscent of the address in *Theodor* which the hero gives on Good Friday.[1] De Wette does not have in mind a supernatural endowment from God, but rather the example of Christ in giving inspiration and strength to his followers. De Wette praises the Reformation as a time of the upsurge of the spirit, and regrets that it is not so apparent in his own times. On the positive side, de Wette mentions great periods in the history of humanity when men of spirit, displaying a variety of gifts, have been evident. Men of spirit are to be tested by their attitude to Christ, since it is his spirit that stands above all others.

In New Testament times, spirits were not tested by conformity to credal formulae. These latter became necessary in later times, and must not be discarded. However, they have their limitations:

> all such credal statements carry the characteristic of human incompleteness, because they were brought into being by the needs of the time, and are the work of humans.[2]

Thus the criterion for testing spirits must be the free spirit of enquiry exercized by those who truly believe in Christ. Such people will agree together about the essentials of salvation.

The sermon had several effects. Vinet was so impressed that he translated it into French and had it published, and de Wette began to be trusted by those in Basel who had suspected his orthodoxy.[3] On the other hand, friends in Halle and Zürich accused him of selling out to Basel orthodoxy, a charge which de Wette repudiated.[4] In fact, both parties were mistaken. It is clear from the sermon that de Wette had not shifted his position. He praises the spirit of free enquiry, maintains that doctrinal formularies are incomplete and sees the spirit as human gifts and inspiration stimulated by the example of Christ, whose life and death released his ideals to be taken up by his followers. As usual, and as we shall see later in his controversy with the pietist Spittler, it

Kirche gehalten von Dr Wilh. Martin Leberecht de Wette (Basel, 1822).

1. *Theodor*, II, pp. 332ff.
2. *Prüfung der Geister*, p. 17.
3. *De l'épreuve des esprits* (Basel, 1822).
4. Wiegand, *De Wette*, p. 67; Staehelin, *Dewettiana*, pp. 120-21.

was de Wette's personality that convinced people of his Christian sincerity, such that his particular form of heterodoxy could easily be taken for orthodoxy.

By 2 October 1822, Vinet was writing as follows:

> You know that I have been attending the theological lectures of the celebrated Professor de Wette for six months. . . They have given me great pleasure; it seems that I have been doing exegesis for the first time. We have read in the original the Epistle to the Galatians and that to the Romans. Doctrine pure and firm, judicious and cautious criticism, fine and profound insights, a talent for seizing the connection of the passages and the overall view of Scripture, precise and methodical exposition—these are the merits that strike me in the lectures of this professor. . . His doctrine has not always been the same, he has searched for the truth in good faith and has progressively found it. He has eventually arrived at the end of his researches at the result which God always grants to good faith.[1]

For his part, de Wette was very satisfied with his lot in Basel. On 4 June, he wrote to Fries to say that his reception (on arrival) was good and that he was daily winning more trust. Although he had few hearers there was no other difference between Basel and Germany. The people were well educated and the surroundings like paradise, and far better than in Heidelberg.[2] The day before, de Wette wrote to Amalie von Voigt to say that not only was he well satisfied with his situation, but that being reunited with his family his good fortune was doubled. However, he added a prophetic note of pessimism:

> In this situation I must be ready for any sacrifice that my concern to maintain my good fortune demands.[3]

De Wette evidently had in mind the possibility that being attentive to his wife would give him less time for things such as correspondence with friends. In the event, his luck was not to last very long.

On 15 September, he wrote to Amalie von Voigt to say that his wife had decided to return to Heidelberg:

> A short dream that I might win back my domestic good fortune cheered me up; but it was only a dream![4]

1. Vinet, *Lettres*, p. 159.
2. Staehelin, *Dewettiana*, p. 120.
3. Staehelin, *Dewettiana*, p. 120.
4. Staehelin, *Dewettiana*, p. 122.

The real problem had been the fate of the children, Anna, nearly twelve, and Ludwig, ten. De Wette was left with his stepson Karl Beck, now aged twenty-four, who obtained a part-time teaching post, and the ten-year-old Ludwig. He would dearly have loved Anna to stay with him but was unable to influence her decision, which was to go with her mother. All he could do was to praise her and commend the outcome to heaven.[1]

De Wette's new domestic circumstances seemed to galvanize him into action to do something about the university, and to bring his friends to Basel to compensate for his sense of isolation. His first main target was Fries. Only the day after de Wette wrote to Amalie von Voigt about his wife's departure, the board of trustees of the university (*Kuratel*) was considering a request from de Wette that Fries should be appointed to a chair of logic.[2] The Education Committee gave its approval on 19 September, and on 21 September de Wette wrote to ask Fries if he would accept the appointment, which would command a salary of 1,600 francs or 1,100 marks (about 850 thalers).[3]

At this precise moment, Fries was suspended from his post in Jena pending the outcome of a commission appointed to investigate the connection with Sand and the student unions.[4] The temptation to go to Basel may appear to us to have been great; but not only was the salary low (850 thalers compared to his Jena salary of 1,100 thalers),[5] Fries had reason to be grateful for the support that he had received from the Weimar government. He was also given assurances that he would not be dismissed, and advised that he should reject the call to Basel.[6] In declining the appointment, Fries seems to have stressed the financial disadvantages to de Wette; but there may have been more than that behind his refusal to move. On 14 November de Wette wrote to Fries, 'come to us, I implore you'.[7] Fries was not be be persuaded, and on

1. De Wette to Amalie von Voigt, 15 Sept. 1822; De Wette Nachlass S (b) 4. Material not in Staehelin, *Dewettiana*, p. 122.
2. Staehelin, *Dewettiana*, p. 122 n. 208b.
3. De Wette to Fries, 21 Sept. 1822; De Wette Nachlass B4. Material not in, Staehelin, *Dewettiana*, p. 122.
4. Henke, *Fries*, pp. 209ff.
5. Fries, *Henke*, p. 210.
6. Fries, *Henke*, p. 219.
7. De Wette to Fries, 14 Nov. 1822; De Wette Nachlass B5.

22 February 1823 de Wette was to express his own disappointment to Fries at the outcome.[1]

At the same time that de Wette was head-hunting for Fries, he was also wondering whether Schleiermacher would be willing to move to Basel if it turned out that he had an 'accident'. Schleiermacher's own position in Berlin was far from secure at that moment; but de Wette was realistic enough to realize that he was betting on an outside chance:

> I have indeed considered trying to win you to us in such a case [i.e. dismissal from Berlin], but there is not much opportunity and less income. Otherwise, you would really like it here.

De Wette went on to say that he was trying to persuade the faculty to support the appointment of a fourth professor, and that Ullmann from Heidelberg would be his first choice for the post.[2] In fact de Wette's attempts to gain approval for the appointment of Ullmann and of Bleek (to replace Buxtorf) were rejected by the City Council.[3]

In spite of these setbacks, de Wette was determined to reorganize the teaching in the theological faculty. His two professorial colleagues were old. Johnann Rudolf Buxtorf, who occupied the Old Testament chair was seventy-five, while Emmanuel Merian, holder of the New Testament chair, was approaching sixty. Merian had previously been professor of mathematics in Basel, and then a parish clergyman. Although the teaching had been reorganized in 1817 everything remained deficient, and needed the drive and vision of de Wette.[4]

At a meeting of the faculty of theology on 16 December 1822, a proposal from de Wette was considered that would produce a four-year course according to the following plan:[5]

Year I	Exegetical Theology
Year II	Historical Theology
Year III	Systematic Theology
Year IV	Practical Theology

1. De Wette to Fries, 22 Feb. 1823; De Wette Nachlass B6.
2. De Wette to Schleiermacher, 28 Sept. 1822; De Wette Nachlass N (a) 18. Part is given in Staehelin, *Dewettiana*, p. 67.
3. Wiegand, *De Wette*, p. 67.
4. See A. Staehelin, *Universität Basel*, pp. 29-33; Hagenbach, *Gedächtnisrede*, p. 89.
5. Universitätsarchiv: Staatsarchiv Basel, OI, 'Protokolle der Sitzungen der theologischen Fakultät von 1744–1923', pp. 55-57.

The years were subdivided as follows:

Year I	1.	Study of 4 of the most important books of the OT
	2.	Study of all or the majority of the NT books
	3.	Introduction to OT and NT
	4.	History and antiquity of the Hebrews
	5.	OT and NT Hermeneutics
Year II	1.	Church history, including the Swiss Reformation
	2.	Selected texts, e.g. Origen
	3.	History of dogma
	4.	Study of dogmatic formularies
	5.	Study of ecclesiastical formularies
Year III	1.	Encyclopaedia
	2.	Belief (*Glaubenslehre*)
	3.	Morals
Year IV	1.	Theory of practical theology
	2.	Homiletics, with practicals.

Each discipline was to be taught at least twice every four years.

This detailed proposal, which was further broken down into the number of courses and hours that would be needed over the four years, required a fourth member of staff, in the field of church history. It was accepted by the faculty on 24 February 1823,[1] and although it was not possible to appoint to a fourth chair, K.R. Hagenbach was appointed as a lecturer to begin work in the winter semester of 1823, at the age of 22.[2] Thus de Wette established the curriculum that would be used for the next quarter of a century at least.

De Wette's other notable activity in the last months of 1822 was the beginning of a course of public lectures on morals. These were given in the Hospital Church (Spitalkirche), which was not the elegant Predigerkirche near today's hospital, but a hall on the site of the then hospital in the centre of Basel.[3] In the first instance, de Wette gave these lectures to a paying public in order to supplement his meagre salary. From this point of view, the venture was a resounding success. He was able to write to Hirzel on 4 January 1823 that he had 170 paid up members of his audience. There were also twenty non-paying

---

1. *Protokolle der theologischen Fakultät*, p. 58.
2. Wiegand, *De Wette*, p. 67.
3. Staehelin, *Dewettiana*, p. 125 n. 222.

members of the public and numerous guests.[1] But what was more important was that the occasion gave him important exposure to the Basel public in general which, as de Wette said, was incalculable when it came to the influence that he could exert. Also important for de Wette was the fact that between fifty and eighty of his hearers were women.

The first of these public lectures was published in the first number of a new scholarly journal, the *Wissenschaftliche Zeitschrift*, which appeared in 1823 with a foreword by de Wette on the inside wrapper, dated February 1823.[2] The first volume of the lectures, including the first, was published in 1823 with a foreword dated to the end of September 1823.[3] Although it is not possible here to expound the lectures in any detail (forty-six lectures were published in four volumes in 1823–24), we can say that this medium suited de Wette, and that he rose to his audience in these lectures. They represent his mature Friesian-Christocentric theology, and they owe much to Fries's *Handbuch der praktischen Philosophie* of 1818.[4] Although they must have required concentrated and attentive listening, they also have a lightness of touch and an abundance of apt illustrations or analogies.

The lectures encompass every aspect of life. Although they begin by analysing the nature of morality in terms of the various impulses (*Triebe*) and how the will and knowledge are to produce a rounded character, they move from the individual to embrace the state and public life, not forgetting the aesthetic dimension, whether that dimension is found in the world of nature or in the world of art. The lectures touch on family life, marriage, vocation and the acceptance of one's lot. There is a discussion of the so-called conflict of duties (which is no conflict) and of human perception of evil and of hopes for a better world. However, the position is thoroughly Christocentric, in de Wette's sublime exemplarist fashion:

1. Staehelin, *Dewettiana*, p. 125. See also *Journal für Literatur, Luxus, Mode und Kunst* 38 (1823), p. 328.

2. *Wissenschaftliche Zeitschrift* (herausgegeben von Lehrern der Baseler Hochschule; Basel, 1823).

3. *Vorlesungen über die Sittenlehre* I. 1, 2 (1823), II. 1, 2 (1824).

4. J.F. Fries, *Handbuch der praktischen Philosophie oder der philosophischen Zwecklehre*, I (Heidelberg, 1818). Reprinted in *Sämtliche Schriften*, X (Aalen, 1970).

the Son of God himself appeared in human form to save humanity from the bonds of the flesh and the service of error. He unveiled the laws of eternal truth, came as a shining example of wisdom and virtue, showed in his own example how humanity can and ought to overcome the sins of the flesh, and, with the call of love, gathered around himself a group of erring men to follow him in the way of truth and justice. In him, freedom celebrated its highest victory and in him humanity was transfigured into divine glory. We, and millions before and with us, have acknowledged him as the lord and master of humanity and strive according to his example to become like him, so as to complete salvation in ourselves.[1]

It is no exaggeration to say that these lectures represent de Wette's best writing, and that they are one of the best introductions to his mature theological thought. A plan for Vinet to translate the lectures into French, as he had translated de Wette's sermon on the testing of the spirits, foundered. In spite of Vinet's respect for de Wette, he quickly discovered, as he began the translation, that de Wette's fundamental position was very different from his.[2]

It has been remarked that de Wette was impressed by the number of women attending his lectures. Women, and their company, were important to de Wette throughout his life, and compensated to some extent for his disappointed desire for domestic happiness. Amongst the women who heard his lectures was Anna Margaretha VonderMühll, wife of a prominent Basel trader.[3] We do not know exactly how and when de Wette became acquainted with the VonderMühll family, or with the family of Carl Burkhardt, whose daughter Anna Margaretha was.[4] In a letter of 29 April 1823 to Amalie von Voigt, de Wette says that he has already written to her about 'Frau V d M'; and it is clear that the friendship is not entirely new.[5] For the next few years de Wette was to be obsessed with this woman thirteen years his junior, and to compensate in this way for the absence of his wife. Indeed Gritly (as de Wette was sometimes later to call her in his correspondence) is mentioned in de Wette's letters until 1840, although in latter years he saw little of her. She seems never to have been a well person, and she died in 1843 aged fifty.

1. De Wette, *Sittenlehre*, I.1, p. 18.
2. Staehelin, *Dewettiana*, p. 128.
3. Anna Margaretha VonderMühll (née Burckhardt) 1793–1843. Her husband was Johann Georg VonderMühll (1789–1853).
4. Carl Burckhardt (1767–1846).
5. Staehelin, *Dewettiana*, p. 129.

It is possible that Anna Margaretha reminded de Wette of his first wife Eberhardine, if the argument in Chapter 2 is correct in identifying her with Euphosyne in the novel *Heinrich Melchthal*. In a letter to Amalie von Voigt of 21 September 1823, de Wette described her thus:

> [she] is thirty years old and has become very sickly, and thus faded [*verblüht*]. Tall of stature, very thin and awkward [*ohne Anmuth*] in bearing and movement, with strong features, she can be considered neither beautiful nor attractive. Her exterior did not draw me to her, and I confess that I would never have got to know her wonderful nature [*Gemüth*] had not her opinion about me to others made me aware of her.[1]

He went on to say that only occasionally did he get the chance to speak to her informally, and that Amalie von Voigt must not suspect anything else about their relationship—a remark which indicates that Amalie von Voigt valued de Wette's friendship to the point where perhaps she became jealous of de Wette's relationship with Anna Margaretha. Indeed, de Wette may have exaggerated the latter's lack of physical attractiveness for this reason.[2] On the other hand, de Wette wrote to Henriette Schleiermacher on 11 June 1823 that he had so much confidence in Anna Margaretha 'that I could open my whole heart to her, if circumstances allowed'. He added that when he ended his (first series of) public lectures, it was for her a day of sad leave-taking.[3]

In the event, de Wette was to see something of Anna Margaretha at St Margarethen, in those days a tiny hamlet about half-a-mile outside the city walls to the north. Here, Anna Margaretha's father had a house, to which the daughter often went for the sake of her health. In the letter of 29 April to Amalie von Voigt, de Wette says that he often goes there in the evening. He relates a recent visit:

> She saw me at the window and came to meet me at the door of the house. What lively joy! The weather was stormy and she could not sufficiently wonder that I had not been deterred. We sat at the tea table on which lay Goethe's *Tasso*. Previously she had had no liking for Goethe; but since reading my *Theodor* she had taken him up again, and said that I was right. She is a clever pupil.[4]

---

1. Staehelin, *Dewettiana*, pp. 133-34.
2. Amalie was the same age as de Wette, and, by now, a widow.
3. Staehelin, *Dewettiana*, pp. 131-32.
4. Staehelin, *Dewettiana*, p. 129.

In the first part of 1823, then, de Wette was delivering his public lectures in addition to his university classes, which amounted to twelve hours per week, and he was also spending time visiting Anna Margaretha. He was also revising his Psalms commentary, the second edition of which appeared in 1823, with a preface dated to the end of October 1823. This will be considered shortly. In May, de Wette became rector of the university, and on 12 May 1823 delivered the customary inaugural address at the beginning of his year of office.[1] It was a noble address, which praised Basel for it surroundings and for its republican constitution, as well as for its readiness to receive foreigners. Among eminent foreigners who had worked in Basel de Wette could name Reuchlin, the great Hebraist of the immediate pre-Reformation period and Oecolombad the city's reformer. But there was criticism as well. The temporary closure of the university in 1813 had been a loss for the life of the people. Its reopening with a new constitution in 1817 had been good, but five years later the constitution had not yet been fully implemented. There were unfilled chairs in law, medicine and philosophy. Not only theology needed to be reconstituted and reorganized, but all the faculties, for each science sent its rays into the various aspects of the life of the people. Thus de Wette made clear his deeply-held conviction that learning, scholarship and the search for truth were essential and that a properly-functioning university was not a luxury but a necessity.

On 12 October (Trinity 20), de Wette preached in the tiny church at St Margarethen.[2] The text was the story of Martha and Mary (Lk. 10.38-42) and it is difficult to read it without being aware that it was particularly intended for Anna Margaretha. In sketching the biblical story, de Wette suggested that, from small beginnings, the friendship of Jesus with the two women developed to the point where they recognised Jesus as the Christ. Perhaps de Wette was wondering where his friendship with Anna Margaretha would lead. Next, de Wette stressed the difference between Martha representing the outward, worldly things in terms of which others judge us, and Mary representing the more important inward things. He noted that some outward relationships, for example, between spouses, could be purely formal: and one

1. 'Rede, nach dem Antritt des Rectorats der Universität den 12. Mai gehalten', in *Wissenschaftliche Zeitschrift*, I.2 (1823), pp. 1-36.
2. *Predigten, theils auslegender theils abhandelnder Art* (1st collection; Basel, 1825), pp. 2-17.

wonders whether he had in mind Anna Margaretha's relationship with her husband as well as his own with Henriette Beck. Of Anna Margaretha's marriage we know only that de Wette regarded her husband as 'slow and broad' for so lively a wife, although the husband was not uncultured.[1] But the marriage may well have been one of convenience designed to link two Basel trading families, and one wonders what Johann Georg VonderMühll really made of his wife's predilection for literature and theology. That she spent much time at her father's country house may also be indicative.

The sermon, then, stressed the importance of the inward and the spiritual in relationships. Mary was the model of those

> who soon recognized Jesus as what he was, as the man who carried in himself the fulness of the spirit.[2]

Mary represented the higher way to which we must aspire: in the bringing up of children and in the treatment of guests. There can be little doubt that if Mary was the model for inwardness in the Gospel story, Anna Margaretha was the model for inwardness among de Wette's hearers, and perhaps she was not unaware that he was preaching primarily to her.

The main literary event of 1823 was the appearance of the second edition of the Psalms commentary, a work that would eventually go to five editions. A comparison with the first edition of de Wette's young and pre-1817 'discovery' days would indicate any alterations in his practice of critical scholarship. In fact, the differences between the two editions are not great, and apply more to the detailed exegetical points than to the overall approach.[3]

The most noticeable critical difference is that de Wette no longer allows that there are Maccabaean psalms. This is on the ground that the completion of the canon cannot be put so late. Thus, he prefers 'late-exilic' to Maccabaean as a designation, and in the case of Psalm 44 the date is put in the pre-exilic period.[4] In one or two cases a slight concession is made in the direction of connecting a psalm with David,

---

1. De Wette to Amalie von Voigt, 16 Jan 1824; see Staehelin, *Dewettiana*, p. 134. Staehelin suggests 14 Jan., but 16 Jan. is clear in the photocopy, and there is a postscript dated 17 Jan.
2. *Predigten*, I, p. 11.
3. The fifth edition was edited after de Wette's death by Gustav Baur (1856).
4. *Commentar über die Psalmen* (Heidelberg, 2nd edn, 1823), p. 334.

for example, in the case of Psalm 3 where he writes 'if we wish to connect this with David. . . ' But the main positions of the 1811 edition are scarcely changed.

The one area in which there is fuller discussion is in the case of messianic psalms, and it is interesting that the 'discovery' of 1817 sharpens de Wette's position in some cases. For example, in discussing Psalm 22, de Wette rejects a direct messianic interpretation on the grounds that, in the psalm, the psalmist hopes for deliverance. De Wette argues that Christ established the Kingdom of God not on the basis of deliverance but through suffering. Because of this, the psalm cannot be messianic in that it does not match what de Wette understands to be the *Christian* idea of the messiah. Thus, as in the first edition of the commentary, Psalm 22 is messianic only in so far as v. 28 envisages an extension of the knowledge of God to the Gentiles.[1]

In the case of Psalm 16, the second edition has a much expanded discussion of its messianic implications, in which recent defenders are refuted by de Wette. Although he admits that, in the New Testament, Psalm 16 is used in reference to Christ, de Wette insists that this is an ideal point of view, since all hopes are fulfilled in Christ.[2] Thus, messianic interpretations do not properly belong to a historical-critical exposition of the Psalms. Otherwise, the approach as a whole lays far more stress upon the aesthetic and religious dimensions of the Psalms, and it is noteworthy that the Introduction is scarcely altered at all.

At the end of September or the beginning of October 1823, de Wette was visited in Basel by the young E.W. Hengstenberg, who arrived in Basel on 26 September to work as a tutor to J.J. Stähelin.[3] Hengstenberg had studied in Berlin, and at this stage in his career was much more liberal than would later be the case. In fact, in 1826, he filled the chair in Berlin that had been vacant since de Wette's dismissal in 1819, and was to be a leading member of the neo-orthodox school which held sway in Berlin and elsewhere for more than three decades. Stähelin would later join the Basel faculty, and be a close colleague of de Wette. Of his meeting with de Wette, Hengstenberg wrote:

1. *Psalmen* (2nd edn), pp. 193-94.
2. *Psalmen*, pp. 193-94.
3. J. Bachmann, *Ernst Wilhelm Hengstenberg: Sein Leben und Wirken* (Gütersloh, 1879), I, pp. 124-38; Lenz, *Universität Berlin*, II, pp. 330ff.

De Wette is very depressed and his circumstances (*Umgang*) are not very pleasant. His misfortune is, in addition, increased by domestic strife[1].

Of the theological situation in Basel, Hengstenberg wrote:

> From a theological standpoint, things are not at their best in Basel. The clergy are ultra-orthodox and very intolerant. I have visited several clergy who spoke of nothing but the temptations of the devil and the like, and also went so far as to say that the true Christian is above the love of the fatherland. For all these people, de Wette, who is greatly respected by many, is a thorn in the flesh. They claim that he is not a Christian. . . and they seek in many ways to malign him.[2]

1824 would be another year of disappointment for de Wette although it had its pleasures also. On his birthday, 12 January, he visited Anna Margaretha (the only festive aspect of the day); and on 28 February he was writing to say how much he was beginning to become a part of the family of Anna Margaretha's father at St Margarethen.[3] He mentions a plan for an outing of the entire family to Chamonix, which was presumably his idea because in the July of 1823 he made a journey of his own to Chamonix and the Simplon pass, only to be frustrated by very poor weather.[4]

On Maundy Thursday, 15 April 1824, he preached at the St Elisabeth Church on the story of Jesus washing the disciples' feet, emphasizing that, for Jesus, it was his humility and suffering that displayed the image of God.[5] Immediately after preaching de Wette went to Zürich, where he spent Easter and Easter week with the Hirzel family, returning to Basel on 23 April.[6]

Not long after his return, the aftermath of the Sand affair struck two further blows. Prussia was able to exert sufficient pressure on Basel to force the city council to investigate certain young men suspected of 'demagogic intrigues', with a view to their extradition. Among those affected were Karl Follen, who had been one of the leaders of the students union in Jena, and de Wette's step-son Karl Beck.[7] It was in Beck's company that de Wette had visited the Sand

1. Bachmann, *Hengstenberg*, p. 124.
2. Lenz, *Universität Berlin*, II, pp. 330-31.
3. De Wette to Amalie von Voigt, 28 Feb. 1824; Staehelin, *Dewettiana*, pp. 134-35.
4. *Journal für Literatur, Luxus, Mode und Kunst* 87 (1823), p. 719.
5. *Predigten*, I, pp. 22-36.
6. De Wette to Hirzel, 24 April 1824; Staehelin, *Dewettiana*, p. 135.
7. Staehelin, *Dewettiana*, p. 31 n. 79. In fact, Follen helped de Wette to edit the

family. The cloud that now hung over de Wette was only dispersed in October, when Beck and Follen left Basel and emigrated to America in order to be totally out of reach of the arm of Prussia. This was, of course, a further blow to de Wette's domestic arrangements. Karl Beck had lived with his step-father in Basel since July 1822 and had contributed to the family income.

The second blow was the Prussian cabinet order of 21 May 1824, binding on all Prussian citizens, which forbade them to study at the universities of Basel or Tübingen. Offenders would forfeit the right to an appointment in Prussia, and parents and guardians of offenders would be fined.[1] This order was presumably intended, among other things, to shut de Wette out of influence in theological scholarship by preventing any young men from the Prussian parts of Germany from going to Basel to study. It is difficult to know whether, in the absence of this order, de Wette would have attracted students from Prussia. Be that as it may, the number of de Wette's hearers remained very small for the remainder of his life.

While de Wette was absorbing the shock of these blows, he was looking forward to his summer holidays, and a visit to Badenweiler with Anna Margaretha in order to meet Amalie von Voigt.[2] This took place over the weekend of 24 July in the village near Müllheim in the Black Forest some 32 km north of Basel. The occasion was not without its tensions, to judge from a letter from Anna Margaretha included with one written by de Wette to Amalie and dated 5 August from St Margarethen. Anna Margaretha notes that, in spite of being so close to Switzerland, Amalie declined to enter it, and would only promise to do so on a future occasion. For his part, de Wette did not follow his usual practice of writing immediately after the meeting. He excused himself on the grounds that, from Monday evening to Thursday afternoon, he had had an unexpected visit from Hirzel and his son. This must have been from 26 to 29 July because, writing on 5 August, de Wette says that he had been at St Margarethen since Tuesday evening. In between, he had been involved in comforting the Streckeisen family, in which a suicide had taken place. Thus the

---

Wissenschaftliche Zeitschrift in Basel. For this, together with Follen's account of his and Beck's journey to America see *The Work of Charles Follen* (ed. E.L. Follen; Boston, 1842), I, pp. 113-14, 121-22, 127-39.

1. Bachmann, *Hengstenberg*, I, p. 148.
2. De Wette to Amalie von Voigt, 22 Nov. 1824; De Wette Nachlass S (c) 8.

meeting at Badenweiler had been over the weekend of 24–25 (26) July, and it was ten days before de Wette then wrote to Amalie. On the other hand, the letter from Anna Margaretha speaks of the beautiful hours that they enjoyed together, and expresses the hope that she may be able to call Amalie her friend. Nonetheless, even in her contribution it is possible to detect some of the tensions that must have attended the meeting, and which made Amalie von Voigt refuse to make the short journey to Switzerland.[1]

Ten days later, on 15 August 1824, de Wette preached at the St Elisabeth Church on Gal. 5.22.[2] In view of his belief that the antithesis between flesh and spirit was the perceived conflict between the natural inclinations and the duties and obligations disclosed by critical reflection, de Wette admitted in the sermon that the flesh was an uncontrollable drive in human nature. He likened it to a wild animal hurting itself in lust for blood upon its prey; or to a swollen mountain stream being assisted rather than restrained by the dam constructed to contain it. One wonders whether this sermon, probably written only a few days after the letter to Amalie, expressed something of the conflicting emotions of love and perhaps jealousy that he had experienced at Badenweiler.

De Wette now entered a difficult period in his Basel existence, a period which was to include a very cold winter, illness, the death of his wife and a renewed theological controversy, this time with the founder of the Basel Mission, Christian Friedrich Spittler.

The winter semester began badly in that he was no longer giving his public lectures and thus was missing this particular outlet. Instead, there was a series on the French Revolution which was attended by Anna Margaretha who, for her part, missed de Wette's lectures. This, and other things, made him often ill tempered, and in a sad letter to Amalie von Voigt of 22 November, he begged for understanding, on the grounds that he had had a sad life.[3] Further, not only was he not giving lectures that Anna Margaretha could attend, but he had little other opportunity of seeing her, since she was spending three of four days each week in family circles. The winter also brought hardship, no doubt because of economies made necessary by the fact that he was not earning money from public lectures for the first

1. Staehelin, *Dewettiana*, pp. 135-36.
2. *Predigten*, I, pp. 58-67.
3. De Wette to Amalie von Voigt, 22 Nov. 1824; De Wette Nachlass S (c) 8.

time since his arrival in Basel. He was also depressed.

Christmas was not spent, as he would have liked, at St Margarethen, but in his constrained home surroundings. On 24 December he preached in the St Elisabeth Church, and it must be said that the sermon showed no sign of his depression.[1] Beginning from the observation that mid-winter is a dreary time of sorrow, cloud and little sunshine, de Wette observed that this was a picture of the state of the world at the time of Christ's birth. But as spring follows winter, so Christ's birth was the beginning of the shining of a light that has never been put out. This light was spoken of by Isaiah in 9.2 and fulfilled in Christ, so that all who live in fellowship with him have a hope that comes from God alone.

The theme that hope should rely on God alone led to a concluding passage that no doubt reflected de Wette's own losses, including his present estrangement from his wife and his daughter Anna:

> do not cry, you parents, whose children God has taken. Do not complain you husbands, whose marriage has not been blessed with the fruit of love. God took your loved-ones so that you might recognize him; that you are not your own but belong to God, so that you might direct your love and hope to him alone.[2]

The strain under which de Wette was living and working finally took its toll in March. On the 6th of that month he was due to preach at the St Theodor Church, and he began to memorize the sermon on the Friday. At about six in the evening, as he came in from the garden he felt a pain in his left foot which increased in intensity, gave him no sleep and continued on the Saturday. The sermon was postponed, although it was later published. He was also obliged to cancel his lectures for a few days. No sooner had he got over this illness than he succumbed to a fever which made it difficult for him to work, right through to mid April. Over Easter, which was on 3 April, he was able to make a short journey to nearby Alsace and to visit Charlotte Kestner, and on 17 April he preached in the St Theodor Church, albeit after a sleepless night.[3]

This is a sermon which, once again, takes on a new light if read in

1. *Predigten*, I, pp. 98-115.
2. *Predigten*, I, p. 115.
3. De Wette to Amalie von Voigt, 14 May 1825; De Wette Nachlass S (c) 10. Part in Staehelin, *Dewettiana*, pp. 137-38.

connection with de Wette's circumstances.[1] The text is Jn 14.1-6, and the theme is that of Jesus preparing a place for those who die. But there is so much reference in the sermon to the experiences of those who lie upon sick beds and look death in the face, that there can be little doubt that de Wette had thought that he might die. In particular, he speaks of those whom death prevents from completing their life's work:

> with noble pain he leaves his course and looks with longing at the goal which he has not reached.[2]

He also speaks of those whose outward circumstances do not satisfy their desires, whose circumstances drag down their aspirations, and hinder their spiritual development. There are surely, again, hints here of de Wette's inner feelings.

De Wette felt the need for a spell away from Basel, and left on 17 April for a journey that would last nearly three weeks. The first part of the journey was to Zürich on foot, via Brugg, where he saw the confluence of the rivers Aare, Reuss and Limmel, and climbed the Habsburg. He reached Zürich on 23 April and stayed a week before setting out, on 30 April, on a visit to the cantons of Schwyz and Zug with Ludwig Hirzel. The visit took in Horgen, Cham, Zug, Arth and Steinerberg, including boat trips on the Zugersee, and views of the Rigi.[3]

The journey was obviously beneficial, but his problems were by no means solved. On 14 May he wrote to Amalie von Voigt that he could not envisage remaining in Basel without Anna Margaretha.[4] On 11 July he complained to Amalie that he was without work, having finished all that he had begun, and not feeling able to start anything new.[5] Presumably, this means that he had completed the work both on the critical edition of the letters of Luther and on the *Andachtsbuch*. These two books appeared later in 1825, with prefaces dated in September of that year, and he was presumably preoccupied with correcting the proofs during the summer. In his letter of 14 May he wrote that he had lost two months of work because of illness and that he would not be travelling in the summer because of the printing of the Luther letters. The *Andachtsbuch* is most likely a work also

---

1. *Predigten*, I, pp. 140-61.
2. *Predigten*, I, p. 148.
3. See p. 207 n. 3.
4. See p. 207 n. 3.
5. De Wette to Amalie von Voigt, 22 Nov. 1824; De Wette Nachlass S (c) 8.

mentioned in the 14 May letter that he was writing with his daughter Anna's confirmation in mind. From 19 July to about the middle of August, de Wette went to St Margarethen, and later in the month he was visited by his publisher, Reimer.[1] In September he was able to report to Amalie von Voigt that his health was much better; and no doubt this was improved by the prospect of the imminent appearance of the edition of the Luther letters and the *Andachtsbuch*.[2]

Of the Luther letters, little needs to be said. They had cost de Wette much labour, and would continue to do so, and the public response would be a disappointment. They enabled readers to gain a glimpse of Luther through the chronological sequence of his letters, and as such remain an interesting work. The *Andachtsbuch* was a new venture for de Wette, and one that was not wholly successful.[3]

The origin of the *Andachtsbuch* is to be sought in de Wette's own preaching (a good deal of the material is taken from his sermons) and in his homiletic classes at the university, to which he devoted much time. Its rationale was that there was a gulf between historical-critical and philological interpretation of the Bible on the one hand, and its practical interpretation on the other. The purpose of the *Andachtsbuch* was to provide material of a spiritual nature for use in the home and by preachers and school teachers. The 1825 volume on John 1–17 was over 400 pages long, and was followed by a second volume in 1828 on the Synoptic Gospels. However, de Wette's plans to cover the whole New Testament (or most of it) in eight volumes was not to be realized, presumably because of lack of a good response. Instead, as we shall see later, de Wette devoted the last thirteen years of his life to producing a critical commentary on the whole of the New Testament.

Volume I of the *Andachtsbuch* was published anonymously, so that readers would not be put off the work by biased views about the author. Whatever its impact in 1825, it strikes the reader of today as unsuccessful. It entirely ignores critical questions and seeks to extract 'spiritual' insights from the text, insights that seem to owe more to the interpreter than to the writer of the Gospel. However, as the work progresses, it seems to become more and more critical, as though

---

1. De Wette to Amalie von Voigt, 31 Aug. 1825; De Wette Nachlass S (c) 12.
2. De Wette to Amalie von Voigt, 14 Sept. 1845; De Wette Nachlass S (c) 13. De Wette to Amalie von Voigt, 14 Sept. 1845; De Wette Nachlass S (c) 13.
3. *Die heilige Schrift des neuen Bundes, ausgelegt, erläutert und entwickelt: Ein Andachtsbuch für die häusliche Erbauung und Schullehrer*, I (Berlin, 1825).

de Wette finds it difficult to suspend his critical instincts.

On commenting on the miracle of changing the water into wine, de Wette seems to accept the miracle with ease:

> Jesus makes water out of wine through an authority over nature which is granted to him, which is quite impossible for us to grasp.[1]

But already in his comment on Jn 4.48 we find de Wette arguing that the desire to see visible demonstrations of Jesus' power was a hindrance to the inner experience of discerning the power of his (human) spirit.[2]

In expounding the healing of the lame man at the Pool of Bethesda de Wette accepts that the word of Jesus healed him without help from other people. He makes much, however, of the people who helped the sick people into the pool when its waters were disturbed, concluding that for us healing depends on the help of many.[3] The meaning of the feeding of the 5,000 is that what little we give to God can be multiplied for the sake of others.[4] Jesus walking on the water is an inspiring picture of the power of his soul to rise above earthly difficulties and constraints.[5] On the raising of Lazarus, de Wette makes the point that Jesus did not pray in order to alter the will of God, but to discover that his wish was in accordance with God's will. Therefore, the 'answer' to our prayers is that we gain the certainty that what we desire is obtainable and will be obtained.[6]

As examples of aesthetic and symbolic interpretation of the Bible, the *Andachtsbuch* is hardly convincing, and reveals a difficulty at the heart of de Wette's theological position. As a critic at the level of grammar, text and original meaning he was virtually without an equal. However, the mystical side of his personality was satisfied by philosophy and aesthetics, with his view of the aesthetic nature of the life of Christ providing a theological centre. This did not enable him to bridge the gap between criticism and edifying use of the Bible, and the *Andachtsbuch* strikes today's reader as artificial and forced. It is perhaps his most noteable failure, and all the more significant as a result.

---

1. *Andachtsbuch*, I, p. 48.
2. *Andachtsbuch*, I, p. 114.
3. *Andachtsbuch*, I, pp. 118-21.
4. *Andachtsbuch*, I, pp. 148-55.
5. *Andachtsbuch*, I, p. 156.
6. *Andachtsbuch*, I, pp. 306-307.

As 1825 came to an end, de Wette found himself caught up in renewed theological controversy . On 9 October he preached in the St Elisabeth Church on Lk. 12.16-21, the story of the Rich Fool.[1] Much of the material was re-used for the second volume of the *Andachtsbuch*, and dwelt on the dangers of using various kinds of riches other than for the glory of God. Thus scholars who pursued their learning for their own sake and parents who enjoyed bringing up their children purely for human reasons were censured. Possibly, de Wette was trying to console his own pecunious and lonely situation.

Then, by a totally unexpected stroke his domestic fortunes changed. On 25 October his wife Henriette died at the age of fifty-one. A sermon written to be preached on Acts 17.22-31 in Bern could not be delivered, and four days after the funeral, de Wette returned to Basel with his daughter Anna, who was now aged fourteen years and nine months. The undelivered sermon, incidentally, was one of de Wette's best, and showed how much better he was when he applied his philosophy to the text than when he tried simply to be edifying. His contrast between the uncertain graspings after truth on the part of the Greeks and the fullness of revelation in Christ was expressed most effectively.[2]

The reunion with Anna easily outweighed his grief at the death of Henriette; but initially it filled him with anxiety. In a letter to Ottilia Hirzel of Zürich, three days after his wife's death, he wrote:

> I am uneasy and anxious. How will it go when I take Anna to myself?. . . Wish me luck in the new life that I am now beginning.[3]

While all this was happening, de Wette was engaged in a theological controversy with Christian Friedrich Spittler.[4] Spittler, who was two years younger than de Wette, had been brought up in a pietist manse in Württemberg, and at the age of nineteen had come to Basel to work for the Deutsche Christentumsgesellschaft. He had had no academic or formal theological training, and he represented what we would call today a fundamentalist orthodoxy. He regarded any attempt to discuss sources or the historical reliability of the Bible as an attack on its authority and inspiration, and similarly required belief in traditional

1. *Predigten*, I, pp. 185ff. Cf. *Andachtsbuch*, II (Berlin, 1828), p. 256.
2. *Predigten*, II, pp. 6-40.
3. De Wette to Ottilia Hirzel, 28 Oct. 1825; De Wette Nachlass T8.
4. For what follows see J. Kober, *Christian Friedrich Spittler's Leben* (Basel, 1887), pp. 94-101; Lindt, 'C.F. Spittler und W.M.L. De Wette', pp. 363-84.

views of the authorship of biblical books. Jesus was the messiah foretold in the Old Testament, the divine son of God, whose words were
infallible and whose sacrificial death had brought forgiveness of sins.
During his years in Basel, until his death in 1867, Spittler founded
numerous agencies that are still active in Basel, and in particular the
Basel Mission, and the St Chrischona Mission. It is worth noting that,
whereas the latter mission has retained something of the outlook of its
founder, the Basel Mission has become much more liberal in its
outlook.

For Spittler, de Wette's arrival in Basel had been an unfortunate
and dangerous event, and Spittler's circle had been involved in the
attempt to block the appointment. In March 1823 Spittler had written
to a friend in Zürich about de Wette's 'heathen lectures', which students at the mission had been forbidden to attend. In one lecture
de Wette had said that Christ came into the world to play the role of
messiah. Spittler added:

> I shall remain an eternal enemy of such men until they are converted to
> Christ; for only in him [Christ] is salvation and blessing whereas in the
> accursed neology there is misery and destruction, which makes children
> and children's children unfortunate for time and eternity.[1]

During 1823 Spittler and his friends had been gathering objectionable
statements from de Wette's works, with special attention to a German
translation of parts of the 1813 Latin work *De morte Jesu Christi
expiatoria commentatio*. This writing, it will be remembered, with its
claim that neither in the Old Testament nor in Judaism nor in the
teaching of Jesus could belief in the expiatory death of the (or a)
messiah be found, but that this belief was the invention of the early
church, had already caused trouble for de Wette in Berlin. It was not
likely to endear him to Spittler, and by the end of 1823 he was ready
to send to de Wette a call from Christian citizens of Basel to renounce
the blasphemous utterances of this work.

For some reason, Spittler did not send this material to de Wette
until 29 September 1825, on which date de Wette received the address
of the Christian citizens dated 24 December 1823, Spittler's accom-
panying letter written on Christmas Day of 1823, and a new letter of
29 September 1825.[2] The last urged de Wette to consider those for

---

1. Kober, *Spittler*, p. 84.
2. See Staehelin, *Dewettiana*, p. 140.

whom the Holy Bible was the chief authority in matters of belief, to listen to them and to change his false opinions so that young men would not be led astray and denied the anchor for their faith.

The situation was ironical in several ways. De Wette had written *De morte Jesu Christi* at a time of great confidence in his philosophical convictions, and before the 'discovery' of 1817. Although the 'discovery' had not altered the actual conclusions in *De morte Jesu Christi*, it had placed them in a new context. De Wette's reverence for the person of Christ could convince a pietist such as Anna Schlatter of his sincerity, for all that de Wette still held that Christ's death was exemplary and not atoning. Further, de Wette had recently completed Volume I of the *Andachtsbuch* precisely in order to offer to readers something more 'spiritual' than bare historical criticism.

In a reply to Spittler, dated 3 October, de Wette defended himself by claiming that the book was not intended for general readers but for experts, that that was why he had written it in Latin, and that for Spittler to circulate a German version was mischievous. Experts did not find it so alarming, as witness the reaction of Alexander Stein, one of those who had suggested de Wette's appointment to Basel.[1]

Spittler replied five weeks later, on 11 November, one day after de Wette had been ordained to the ministry of the Reformed Church in Basel by its head (Antistes) Hieronymous Falkeisen.[2] Spittler felt that de Wette was on dangerous ground in dividing believers into experts and non-experts, with the latter excluded from certain types of theological discussion. Luther had put an end to the compulsive power of learned clerics. Further, it was not the case that experts would not be troubled by de Wette's writing. Many Basel theologians had been disturbed by the prospect of his appointment. Also, it was not only in *De morte Jesu Christi* that objectionable passages could be found. Spittler called once again for de Wette to renounce his dangerous views so that people known to Spittler would enjoy rest and peace. Attached to the letter was a long memorandum, probably written by Christian Zeller, which showed, among other things, how de Wette's critical conclusions were contradicted by the testimony of the Bible.

When de Wette received this material it was only just over a fortnight since his wife had died. If Spittler knew this, his timing was not distinguished by sensitivity. In the event, de Wette did the only

1. Staehelin, *Dewettiana*, pp. 140-41.
2. Staehelin, *Dewettiana*, p. 141.

sensible thing, which was to suggest a meeting between Spittler and himself. The positions of the two parties were so fundamentally different that continued correspondence was pointless. The meeting took place on Monday 21 November and lasted about three hours. Once again, de Wette was able to convince someone with fundamentally different views of the sincerity of his Christian convictions. We know from a minute written by Spittler after the meeting that they discussed offensive passages in the *De morte Jesu Christi* as well as the work of the missions, and we can surmise that de Wette spoke honestly about his devotion to Christ. At all events, the first steps were taken that were to lead to friendship between the two men. De Wette, as we shall see later, supported Spittler's concern for the liberation of the Greeks from Turkish rule, and three days after their meeting, de Wette wrote to Spittler, addressing him as 'esteemed friend' (*hochgeschätzer Freund!*).[1]

At the end of 1825 de Wette was able to write one of his most cheerful letters for a long time. He described to Amalie von Voigt his Christmas and New Year celebrations, the cultural circles to which he belonged, and, above all, his relationship with his daughter Anna. This had become the most important female relationship in his life.

I am to some extent father and lover at the same time.[2]

Anna's presence was also a new meeting-point for de Wette and Anna Margaretha, who was able to express her feelings towards de Wette by giving Anna expensive presents and by paying her a good deal of attention.

In January 1826 Basel was visited by James R. Reily in his capacity as ambassador to Europe on behalf of the Synod of the German Reformed Church in America.[3] This association of over 400 German-speaking congregations traced its constitution back to 1747, and to the missionary activity of Michael Schlatter of St Gallen. It had sent Reily to Europe to enlist support for the founding of its own seminary for the training of clergy. Reily's speaking and preaching made a considerable impact in Basel. The congregations of the German synod

---

1. See the Spittler-Archiv in the Staatsarchiv Basel.
2. De Wette to Amalie von Voigt, 28 Dec. 1825; De Wette Nachlass S (c) 15.
3. For what follows see W.M.L. de Wette, *Die deutsche theologische Lehranstalt in Nord-Amerika: Aktenstücke, Erläuterungen, Bitten* (Basel, 1826).

were widely scattered, seventy had no minister, and Reily had twice undertaken the role of *Reise-Prediger* (itinerant preacher) in 1822 and 1823. He was able to tell gripping stories of dangerous journeys through Indian territory, and in 1822 he had travelled over 1400 miles in three months and had preached forty-six times.

The main need of the synod was for a seminary, and an offer had been received from Dickenson College, Carlisle, Philadelphia, for a seminary to be founded there. This had been inaugurated in 1824, and the first professor, Ludwig Maier, had delivered his inaugural address on 6 April of that year. De Wette commended this cause to the Basel and other public in a book entitled *Die deutsche theologische Lehranstalt in Nord-Amerika*, whose preface was dated February 1826. De Wette had, of course, a personal interest in North America since his step-son Karl Beck had gone there, together with Karl Follen. But his high profile in the matter was also a demonstration of the understanding that he had reached with C.F. Spittler. Among the names of those who were listed at the end of the book to whom reference could be made, de Wette and Spittler were mentioned as representing Basel.[1]

On the other hand, this was a project which de Wette could accept without reservation. He was worried by the fact that Professor Maier, in his inaugural address, had had to appeal to the Bible and early Church history in order to justify the establishment of the seminary. In de Wette's view, the seminary needed no justification, and it was a bad sign that Maier had needed to provide some. De Wette saw in the appeal for help from German-speaking countries a heaven-sent opportunity. German-speaking scholarship in general and its theological scholarship in particular led the world. It was therefore ideally placed to help North America to achieve great advances in learning and education. In the field of theology, these would unite the various denominations in a common appreciation of the truth. Further, the enterprise would help to extend the use of German and the spread of German culture in North America. Thus de Wette could wholeheartedly support an enterprise that would further the cause of truth, and enable him to be seen to stand alongside the influential Spittler.

De Wette was to stand alongside Spittler later in 1826 when, in July, he chaired a meeting which established a 'Society for Ethical and

---

1. Schleiermacher is named for Berlin (pp. 76-77).

Religious Work among the Greeks'. The freedom struggle of the
Greeks against the Turks attracted much attention in Europe at the
time, and it was bound to be of interest to de Wette given his views on
freedom and democracy. For Spittler and his supporters, Greek independence opened up a new mission field, and thus the society was
founded to support this work.

In the August 1826 issue of the *Baslerische Mittheilungen* a writer
had criticized the society on two grounds, linguistic and ecclesiastical.
In what language would the society's workers give instruction, and
was it not ironical that non-Greeks would seek to awaken the Greek
church to true and active Christianity? De Wette replied to this criticism in the September issue of the same journal and again it is clear
that his support for the society was entirely consistent with his principles.[1] He argued that the Byzantine kingdom fell and the Greeks lost
their freedom because of the impoverishment of their spiritual life. It
followed that, with the attainment of independence, there was a need
for the renewal of spiritual life which, for de Wette, included
intellectual life. There was a need for the Bible to become known and
for it to be preached. Thus the aims of the society could be fully supported. It would contribute to the building up of the religious and
national life of the Greek nation after independence.

That de Wette played such a prominent role in the establishment of
the society surprised many in Basel. Rudolf Stier, who taught at the
Basel mission, confessed in a letter dated 13 August 1826 that he
found it difficult to think as well of de Wette as Spittler now did.[2] He
added that, although he fully sympathized with de Wette's personal
circumstances, he could not forget that de Wette had treated him in a
most unfriendly manner when they had come into contact with each
other. Alexandre Vinet wrote on 20 September:

> the people are not the slightest bit grateful to M. de Wette for an enterprise
> which puts him in contact with the work of the missions.[3]

All this goes to show that, for those who did not know de Wette, or
who had experienced only his brusque manner, he was to be judged by

1. 'Über den Zweck des Vereins zur sittlich-religiösen Einwirkung auf die
Griechen', *Baslerische Mittheilungen zur Förderung des Gemeinwohls* 18 (1826),
pp. 409-19.
2. Staehelin, *Dewettiana*, p. 142.
3. Vinet, *Lettres*, I, pp. 276-77.

his lack of adherence to orthodoxy. Those who had come to know him better found themselves respecting his sincerity while disagreeing with his theology. At the same time, we see de Wette moving more confidently into the life of the Basel community.

While he was taking a lead in these initiatives, de Wette was planning another course of public letures to be given in the winter of 1826–27. We first learn of this project from a letter to Amalie von Voigt, dated 10 July 1826. The letter implies that he had begun writing the lectures and states that, in eight days' time, he will be journeying to the Alps.[1]

These lectures would become one of de Wette's major works, the *Über die Religion*, which would appear in 1827.[2] We can easily surmise why it was that he decided to deliver a new set of public lectures. The first reason was financial; for, although he no longer had a wife and two houses to support, he was still very poorly paid. The second reason was that public lectures brought him hearers such as Anna Margaretha, whose adulation meant much to him. Thirdly, the lectures would give him another opportunity to state his theological position publicly, something that he probably wished to do following his rapprochement with Spittler.

In embarking on this major project (the published version of the twenty-one lectures runs to over 540 pages) de Wette was taking a risk with his health, which had not really recovered from the setbacks of the previous year. On 13 September he described to Amalie von Voigt a holiday that he had taken at the health resort of Gais, six kilometres to the north east of Appenzell. It had not been a successful holiday. He returned less well than when he went, did not really find any congenial companions, and then received the sad news of the sudden death of Ottilia Hirzel. Ottilia, who was only thirty-four, had been a travelling companion of de Wette in the Zürich area in 1825 and he had visited her on his way to Gais.[3]

In these circumstances, de Wette set about mounting a major series of public lectures and on 29 October he informed Amalie von Voigt that the lectures would begin on Saturday 4 November.[4] His request

---

1. De Wette to Amalie von Voigt, 10 Jul. 1826; De Wette Nachlass S (d) 4.
2. *Über die Religion, ihr Wesen, ihre Erscheinungsformen und ihren Einfluss auf das Leben* (Berlin, 1827).
3. De Wette to Amalie von Voigt, 13 Sept. 1826; De Wette Nachlass S (d) 5.
4. De Wette to Amalie von Voigt, 29 Oct. 1826; De Wette Nachlass S (d) 6.

for her to wish him luck did not bring the hoped-for result. On
26 December he wrote to say that the lectures were not as well
attended as he had hoped.[1]

The published version of the lectures gives no indication of
de Wette's health and other problems, and the work is a considerable
achievement. It is true that some of the material was not new. Thus,
the exposition of the nature of religion in Friesian philosophical terms
followed familiar lines, as did his account of the history of
Catholicism and Protestantism. Also, in his *Über Religion und
Theologie*, de Wette had discussed fetishism, which was to receive
detailed attention in the 1826–27 lectures. But there were new discussions and, in some cases, de Wette explained some of his established
views with greater clarity than hitherto.

At the time of preparing the lectures, the comparative study of
religions and of their history was attracting scholarly interest. Charles
de Brosses (1709–77) had published a book in 1760 on fetishism as the
primordial form of religion, and this theory had been refined and
elaborated by C. Meiners (1747–1810) in a general history of religions published in 1806–1807.[2] In 1824 Benjamin Constant (1767–
1830) had begun to publish a work in several volumes which argued
that feeling was both the essence of religion and the foundation of
human nature.[3] This position was, of course, similar to that of
de Wette. Another important work of this period was G.F. Creuzer's
study of the symbolism and mythology of ancient people, which
appeared from 1810–12.[4] De Wette's lectures were based upon the
latest research, combined with his distinctive viewpoint.

Basically, the argument of *Über die Religion* is that all religions are
an expression of the revelation of eternal truths that God has given to
every person's reason (*Vernunft*). There is thus no religion that is
completely false, even if there are many forms of religion that grossly
misunderstand the truth both in theory and in practice. For de Wette,

1.   De Wette to Amalie von Voigt, 26 Dec. 1826; De Wette Nachlass S (d) 7.

2.   C. de Brosses, *Du culte des dieux fétisches: Ou parallèle de l'ancienne religion
de l'Egypt avec la religion de Nigritie* (Paris, 1760); C. Meiners, *Allgemeine kritische Geschichte der Religionen* (Hannover, 1806–1807).

3.   B. Constant y de Rebecque, *De la religion considerée dans sa source, ses
formers et ses developpements* (6 vols.; Paris, 1824–31).

4.   G.J. Creuzer, *Symbolik und Mythologie der alten Völker, besonders der
Griechen* (4 vols.; Leipzig, 1810–12).

not surprisingly, the highest form of religion is philosophically-informed (German) Protestantism, and the purpose of the lectures is to describe the basis of religion, and to trace its development from fetishism to polytheism and nature religion, to its most complete manifestation in Christianity. In this development, important contributions are made by the Greeks and the Israelites.

The first seven lectures describe the nature of religion, and they begin with material that echoes de Wette's 1821 sermon in the St Katherine Church in Braunschweig. He criticizes those whose zeal for their own religion blinds them to the truth that there is in other religions; and he condemns those whose recognition of truth in other religions leads them to indifference about the competing claims of the various religions. What is called for is tolerance combined with the ability to discriminate the true from the false in religions.

It is clearly the de Wette who had recently publicly supported the work of Spittler's missions who is speaking here; but it is a de Wette who has not compromised his position. It is doubtful whether Spittler could have accepted de Wette's view that there was truth in all religions. On the other hand, de Wette could both accept this and support the need for missions to spread the complete knowledge of the truth of religion as known in Protestant Christianity.

De Wette next stresses that religion is not something derived from sense experience, but that it is given in reason. However, this familiar position is presented with freshness and vigour, and with some powerful statements. Thus he elegantly cuts the Gordian knot of the conflict between reason and revelation by declaring that the apprehension of religion that is given to human reason *is* a divine revelation, and he goes on to criticize those who believe that the divine revelation is given objectively.[1] They believe that miracles prove the truth of revelation; the truth is that only those who are illuminated by the inner revelation of reason can understand what miracles are. They believe that history can be a revelation; the truth is that only those who are illuminated by the inner revelation of reason can perceive the divine in the historical.

De Wette further elaborates his position by describing feeling (*Gefühl*) as the basis of religion, while placing this facility firmly in the area of intuitive reason and not in the area of understanding

---

1. *Über die Religion*, p. 40.

stimulated by external impressions. He credits Jacobi, Fries and Schleiermacher with having made the discovery that religious feeling was a distinctive category independent of sense-initiated understanding. He also says that Hamann had claimed this even earlier.[1] This meant that, even in regard to the life of Christ, it had to be said that it was the prior inner revelation that enabled people to see that Christ expressed the highest truth about God. It was not the case that the historical records in the Gospels about Christ created faith. These records were an indispensable introduction to faith in Christ and an occasion (*Veranlassung*) of faith in Christ; but, being historical records and belonging to the realm of understanding, they could not themselves produce faith. It was faith that recognized them for what they were, namely, a testimony to Christ as the highest truth about God.

In these lectures so far, we have what was probably de Wette's clearest exposition to date of how his distinction between reason and understanding affected his attitude to biblical criticism and to Christian belief and practice. Faith, as given in human reason, was prior to understanding, although the form in which faith was expressed, both in idea and in practice, was a matter for the understanding and thus was open to criticism. Supernaturalists and rationalists both made the same mistake of locating revelation in the area of the understanding. The former accepted it uncritically, the latter rejected it and were left only with morality. De Wette's approach alone could enable believers to be both critical and devout. It was also in harmony with what was best in recent philosophy .

The second, and main, part of *Über die Religion* comprises lectures 8 to 21, and is a comparative study of the origin and development of religion based on de Wette's views of the nature of religion. He begins with fetishism, as practised by peoples in the most elementary state of civilization, the hunter-gatherer stage.[2] Their worship of natural objects on which their life depends comes from an intuition (*Ahnung*) of the divine that is expressed crudely because the intuition of reason is overpowered by the overwhelming impression made upon them through their senses. Theirs is a sensual pantheism. The worship of a man-made fetish, in the form of a human representation of a natural object, is regarded by de Wette as an advance, because the worshipper

1. *Über die Religion*, p. 80.
2. *Über die Religion*, p. 190.

is less immediately dependent upon nature and is trying to grasp and express something through his own efforts. This is even more true where the man-made fetish has no resemblance to an object in the world of nature. Then the latter are the forerunners of fetishes in human form, which express the idea that divine powers are human-like. This is a step away from pantheism to the idea that the divine has personality.[1]

Because one of de Wette's aims is to show the effect of religion upon people's lives, he describes the religious practices of fetish worshippers. Their sacrifices express the important notions of thanksgiving and self-denial (*Entsagung*), while various rites of fasting, in preparation for manhood or high office, express dependence (*Abhängigkeit*) upon the divine.[2] De Wette also discusses the moral life of fetish-worshippers, which is only rudimentary because their social life is rudimentary; he also discusses their apprehensions of life after death. Although they have no priesthood, they have holy men whom de Wette calls shamans. Increasingly, these assume functions that are later found to be the exclusive property of priests, such as the right to offer sacrifices.[3]

De Wette's account of fetish worship was dependent for its actual information upon descriptions of contemporary so-called primitive peoples. For his account of the next stage of religion, nature religion, he concentrated upon ancient religion, especially that of the Egyptians and of texts from India.[4] In nature religion there were remnants of fetishism, as in the animal forms of gods in Egyptian religion. But nature religion had distinguished the elements of nature from each other, was practised in the context of agriculture and of its seasons, had developed a powerful priesthood, and had a more substantial view of life after death. It was also more morally developed, corresponding to its setting in more formal political structures.

In treating nature religion, de Wette expounded some of the Egyptian and Indian sagas, giving to the story of Isis and Osiris, for example, an interpretation in terms of the annual vegetation cycle.[5] Because these religions had written traditions, de Wette traced the

1. *Über die Religion*, pp. 201-203.
2. *Über die Religion*, pp. 210-11.
3. *Über die Religion*, pp. 228-31.
4. *Über die Religion*, pp. 247ff.
5. *Über die Religion*, pp. 261-67.

importance of these as transmitting religion, as well as the importance of the priesthood. De Wette also saw in these religions anticipations of important elements of more developed religions: first, symbols for belief, and doctrines and dogmas; second, symbols for worship and ethical instructions; third, social forms for belief and life. By symbols for belief de Wette meant objects such as the sun and by doctrines he meant myths and sacred sagas.

An entire lecture is devoted to the polytheism of the Greeks, and it is interesting, first, for the manner in which the subject is treated, and second, for the possible light that it throws upon de Wette's understanding of myths in his youthful *Beiträge* of 1806–1807.

To take this latter point first, it was argued in Chapter 2 that de Wette's view of myths was influenced by writings on this subject in literary circles of the late eighteenth century. Some of these saw myths as poetic and literary expressions of moral virtues, and thus demanded that myths be interpreted accordingly. In *Über die Religion*, this view comes strongly to the fore. De Wette believed that the Greek gods were mostly originally nature gods, but that this background had receded to vanishing point and that the gods had come to stand for virtues that humans could and should emulate:

> Achilles is the picture of youthful gallantry, Odysseus of thoughtful patience, Nestor of wisdom born of experience, Agamemnon of the value of kingship. The gods. . . are nothing more than noble human figures that come from the sacred darkness of the unseen world; but their appearance is uplifting indeed, and calls to mind the high dignity of humanity.[1]

De Wette praises Greek religion for its achievements of literature, art and drama and, in particular, its concern for beauty. Also, it did not develop a priesthood, and it was ever open to receiving gods and ideas from other nations. This strength was also a weakness, in that Greek religion never developed a definite theology and was thus indifferent to whether an aspect of religion was true or not. This was why, for all their achievements, the Greeks were not to be the supreme benefactors to the human race in things religious. It would fall to the Judaeo-Christian tradition to fulfil this role; but before dealing with Israel, de Wette devotes a lecture to Roman religion and to Zoroastrianism, which latter he strongly commends because of the way it teaches the importance of human participation in the struggle of good to over-

---

1. *Über die Religion*, p. 381.

come evil. It is a thoroughly moral religion with strong emphasis upon freedom. It has a developed view of afterlife, and a hope in the ultimate reconciliation of the dualistic powers whose endless struggle lies at the heart of its world view. It has a transcendent view of God. It stands 'closer to the truth than any other religious teaching of the ancient world'.[1] Its major failing was its intolerance towards other faiths, and that it forced subject peoples to accept it. Religion could not properly be a matter of necessity as opposed to free choice.

In commending Israelite religion, de Wette stressed first its exalted idea of God as the one on whom the world depended, and whose character was seen more clearly than in any other ancient religion. It also combined with this sense of transcendence a belief in the nearness and approachability of God, who was the protector of the tribe. The religion of Abraham is described in glowing terms. He was descended from a line that had preserved something of the original, childlike trust in God that the human race had once had, and had remained free from fetishism, nature worhip or idolatry. He had a future hope for the expansion of his people, and his religion was profoundly moral. Its only deficiency was lack of belief in a future life.[2]

At first sight, it seems that de Wette had moved a long way here from his treatment of the patriarchal narratives in the *Beiträge* of 1806–1807. Here, he is taking them at face value as historically reliable. But the problem may be more apparent than real. De Wette was always impressed with the 'inner' characteristics of narratives, and no doubt felt that the Abraham stories exhibited a type of religion that must be authentic even if the stories as we now have them mediated the spirit of Hebrew religion to the Israelites of the period of the monarchy. The account of the religion of the patriarchs was also important because it paved the way for the treatment of Moses, who fashioned something new from his combination of an Egyptian priestly-instructed upbringing, with his share in the religion of the patriarchs. Thus Moses gave to his people a theocratic state with a moral constitution based upon a cult freed from idolatry, nature worship or superstition. Other contributions were made later by the prophets and the psalmists, who contributed inspiration and personal piety respectively. After the return from exile, Hebrew religion was

1. *Über die Religion*, p. 402.
2. *Über die Religion*, pp. 413-15.

replaced by Judaism. This, de Wette describes in familiar terms.[1]

In his treatment of Christianity de Wette gives us at least one surprise, which is an apparent affirmation of Christ's resurrection. He
describes how Christianity as preached by Christ—a spiritual kingdom
of love and freedom—fulfils not only Judaism but the other religions
as well. The intimations of truth that they contain receive full expression in Christ. In particular, the ingredient of life after death receives
new confirmation:

> he [Jesus] taught people to know God as a loving father and he under-
> stood resurrection in a more spiritual sense than his contemporaries.
> Further, the hope of immortality received confirmation through his own
> wonderful resurrection, something that it had previously lacked.[2]

As we shall see, de Wette affirmed the resurrection in various subse-

---

1. *Über die Religion*, pp. 432ff.
2. *Über die Religion*, p. 445. The following points can be made about de Wette's
views on the Resurrection. In the first edition of the *Biblische Dogmatik* (1813),
p. 219, de Wette stated simply that, unexpectedly for Jesus and his disciples, the
cross was not fatal (*tödtlich*) and Jesus showed himself again to the astonished
disciples. In the second edition (1818), and after de Wette's 'discovery' of 1817, the
section (para. 200 in 1st edn, para. 224 in 2nd edn) is re-written thus: 'the shattered
faith of the disciples was restored when they found their Master's grave empty, and
when they saw in his own appearance to them confirmation of the news that he had
risen'. The note to this paragraph in the second edition shows that de Wette was
worried about the implication of the Gospel accounts that Jesus' appearance had been
a physical not a spiritual appearance. He put this down to the fact that the Gospel
accounts were based upon tradition, i.e. they were incorrect in asserting a physical
appearance. The same problem is addressed in *Theodor*, II, pp. 185ff., where
Theodor (de Wette) is in dialogue with a well-known theologian (Schleiermacher).
Theodor is worried by his teacher's assertion that Christ's risen body was physical
but transfigured; this does not make it clear whether it was material or not, and if it
was material then it would have had to die. To Theodor's statement that he will
understand the Resurrection as a symbol, the teacher replies that this will deny the
historic faith of the church, and that membership of the church implies acceptance of
a shared understanding of feeling (*Gefühl*) articulated through historical statements.
How far this satisfied de Wette is not clear. This whole section in *Theodor* together
with the following section is important for understanding de Wette's view of his
differences with Schleiermacher. De Wette's view of the Resurrection as articulated
in his commentaries on the New Testament (see below pp. 244-45) seems to have
been that he accepted that it must have happened but remained uncertain about most
of its details. Also, de Wette probably believed in the Resurrection because he
believed in Christ, and not vice versa.

quent writings, even if he held that we could know little about it as a historical event.

In his treatment of Catholicism, de Wette criticizes its development of a priesthood and its compromising of monotheism through the worship of Mary and the saints. This was the occasion for the rise of Islam with its uncompromising monotheism. De Wette sees Catholicism as almost a superior version of the religions of Egypt and India; but he regards it also as the necessary preparation for the rise of Protestantism in which Christianity is to attain its purest form.[1]

De Wette's treatment of Protestantism brings no surprises, and his final chapter, on the relations between church and state, adds nothing to his previous views. He defends the rights of the canton of Basel to exclude Catholics, Jews and Anabaptists from full citizenship.

Taken as a whole, *Über die Religion* is a considerable achievement. It is executed with intellectual clarity and rigour, its argumentation is impressive, and it exhibits itself as the work of a mature, confident and gifted scholar. The verdict of Alexandre Vinet is not overdone, in spite of his reservations about de Wette's approach:

> I cannot but admit the talent, the knowledge and the fine style of this man who is a writer of the first rank as well as a celebrated scholar.[2]

The achievement was all the greater, given the poor health that de Wette had experienced in 1826 and his continuing financial worries.

Another work which had occupied de Wette in 1826 and earlier was his New Testament Introduction, which appeared in 1826 as the second volume of his *Lehrbuch der historisch-kritischen Einleitung in die Bibel Alten und Neuen Testaments*. Its foreword was dated 18 August 1826. In fact, in 1817, this volume had been promised for Easter 1819, and de Wette had been chided by Schleiermacher for not completing it.[3] De Wette seems also to have been reluctant to finish it, suspecting, rightly, that it would stimulate further opposition to him in Basel.[4] However, its appearance was part of a process which saw

1. *Über die Religion*, p. 479.
2. Vinet, *Lettres*, I, p. 337.
3. Staehelin, *Dewettiana*, p. 128. Schleiermacher to de Wette, March 1823: 'Wann wird dann aber Deine neutestamentliche Einleitung erscheinen? Sieh doch diese Schuld als recht dringend an. . . '
4. Staehelin, *Dewettiana*, p. 32, indicates that, on 29 September 1828, a commission set up to investigate complaints about de Wette's lectures on New Testament introduction recommended that he be sent 'a brotherly communication'.

him moving decisively from being an Old Testament scholar to devoting to the New Testament that time allocated to biblical studies.

In 1827 de Wette's domestic front was disturbed by the illness of his daughter Anna, and there was more than a hint of romance as the possibility presented itself of marriage to a woman twenty-five years de Wette's junior. Unfortunately, we do not know her name or her circumstances, but it appears that she was urged to consider marrying de Wette, but rejected the idea; de Wette responded philosophically.[1] In the midst of all this, he was working on later volumes of the Luther letters and the second volume of the *Andachtsbuch*, was preaching occasionally, was preparing a new edition of *Theodor* and now planning a second novel, *Heinrich Melchthal*, which appeared in 1829.[2] As early as 1823 de Wette had contemplated writing a second novel, one that would set out what de Wette regarded as the ideal calling and education of a citizen.[3] That he now produced another long novel is a tribute to his industry.

Heinrich Melchthal has been much less read than *Theodor*, and although Handschin, for one, regards the characterization to be superior to what is found in *Theodor*, the neglect of the second novel is not surprising.[4] Whereas *Theodor* is clearly semi-autobiographical, and is written out of de Wette's own struggle from doubt to faith, *Heinrich Melchthal* is autobiographical only in regard to the relationship between the hero and Euphosyne; and this autobiographical aspect was not clearly established until the present work.[5] Stripped of autobiographical interest, *Heinrich Melchthal* cannot claim to be great literature; it is too obviously didactic for that. It must also be questioned whether de Wette's ideal for a Christian, educated Swiss citizen is realistic.

Basically, the novel describes how Heinrich, who is sent from Switzerland (presumably Basel) to Germany to learn commerce,

This, however, was not done. See later in this chapter for de Wette's views on aspects of New Testament introduction in the discussion of his commentary on the complete New Testament.

1. De Wette to Amalie von Voigt, 17 Sept. 1827; De Wette Nachlass S (d) 11.
2. *Heinrich Melchthal, oder Bildung und Gemeingeist: Eine belehrende Geschichte* (Berlin, 1829).
3. Staehelin, *Dewettiana*, p. 132.
4. Handschin, *De Wette als Prediger*, p. 124.
5. See above, pp. 43-44.

receives an education in literature, philosophy (Fries), and biblical theology (that of de Wette), before he marries Cölestine and becomes a prominent business man. De Wette thereby expresses his view of the relation between church and state. The two should complement each other in producing citizens whose prowess in commerce is informed by sensitivity to literature and art, and who have a mature, philosophically-informed Christian faith.

From the context in which the novel was written, it is noteworthy that, in his adventures, Heinrich fights in Greece in the struggle for the freedom of Greece from Turkey. There are adverse comments about pietist Christianity. De Wette thus both justifies his support of the *Griechenverein* in Basel and indicates his theological distance from Basel pietists such as Spittler.

The period 1820–34 was to be troubled and significant for de Wette. It was the time of the civil war between Basel-Stadt and Basel-Land, there was the possibility of appointments for de Wette in Strasbourg, Leipzig and Marburg, and de Wette married a third time and decided to stay in Basel for the remainder of his life. This troubled period would usher in the last fourteen years of his life—a period of undiminished literary and scholarly activity.

The first difficulty was the weather, in that the winter of 1829–30 was the coldest in Basel for 100 years.[1] Frost was experienced on 16 November 1829, and there were then some warmer days towards the end of the month before the cold really set in. From 4 December to 8 February average temperatures were well below zero. On 30 January the maximum and minimum temperatures were minus eight and minus thirteen degrees centigrade, while on 3 February they were minus twelve and minus twenty-one degrees. The extreme cold was followed by a mild spring which bore the scars of the winter. There was then an unpleasant summer with destructive floods and an outbreak of cholera. Schleiermacher, who visited Basel in September 1830, complained of the changeable weather that he was experiencing on his journey[2] and found his visit spoiled by the presence of cholera.[3]

The weather was not the only problem. The July revolution in Paris in 1830 generated shock waves that were felt all over Europe. 'From

1. *Baslerische Mittheilungen* 5 (1830), p. 113.
2. Schleiermacher to de Wette, 8 Sept. 1830, in *Aus Schleiermachers Leben*, IV, pp. 401-402.
3. Staehelin, *Dewettiana*, p. 33 n. 91.

the Iberian peninsula to the Russian frontier, social conflicts and political demonstrations threatened public order.'[1] In so far as Basel was
affected, the troubles took the form of a demand by the landowners of
Basel-Land for more equality between the city and the *Land*. The
land-owners were under represented in the Basel parliament in relation to their numbers and the taxes that they paid. Further, they
resented having to support the university to the extent that they did,
given that they derived little benefit from it. Their grievances were
expressed at a meeting in the village of Bubendorf on 18 October
1830. On 20 December the Basler Rat decided that there could be no
lowering of indirect taxes.[2]

At the end of the year, de Wette preached a sermon on Heb. 13.14.
He referred to the appalling weather and then went on to the political
crisis:

> One throne fell and another rose. . .even our fatherland is still in the pro
> cess of change. . .war and rumours of war disturb the tranquillity of
> peace and the torch of disunity threatens to set light to Europe.[3]

He went on to criticize those who wanted to alter things so that they
did not have to contribute so much to the common good. It was a
Christian duty to seek the common good, and not to complain about
the expensiveness of institutions devoted to ennobling and fulfilling the
common good. De Wette concluded by re-stating his view of the
relation between church and state:

> The kingdom of Christ is heavenly, but it must begin here below; and not
> just in the church, but also in the state. . . The state is the outer periphery
> [*Umfang*] of the church.[4]

Within days of this sermon, on 4 January 1831, an ultimatum was
brought by two to three thousand armed men, demanding that there
should be a new parliament representative of the population. On the
same day, the people of Basel were addressed in St Martin's Church
by Pastor Daniel Kraus. A militia was organized in which de Wette
enlisted. In a letter to Amalie von Voigt of 13 January 1831, he

1. Sheehan, *German History*, p. 604.
2. For this, and what follows, see A. Staehelin, *Universität Basel*, ch. 8 : 'Die
Universität in den Dreissigwirren'.
3. *Predigten*, III, p. 20.
4. *Predigten*, III, p. 30.

describes how the militia had been called out at three in the morning, and how the inhabitants of the city were resolute in their opposition to the unreasonable demands of the land-owners. Given de Wette's position as presented in *Heinrich Melchthal* it is quite understandable that he believed it to be his duty to defend the city. One of the consequences of its defeat could be the closing of the university so vital to the education of the public.[1]

However, not everyone agreed with de Wette on this point. Already in 1829–30 there had been demands for the establishment of a single university for Switzerland and for the closure of the rest. De Wette had defended the continuance of his own institution.[2] Two Basel professors who sided with the opposition were Wilhelm Snell, professor of law, and Ignaz Paul Vital Troxler, professor of philosophy.[3] In the first instance, they were suspected of being Basel correspondents of the *Appenzeller Zeitung*, a journal hostile to Basel-Stadt. Further, Troxler was rector of the university and argued that students who enlisted in the militia should come under his authority and not that of the city. There was a strong suspicion that Troxler would use such students against the city. On 15 January he began to be investigated, whereupon he refused to undertake any university or rectorial duties. Since the university could not function without a rector, a group of professors including de Wette, Hagenbach and Jung pressed the Kuratel for the appointment on an interim rector. The application succeeded, and professor Gerlach was appointed. On 9 May, Troxler was cleared of the suspicions against him, and he proceeded to write articles denouncing his colleagues, including de Wette. However, he did not resume his duties, and on 9 June he was finally deposed from the rectorship.

In the run up to these troubles, and during their first phase, de Wette's main work was the preparation of a new edition of his translation of the Bible. This involved translating those parts that Augusti had undertaken for the first edition, as well as revising the rendering of the poetic books that he had made for the first edition. These now had a less 'raw' and a more poetic form in the German

---

1. Staehelin, *Dewettiana*, p. 151.
2. See de Wette's 'Basels Hochschule und die Schweiz', in *Neue Zürcher Zeitung* 1 (1830); and *Allgemeine Schulzeitung* (1830), pp. 257ff.
3. See de Wette to Fries, 7 Mar. 1831, in Staehelin, *Dewettiana*, p. 152.

version. The second edition appeared in 1831 with a preface dated in March of that year.

On 20 August 1831 trouble flared up again. There was a fresh uprising in Basel-Land, on which day Troxler left Basel; he was dismissed on 21 September and, from 1834, held a professorship in Bern. The uncertainties dragged on through 1832 into 1833. On Sunday 12 May 1833 (*Rogate*), with the prospect of renewed fighting between Basel-Stadt and Basel-Land looming ominously, de Wette preached on Jn 16.23—'whatever you shall ask the father in my name, he will give it'. How did this text relate to the situation faced by Basel-Stadt? Prayer in the name of Jesus was prayer designed to further the cause of Jesus; and de Wette had no doubt that Basel-Stadt's stand was in harmony with the cause of Jesus. Thus,

> we may implore God at this time that he will protect our city against the havoc of that destructive plague, and spare the lives of our loved ones and friends, as well as our own.[1]

He added, however, that although all prayers were heard (*gehört*) they were not all granted (*erhört*). On a later Sunday, with the storm-clouds darkening, de Wette preached on 1 Pet. 5.6 ('humble yourselves under the mighty hand of God, that he may exalt you in due time'). He suggested that God's hand was to be seen in the troubled events of the time, and that God was calling on Basel-Stadt to wage its unequal struggle, which so far had met with so little outward success. But he drew on examples from the Bible (Elijah, Jeremiah and Christ) to show that God's servants were obliged to suffer and that suffering was part of the Christian vocation. He commended the stand taken by Basel-Stadt:

> What would have happened to our good city if our government, out of a false love of peace, had surrendered to the mercy of impertinent arrogance? We would now be groaning under an unworthy authority [*Herrschaft*].[2]

On 3 August 1833, the worst happened. Basel-Stadt was defeated by Basel-Land, and the city was then occupied by the troops of the Swiss Confederation pending a settlement. It was decided that Basel-Stadt and Basel-Land should be separated and that the property of the university should be divided between them. Fortunately, this latter decree

1. *Predigten*, III, p. 92.
2. *Predigten*, III, p. 114.

was not to be carried out in that precise form.

It was in this situation that a real possibility of a move for de Wette from Basel to Germany or France presented itself. The first intimation was in a letter to de Wette from Hermann Hupfeld of Marburg, dated 9 July 1831:

> Last winter there was a lot of talk about you here. Among the public matters with which enlivened minds concerned themselves was naturally discussion about what should be done for the improvement of the university. For this there went up a general cry from the students and from there to the citizens and others, that you should be invited here.[1]

Hupfeld went on to say that the outcome would depend on the new budget, but that an invitation was a real possibility and one that he would try to help bring about.

So far as we can tell, de Wette did not reply to this letter. The strain of events was beginning to affect him. On 15 December he wrote to Amalie von Voigt that he was suffering from nervous stress, and he voiced his anxieties about the state of affairs in Basel and Switzerland.[2] The situation was not helped by a renewed attack on de Wette from the *Appenzeller Zeitung* of 4 January 1832.[3] The complaint of this newspaper was that de Wette was supporting the reactionary citizens of Basel against the democratic wishes of Basel-Land. This behaviour was contrasted with de Wette's excerpt from Jean Paul's essay on Charlotte Corday in his letter to Frau Sand, and with sections from his public lectures on ethics in Basel.[4]

It must have been with some relief that de Wette received a letter from Hupfeld, dated 1 February 1832, that seemed to hold out a real prospect of an invitation to Marburg. Hupfeld wrote:

> I shall soon be given authority [*in den Stand gesetzt sein*] to send an *official* invitation to you as dean of the theological faculty for the current year.[5]

Hupfeld went on to say that, although official discussions about the

---

1. R. Hupfeld, 'W.M. Leberecht de Wette und Hermann Hupfeld: Ein Briefwechsel aus theologisch und politisch bewegter Zeit', *Neue Zeitschrift für systematische Theologie und Religionsphilosophie* 5 (1963), pp. 64-67.

2. De Wette to Amalie von Voigt, 15 Dec. 1831; De Wette Nachlass S (f) 6.

3. Staehelin, *Dewettiana*, pp. 153-54.

4. See *Vorlesungen über die Sittenlehrer*, II.1, pp. 317-18.

5. Hupfeld, 'Briefwechsel', p. 68.

budget for the university were dragging on, he had been to Kassel (the capital of Kurhessen) and had privately obtained authority to ask de Wette under what conditions he would accept an invitation to Marburg. He accepted that Marburg was not a first-rank university, but said that theology students numbered 120–130 and could easily rise to 200.

De Wette answered by return on 6 February.[1] He apologized for not replying to previous correspondence (the translation of the Bible is given as an excuse) and expressed his gratitude for the real possibility of the invitation to Marburg. He stated that, in between times, he had had a very indirect enquiry from Leipzig as to whether he would be prepared to go there, but, although such a post would be more prestigious than one in Marburg, it was not a specific offer. If he left Basel, it would upset his friends there, especially those who had enabled him to become a Swiss citizen in 1829. However, his duty was to himself to seek a better sphere for his work, and thus he would gladly accept the invitation to Marburg. At the end of the letter, de Wette confessed that he knew very little about the Marburg theological faculty and its personnel.

The lukewarm tone of this reply to what seemed to be an answer to his prayers suggests that de Wette was beginning to be more hopeful about the future in Basel. In a letter to David Hess just over a week later he spoke of the election of Burkhardt as mayor of Basel, and regarded it as 'a sign of the good spirit that predominates in Basel and the pledge of a better direction of communal affairs', even though its implications for education were still not known. He was thus pleased that it seemed as though there was a future for him in Basel, although it was too early to be sure. He speaks of Leipzig, of which he knows nothing further, and of Marburg, from where he definitely awaits an invitation. If he stays, it would be out of gratitude to Basel for the opportunity of work that it had given him.[2]

However, and typically, de Wette was in several minds. If in writing to Hess he seemed to prefer to stay in Basel, he was still entertaining real hopes about Marburg, as a letter to Hupfeld of 19 March 1832 shows.[3] In this letter we have the first mention of a possible move to Strasbourg. This last possibility was the idea of

1. Hupfeld, 'Briefwechsel', pp. 69-70.
2. De Wette to David Hess, 14 February 1832; De Wette Nachlass E3.
3. Hupfeld, 'Briefwechsel', pp. 70-71.

L. Verny, and our fullest information about it comes from the unpublished autobiographical *Erinnerungen* of the Strasbourg Old Testament scholar Eduard Reuss.[1] Reuss indicates that he was let into the secret about a position for de Wette, a move about which he had some reservations, but which he welcomed on the whole. The idea was for a well-salaried special post in New Testament literature to be created until such time as an official position could be offered. In apparent disagreement with Reuss's memory is de Wette's statement in his letter to Hupfeld of 19 March that he had received an invitation from the rector of the Strasbourg Academy to fill the position of Isaak Haffner. De Wette was attracted by the salary (250 Carolines) and free accommodation. On the other hand, he stated to Hupfeld that he would rather go to Germany. Reuss hints that the matter was not entirely straightforward at the Strasbourg end since the Catholic authorities would want Protestant assurances about de Wette, which might be difficult to obtain.

The following day, de Wette was writing to Amalie von Voigt to say that the Leipzig possibility was the one that he preferred, and that he understood that the theological faculty there was willing to support him, although he had not received an outstanding recommendation. To have to go to France would be bitter. He also added that he had been ill now for some weeks, first with a cough and later with diarrhoea.[2]

On 2 April, Hupfeld wrote that although the education minister was interested in de Wette's possible move to Marburg, questions were being raised about the fateful letter to Frau Sand and its implications for de Wette's suitability. An enquiry from Hupfeld to a member of the ministry had brought the reply that:

> it would be hazardous [*bedenklich*] to invite de Wette because he had written the well-known letter of comfort. All attempts to wipe away this semblance of blame have not yet had any success.[3]

Hupfeld added that the cry had also gone up that de Wette was a

---

1. J.M. Vincent, *Leben und Werk des frühen Eduard Reuss* (Göttingen, Vandenhoeck & Ruprecht, 1990), p. 170. See also for what follows Reuss's own unpublished *Erinnerungen*, III, pp. 169-71. This material is in the library of the Séminaire Protestant de Strasbourg. I am indebted to Dr. Vincent for providing me with a photocopy of the relevant passage.

2. De Wette to Amalie von Voigt, 20 Mar. 1832; de Wette Nachlass S (f) 8.

3. Hupfeld, 'Briefwechsel', p. 72.

rationalist. On the other hand, he was still determined to do all that he could to further de Wette's cause in Marburg.

De Wette again answered by return, and this time it was a very long and angry letter.[1] Once again, he protested at the fact that he was to be judged not on his published work, but on a private communication whose purpose was to comfort a grieving mother, and which clearly stated that Sand's act was wrong. He cited the support he had received in Braunschweig and from the theological faculties in Leipzig and Jena. In *Heinrich Melchthal* he had opposed all revolutionary movements, and his main principle had always been reform not revolution. Indeed, he complained about the unlimited freedom of the press in Switzerland, and how it could be misused. The attacks upon him in the *Appenzeller Zeitung* were no doubt in his mind. He also reacted angrily to the charge of being a rationalist and insisted that his sermons were regarded by Swiss Methodists as evangelically pure, that they did not contradict what he taught in the academy, and that all the central doctrines of Christianity featured in his theological system. He professed to be a follower of Schleiermacher. On the other hand, he was quick to point out where he thought that Schleiermacher was wrong, and he also stated that traditional church interpretations of the central dogmas of Christianity were based upon false logic.

Five days later he was penning another long letter setting out his ethical position. It ended with an interesting postscript:

> I have said above: I want to sail with both winds [i.e. Marburg and Strasbourg]. Do not take this as equivocation. I *cannot* give up Strasbourg and must let my man there operate, because I *must* leave Basel if I am not to succumb to despondency. My preference is for Marburg if the conditions are tolerable and the decision does not come too late.[2]

Less than a month later, the Marburg affair was settled. On 7 May Hupfeld wrote to say that de Wette would not receive an invitation. The government of Kurhessen needed the good will of Prussia for its survival, and could not, therefore, risk the appointment. Hupfeld tried to sweeten the pill by saying that it was the political crisis of the times that had counted against de Wette, and that had the whole matter been acted upon six months earlier, when the faculty first made the suggestion, all would have been well. The embarrassed Hupfeld ended

1. Hupfeld, 'Briefwechsel', pp. 73-79.
2. Hupfeld, 'Briefwechsel', p. 82.

with a plea that de Wette would not withdraw his good will from him, and would remain in touch by correspondence.[1] De Wette did not reply until January 1833.

As the summer continued, de Wette's mind must have turned more and more to Basel, assuming that his outburst to Hupfeld about the necessity of leaving represented what he really felt. In all probability he regarded every eventuality, staying or moving, as undesirable. Marburg was now out, as was presumably Leipzig. Strasbourg remained, but there were still difficulties.

However, there was a new development in the offing. We do not know exactly when Sophie von Mai, the widow of a pastor in Bern, re-entered de Wette's life. He had known her for some time, for her maiden name was Streckeisen, and we know from a letter dated 5 August 1824 that de Wette had connections with this family. He had been called in shortly before writing that letter to give pastoral comfort following a suicide in the Streckeisen family.[2] Wiegand adds that de Wette had met Sophie at the Burkhardt villa (presumably St Margarethen) and had given religious instruction to her elder daughter Emma.[3] Some time in 1832 (Wiegand says autumn, but it was almost certainly earlier) Sophie returned from Bern to live in Basel, accompanied by her seven-year-old daughter Clara. The prospect of a third marriage and a chance to achieve domestic happiness presented itself. This was a significant factor in whether or not de Wette should leave Basel; for if he did marry Sophie it was likely that she would want to stay in Basel, where her mother still lived.

De Wette, as usual, was in several minds. During August of 1832 he went with his daughter Anna for a cure at Baden. He was also accompanied by the twenty-year-old Sophie Frey, daughter of the Basel Bürgermeister, who was given into his care for the occasion.[4] He was very taken by Sophie Frey, and after they had parted, and de Wette had arrived at Seengen on the Hallwilersee, he wrote a very long letter to her on receipt of a letter from her. It ended with as strong a statement of affection as convention allowed:

1. Hupfeld, 'Briefwechsel', pp. 82-83.
2. Staehelin, *Dewettiana*, p. 136, and see above, p. 205.
3. Wiegand, *De Wette*, p. 82.
4. De Wette to Amalie von Voigt, 6 Sept. 1832, in Staehelin, *Dewettiana*, p. 156.

> Live well my dear, good Sophie, and allow me to say to you what you
> already know, that I have felt an inner attraction [*Zuneigung*] and
> friendship for you, which time will never be able to extinguish.[1]

The sincerity of these remarks can be confirmed by the fact that,
among the very last letters that de Wette wrote before his death, were
some intimate ones to Sophie Jung-Frey, as she had become.[2]

But in this same letter, de Wette mentions the one thing, marriage,
that is missing from his old, joyless life, and speaks of his dear female
friend who wants to return to him. He then goes on to say that she
does not have the charm (*Reiz*) that immediately grips one, and he
speaks of an emptiness and coldness of heart that seems to come with
age. He contrasts this with the liveliness of his youth.[3] Reading
between the lines, he is saying that he would much prefer to have
friendship, even married life, with a younger rather than an older
women; and it is noteworthy that Sophie later married de Wette's
colleague Carl Gustav Jung, who was eighteen years her senior.

On 29 December, de Wette wrote to tell Amalie von Voigt of his
engagement to Sophie von Mai. Understandably, it was not an easy
letter to write, and de Wette said little about his intended third wife
beyond that she was an old friend whose mother Amalie had met, that
she had an income, that Anna had inquired whether she would accept a
proposal, and that Anna knew her elder daughter well.[4] To Reimer, in
a letter of 8 February 1833 cited by Wiegand, de Wette was more
forthcoming:

> I hope that I shall be really happy with my dear Sophie. She is no longer
> young and could be the mother of my children, which fact alone is appro-
> priate. . . She has a good and loving character and has understanding and
> education. Her younger daughter, Clara, is a loveable child, who will add
> much to my happiness. She is not rich, but sufficiently well off that, with

1. De Wette to Sophie Frey, University Library Basel; Nachlass Jung 14, 1.
2. Nachlass Jung 14, 3-10.
3. Nachlass Jung 14.1:

    > sie hat nicht den Reiz der sogleich anzieht und festhält, und immer bleibt das Herz dabei
    > leer, das mir bei kalten leeren Menschen mit dem Alter alt und kalt wird und seine
    > Ansprüche aufgibt. Ich habe mich in jenen Tagen des frohsinnes, der selbst zu meiner
    > grossen Freude wenigstens auf Augenblicke meine Anna anlächelte, von Ihrem
    > jugendlich heiteren Wesen umspielt, in einenlieblichen Traum hinein täuschen lassen;
    > der Traum ist zeronnen. . .

4. Staehelin, *Dewettiana*, p. 158.

her, I shall enjoy a comfortable situation and have about the same extra income as I have previously had to earn from writing.[1]

Anyone familiar with de Wette's descriptions of ideal women will feel that his references to Sophie von Mai are slightly restrained. Although it would be unfair to say that de Wette was marrying her for her money, this aspect cannot be overlooked. Ever since his dismissal from Berlin in 1819 he had had to struggle financially. In Basel he had relied upon public lectures to supplement his income; the future arrangements for the university were uncertain. Whatever his hopes for a loving relationship for the remainder of his life, he would now have added financial security, and this played no little part in his decision to stay in Basel.[2]

On 12 January 1833 he replied at long last to Hupfeld, detailing the reasons why he was not going to Strasbourg, and speaking of his engagement:

> I am now a bridegroom and shall stay in Basel for ever. Live well Germany! You have rejected me and I know that I must comfort myself.[3]

The die was cast, and on the same day that he wrote to Hupfeld, de Wette bought a house from Alexandre Vinet. It was Brunngässlein 11, in an area today behind the Kunstmuseum in Basel. A coloured print of 1845 shows the area to be beautifully laid out with trees and gardens, and de Wette would have had a pleasant walk to the university through the city gate, along the Rittergasse and past the cathedral. In a letter to Amalie von Voigt of 29 May 1833 he described the house, a three-storey house with a wing. Anna and Clara would have a room each on the ground floor, the reception rooms were on the first floor, and de Wette's bedroom and study were on the second floor.[4] Thus de Wette's personal future was settled; what of the university?

1. Wiegand, *De Wette*, p. 83.
2. On de Wette's income, Wiegand (*De Wette*, p. 90 n. 1) says that it was initially 2,400 francs, which was later doubled. His wife's income and that from his writings increased his income to 10,000 francs. In the biography of J.T. Beck, it is noted 'Es kam öfters vor, dass De W. aus den Stürmen seiner nicht eben lieblichen Häuslichkeit zu dem unweit von ihm wohnenden Kollegen floh'. See B. Riggenbach, *Johann Tobias Beck, ein Schriftgelehrter zum Himmelreich gelehrt* (Basel, 1888), pp. 203-204.
3. Hupfeld, 'Briefwechsel', pp. 83-84.
4. De Wette to Amalie von Voigt, 29 May 1833; de Wette Nachlass S (h) 4. The year has been wrongly read as 1831 in the numbering in the Staatsarchiv Weimar.

The original decision, that the property of the university should be divided between the city and the *Land*, proved to be impossible in practice, quite apart from the undesirability of the proposal. Instead, the city kept the university and became wholly responsible for it, and made a payment to the *Land* of 331,451 francs. At the university's reopening under the new arrangements, de Wette, as rector, issued a noble call to the citizens of Basel to see the university not as an unnecessary drain on public expenditure, but as an investment on which Basel's future depended. Basel's hope lay in an educated citizenry that would appreciate the things of the mind and spirit.[1] Some, for example Alexandre Vinet, felt that the hope was false.[2] He was to be proved wrong. In the words of Andreas Staehelin, 'the university did not die; just the opposite. Supported ideally and materially by the citizenry as never before in the history of the city, it quickly regained its strength.' Staehelin goes on to describe how the danger which threatened the university made it a cause close to the hearts of many citizens in a way which had not been the case before.[3]

It seems as though de Wette's troubles were now over; but this was not so. Leaving aside the attack upon him in 1833 by a 'Bible-believing clergyman', an attack to which de Wette's colleagues Hagenbach and Fischer replied,[4] there was the case of the *Grey Man*.[5] The *Grey Man* was a journal edited by Ernst Joseph Gustav de Valenti, a Basel resident who, in November 1832, had failed to gain the approval of the Basel theological faculty to give lectures in church history.[6] On 3 August 1833 an edition of the *Grey Man* gave an account of why it was that Basel-Stadt had recently been humiliated in its struggle with Basel-Land. The reason was that it had given hospitality to enemies of public order who had fled from Prussia. Basel had thus shared in the sins of these people. Moreover, these so-called martyrs to the cause of freedom in north Germany had themselves become despots in Basel, and were responsible for the bloodshed that had recently taken place.

1. These sentiments are repeated in de Wette's *Über den Angriff des grauen Mannes gegen Lehrer der hiesigen Universität* (Basel, 1834), pp. 22-23.

2. 17 Sept. 1834, Vinet, *Lettres*, II, p. 249.

3. A. Staehelin, *Universität Basel*, p. 148.

4. Staehelin, *Dewettiana*, pp. 159-60.

5. See note 1 above.

6. Staehelin, *Dewettiana*, p. 157.

De Wette and his colleague C.G. Jung were stung by this attack into writing to Valenti to clarify whether he was referring to them. Valenti replied on 5 December 1833 that he was basing his article on a speech given to over 1,000 people by Dekan Linder from Zyfen in Basel. Why did he, Valenti, need to justify publishing what was said openly by a man 'who had so clearly established his credentials as a Christian and true citizen?' Further, it was up to readers to interpret these words as they wished. De Wette and Jung were not satisfied and initiated an action for libel against Valenti. This was rejected by the court, and de Wette and Jung had costs awarded against them.

In 1834 de Wette published an account of the affair with the aim, so he argued, not of clearing his own name so much as trying to counter smears against the university and claims about the financial burden that it placed upon the citizenry.[1] As de Wette pointed out, the words of the article in the *Grey Man* did not fit his case, since he did not flee from Prussia; but they could be taken to refer to him even if the balance of probability was against this. It was, however, his concern about the future of the university that motivated de Wette chiefly, and he repeated the sentiments of this rectorial address of 1834. He cited the example of Prussia in founding a university in 1810 to be the spearhead for its regeneration after its defeat by Napoleon. He stressed the need for Basel's citizens to be intellectually and spiritually awakened, and for the university to be the spearhead of the future based upon the love of God and of the spirit of truth. That this was truly his intention as opposed merely to the desire to clear his name can be accepted. De Wette's position in this regard had been made clear many times, for instance, in *Heinrich Melchthal*, and the sincerity of his convictions must have played a part in the response of the people of Basel to the saving of the university.

Shortly after losing the case against Valenti, de Wette received the sad news that Schleiermacher had died on 12 February 1834. In personal relationships, the two men had drawn close together, there had been a bond of affection between de Wette and Schleiermacher's wife Henriette, and de Wette had been the godfather of their son Nathaniel. Although differences of opinion remained, de Wette penned a noble tribute to Schleiermacher, which appeared in the *Baseler Zeitung* for 20 February 1834.[2] He placed Schleiermacher close behind Calvin and

---

1. See p. 238 n. 1.
2. Staehelin, *Dewettiana*, pp. 162-63.

Melanchthon as a Protestant theologian, and called him a Christian Plato. He referred to the impact that Schleiermacher's 1799 *Reden* had made upon those brought up in the Semler-Kantian school, how he had pioneered a new way for Christian theology and how his sermons had inspired many listeners. Because of his contribution to the renewal of Prussia, Schleiermacher deserved a monument alongside that of Blücher to show that the sword of the spirit had achieved as much as and more than the sword of the hero. He hoped that, just as the sculptor Christian Daniel Rauch had produced a fine bust of Schleiermacher (de Wette had a copy of it in his study), so there would be a worthy biographical description of his many-sided and outstanding character.[1]

It was probably in 1834 that de Wette began to work on a project to which he would devote his major, but by no means his entire, attention for the fifteen years of life that remained to him. This was the *Kurzgefasstes exegetisches Handbuch zum Neuen Testament*, a commentary on the whole of the New Testament. What is remarkable about this project is not only that he completed it, but that he produced second editions for nine of the eleven volumes, third editions for five and a fourth edition for one volume. Had he written just one edition of each commentary on each book, the total number of pages would have come to just over 2,500. As it was, he did much more than write a single edition, although it must be added that, once the first editions had been completed, their revisions amounted to alterations and amendments occasioned by newly-published books and articles. An overview of the dates of the various volumes and editions will indicate how fully de Wette committed his time to the enterprise between 1834 and 1848:

Volume	1st edn	2nd edn	3rd edn	4th edn
Romans	1835	1838	1841	1847
Matthew	1836	1838	1845	
Luke + Mark	1836	1839	1845	
John + Letters	1837	1839	1846	
Acts	1838	1841	1848	
Corinthians	1841	1845		
Galatians + Thessalonians	1841	1845		

1. A rare print, in the possession of Professor L. Perlitt in Göttingen, shows the bust in de Wette's study.

Volume	1st edn	2nd edn	3rd edn	4th edn
Colossians, Philemon,				
Ephesians, Philippians	1843	1847		
Titus, Timothy, Hebrews	1844	1847		
Peter, Jude, James	1847			
Revelation	1848			

Among the first of the volumes to appear, and by far the most important, was that on Matthew, because it appeared in the year after the publication of D.F. Strauss's *Leben Jesu*, a book which provoked a storm of criticism. De Wette took full account of it, and often approved its results. Indeed, in the second edition of the commentary on Matthew de Wette noted that his agreement with Strauss had offended some reviewers, and that one had written of Strauss's 'overpowering influence' upon de Wette. Because of the importance of the matter, not only for understanding de Wette but for the history of interpretation, this matter will be examined closely, together with de Wette's treatment of Matthew.

In an important introduction, omitted in the second edition, de Wette reacted to Strauss's book as follows:[1] (1) oral tradition is the basis of the Synoptic Gospels, subject to variations within itself, and used differently by the three evangelists although Matthew was probably the basis for the other two; (2) de Wette agrees with Strauss that the Synoptics cannot be harmonized: differences are more significant than similarities; (3) with Strauss, he rejects the explanation of miracles in natural terms; and (4) 'whether the belief in miracles of the early Christians can or should be ours' is a question that can only be answered (a) on the basis of historical criticism, in which area there will be no agreement, (b) from a metaphysical standpoint, where again there are various views, (c) out of differing religious convictions. De Wette believes that here he has something to offer to all sides:

> whatever people's views on miracles may be, the factor that could unite them is the ideal-symbolic meaning of miracle, to which I have drawn attention here and there, without wanting to assert that the miracle stories have been woven together simply out of ideas [the view of Strauss].[2]

---

1. *Kurzgefasstes exegetisches Handbuch zum Neuen Testament.* I.1. *Kurze Erklärung des Evangeliums Matthäi* (Leipzig, 1836), pp. v-viii.
2. *Matthäi*, p. vi.

His view of Strauss's picture of Jesus was that it was too negative:

> I believe that those who have freed themselves from the naivety [*Unkritik*]
> and arbitrariness of so-called orthodoxy, but who have at the same time
> preserved the true historical belief in Christ, can achieve other results.[1]

By 'true historical belief' de Wette meant

> a sound, thoroughly moral belief which, on the basis of the historical
> church community, holds fast to the fact that the spirit, which has become
> the life-principle of the new world, had its source in the personality of
> Christ, and that he is the creator of our religious life.[2]

De Wette added that the revelation in Christ rested on facts
(*Thatsachen*) that were certain without the testimony of Scripture.

On the authorship of Matthew, de Wette noted that Strauss's attack
on the Gospel of John had weakened the view that Luke and John
together were to be preferred as more accurate than Matthew. This
disposed of one argument against the apostolic authorship of Matthew;
but de Wette was worried by the following material in Matthew that
argued against the apostolic authorship of Matthew in its present
form: the resurrection of dead bodies after the death of Christ, the
coin in the fish's mouth, the setting of the watch over Christ's tomb,
the second account of the feeding of the multitude, and the use of Old
Testament prophecies. De Wette preferred Matthew to Luke and Mark
as the first Gospel to be written, although Luke was more accurate on
some occasions.

Of narratives in Matthew, de Wette wrote as follows.[3] The account
of the Virgin Birth was unhistorical, but this did not prevent it from
containing ideas that could profitably be handled symbolically. Similarly, the story of the Magi was unhistorical (de Wette was sharply
critical of the idea of a moving star that could identify a particular
house), as was the account of the slaughter of the children in Bethlehem.
But, again, both could be handled symbolically, with the latter expressing the tragic idea of danger and suffering for the messiah and the
church. The baptism of Jesus was a historical fact. Jesus was baptized
because he could have sinned, although he did not sin. The Temptations are a myth expressing the struggle of Jesus against the evil that
follows from his dedication to his ministry at baptism.

---

1. *Matthäi*, p. vii.
2. *Matthäi*, p. vii.
3. *Matthäi, passim.*

De Wette's view of the Sermon on the Mount was that it was a compendium of sayings of Jesus, and probably an enlargement by Matthew of an actual discourse. Within the discourse, de Wette was worried by sayings such as 5.45 ('God makes the sun rise on the evil and the good') and 6.24-34 ('consider the lilies of the field'). It was contrary to fact that God provided for everything in the world of nature, and nature knew want as well as plenty. Further, nature was a far less reliable guide to faith in God's providence than was critical reflection. The appearance of the phrase Son of Man in 8.19 enabled de Wette to affirm that Jesus used this title derived from Dan. 7.13 to show that he represented the messiah in his own individual person.

The casting out of the Gerasene demoniac (8.28-34) enabled de Wette to argue for the superiority of Matthew over Luke. Luke's account was more complete, and thus later because it was typical of tradition that it tried to clarify obscurities in stories. The collection together of parables in ch. 13 was unhistorical.

In chs. 14–16 de Wette had to deal with a series of miracles. The first, the feeding of the 5,000, had been rationalized by de Wette's teacher Paulus to suggest that the people fed each other. De Wette preferred the approach of Strauss, that an ideal not a natural historical basis for the story was to be sought. This de Wette found in the ideas of the bread of unity of the Christian community (1 Cor. 10.16), Christ as the bread of life (Jn 6.32-35), and the Old Testament ideas of the manna and quails in the wilderness, and the feedings provided by Elijah (1 Kgs 17.10-16) and Elisha (2 Kgs 4.42-44). For Jesus' walking on the water (14.22-36), de Wette offered no view, but merely outlined the difficulties. The second account of the feeding of the multitude (15.29-39) was impossible, otherwise the response of the disciples showed that they had learnt nothing from the first miracle.

The prediction by Jesus of his death and resurrection (16.21) was unlikely, given the evidence elsewhere in the gospels that the disciples did not expect a resurrection. What de Wette thought about the Transfiguration is not easy to determine. Again, the possibilities are discussed, and Strauss is praised for having demonstrated that Luke's fuller account is inferior to that of Matthew. It may be that de Wette saw the Transfiguration as a symbol of that purifying of his humanity that Jesus achieved through his obedience and death.

Moving now to the close of the Gospel, it was important both for de Wette's view of the resurrection and for his belief that Matthew was the earliest gospel, that there is only one appearance of Jesus after his Passion in Matthew, an appearance in Galilee. Further, there is no ascension in Matthew. Because John and Luke provided Resurrection appearances in Jerusalem, de Wette regarded them as later, and as trying to make explicit a mystery. 'In the earliest time, people were satisfied with the simple idea: Jesus has gone to the father.'[1]

This statement could be consistent with the view that the Resurrection had not happened, an opinion which de Wette had seemed to hold earlier. But in the commentary on John of 1837, de Wette expressed a more positive, if uncertain, view of the Resurrection.[2] His view of the Fourth Gospel was that it was late, anti-Jewish, gnostic-mystical and Hellenistic. Yet it contained historically accurate material, especially in showing Jesus to be active in Jerusalem and Judaea before Holy Week, and in the dating of the Last Supper and the Passion, and it contained authentic sayings of Jesus such as 1.52 [sic], 2.16, 19, 4.48 and 7.37. The author was probably the disciple of an apostle, and he had written the Gospel out of the needs of his situation but in the spirit of Christ. This gave the Gospel many distinctive features, especially in the discourses ascribed to Jesus.

On miraculous incidents in the Gospel, de Wette's negative criticism was apparent. He could not rationalize incidents such as the turning of water into wine or the raising of Lazarus, nor follow Strauss in supposing that they were entirely 'ideal'. He was worried by the fact that such miracles were unknown to the synoptic tradition, and by the profligacy of the miracle at Cana. He stated the views of others, and their difficulties, and preferred to live with uncertainty about what lay behind the narratives. De Wette justified this stance in his dedication of the commentary to his former Berlin colleague Lücke. At least negative criticism left open the door for further investigation, whereas the once highly-praised positive criticism of Eichhorn had only produced confusion.

In dealing with the Resurrection, de Wette followed a similar line in an extended treatment of all the Resurrection appearances in the New Testament. For all their difficulties and contradictions, they indicated the undeniable fact that the early church believed in the Resurrection, had proclaimed it in the face of martyrdom, and had been helped by it

1. *Matthäi*, p. 247.
2. *Kurzgefasstes exegetisches Handbuch zum Neuen Testament. 1.3. Kurze Erklärung des Evangeliums und der Briefe Johannis* (Leipzig, 1837), *passim.*

to change their attitude from fear to boldness. Further, it would have contradicted the absolute honesty of Jesus if he had merely physically survived crucifixion, and had then tried to persuade his followers that he had overcome death. On the other hand, de Wette could offer no positive account of the Resurrection, and advised simply that it was necessary to accept the testimony of the early church without being able to understand it in terms of the explanations available to the modern understanding of reality.

This same uncompromising honesty is to be found in probably the most important part of the commentary on John, the appendix dealing with the historical criticism of the Gospels and its relation to Christian belief.[1] It is written with a realism and honesty which make it as relevant to the end of the twentieth century as to the first third of the nineteenth, and it was reprinted in all subsequent editions of the commentary.

The appendix begins with the point that no critical investigation can be attempted without presuppositions. Strauss's claim to have written a presuppositionless life of Jesus is rejected. The criticism of the Gospels must entail two presuppositions; it must look for undisputed facts and it must rest on general basic principles. Regarding the first, de Wette confessed that Strauss had destroyed the previous critical consensus that John was a reliable Gospel, and had thus created a very uncertain situation when it came to evaluating the Gospels as historical sources. Material outside the Gospels, such as Paul, Josephus or Tacitus, gave no help for the criticism of the details of the Gospel narratives, but did establish certain limits (*Schranken*) which could not be violated. One had to rely, therefore, on the general basic principles.

The first of these, rightly maintained by Paulus and Strauss among others, was that Jesus was subject to all the limitations of humanity in this world, and was not all-knowing and all-powerful. On the other hand, it was not possible to say precisely what Jesus' limitations were, and thus it would be wrong to hold that none of the miracles could have happened.

The most important basic principle was that Jesus was the founder of Christianity. This was secured by the existence of the church and the gospel history, as well as the fact that any movement required an

1. *Johannis*, pp. 214-22.

individual to set it in motion, however important other more general factors might be.

The statement that Jesus was the founder of Christianity did not entail acceptance of the ecclesiastical dogmatic view of Jesus, which had plucked him from the ground of history. Nor did it make him the founder of everything that we associate with Christianity. He had simply laid the foundation. He had done this by communicating to his followers his own conviction of the need for harmony between the divine and the human, a need that his own life achieved and expressed. That he made this impression upon his followers was a fact. Belief in him as a saviour could only have resulted from the impact of his own belief that he was the pioneer of a new way of life and that he was to be the head of a new and better community.

De Wette now deals with three matters, the teaching of Jesus, the death of Jesus and the remaining facts of his life. For the teaching, we are dependent upon oral tradition, some of which altered the form of the teaching while retaining the essence. Some questions could not be decided, for example, how clearly did Jesus declare himself to be the messiah? On the other hand, it could not be doubted that Jesus wished to found a spiritual kingdom based upon self-sacrifice, modesty, and resignation, and freedom grounded on truth and love. The death of Jesus and its circumstances were above all doubt. He died as an innocent and just man out of love for truth and humanity, and out of a commitment to duty. Also indisputable was that his death had brought about in his disciples a change to selflessness, and a love for truth and justice.

Regarding other facts in the life of Jesus, de Wette accepts the ministry of John the Baptist, Jesus' ministries in Judaea and Galilee, some miracles (although their accounts present problems) and the Resurrection, even if that is shrouded in an impenetrable darkness. The Transfiguration is problematic, but not vital to any truth, and the dubious infancy stories are not necessary to prove Jesus' divine worth.

De Wette sharply criticizes those who cannot separate the acceptance of all the details of the Gospels from the practice of Christianity. None of the apostles had such a clear, historical view of the life of Jesus as is presupposed in the Gospels, and to insist on acceptance of the detail of the latter is to ignore what is vital in order to concentrate on inessentials:

how does it come about that we, who stand so far away from the mysterious beginnings of Christianity, make so much of a historical knowledge
about those beginnings which none of the first Christians had?[1]

In a concluding section de Wette makes an appeal for a symbolic-
poetic handling of the Gospels as an alternative to the uncritical har-
monizing of conservatives, or to the rationalizing which ends up with
the position of Strauss. He recognizes the pastoral problems entailed in
confronting ordinary people with critical scholarship; but he believes
that there can be no substitute for Christian leadership filled with the
love of truth and firmly rooted in the spirit of Christ.

It is typical of the conflict that de Wette felt between the uncompromising search for truth and the need to build up people's Christian
faith that, while he was treating the Gospels in a radical fashion he
was wrestling with the use of the Old Testament in general and the
Psalms in particular in Christian instruction. 1836 had seen the
publication of the fourth edition of his Psalms commentary; but he felt
that this was inadequate as an aid for Christian instruction, nor could
he see how to embody such an aid in the commentary. As a result he
published a short book of some eighty pages in 1836, entitled *Über die
erbauliche Erklärung der Psalmen: Eine Beilage zum Commentar
über diesselben.*[2] This book was based upon the practical classes in
homiletics that he had regularly held since coming to Basel. It was
also prompted by several recent publications, especially Stier's *Siebzig
ausgewählte Psalmen* of 1834.[3] This latter was written from a strong
neo-orthodox standpoint which imported Christian meaning into the
Psalms, and argued that the interpretation of Psalms in the New
Testament was binding upon Christian interpreters.

In his reply, de Wette emphasized both the importance of the Old
Testament for Christian edification and its inferiority to the New
Testament, as well as both the necessity of the historical-critical study
of the Old Testament and the need for this method to be comple-
mented by an approach that would build up faith. De Wette solved
these dilemmas by arguing that the sense of the Old Testament had

---

1. *Johannis*, p. 221.
2. *Über die erbauliche Erklärung der Psalmen: Eine Beilage zum Commentar über
diesselben* (Heidelberg, 1836).
3. E.R. Stier, *Siebzig ausgewählte Psalmen nach Ordnung und Zusammenhang
ausgelegt* (Halle, 1834).

two sides, a conscious and an unconscious.[1] The conscious was what
the writer intended. It was to be understood within the context of his
time and circumstances, and where it looks forward to the future, this
was necessarily thought of in terms dictated by the circumstances, e.g.
an actual restoration of Jerusalem and Israel.

The unconscious sense of the Old Testament was rooted in universal
human experience. Given that humans had intuitions of ideal harmony
and purposefulness, their expressions of these hopes or feelings had a
significance beyond the particular form in which the hopes and feelings were expressed. In this way, material in the Old Testament that
expressed an earthly, national hope for Israel could be taken, at the
unconscious level, to be an expression of hope for God's kingdom in a
universal, spiritual or ideal sense. In this case, it could well have a
fulfilment in the New Testament and could be said to be a prophecy of
the same. But it had to be emphasized that prophecy and fulfilment
worked at the unconscious level only. If Isaiah 53 seemed to be a
prophecy of the sufferings of Christ, this was not because the writer
had Christ in mind as an individual who would live some centuries
later. It was because at the unconscious level of meaning, Isaiah 53
expressed the 'law' that resignation and self-sacrifice on behalf of
others brought them salvation. If Christ fulfilled Isaiah 53 it was by
exemplifying that same 'law'.[2]

Thus, while clearly indicating that the Old Testament was inferior
to and superceded by the New Testament, de Wette was asserting a
bond between them. But this bond was grounded in anthropology, that
is, in a common human experience underlying both. Of course,
de Wette did not rule out the work of the spirit of God; but the role of
the spirit of God was to illumine the human spirit and to impart the
intuitions of harmony and of purposefulness which were expressed
consciously in specific this-worldly terms, while carrying unconscious
undertones that referred beyond the time and circumstances of
writing. De Wette strongly criticized those who confused the scheme

specific meaning—conscious intention
deeper meaning—unconscious intention

by believing that Isaiah 53, for example, consciously referred to

1. *Erbauliche Erklärung*, pp. 14-21.
2. *Erbauliche Erklärung*, p. 20.

Christ's sufferings in his Passion.[1] If this connection was to be made, it could only be at the level of unconscious intention.

Having established this point, de Wette went on to say that a complete interpretation of the Old Testament required both grammatical and historical critical work in order to establish the conscious intention, and a further approach that paid attention to the unconscious intention and its wider meaning. This would enable the Psalms to be used in an edifying manner. The last half of the book is devoted to classifying the Psalms from this standpoint, and in some cases there are 'edifying', detailed interpretations of psalms based upon lecture notes taken by a student at de Wette's homiletics classes.

It has to be said at once that the results are, on the whole, disappointing, and could have been achieved without the hermeneutical theory advanced by de Wette. The exercise also makes de Wette appear to be more conservative than was actually the case. For example, he allows that, at the level of wider application/unconscious intention it may be justifiable for an interpreter to uphold a traditional interpretation even if this presents difficulties at a critical level. A specific instance is Psalm 3 which, according to its 'title', is a psalm of David when he fled from Absalom. De Wette holds that this 'title' does not do full justice to the psalm, but he accepts that it could yield an acceptable 'edifying' sense if one dwells on the uncertainties that David would have experienced in his flight.[2] One has to ask here whether de Wette has been guilty of confusing his own categories. Surely, it would be better to say that, at the critical level, we do not know the psalmist or his circumstances but at the more general level the psalm can be applied to hopes for deliverance from trouble. But de Wette does not do this. In one of the interpretations noted down by the student, he adheres to the interpretation within the life of David.[3] On the other hand, and to be fair to de Wette, he probably thought that the identity of the psalmist could not be known, and that it did no harm to place the psalm in the life of David, especially if that is what many people wanted to accept. In another section, de Wette deals with imprecatory psalms by finding the deeper sense in a desire to see God's justice vindicated.

It is on the basis of writings such as *Über die erbauliche Erklärung*

1. *Erbauliche Erklärung*, p. 25.
2. *Erbauliche Erklärung*, p. 38.
3. *Erbauliche Erklärung*, pp. 75-76.

der Psalmen that it has been suggested that de Wette became more conservative or traditional in the last main period of his life. The truth probably is that he became more aware of the need to enable ordinary church members to be built up in their faith, and realized that historical criticism on its own could not do this. He thus became more willing to tolerate traditional or conservative positions, while his critical sharpness was never blunted. Whether he succeeded in solving the problem raised by the historical-critical method for 'edifying' ordinary believers is another matter. The dilemma is one that remains acute today.

In the period 1835 to 1837 de Wette was also reading three Old Testament works that had been published in 1835: W. Vatke's *Biblische Theologie*, P. von Bohlen's *Die Genesis*, and J.F.L. George's *Die älteren jüdischen Feste*.[1] These three books owed much to de Wette's early critical work, but they all disagreed with him on several essential points. Vatke held that very little could be known about the history of Israel before the time of David, and assigned to Moses a more limited achievement than even de Wette allowed. Vatke also rejected de Wette's view of a degeneration of Israelite religion after the exile. Von Bohlen and George had taken to its logical conclusion the assumption that the Levitical institutions had reached the form described in the Old Testament only after a long phase of development. In so doing they placed the final stages of the development after the exile, in the process rejecting de Wette's belief that Deuteronomy was later than Leviticus and that Deuteronomy was to be dated to the seventh century.

De Wette reviewed these three works in a major review of fifty-six pages in the *Theologische Studien und Kritiken* of 1837.[2] He presented the contents of the books fairly with more attention to Vatke and George than to von Bohlen. Perhaps the lesser treatment of von Bohlen owed something to the fact that von Bohlen had sent de Wette a copy of *Die Genesis* in 1835 together with a letter addressed to Gesenius (!), and de Wette had replied in sympathetic and encouraging terms.[3] In criticizing Vatke and George, de Wette argued that they

---

1. See my *Old Testament Criticism*, pp. 63-67, 69-78, 175-77.

2. *Theologische Studien und Kritiken* (1837), pp. 947-1003.

3. *Autobiographie des ordent. Professor der orientalischen Sprachen und Literatur an der Universität zu Königsberg Dr Peter von Bohlen* (ed. J. Voigt; Königsberg, 1842), pp. 149-50, prints a letter of de Wette of 11 October 1835.

both relied too much on the principle that the more developed something was, the later it was. De Wette certainly wanted to attribute more to Moses than Vatke was prepared to do:

> Moses gave not only the two tables of commandments but other laws, and if he did not establish the most important institutions of the theocratic state he had at least commanded and arranged them.[1]

Although he disagreed with Vatke, de Wette was characteristically generous to a man whose critical acumen he could admire:

> he cannot be denied the praise of acuteness (*Scharfsinn*), or the gift of synthesis and of a comprehensive use of everything that is favourable to his views. Neither can he be charged that he has done his research in an irreligious or untheological spirit. . . He has highlighted the power of the spirit of religion at work in the people, and has given to the pious observer an exciting deep insight into the secret leading of the divine spirit.[2]

The orthodox verdicts on Vatke were much less generous!

In comparison with earlier years, the decade from 1839 to 1849 was one of comparative peace and quiet for de Wette. His third marriage did not bring him the happiness that he had hoped for, but there were other consolations on the family front. Anna had married in March 1835 and a son, Ernst Ludwig, and a daughter, Sophie, were born to her and her husband Dr August Christoph Heitz, as well as three other sons. Ludwig, after completing his study of medicine, had visited his step-brother Karl Beck in America, and on his return to Basel in 1838 had married Amalie Jersing. They had a son, August, a daughter, Emma, and one other child. We can assume that de Wette took great delight in his grandchildren.

He was able to continue his travelling, something that was considerably facilitated by the expansion of the railway network. Journeys by rail took only one eighth of their previous time. Visits to Germany became more frequent, especially as de Wette became associated with the work of the Gustav Adolf Verein. This all-German association for the support of needy Protestant congregations was inaugurated in Frankfurt-am-Main on 21 September 1843, and on Sunday 24 September de Wette preached at a service in the German Reformed Church in Frankfurt.[3] Other visits to Germany were made in 1842,

---

1. *TSK* (1837), p. 973.
2. *TSK* (1837), p. 981.
3. See *TRE* 8, pp. 719-20, and de Wette's *Die Ausschliessung des D. Rupp von*

1844, 1846, 1847 and 1848, in which last year de Wette attended some of the meetings of the German National Assembly in St Paul's Church in Frankfurt. In October 1845 he began a visit of six months to Rome and Naples.

This Italian visit was undertaken because of his health. According to Wiegand, de Wette had had frequent headaches and lung infections, and was advised that a visit to a warmer climate would be beneficial.[1] In the Autumn of 1848 he spent some weeks near Lake Geneva in order to improve his health. This increasing loss of health coincided with the death of some of his closest friends. Amalie von Voigt had died in 1840, and in 1843 de Wette lost both Anna Margaretha VonderMühll and his old friend Fries. In 1842 his publisher Georg Reimer died. It was not only his old friends whom he lost. In 1844 his godchild Emma Jung died at the age of twenty, and de Wette gave the address at her funeral.[2] During these years, his wife and his stepdaughter Clara were often ill, and his wife spent much time taking cures at health resorts. De Wette was thus well aware that his own life was drawing to a close, and it is remarkable that he was able to continue to write so much in his last ten years.

Among high points during this period was the celebration in 1847 of his twenty-five years in Basel as a professor, and the visit to Basel in 1845 of Franz Liszt, who gave three concerts.[3] Also, in 1847 his stepson Karl Beck travelled from America to Europe to visit him. De Wette accompanied him to Ostend to see him off on his return to America.

For the remainder of this chapter, four of de Wette's writings from this last period of his life will be examined: the remainder of the commentary on the New Testament, his last big theological book *Das Wesen des christlichen Glaubens* of 1846, and two smaller works, *Gedanken über Malerei und Baukunst* and *Die biblische Geschichte als Geschichte der Offenbarung Gottes*, both also published in 1846. In addition, mention will be made of a series of sermons on Christian faith that de Wette preached at the end of his life and of which his

---

der Hauptversammlung des Gustav-Adolf Vereins zu Berlin am 7. September 1846 (Leipzig, 1847). This is de Wette's account of a famous case of the eligibility of someone who had been elected by a church which he had then left.

1. Wiegand, *De Wette*, pp. 86ff.
2. The text is given by Handschin, *De Wette als Prediger*, pp. 143-46.
3. Staehelin, *Dewettiana*, p. 182 n. 436.

death prevented him from delivering the last two, although he had already written them.

De Wette completed his commentary on the New Testament in three phases. The first saw the completion of 1 and 2 Corinthians (1841), Galatians and 1 and 2 Thessalonians (1841), and the second the publication of Colossians, Philemon, Ephesians and Philippians (1843) and Titus, 1 and 2 Timothy and Hebrews (1844). There followed an interval of several years before the two final volumes appeared: 1 and 2 Peter, Jude and James (1847), and Revelation (1848). In spite of ill-health and frequent travelling, this writing showed no signs of diminishing powers. No critical problem was inadequately dealt with, nor was any matter that raised difficulties for modern belief brushed aside. Commentators of all persuasions were utilized, and whereas de Wette could criticize the orthodox Tholuck for completely ignoring Bleek's commentary on Hebrews in the second edition of Tholuck's commentary, de Wette could also express his own gratitude to Tholuck even if he disagreed with him. Again, we find de Wette making use of Baur's so-called 'Tübingen Hypothesis' in his commentary on the Pastoral Epistles (and in the second edition of the Acts commentary of 1841), even if he regarded its conclusions as highly improbable. The critical positions had, of course, been presented in the New Testament Introduction of 1826. Here, they were defended in the context of complete commentaries. In a number of cases, de Wette believed that he was providing original and definitive solutions to the exegesis of difficult passages. What follows now can only be a subjective sampling of the material.

On 1 Corinthians, de Wette used the theory of D. Schenkel (1838) that the parties in Corinth were the following:[1] the Christ party rejected apostolic leadership and claimed direct inspiration from Christ; the Paul and Apollos parties had apostolic authority; the Cephas party was a group of Jewish Christians. Of special interest is de Wette's treatment of the Resurrection in chapter 15. De Wette rejected the suggestion that Paul believed the Resurrection was necessary for immortality, appealing for support to Phil. 1.21-23. The argument of 1 Cor. 15.32, that if there was no Resurrection one should eat, drink and be merry, depended just as much on belief in immortality and retribution as it did on Resurrection; that is, one

---

1. *Kurze Erklärung des Briefes an die Corinther* (Leipzig, 1841), pp. 4-5, and *passim*.

could only eat, drink and be merry if there were no Resurrection or
immortality or retribution. Paul, according to de Wette, believed this,
but chose in 1 Corinthians 15 to deal only with the Resurrection
aspect. Because de Wette believed in immortality, he was disturbed by
the implications of vv. 12-20, that the Resurrection of Christ was
necessary and sufficient for the Resurrection of the human race.
According to de Wette the verse 'if the dead rise not, then is not
Christ raised' (v. 16) means that if there is no general Resurrection,
then Christ's Resurrection has not achieved its purpose. But its
purpose is not fulfilled in a causal way. As the one who died without
having sinned, Christ cannot enable those who have sinned to rise. If
this seems to be very tortuous, it is at least an indication that de Wette
could not suspend his own deeply-held convictions when trying to
expound what Paul had written.

On 2 Corinthians, de Wette rejected the theory that had been proposed by Semler in the eighteenth century that chs. 10–13.10 were a
separate letter.[1] On 5.14, he acknowledged that Paul spoke of Christ's
death as being on behalf of others (*stellvertretend*), but denied that
this entailed a satisfaction theory. Christ, as the highest embodiment of
humanity, died in conscious solidarity with humanity, and in this sense
he died for all and all died in and with him. Commenting on Paul's
'thorn in the flesh', de Wette suggested that it was a recurring physical
ailment such as headache or migraine. This makes one wonder
whether de Wette was a migraine sufferer.

In the commentary on Galatians, de Wette interprets the passage in
ch. 5 about the flesh and the spirit in terms of his Friesian anthropology.[2] The two tendencies are instinct-led behaviour and behaviour
based upon the duties disclosed by critical reflection. In commenting
on Thessalonians, de Wette rejects Kern's doubts about the authority
of 2 Thessalonians but sets out fully Kern's grounds for suspicion.

The most important feature of the commentary on Colossians,
Philemon, Ephesians and Philippians is the continued rejection of
Ephesians as an authentic Pauline epistle.[3] De Wette argued that
Ephesians is dependent on Colossians (he rejects Meyerhoff's attack on

1. *Corinther, passim.*
2. *Kurze Erklärung des Briefes an die Galater und die Briefe an die Thessaloniker*
(Leipzig, 1841), *passim.*
3. *Kurze Erklärung des Briefes an die Colosser, an Philemon, an die Ephesier
und Philipper* (Leipzig, 1843), *passim.*

the authenticity of Colossians), there are hapax legomena, and the
method of writing shows 'an evident decline from that of Paul'.
De Wette also finds a few elements in common between Ephesians,
and the Pastoral epistles and the Petrine Epistles. Like these, it bears
an apostle's name but was probably written by a pupil of the apostle.

De Wette returned to this theme in the commentary on the Pastoral
Epistles and Hebrews.[1] The former were not by Paul. They have too
much in common, and they address similar general points. Further,
they contradict the Pauline view of grace (see 2 Tim. 4.8) and have an
unhealthy stress upon law (1 Tim. 1.8). De Wette follows Baur in
seeing the Pastorals as the work of a follower of Paul in the period
when Gnosticism was a danger, but places their time of composition at
the end of the first century, certainly not as late as Baur's date. On
Hebrews, which is also non-Pauline, de Wette is anxious to deny a
crude metaphysical interpretation of the opening of the epistle, where
Christ is said to be the one through whom God created the world.
This type of language (similarly that in Jn 1.1-14 and Phil. 2.6-11)
was not about the pre-existent Christ or the eternal Logos. It was
about the historical Christ who, in his life, had displayed anticipations
of divine characteristics and eternal realities without himself becoming divine or having been pre-existent. The preface to this volume
contains a robust defence of the right of criticism to show that books
within the canon of Scripture are not authentic. Such criticism sets the
church free from false beliefs and enables it to find the Christ who
continues to live within the Christian community.

In the volume on 1 and 2 Peter, Jude and James, de Wette accepted
with some reservations that James the brother of Jesus had written
James, but denied apostolic authorship to the others.[2] These writings
are valuable for the history of early Christianity, de Wette believed.

The final volume, on Revelation, has a most interesting introduction.[3] The commentary had been begun during the civil war in
Switzerland, continued with the demise of the French throne, and
completed during the anarchy of the 1848 revolution in Germany. Of
the biblical book itself, de Wette held that it occupied the second rank
as a document of Christian revelation. It lacked freedom of spirit and

---

1. *Kurze Erklärung der Briefe an Titus, Timotheus und die Hebräer* (Leipzig,
1844), *passim*.
2. *Kurze Erklärung der Brief des Petrus, Judas und Jakobus* (Leipzig, 1847).
3. *Kurze Erklärung der Offenbarung Johannis* (Leipzig, 1848).

originality, and not only was it too dependent on Old Testament images, but it had not completely freed itself from Old Testament ideas of the theocracy in its concept of the kingdom of God.

It is important to note this radical and dismissive stance, because there is in the preface a phrase which, taken out of context, could be interpreted to mean that de Wette had arrived at a very orthodox type of belief just under a year before he died. Wiegand certainly misrepresents de Wette in this way in his well-intentioned caricature. The passage by de Wette is as follows:

> I know only that there is salvation in no other name except the name of Jesus Christ the crucified, and that there is nothing higher for humanity than the divine humanity that was achieved in him, and the kingdom of God that was planted by him. This is an idea and task which is still not properly recognized and introduced into life, not even by those who are otherwise rightly regarded as the most active and devoted Christians.[1]

The second part of the quotation warns us that we are not dealing with a de Wette suddenly converted to an orthodox pietism. We recognize de Wette as he had substantially been since late 1817, with his belief in the achievement of Christ's life and death as the greatest example to which humanity should aspire. In the context of the whole preface, this passage is a call to the church to follow the path for which de Wette had so often argued and pleaded—a path of free enquiry and inspiration ever holding before it the sublime example of Christ. The whole of the commentary on the New Testament was permeated with this same conviction.

Das Wesen des christlichen Glaubens is de Wette's last major work of theology, and is his proverbial swan song.[2] Five hundred pages long, it is intended as a simple and understandable account of the certainties of Christian belief for those who need an alternative to narrow orthodoxy and unrestrained rationalism. As de Wette remarks, nothing is rarer than a Christian layman who is both free-thinking and firmly-believing (*warmgläubig*). To what extent the non-academic Christian reading public would have found this a simple and understandable book is hard to say. While it lacks the complicated vocabulary of de Wette's scholarly works, it also lacks the lightness of

1. *Offenbarung*, p. vii.
2. *Das Wesen des christlichen Glaubens vom Standpunkte des Glaubens* (Basel, 1846).

writings such as the *Vorlesungen über die Sittenlehre* that were designed as public lectures. For the modern reader, it constitutes de Wette's definitive statement of belief, albeit one that is designed for the general public. This fact no doubt affects the writing; for while, in typical de Wette fashion, no difficulty is avoided, and everything is tackled openly and honestly, de Wette is restrained by the self-imposed need not to damage the faith of those for whom untempered words of criticism might prove fatal.

In form, *Das Wesen des christlichen Glaubens* follows Schleiermacher's *Glaubenslehre* within the limitations of the fundamentally different standpoint which de Wette maintains.[1] This is most noticeable in the three great sections

I	The original union of man with God
II	The disrupted (*gestörte*) union of man with God
III	The restored union of men with God through Christ.

These correspond to Schleiermacher's sections: (1) the religious self-consciousness of the relation between the world and God; (2) first antithesis, consciousness of sin; and (3) second antithesis, consciousness of grace.[2] If these titles do not appear to be similar, the content makes the sections closer. For example, de Wette's first section deals with the nature of God and the created order, as does Schleiermacher's first section, and in the second sections of both men, subjects such as original sin and the holiness of God are treated. In the respective third sections, the redeeming work of Christ, and the church with its worship and sacraments are dealt with. Both works end with a discussion of the doctrine of the Trinity, and de Wette explicitly mentions that he is following Schleiermacher in doing this. In adapting something like the form of Schleiermacher's *Glaubenslehre*, de Wette was no doubt acknowledging his admiration of his former colleague; but he may also have been making a bid to outdo Schleiermacher by putting the latter's approaches to better use. The most notable difference between the two works is that Schleiermacher based his account of the relation of God to the world on a religious consciousness, whereas de Wette based it upon a Friesian philosophical awareness.

---

1. F.D.E. Schleiermacher, *Der christliche Glaube nach den Grundsätzen der evangelischen Kirche* (Berlin, 2nd edn, 1830–31).

2. For the purposes of comparison, I have simplified the actual structure of the two works.

In part I, then, de Wette employed his Friesian position without the explicit philosophical language. The ideal union between man and God is one in which there is a perception of eternal unity and purposefulness, and de Wette believes that the human race had this perception in its infancy before it began to grow in freedom towards adulthood. De Wette tackles in a familiar way the problem of natural evil as denying God's providence. We do not complain when a cloud obscures the sun or there is a storm. Why should we complain at more drastic and destructive occurrences in nature? They should increase our sense of dependence, and we should not doubt the purposefulness of natural disasters.[1]

Part II, dealing with the distorted unity of humanity and God, is based upon Friesian anthropology. De Wette contrasts the natural drive (*sinnliche Trieb*) with the moral drive (*sittliche Trieb*). One notices, however, a great stress on the communal aspect of wrongdoing. Sin is inherited in the sense that it is learned from the community into which one is born. De Wette's treatment of the 'fall' mentions the views of Kant and Schiller.

In part III, on the new union made possible by Christ, there is much on the life of Jesus, his messianic consciousness, his miracles, the Resurrection and the Atonement. De Wette's treatment begins from the fact of the existence of the early church as witnessed in the New Testament epistles. That a new community filled with a new spirit of love and self-sacrifice, reaching out to all humanity, came into existence cannot be denied. From this, de Wette infers that it must have had one founder who intended it to be as we find it at its best in the New Testament. This enables de Wette to go back to the Gospels and to sketch a life of Jesus which provides the credible foundation for the existence of the Christian community. Jesus is presented as one who did not speak of himself as messiah (this would have aroused false, this-worldly expectations), and who worked out the need for his death in his confrontation with the religious leaders. His death was a conscious self-offering on behalf of humanity, and Jesus had taught his disciples the necessity of his path of suffering. In treating miracles de Wette notes that Jesus was not alone in working miracles at that time, citing the verse, 'if I by Beelzebub cast out devils, by whom do your sons cast them out?' (Lk. 11.20). He allowed that, in the Gospels,

---

1. *Wesen*, p. 151.

some accounts could well be exaggerated and that, in any case, the purpose of recounting miracles was theological not historical. Christian apologetics should certainly not try to appeal to miracles as evidence for Christianity. On the Resurrection, de Wette's view can be summed up in the statement that he believes in the Resurrection because he believes in Christ, not that he believes in Christ because he believes in the Resurrection. Also, he states that those who find difficulty in accepting the Resurrection should not feel dismayed; but neither should they try to disturb the faith of those who do believe in it.[1]

The Atonement and Christology are also treated in familiar fashion. Christ's death is for others, in that Christ willingly identified himself with humanity in choosing the crucifixion. His death reveals the awfulness of evil but is a victory of self-giving love over it. De Wette firmly rejects theories that hold that the death of Christ resolves a conflict in God between his justice and his love. To say that Jesus is the son of God and is divine is to assert that, in his historical life, Jesus achieved and lived out the perfect fulfilment of the will and knowledge of God in a human being. He thus showed what true humanity was like, and was an expression of the divine love towards the human race.

Given his denial of traditional Christology, what does belief in Christ mean for de Wette? He sums it up as

> the firm, living conviction, that a man appeared in whom once again after a long break, the ideal [*Urbild*] of a pure humanity pleasing to God and at one with him was seen, who served the cause of God and humanity without wavering or failure, with perfect obedience and self-giving love to all. He went to his death for this cause, and established the kingdom of God among humanity through this most perfect act of obedience and love, and has established a new life.[2]

Given that this is belief *about* Christ rather than *in* him, it is no surprise that de Wette's concluding words about the Trinity state that belief in the Son and the Holy Spirit are designed to lead us to belief in the Father, and that this is the complete belief in God.[3] Thus we have in this mature exposition of de Wette's faith an unorthodox account which rejects many traditional orthodoxies, and which is subordinationist in its Christology and Trinitarian theology. Yet it is

1. *Wesen*, p. 318.
2. *Wesen*, p. 396.
3. *Wesen*, p. 492.

impossible to impugn de Wette's sincere conviction, and many of the observations that he makes in the book are of relevance for those who may disagree with him.

The two small works *Die biblische Geschichte als Geschichte der Offenbarung Gottes* and *Gedanken über Malerei und Baukunst* were written during de Wette's visit to Italy from October 1845 to April 1846. Rome, in particular, made a deep impression upon him, with its many churches and paintings, and he was exposed as never before to the rites, ceremonies and ethos of the Roman Catholic Church. The two books were responses to his Italian experience in two ways. First, de Wette had an admiration for much Italian and Catholic art, and lamented that Protestantism had no comparable religious artistic tradition. Yet he was faced with the problem that, on his view of aesthetics, the truly great piece of art needed to combine beauty of form with true understanding of the idea of beauty. But much Catholicism, for de Wette, displayed a flawed idea of truth, and to this extent its art could not achieve a perfect unity between the ideal and its representation. De Wette had the same problem with Greek sculpture. He marvelled at its beauty but was disturbed by his intellectual conviction that, for the Greeks, reality and the ideal did not achieve a perfect union. There is nothing in this 1846 essay that cannot be found in his earlier writings on this subject, for example, in *Theodor*; but he felt it necessary to re-state his views, given that art and architecture were so important in the Catholic ethos in Rome.[1]

De Wette's second reaction to Italy was in regard to the Christian instruction of the young. He could appreciate that Catholic ceremonials were a potent influence in the nurture of children. What was to be the Protestant equivalent? Here, de Wette decided to fulfil an old ambition and a request once made by his late friend and publisher, Reimer, to produce a book on the Bible designed for the instruction and nurture of Protestant youth. This is what he now attempted in *Die biblische Geschichte*.[2] An imaginative presentation of the content of the Bible to young Protestants would fulfil the same function as Catholic rites and ceremonies for Catholic nurture.

However, de Wette was well aware of the dangers of such a project.

1. *Gedanken über Malerei und Baukunst besonders in kirchlicher Beziehung* (Berlin, 1846).
2. *Die biblische Geschichte als Geschichte der Offenbarungen Gottes: Leitfaden für Lehrer* (Berlin, 1846).

It might inculcate a biblical literalism which would be far from de Wette's view of sound Christian faith. It might encourage false hermeneutics, for example, by justifying immoral deeds in the Old Testament on the ground that they could not be immoral, because they were in the Bible. De Wette's solution to these dilemmas was to advocate what we might call a censored version of the Bible, one that left out anything immoral (e.g. Genesis 19), obscure (e.g. Gen. 32.22-32) or unedifying (e.g. genealogies). Further, in dealing with passages whose literal interpretation raised difficulties, stress was to be laid upon the underlying symbolic meaning.

In his introduction, de Wette laid down some clear theological principles.[1] The only revelation of God in history is that given in the life and death of Christ. This is the centre-point in relation to which everything else has to be understood. Thus, the Old Testament is inferior to the New for, although it contains anticipations of God's kingdom in the form of the Israelite theocracy, these are expressed through incomplete institutions. God's revelation in Christ, on the one hand, is expressed through a completely fulfilled and pure life. Another distinction, this time pertaining to the New Testament, is between revelation and its appropriation (*Aneignung*). From this standpoint, Acts and the New Testament letters are not God's revelation, but an account of how this revelation was appropriated by the first disciples. Miracles are not regarded as revelations, and de Wette states his familiar views about their dubious role in creating Christian belief. In the Old Testament, the fundamental ideas of the Mosaic theocracy are the high point, in terms of which other material is to be read, and the Old Testament itself must be handled scrupulously so as to sustain the moral values disclosed in the life of Christ.

In view of this introduction it has to be said that the title of the book is misleading. It invites us to think that biblical history is the history of God's revelation, but this is not at all the case. De Wette's introduction is designed to argue that very little of the history in the Bible is actually God's revelation. What remains of the Old Testament after de Wette's censorship is background to and anticipation of the revelation in the life and death of Christ. Even the greater part of the New Testament is appropriation, not revelation. The important word in the title appears to be the word *als* ('as'). The title is not claiming that

---

1. *Biblische Geschichte*, pp. 7ff.

biblical history is God's revelation, but rather, it is advertising how the biblical history may be seen as God's revelation; and in practice, this 'how' is by way of making careful distinctions in relation to the 'centre' of the Bible, the life and death of Christ.

These qualifications are vital, for without them *Die biblische Geschichte* looks like a very conservative writing. The biblical material begins with the creation in Genesis 1, and continues through the 'fall' in Genesis 3 and the call of Abraham to the exodus and the Mosaic establishment of the theocracy. This is a far cry from the radical treatment of the patriarchal and exodus narratives in the youthful *Beiträge*, and can create the impression that de Wette had become far less radical in his old age. There is no doubt that, as he grew older, de Wette had become more positive about the work of Moses compared with the *Beiträge*. But it would be wrong to point to a retreat from his basic radicalism. The New Testament commentary is fully critical, as are de Wette's views on the Bible as revelation in the introduction to *Die biblische Geschichte*. The appearance of conservativeness is more a function of the use to which de Wette intended this book to be put, than an indication of a fundamental change in his convictions.[1]

On Sunday 14 January 1849, de Wette began a series of twelve sermons in the St Elisabeth Church in Basel entitled *Die Hauptstücke des christlichen Glaubens*.[2] These he proceeded to deliver at roughly fortnightly intervals until his final illness, which began on 7 June, and curtailed the series. Not all sermons were preached on Sundays. We know that the ninth was preached on Ascension Day, 17 May 1849, and it is likely that the sixth was preached on Good Friday, 6 April. The last sermon that de Wette preached was on Whit Sunday 27 May, ten days before his last illness.

The sermons present all of de Wette's favourite and familiar theological positions, in some cases in striking language. In the first, on the necessity of faith, we find reference to Fries's favourite text Heb. 11.1. Faith is necessary because, without it, we will only see Jesus as the Pharisees saw him, or as those who have simply taken him to be a great man.[3] De Wette stresses the link between faith

---

1. *Biblische Geschichte*, p. 15.
2. *Die Hauptstücke des christlichen Glaubens in einer Reihe von Predigten von Dr W.M.L. de Wette* (Basel, 1849).
3. *Hauptstücke*, pp. 5-6.

and love, and in the second sermon defines faith as

> being convinced of truths that do not rest only on the testimony of the
> senses or on the basis of reason, but find recognition [*Anerkennung*] in
> the heart.[1]

In this connection between faith and love, Jesus plays a crucial role in
enabling us to believe in the love of God, but this does not mean that
we worship Jesus as God. We must only believe in Christ because and
in that he leads us to the Father. De Wette criticizes those whose belief
is too Christ-centred.

The third sermon, on the Bible, reiterates much that is in the intro-
duction to *Die biblische Geschichte*, while numbers four and five
describe how the life and sufferings of Jesus began the kingdom of
God, a kingdom anticipated in the Israelite theocracy. The sermon on
Christ's death takes up the theme expressed so nobly in Theodor's
Good Friday reflection:

> any other victory. . . would not have been pure.[2]

The death of Jesus is the ultimate victory of the spirit of truth and
love, and the most victorious revelation of this spirit, which could
have occurred in no other way. The Resurrection of Christ was the
inevitable consequence of the love shown in the life and death of Jesus:

> a soul in which there was such love could not fall to death. With this ful-
> ness of love was included the fulness of life, immortal life.[3]

This is perhaps the clearest indication of how de Wette's belief in the
Resurrection was arrived at. It enabled him to accept the New
Testament witness to the Resurrection. It was not the case that this
witness had itself convinced de Wette of the Resurrection.

Sermons eight and nine dealt with Jesus as the son of God and of
his exaltation to God's right hand. To believe in Jesus as son of God
was to accept that God had spoken and worked through him. To
believe in his exaltation is to identify him with the eternal word of
God, which was in Christ but which also created the world. De
Wette's final preached sermon, on the Holy Spirit, stressed that the
spirit had been imparted to a community of believers, and he called
upon the church to recover that same sense of community, especially

1. *Hauptstücke*, p. 22.
2. *Hauptstücke*, p. 87.
3. *Hauptstücke*, p. 101.

in imitating the early church in its care of the poor.[1]

As a young student, de Wette's first two sermons in his father's church had been empty exercises in Kantian moralism. His last sermons, nearly fifty years later, showed a sincere, robust and positive, if unorthodox, Christian faith.

We owe our knowledge of De Wette's last illness to Wiegand, who had available a letter from de Wette's daughter, Anna.[2] On Thursday 7 June, de Wette, who was serving his fourth term as rector of the university, returned home from chairing a long meeting, presumably of the senate. He complained of rheumatic pains and was unable to begin his accustomed work. His ailment developed into typhoid fever, whose symptoms were recognized on 13 June. As his condition worsened, he experienced periods of delirium interspersed with periods of normal consciousness. He was cared for constantly by his daughter Anna (de Wette's wife excused herself lest she should be infected) and was given medical treatment by his son Ludwig and his old friend and colleague Jung.

It was Jung who recorded the following poem composed by the dying de Wette:

> Angel voices sound
> 'Come into our choir, loved-one;
> your songs press
> high up to the throne of God'.
> And the singer inclined
> his head gently to their song.
> He, the incomparable singer
> of sacred songs inclined
> his dear head gently, and departed.[3]

On Saturday 15 June he rallied, and was able to say farewell to family and close friends. On Sunday 16 June, he died at five o'clock in the evening.

The funeral took place on Tuesday 19 June at the St Elisabeth Church. The address was given by de Wette's colleague Hagenbach, and the service was attended by a great number of students, colleagues from the university, and citizens of Basel. The coffin was carried by

---

1. *Hauptstücke*, p. 148.
2. See Wiegand, *De Wette*, pp. 93-97, for what follows.
3. Staehelin, *Dewettiana*, p. 200. De Wette, if this poem is about himself, seems also to be referring to David (the incomparable singer).

students. Following the service in the St Elisabeth Church, the assembly moved to the St Elisabeth churchyard were the interment took place.[1] The movement from Ulla to Basel, a movement that had seen much grief, sadness and disappointment, as well as achievement in scholarship and pleasure in art, literature, music and travel, had ended. It had begun in the piety of a Lutheran manse and it ended in a sincere faith and hope which had been conceived by feeling, and given substance by uncompromising honesty.

---

1. The St Elisabeth Churchyard was built over at the end of the 19th century (Staehelin, *Dewettiana*, pp. 211-12). De Wette's tombstone is now in the Wolf-Gottesacker, but where he was buried there is now a De Wette street and a De Wette school.

Chapter 8

RETROSPECT

'A man of the future.' Was Adalbert Merx correct to describe de Wette in this way?[1] If we pay attention to how de Wette's reputation has fared in subsequent scholarship, the answer must be no. Among Old Testament scholars, de Wette is best known for that part of his doctoral dissertation that argued for a seventh-century date for Deuteronomy, while the small constituency that specializes in Chronicles acknowledges his pioneering work in the *Beiträge*. In New Testament studies he is referred to mainly as one of the first to dispute the Pauline authorship of Ephesians. In systematic theology he is at present merely noted as a 'mediating' theologian, while his contributions to ethics are totally unknown. His work as novelist, poet and writer on aesthetics has been forgotten, and even in the political and historical sphere he is usually ignored in accounts of Sand's assassination of Kotzebue and its aftermath.[2]

In some of these cases, his oblivion can be explained and understood. He attached himself to positions that were superseded by later scholarship, and thus his work was forgotten. In the field of Old Testament, his failing was his reluctance to accept that Levitical-priestly material in Exodus–Numbers could be later than Deuteronomy. Thus, having pioneered the way for the theory of Israelite religion to be advocated by Wellhausen, he refused to take the final step which was needed for that theory's coherence. As a New Testament scholar it was his attachment to the Griesbach hypothesis of Matthaean priority that ensured his obscurity once the rival theory of Markan priority was almost universally accepted. In the fields of theology and ethics, the Friesian philosophy that he embraced so wholeheartedly was never a widely-adopted position in his own day let alone

1. Merx, 'Die morgenländischen Studien', p. 41.
2. Thus Sheehan, *German History*; Nipperdey, *Deutsche Geschichte*.

later in the nineteenth century. It is true that, when Fries's philosophy enjoyed a brief revival early in the present century, de Wette's reputation benefitted, and the scholarly world was made aware of him in Rudolf Otto's *Kantisch-Fries'sche Religionsphilosophie*; but this was to be short lived.

De Wette also had the disadvantage of being overshadowed by other figures in the nineteenth century, in comparison with whom his own work seemed to be unimportant. Thus, Wellhausen was to become the dominant figure in nineteenth-century Old Testament scholarship (how many students know what happened *before* Wellhausen?) and de Wette's reputation suffered because he had done so much to make Wellhausen's position possible. Why worry about predecessors when we have in the *Prolegomena zur Geschichte Israels* a book which has become a classic? In New Testament scholarship, de Wette has been overshadowed by Strauss, precisely because Strauss presented such a formidable and radical challenge to Christian belief. On the theological front it is de Wette's Berlin colleague Schleiermacher who has exerted a hold on the scholarly imagination that continues unabated even today.

Thus far the verdict of 'history'. But is this verdict correct? In what follows, I shall attempt to justify Adalbert Merx's view of de Wette as a 'man of the future' not so much from what he achieved, as from what he failed to achieve; from a good deal of unfinished business with which he concerned himself and which ought to be our concern today.

I begin with de Wette's most conspicuous weakness, his adherence to the philosophy of Fries. If only he had been more eclectic or more obscure (one is tempted to add 'like Schleiermacher') he may have retained a greater reputation. But this was not de Wette's way, and it is possible to see, in this weakness, a strength. De Wette was convinced that biblical interpretation and theology were concerned with reality, and that reality could only be understood with the help of philosophy. In this he was surely right. Implicit in Christian belief are claims about the nature of reality, about the sort of world in which we live and about the sort of things human beings are. Although philosophy in a broad sense does not seek to provide answers to these questions, it does offer critiques of attempted answers, it exposes contradictions and tautologies and offers conceptual frameworks for deeper reflection. Those who claim to have no philosophy are simply unaware of their philosophical presuppositions.

In using philosophy so unashamedly in his biblical interpretation, theology and ethics, de Wette was standing in an honourable tradition reaching back through Protestant scholasticism to Aquinas and to the church of those centuries that produced the classical creeds of Christian orthodoxy. This was one reason why de Wette rejected such orthodoxy, believing that it was based upon inadequate philosophy. But in advocating the use of a philosophy that tried to account for reality as it was thought about in his day, de Wette was heeding an agenda that presents itself afresh to each generation. Are there really such things as demons, and a devil? What is the ontological status of evil and wickedness, and if they are more than powerful embodiments of nothing, how do we escape the dilemma of dualism? How do we account for God's love in the face of moral and natural evil?

De Wette faced up squarely to all these questions, even if we find some of his answers tragically naive. I find it remarkable that a man who endured so much personal tragedy and disappointment could be satisfied that reality was ultimately harmonious and purposeful. Be that as it may, we cannot fault de Wette's sincerity in making his views about the nature of reality affect his biblical interpretation and his theology; and while we can be grateful for much modern biblical interpretation that illuminates the text by showing what it meant in context in the ancient world, we cannot escape the question of how we appropriate that meaning in the modern world. If we do not believe that 'flesh' and 'law' are 'powers' seeking to establish dominion over humanity, what are we to make of Paul's belief that this was so?

A second area in which de Wette addresses an agenda that cannot be assumed to have been exhausted is that of the relation of biblical criticism to Christian belief. This struggle was central to de Wette's own pilgrimage from doubt to faith, a dilemma that he resolved by a philosophical interpretation of a spiritual/aesthetic experience. It is easy to criticize de Wette for privileging, on the basis of philosophy, a particular view of the significance of the life of Christ, and of using this view to arbitrate in the matter of historical criticism. At least he never concealed what he was doing. Was this any worse than privileging a particular view of the life and significance of Christ because it is held by a believing community? It is probably better, in that de Wette could give reasons for his position, whereas one wants to ask why a believing community thinks about Christ in the way it does. In one respect, de Wette advanced an argument that has found support in modern writing. This was his view that the faith and existence of the earliest Christian community is a datum, and that one can work back from this to a plausible reconstruction of what must have happened to bring this community and its faith into being. De Wette was remarkable in being so sensitive on two fronts: to those for whom faith was impossible unless the Bible was studied critically, and to those for whom the results of biblical criticism were threatening. That sensitivity is needed no less today.

We can deal briefly with the third and fourth aspects of de Wette's modernity. In his writings on religion he succeeded in allowing that there was truth to be found in all religions. Yet not all were equally true. We think here of his strenuous efforts to combine tolerance with commitment to truth. Whatever we think of the philosophical methodology that enabled him to discuss and discriminate among religions, we must concede that it was well thought out and well executed. The *Über die Religion* is a considerable achievement, and raises the question whether we can be satisfied with anything less thorough in our own situation. The other aspect in this paragraph is the ethical/political aspect. For de Wette, Bible and theology were not academic games. Because they were concerned with reality they affected people's lives at the individual and corporate levels. This was why de Wette wrote on ethics, and on politics as they affected the life of the church and the nation. Again, we may think that de Wette was naive to suppose that a well-educated populace would want to espouse nationalism, religion, democracy and the arts, but it is clear that he was not passive in his politics, and that he paid a considerable personal price for his beliefs. It would be nice to think that, in today's world, he would be sympathetic to those who are using the Bible in the struggle to liberate the poor and oppressed.

The fifth point that I wish to discuss is de Wette's interest in art, drama and aesthetics. It is here that he is at his most interesting for the modern world, in which the application of terms such as tragedy and comedy to biblical literature has been a feature of recent research. For all his prowess as a historical critic who never lost his sharpness, de Wette appreciated, as few have before or since, that the Bible has literary and dramatic power. His youthful dismissal of the possibility of reconstructing history from the Pentateuch was precisely so that he could defend the poetic and literary qualities of the material. His Psalms commentary was cool towards reconstructing historical or cultic settings for the same reason. His youthful essay on Job, Psalms and Ecclesiastes was concerned with their meaning as pieces of literature, and in his article on Hosea for the Ersch and Gruber encyclopaedia, he suggested that the material had been put into its present form for literary reasons.

De Wette, then, would have welcomed the recent interest in the application of literary theory to biblical interpretation, and would no doubt have been surprised at the initial hostility that was expressed towards this trend. In one regard, however, his position differs from modern approaches. De Wette tied aesthetics to ontology. For him, literature was not simply literature; it was an attempt, consciously or unconsciously, to grasp and express eternal truths. It is here, it seems to me, that de Wette demands that we add to our agenda an item long since neglected. What is the status of aesthetic experience in theology and biblical studies? Is there nothing 'behind' biblical texts in their literary forms? It is not without significance that one of the most influential books in religious studies this century that has stressed the aesthetic, non-rational dimension of human and religious experience had been Rudolf Otto's *The Idea of the Holy*. Otto was, of course, a careful reader of Fries. Further, there is a continuing interest in modern philosophy in the importance of aesthetics within human experience as conveying non-cognitive insights about our being.[1] There must be a place for an attempt to integrate biblical studies more closely with an aesthetic-literary exploration of reality.

The word 'integrate' brings me to my final point. When one looks at the range of de Wette's work, it is astonishingly wide: biblical studies, theology, ethics, religious studies, art, literature and aesthetics. It is no exaggeration to say that de Wette worked in all these fields because he was a full and rounded human being, and wanted to give consideration to all these dimensions of being human. There is a lack, of course, in the areas of economics and sociology, fields yet to be developed in de Wette's day, yet ones that he would have undoubtedly studied given his known refusal to be satisfied with his state of knowledge. De Wette, then, was a man of the future not by establishing himself unforgettably in a particular field, but by honestly and

---

1.   See, for example, G. Steiner, *Real Presences: Is there Anything in what we Say?* (London: Faber and Faber, 1989); C. Taylor, *Sources of the Self: The Making of the Modern Identity* (Cambridge: Cambridge University Press, 1989).

fearlessly addressing himself to questions that concerned humanity in all aspects of its existence. It is only comparatively recently in biblical studies that we have begun to move tentatively towards that complete agenda that constituted his life's work.

LIST OF WRITINGS BY DE WETTE

This list is as complete as I can make it, based upon the researches of Staehelin, Smend, Handschin and myself.

Books

'Dissertatio critico-exegetica qua Deuteronomium a prioribus Pentateuchi Libris diversum, alius cuiusdam recentioris auctioris opus esse monstratur; quam... auctoritate amplissimi philosophorum ordinis pro venia legendi AD XXVIII.' (Aug. MDCCCV publice defendet auctor Guilielm Martin Leberecht de Wette, philosophiae doctor; Jena, 1805 [repr. in *Opuscula theologica* (Berlin, 1830)]).

Auffoderung zum Studium der Hebräischen Sprache und Literatur; zur Eröffnung seiner Vorlesungen (Jena and Leipzig, 1805).

Beiträge zur Einleitung in das Alte Testament. I. Kritischer Versuch über die Glaubwürdigkeit der Bücher und Gesetzgebung (Halle, 1806). II. *Kritik der israelitischen Geschichte. Erster Teil: Kritik der mosaischen Geschichte* (Halle, 1807 [repr. Darmstadt: Wissenschaftliche Buchgesellschaft, 1971]).

'Vindiciae auctoritatis, qua Augustana Confessio praedita est, symbolicae; oratio solemnis, quam ex instituto Lynkeriano a.d. XV.' (Aug. MDCCCVI intemplo academico habuit Guil. Martin Leberecht de Wette, philosophiae doctor; Jena, 1806).

Beytrag zur Charakteristik des Hebraismus, in *Studien* (ed. C. Daub and F. Creuzer; Heidelberg, 1807), III.2, pp. 261-312.

Die Schriften des Alten Testaments: Neu übersetzt von J.C.W. Augusti und W.M.L. de Wette, I (Heidelberg, 1809).

Commentar über die Psalmen (Heidelberg, 1811 [2nd edn, 1823; 3rd edn, 1829; 4th edn, 1836]).

De Morte Jesu christi expiatoria commentatio (Berlin, 1813).

Lehrbuch der christlichen Dogmatik in ihrer historischen Entwickelung dargestellt. I. *Biblische Dogmatik Alten und Neuen Testaments oder kritische Darstellung der Religionslehre des Hebraismus, des Judenthums und Urchristenthums: Zum Gebrauch akademischer Vorlesungen* (Berlin, 1813 [2nd edn, 1818; 3rd edn, 1831]). II. *Dogmatik der evangelisch-lutherischen Kirche nach den symbolischen Büchern und den älteren Dogmatikern* (Berlin, 1816 [2nd edn, 1821; 3rd edn, 1839]).

Die Schriften des Neuen Testaments: Neu übersetzt von J.C.W. Augusti und W.M.L. de Wette (Heidelberg, 1814).

Lehrbuch der hebräisch-jüdischen Archäologie nebst einem Grundriss der hebräisch-jüdischen Geschichte (Leipzig, 1814 [2nd edn, 1830; 3rd edn, 1842]).

Über Religion und Theologie: Erläuterungen zu seinem Lehrbuche über Dogmatik (Berlin, 1815 [2nd edn, 1821]).

Die neue Kirche oder Verstand und Glaube im Bunde (Berlin, 1815).

'Programma de prophetarum in Veteris Testamenti ecclesia et doctorum theologiae in ecclesia evangelica ratione atque similitudine' (Invitation to award the degree of Doctor of Theology to August Neander; Berlin, 1816).

Lehrbuch der historische-kritischen Einleitung in die Bibel Alten und Neuen Testaments. I. Die Einleitung in das Alte Testament enthaltend (Berlin, 1817 [2nd edn, 1822; 3rd edn, 1829; 4th edn, 1833; 5th edn, 1840; 6th edn, 1844]). *II. Die Einleitung in das Neue Testament enthaltend* (Berlin, 1826 [2nd edn, 1830; 3rd edn, 1834; 4th edn, 1842; 5th edn, 1848]). ET with additions by T. Parker, *Introduction to the Canonical Scriptures of the Old Testament* (Boston, 1843 [2nd edn, 1850]).

Synopsis evangeliorum Matthaei, Marci et Lucae cum parallelis Joannis pericopis (ed. de Wette and F. Lücke; Berlin, 1818 [2nd edn, 1842]).

Christliche Sittenlehre. I. Die allgemeine Sittenlehre (Berlin, 1819). *II. Allgemeine Geschichte der christlichen Sittenlehre. 1. Geschichte der vorchristlichen und altkatholischen Sittenlehre* (Berlin, 1819). *2. Geschichte der römisch-katholischen und protestantischen Sittenlehre* (Berlin, 1821). *III. Besondere Sittenlehre* (Berlin, 1823).

Zur christlichen Belehrung und Ermahnung: Theologische Aufsätze. 1. Katholicismus und Protestantismus im Verhältnis zur christlichen Offenbarung: eine polemische Abhandlung. 2. Die Sünde wider den heiligen Geist: eine biblische Betrachtung (Berlin, 1819).

Die Psalmen. Metrisch übersetzt von W.M.L. de Wette: Besondere Abdruck aus der vollständigen Bibelübersetzung von Augusti und de Wette (Heidelberg, 1819 [repr. 1823 and 1829]).

Aktensammlung über die Entlassung des Professors D. de Wette vom theologischen Lehramt zu Berlin: Zur Berichtigung des öffentlichen Urteils von ihm selbst herausgegeben (Leipzig, 1820).

Der Graf von Gleichen (1820), in Handschin, *De Wette als Prediger*, pp. 299-321.

Theodor oder des Zweiflers Weihe: Bildungsgeschichte eines evangelischen Geistlichen (2 Vols; Berlin, 1822 [2nd edn, 1828]). ET by F. Clarke, *Theodore or the Skeptic's Conversion* (ed. G. Ripley; Specimens of Foreign Standard Literature; Boston, 1841).

Die Entsagung (Play in three acts) (Berlin, 1823).

Vorlesungen über die Sittenlehre. I. Die allgemeine Sittenlehre (Parts 1 and 2; Berlin, 1823). *II. Die besondere Sittenlehre* (Parts 1 and 2; 1824). ET by S. Osgood, *Human Life or Practical Ethics* (Specimens of Foreign Standard Literature; Boston, 1842).

Das erste Kapitel Johannes des Evangelisten, erbaulich ausgelegt als Probe eines biblischen Erbauungsbuches, nebst Ankündigung desselben (Berlin, 1825).

Die heilige Schrift des neuen Bundes, ausgelegt, erläutert und entwickelt: Ein Andachtsbuch für Prediger und Schullehrer. I. Das Evangelium Johannes bis zur Leidensgeschichte (Berlin, 1825). II. *Das Evangelium von Matthäus, Markus und Lukas* (Berlin, 1828).

Dr Martin Luthers Briefe, Sendschreiben und Bedenken (5 vols.; Berlin, 1825 [I], 1826 [II], 1827 [III], 1827 [IV], 1828 [V]).

Die heilige Schrift des Alten und Neuen Testaments: Übersetzt von Dr. W.M.L. de Wette (Heidelberg, 1832 [This rates as the second edition of the translation by Augusti and de Wette of 1809/1814, but in this edition the translation is by de Wette alone] [3rd edn, 1839]).

Die deutsche theologische Lehranstalt in Nord-amerika: Aktenstücke, Erläuterungen, Bitten. Hg. zum Besten dieser Lehranstalt (Basel, 1826).

Über die Religion, ihr Wesen, ihre Erscheinungsformen und ihren Einfluss auf das Leben: Vorlesungen (Berlin, 1827).

Heinrich Melchthal oder Bildung und Gemeingeist: Eine Belehrende Geschichte (ed. W.M.L. de Wette; 2 vols; Berlin, 1829).

Opuscula theologica (Berlin, 1830).

Lehrbuch der christlichen Sittenlehre und der Geschichte derselben (Berlin, 1833).

Über den Angriff des grauen Mannes gegen Lehrer der hiesigen Universität (Basel, 1834).

Rede bei der öffentlichen Feier der Wiederherstellung der Universität am 1. October 1835 im Chor der Münster-Kirche, gehalten von W.M.L. de Wette, Dr und Professor der Theologie, d.Z. Rector (Basel, 1835).

Kurzgefasstes exegetisches Handbuch zum Neuen Testament (Leipzig, 1836–48).

  I. 1. *Kurze Erklärung des Evangeliums Matthäi* (1836 [2nd edn, 1838; 3rd edn, 1845]).
  I. 2. *Kurze Erklärung der Evangelien des Lukas und Markus* (1836 [2nd edn, 1839; 3rd edn, 1845]).
  I. 3. *Kurze Erklärung des Evangeliums und der Briefe Johannis* (1837 [2nd edn, 1839; 3rd edn, 1846]).
  I. 4. *Kurze Erklärung der Apostelgeschichte* (1838 [2nd edn, 1848; 3rd edn, 1848]).
  II. 1. *Kurze Erklärung des Briefes an die Römer* (1835 [2nd edn, 1838; 3rd edn, 1841; 4th edn, 1847]).
  II. 2. *Kurze Erklärung der Briefe an die Corinther* (1841 [2nd edn, 1845]).
  II. 3. *Kurze Erklärung des Briefes an die Galater und der Briefe an die Thessaloniker* (1841 [2nd edn, 1845]).
  II. 4. *Kurze Erklärung der Briefe an die Colosser, an Philemon, an die Ephesier und Philipper* (1843 [2nd edn, 1847]).
  II. 5. *Kurze Erklärung der Briefe an Titus, Timotheus und die Hebräer* (1844 [2nd edn, 1847]).
  III. 1. *Kurze Erklärung der Briefe des Petrus, Judas und Jakobus* (1847).
  III. 2. *Kurze Erklärung der Offenbarung Johannis* (1848).

Über die erbauliche Erklärung der Psalmen: Einladungschrift zur Rede des Zeit. Rector Magnificus Herrn Prf. Dr Fr. Brömmel von Dr W.M.L. de Wette (Basel, 1836). Edition for general sales: *Über die erbauliche Erklärung der Psalmen. Eine Beilage zum Commentar über dieselben* (Heidelberg, 1836).

Wilhelm Gesenius: Hebräisches Elementarbuch. Zweiter Teil: Hebräisches Lesebuch (ed. W.M.L. de Wette; Leipzig, 7th edn, 1839).

Das Wesen des christlichen Glaubens vom Standpunkte des Glaubens (Basel, 1845).

Die biblische Geschichte als Geschichte der Offenbarungen Gottes: Leitfaden für Lehrer (Berlin, 1846).

Gedanken über Malerei und Baukunst, besonders in kirchlicher Beziehung (Berlin, 1846).

Die Ausschliessung des D. Rupp von der Hauptversammlung des Gustav–Adolf– Vereines zu Berlin am 7. September 1846 (Basel, 1847).

Articles

'Über den Verfall der protestantischen Kirche in Deutschland und die Mittel, ihr wieder aufzuhelfen', *Reformations-Almanach* (1817).

'Accommodatio', *AEWK* 1.1 (1818), pp. 266-68.

'Äthiopische Sprache und Literatur', *AEWK* 1.2 (1819), pp. 113ff. 'Amos', *AEWK* 1.3 (1819), pp. 384-85.

'Über den sittlichen Geist der Reformation in Beziehung auf unsere Zeit', *Reformations-Almanach* (1819).

'Kritische Übersicht der Ausbildung der theologischen Sittenlehre in der evangelisch-lutherischen Kirche seit Calixtus', *TZ* 1 (1819), pp. 247ff.; *TZ* 2 (1820), pp. 1ff.

'Über die Lehre von der Erwählung, in Beziehung auf Herrn Dr Schleiermachers Abhandlung darüber in dieser Zeitschrift', *TZ* 2 (1820), pp. 83ff.

'Andreas', *AEWK* 1.4 (1820), p. 36.

'Angelsächsische Bibelübersetzungen', *AEWK* 1.4 (1820), pp. 89-90.

'Antilegomena', *AEWK* 1.4 (1820), p. 301.

'Apokryphen', *AEWK* 1.4 (1820), pp. 412-13.

'Apostel', *AEWK* 1.4 (1820), p. 463.

'Apostolische Briefe', *AEWK* 1.4 (1820), pp. 465-66.

'Aquilen', *AEWK* 1.5 (1820), pp. 29, 30.

'Arabische Bibel-Übersetzungen', *AEWK* 1.5 (1820), pp. 77-80.

'Armenien', *AEWK* 1.5 (1820), pp. 359-60.

'Baruch, Buch Baruchs', *AEWK* 1.7 (1821), pp. 461-62.

'Über die symbolisch-typische Lehrart des Briefes an die Hebräer; in Beziehung auf Herrn Dr Schulzens Bearbeitung desselben', *TZ* 3 (1822), pp. 1ff.

'Der [*sic*] Strassburger Münster, 1820', in *Erheiterungen* (ed. H. Zschokke; 1822), pp. 141ff.

'Rede, nach dem Antritt des Rectorats der Universität den 12. Mai gehalten', *WZ* 2 (1823), pp. 1ff.

'Bibel', *AEWK* 1.10 (1823), pp. 1ff.

'Über den Begriff und Umfang der Sittenlehre' (the first of de Wette's public lectures 1822–23, see p. 198), *WZ* 1 (1823), pp. 1ff.

'Ideen über die christliche, besonders die tragische Dichtung', *WZ* 1.3 (1823), pp. 69ff., 1.4 (1823), pp. 1ff.

'Ein Tag in Basel', *JLKLM* 39 (1824), pp. 17ff., 16ff., 34ff.

'Andeutungen über die Bildung und Berufstätigkeit des Geistlichen, insbesondere über die Kanzelberedsamkeit', *WZ* 2.1 (1824), pp. 52ff., 2.2 (1824), pp. 1ff., 2.4 (1824), pp. 1ff.

'Die Philister', *WZ* 3.4 (1825), pp. 74ff.

'Über den Zweck des Vereines zur sittlich-religiösen Einwirkung auf die Griechen', *BMFG* 1.18 (1826), pp. 409-10.

'Du comité de Bâle pour réveil de la religion et des moerus parmi les Grecs', *NV* 78 (1826), p. 314.

'Uber das Verhältnis der Kirche zum Staate: Eine Vorlesung', *WZ* 5.2 (1827), pp. 1ff.

'Habakuk', *AEWK* 2.1 (1827), pp. 35-36.

'Haggai', *AEWK* 2.1 (1827), pp. 178-79.

'Hagiographa', *AEWK* 2.1 (1827), p. 180.

'Über Mosaismus, Urchristenthum, Katholizismus und Protestantismus. Aus den von Dr de Wette im verflossenen Winter zu Basel gehaltenen Vorlesungen über die Religion, ihr Wesen, ihre Erscheinungsformen und ihren Einfluss auf das Leben', *Der Protestant* 1.3, (1827), pp. 55-77.

'Das Christenthum in seiner ersten Erscheinung', *Der Protestant*, 2.1 (1827), pp. 38-57.

'Der Katholizismus', *Der Protestant* 2.2 (1827), pp. 9-29.

'Der Protestantismus oder der neuere Entwicklungsgang des Christenthums, nebst den Aufgaben, welche der christlichen Kirche für die Zukunft gestellt sind', *Der Protestant* 2.3 (1827), pp. 1-22.

'Die neugriechischen Flüchtlinge in Basel', *WZ* 5.4 (1827), pp. 26-45. (This was published anonymously, but is probably by de Wette. See Handschin, *De Wette als Prediger*, p. 329).

'Einige Gedanken über den Geist der neueren protestantischen Theologie', *TSK* 1 (1828), pp. 125ff.

'Beitrag zur Charakteristik des Evangelisten Markus', *TSK* 1 (1828), pp. 789ff.

'Brief an die Hebräer', *AEWK* 2.3 (1828), pp. 329ff.

'Gedanken eines Theologen über Goethes Faust', *Der Protestant* 3 (1829), pp. 210ff.

'Von der Stellung der Wissenschaft im Gemeinwesen. Rektoratsrede, gehalten den 2. Juli 1829' (Basel, 1829).

'Basels Hochschule und die Schweiz', *NZZ* (2 January, 1830); *ASZ* 7 (1830), pp. 257ff.

'Einsiedlers Morgenlied "Wieder hat das Licht gesiegt"', *Musenalmanach* 1 (1830), p. 134.

'Exegetische Bemerkungen über Jak. 2, 14-16, Röm 14; 5, Mos. 1-3', *TSK* 3 (1830), pp. 348ff.

'Zur Geschichte der Kindertaufe', *TSK* 3 (1830), pp. 669ff.

'Hexapla', *AEWK* 2.7 (1830), pp. 337ff.

'Gedanken über die Lehreinheit der evangelischen Kirche', *TSK* 4 (1831), pp. 221ff.

'Über schwere Stellen der historischen Bücher des Alten Testaments', *TSK* 4 (1831), pp. 303ff.

'Über die geschichtliche Beziehung der prophetischen Reden Hoseas', *TSK* 4 (1831), pp. 807ff.

'Vorarbeiten zu einem christlichen Henotikon', *ZPW* 2, (1831), pp. 566-77.

'Hiob', *AEWK* 2.8 (1831), pp. 290ff.

'Daniel', *AEWK* 1.23 (1832), pp. 1-15.

'Die Baselbieter Revolution' (anonymously published) *AZ* 453, 454 (10 November 1832). See Staehelin, *Dewettiana*, p. 46.
'Abfertigung', *BZ* 3.91 (1833). (Reply to the open letter criticizing de Wette by a 'Bible-believing clergyman'.)
Anonymously published reminisence on Schleiermacher, *BZ* 4.30 (1834), p. 126.
'Einige Betrachtungen über den Geist unsere Zeit. Academische Rede, am 12. September 1834 gehalten von Dr W.M.L. de Wette, d.Z. Rector der Basler Universität', (Basel, 1834).
'Hosea', *AEWK* 2.11 (1834), pp. 80-84.
'Bemerkungen zu Stellen des Evangeliums Johannis', *TSK* 7 (1834), p. 924ff.
'Die Liebe ist grösser als der Glaube', *OJABTUL* (1835).
'Die christliche Hoffnung. Eine dogmatische Betrachtung', *OJABTUL* (1837).
'Die Halle'sche Missionsanstalt', *AKZ* 16 (1837), pp. 601ff, 609ff.
'Echtheit (der Bücher, Authentie)', *AEWK* 1.30 (1838), pp. 403-404.
'Aufruf zur Bildung eines protestantischen kirchlichen Hülfsvereins', *AKZ* 21 (1842), pp. 329ff. (co-signed by de Wette).
'Ein Brief aus Rom', *KRS* 2 (1846), pp. 59ff.
'Festrede, gehalten an dem 14. Februar 1849 begangenen Jubiläum der fünfundzwanzigjährigen Dozententätigkeit von Karl Rudolf Hagenbach, Johann Jakob Stähelin und Friedrich Brömmel', *Literarische Beilage zum Intelligenz-Blatt der Stadt Basel* 8 (1849).
'Bermekungen über die Lehre von der Sünde mit Rücksicht auf das Werk von Julius Müller', *TSK* 21 (1849), pp. 539ff.

Reviews

Über die Religion. Reden an die Gebildeten unter ihren Verächtern, by F. Schleiermacher (2nd edn, 1806). *JALZ* 4.2 (1807), pp. 433-88.
Über den sogennanten ersten Brief des Paulus an den Timotheus, by F. Schleiermacher (1807). *JALZ* 4.4 (1807), pp. 217ff., 225ff.
Geist und Würde des christlichen Religionslehrers, by J.L. Ewald (1806). *JALZ* 4.4 (1807), pp. 231-32.
Vertraute Briefe über die Bibel, by G. Ehrlich (1807). *JALZ* 4.4 (1807), pp. 380-82.
Über den Geist und die Form der evangelischen Geschichte in historischer und ästhetischer Hinsicht, by F.A. Krummacher (1805). *JALZ* 5.1 (1808), pp. 11ff.
Universalgeschichte der christlichen Kirche, by K.F. Stäudlin (1806). *JALZ* 5.3 (1808), pp. 545-50.
Commentar über den Pentateuch, by J.S. Vater (1802–1805). *HJL* 1.1 (1808), pp. 105ff.
Die heiligen Schriften des Neuen Testamentes, trans. C. van Ess and L. van Ess (1807). *HJL* 1.1 (1808), pp. 227ff.
Uransichten des Christenthums nebst Untersuchungen über einige Bücher des neuen Testaments, by H.H. Clusius (1808). *JALZ* 6.1 (1809), pp. 27ff.
Geschichte der Religion Jesu Christi, I-IV, by F.L. Graf zu Stolberg (1806–1809). *JALZ* 6.1 (1809), pp. 201-16.

Anti-Stolberg, oder Versuch, die Rechte der Vernunft gegen F.L.G. zu Stolberg zu behaupten, by H. Kunhard (1808). *JALZ* 6.1 (1809), pp. 201-16.

Bemerkungen über den ersten paulinischen Brief an den Timotheus, in Beziehung auf das kritische Sendschreiben von Hrn. Prof. Schleiermacher, by H. Planck (1808). *JALZ* 6.1 (1809), pp. 401ff., 409ff.

Einleitung in die Schriften des Neuen Testamentes, by J.L. Hug (1808). *HJL* 2.1.1 (1809), pp. 145ff.

Curarum exegetico-criticarum in Nahumum Prophetam specimen, by C.M. Fraehn (1806). *HJL* 2.1.1 (1809), pp. 159ff.

Die Schriften des Alten Testaments. Neu übersetzt von J.C.W. Augusti und W.M.L. de Wette, I (1809). *HJL* 2.1.1 (1809), pp. 257ff.

Scholia in Vetus Testamentum, V, VI, by E.F.C. Rosenmüller. *HJL* 2.1 (1809), pp. 59ff.

Blumen althebräischer Dichtkunst, ed. K.W. Justi (1809), and *Die schönsten Geistes Blüthen des ältesten Orients für Freunde des Grossen und Schönen*, Gepflückt von J.L.W. Scherer (1809). *HJL* 3.1 (1810), pp. 393ff.

Die Schriften des Alten Testaments. Neu übersetzt von J.C.W. Augusti und W.M.L. de Wette, II, III (1809). *HJL* 3.1.1 (1810), pp. 76-77.

Grundriss einer historisch-kritischen Einleitung in's alte Testament, by J.C.W. Augusti (1806). *HJL* 3.1.1 (1810), pp. 171ff.

Siona: Darstellungen das Alte Testament betreffend, by W.N. Freudentheil (1809). *JALZ* 7.1 (1810), pp. 13ff.

Über die bekanntschaft Marcions mit unserem Kanon des neuen Bundes und insbesondere über das Evangelium desselben, by M. Arneth (1809). *JALZ* 7.1 (1810), pp. 220-24.

Briefe, den Werth der schriftlichen Religionsurkunde, als solcher, betreffend, I, II, by C.V. Hauff (1809). *JALZ* 7.1 (1810), pp. 393ff.

Geschichte der Religion Jesu Christi, V, by F.L. Graf zu Stolberg (1809). *JALZ* 7.2 (1810), pp. 7ff.

Amos, trans. and annotated by J.S. Vater (1810). *HJL* 3.2.1 (1810), pp. 154ff.

Bemerkungen über Stellen in Jeremias Weissagungen, by C.G. Hensler (1805). *HJL* 3.2.1 (1810), pp. 159ff.

Hebräisch-deutsches Handwörterbuch über die Schriften des Alten Testaments, I, by W. Gesenius (1810). *HJL* 4 (1811), pp. 65ff.

Einleitung in das Neue Testament, I, II, by J.G. Eichhorn (1804, 1810). *HJL* 4 (1811), pp. 533ff., 545ff.

Einleitung in das Neue Testament, II.2, by J.G. Eichhorn (1811). *HJL* 5 (1812), pp. 695ff.

Ansichten von interessanten, dunkeln und sinnreichen Stellen des neuen Testaments (1810). *JALZ* 9.4 (1812), pp. 182ff.

Die Schein–Widersprüche in der Schrift, by F. Österlen. *JALZ* 10.1 (1813), pp. 22ff.

Über öffentliches Gottesdienst und heiligen Abendmahl, by C.F. Schmidt (1806). *JALZ* 10.2 (1813), pp. 7-8.

Analekten für das Studium der exegetischen und systematischen Theologie, I, ed. C.A.G. Keil and H.G. Tzirschner (1812). *JALZ* 10.2 (1813), pp. 161-68.

Die Psalmen. Aus dem Hebräischen neu übersetzt und erläutert, by M.H. Stuhlmann (1812). *JALZ* Ergänzungsblätter 1.2 (1813), pp. 125-33.

De Daemonologia in sacris Novi Testamenti libris proposita Commentation prima, by D. Winzer (1812). *HJL* 6 (1813), pp. 29ff.

Hebräisch–deutsches Handwörterbuch über die Schriften des Alten Testaments, II, by W. Gesenius (1812). *HJL* 6 (1813), pp. 33f.

Geschichte der Sittenlehre Jesu, by C.F. Stäudlin (1799–1812). *JALZ* 11.2 (1814), pp. 361-71.

Über die Religion der Ebräer vor Moses, by L. Bendavid (1814). *JALZ* 11.2 (1814), pp. 375-76.

Die Psalmen übersetzt und ihrem Hauptinhalte nach erläutert by F.V. Reinhard (1813). *JALZ* 11.3 (1814), pp. 1ff.

Exegetische Bruchstücke (1812). *JALZ* 11.3 (1814), pp. 212ff.

Die Psalmen, übersetzt und metrisch bearbeitet, by M. Lindemann (1812). *JALZ* 11.3 (1814), pp. 347-50.

Theologische Encyklopädie, by J.E.C. Schmidt (1812). *JALZ* 11.4 (1814), pp. 1ff.

Die Leidensgeschichte Jesu, exegetisch und archäologisch bearbeitet, mit Rücksicht auf die neuesten Ansichten, besonders für Prediger und Religionslehrer. JALZ 11.4 (1814), pp. 3ff.

Glückwünschungsschreiben an die hochwürdigen Mitgleider der von Sr Majestät dem König von Preussen zur Aufstellung neuer liturgischer Formen ernannten Commission (1814). *JALZ* 11.4 (1814), pp. 377-88.

Hebräische Sprachlehre, by J.S. Vater (2nd edn, 1814); *Hebräische Grammatik*, by W. Gesenius (1813); *Grammatica Hebraica*, by T.A. Dereser (1813). *HJL* 7 (1814), pp. 1137ff.

Antwort auf unter die Titel 'Glückwünschungsschreiben an die Mitgleider der zur Aufstellung neuer liturgischer Formen ernannten Commission' erschienenen Schrift 1814; Erwiederung auf die Antwort der allerhöchst ernannten Commissarien zur Aufstellung neuer liturgischer Formen auf Veranlassung des an sie erlassenen Glückwunschschreibens. JALZ 12.1 (1815), pp. 349-52.

Die heilige Kunst oder die Kunst der Hebräer, by A. Gügler. *JALZ* 12.2 (1815), pp. 313ff.

Brüchstücke zur Menschen- und Erziehungskunde, religiösen Inhalts, VI-X (1815). *JALZ* 12.3 (1815), pp. 129-47.

Über den christlichen Cultus, by J.C. Gass (1815). *JALZ* 12.3 (1815), pp. 153-68.

Aus welchem Gesichtspuncte muss die in Anregung gebrachte Verbesserung der protestantischen Kirchenverfassung betrachtet werden? Worte der Verständigung und Beruhigung an das über diese Angelegenheit noch nicht unterrichtete Publicum; besonders in Beziehung auf die Schrift: Erwiederung auf die Antwort der allerhöchst ernannten Commission zur Aufstellung neuer liturgischer Formen, by C.H. Neumann. *JALZ* 12.3 (1815), pp. 329-34.

Grundlinien einer künftigen Verfassung der protestantischen Kirche im preussischen Staate, by Küster–Neumann–Tiebel (1815). *JALZ* 12.3 (1815), pp. 334-39.

Ein Wort zu rechter Zeit an meiner Brüder: Veranlasst durch die zu Berlin allerhöchst angeordnete königl., preussische Commission zur Veredelung des protestantischen Cultus, by L. Pflaum (1814). *JALZ* 12.3 (1815), pp. 340-44.

Zur Kirchenvereinigung: Eine Streitschrift gegen eines ungennanten Glückwünschungsschreiben an die hochwürdigen Mitgleider der von Sr Majestät dem Könige von Preussen zur Aufstellung neuer liturgischer Formen ernannten Commission, by L. Beckedorf (1815). *JALZ* 12.4 (1815), pp. 313-23.

Sendschreiben an einen Freund weltlichen Standes über die Erneuerung des Cultus by A.K.Z.K. ('ein preussischer Geistlicher') (1815). *JALZ* 12.4 (1815), pp. 323-26.

Die Bestimmung des evangelischen Geistlichen (1815). *JALZ* 12.4 (1815), pp. 325ff.

Einleitung in das Neue Testament, III.1, by J.G. Eichhorn (1812). *HJL* 8 (1815), pp. 225ff.

De pentateuchi Samaritani origine, indole et auctoritate commentatio philologico-exegetica, by W. Gesenius (1815). *HJL* 8 (1815), pp. 631ff.

Über die Lehrart in Volksschulen, mit besonderer Rücksicht auf die Weissfrauenschulen by A. Kirchener (1814); *Drey Actenstücke, die Weissfrauenschulen betreffend*, by A. Kirchner (1814). *JALZ* Ergänzungsblätter 3.1 (1815), pp. 129-34.

Exegetische Bruchstücke. Zweyter Prodromus einer Darstellung des Christenthums nach Vernunft und Bibel (1812). *JALZ* Ergänzungsblätter 3.2 (1815), pp. 177-88.

Geschichte der hebräischen Sprache und Schrift, by W. Gesenius (1815). *HJL* 9 (1816), pp. 33ff.

Libri sacri antiqui foederis ex sermone hebraeo in latinum translati..., I, by H.A. Schott and J.F.W. Sinzer (1816). *HJL* 9 (1816), pp. 1096ff.

Mysteriosophie, oder über die Veredelung des protestantischen Gottesdienstes durch die Verbindung eines einfach-erhabenen inneren Acts des Cultus mit der Predigt, by G.C. Horst (1817). *JALZ* 13.4 (1816), pp. 169-87.

A Comparative View of the Churches of England and Rome, by H. Marsh (1814). *JALZ* 14.2 (1817), pp. 1ff., 9ff.

A Letter to the Rev. Peter Gandolphy, in confutation of the opinion that the vital principle of the Reformation has been lately conceded to the Church of Rome, and *A Letter of Explanation to the Dissenter and Layman, who has lately addressed himself to the author on the Views of the Protestant Dissenters* by H. Marsh (1813). *JALZ* 14.1 (1817), pp. 14ff.

Analekten für das Studium der exegetischen und systematischen Theologie, II.2, 3, III.1, ed. C.A.G. Keil and H.G. Tzirschner (1814–1816). *JALZ* Ergänzungsblätter 4.2 (1817), pp. 193-203.

Bruchstücke zur Menschen- und Erziehungskunde religiösen Inhalts, XI, XII (1816). *JALZ* 14.1 (1817), pp. 59-64.

Judas Ischariot oder das Böse im Verhältnis zum Guten, I, by C. Daub (1816). *JALZ* 14.1 (1817), pp. 313-26.

Beyträge zur Sprachcharakteristik der Schriftsteller des Neuen Testaments, I, by C.G. Gersdorf (1816). *HJL* 10 (1817), pp. 189ff.

Vorlesungen über die Hermeneutik des Neuen Testaments, by J.J. Griesbach (1815). *JALZ* Ergänzungsblätter 6.1 (1818), pp. 25ff., 33ff., 41ff.

Geschichte der litthauischen Bibel, and *Philologisch-kritische Anmerkungen zur litthauischen Bibel*, by L.J. Rhesa (1816). *JALZ* 15.2 (1818), pp. 1ff.

A Collection of Hymns and a Liturgy for the use of Evangelical Lutheran Churches (1814); *Evangelical Catechism* and *Three sermons*, by F.H. Quitman (1814, 1817). *JALZ* Ergänzungsblätter 8.1 (1820), pp. 4ff.

Sophronizon oder unparteyisch-freymüthige Beyträge zur neueren Geschichte, Gesetzgebung und Statistik der Staaten und Kirchen, ed. H.E.G. Paulus (1819). *JALZ* 17.1 (1820), pp. 81-88.

Die Agape oder der geheime Weltbund der Christen, von Klemens in Rom unter Domitians Regierung gestiftet, by A. Kestner. *JALZ* 17.2 (1820), p. 3.

Monogrammata Theologiae christianae dogmaticae, by G.P.C. Kaiser (1819). *JALZ* 17.2 (1820), pp. 171ff.

De Pentateuchi versione Alexandrina, by J.L. Hug (1818). *JALZ* 17.2 (1820), pp. 391-92.

Analekten für das Studium der exegetischen und systematischen Theologie, III.2, III.3, IV.1, ed. Keil–Tzschirner–Rosenmüller (1816, 1817, 1820). *JALZ* 18.2 (1821), pp. 449-60.

Der Prophet Jesaja, by W. Gesenius (1820–21). *JALZ* 19.1 (1822), pp. 1ff., 9ff., 17ff., 25ff., 33ff., 41ff.

Wörterbuch der Blumensprache: Für Verzierungsmaler und Stickerinnen, by Cäcilie (= Amalie von Voigt). *JLKLM* 37 (1822), pp. 338ff.

Entwickelung des Paulinischen Lehrbegriffes, by L. Usteri (1824). *WZ* 2.4 (1824), pp. 117-18.

A Course of Lectures, Containing a Description and Systematic Arrangement of the Several Branches of Divinity, by H. Marsh (1813). *JALZ* Ergänzungsblätter 13.2 (1825), pp. 201ff., 209ff.

A Letter to the Conductor of the Critical Review on the Subject of Religious Toleration, with Occasional Remarks on the Doctrines of the Trinity and the Atonement, by H. Marsh (1810). *JALZ* Ergänzungsblätter 13 (1825), pp. 211ff.

Das Prinzip der Moral in philosophischer, theologischer, christlicher und kirchlicher Bedeutung, by H. Schreiber (1827). *TSK* (1828), pp. 482ff.

Lehrbuch der christlichen Sittenlehre, by L.F.O. Baumgarten-Crusius (1826). *TSK* (1828), pp. 247ff.

Kritische Geschichte der Entstehung und der Schicksale der ersten Basler Confession, by K.R. Hagenbach (1827). *TSK* (1828), pp. 415ff.

Eine Bemerkung über die von Herrn Dr Steudel aufgeworfene und beleuchtete Frage...: Über die Ausführbarkeit einer Annäherung zwischen der rationalistischen und supranaturalistischen Ansicht. *TSK* (1828), pp. 563ff.

Predigten über sämtliche Sonn- und Festtage-Evangelien des Jahres, by E. Zimmerman (1825, 1827). *TSK* (1828), pp. 669ff.

Logik, by I.P.V. Troxler. *TSK* (1831), pp. 137ff.

Meditations religieuses, by J.L.S. Vincent (1830). *TSK* (1831), pp. 159ff.

Religion et Christianisme, ed. J.L.S. Vincent and Fontanes. *TSK* (1831), pp. 166ff.

Predigten über die sonn- und festtäglichen Episteln des Jahres, ed. G.E.F. Seidel (1830). *TSK* (1832), pp. 660ff.

Nachweis der Echtheit sämmtlicher Schriften des Neuen Testaments, by H. Olshausen (1832). *TSK* (1834), pp. 135ff.

Ostergabe oder Jahrbuch häuslicher Andacht und frommer Betrachtung über Tod, Unsterblichkeit, ewiges Leben und Wiedersehen für das Jahr 1834, ed. J.C. Ernst Lösch (1834). *TSK* (1835), pp. 532ff.

Offenbarungsglaube und Kritik der biblischen Geschichtsbücher am Beispiele des B. Josua in ihrer nothwendigen Einheit dargethan, by G.A. Hauff. *TLAKZ* 23 (1844), pp. 513ff.

Die ewigen Thatsachen, by K. Sederholm (1845). *TLAKZ* 24 (1845), pp. 1161ff.

Einleitung in die Schriften des Neuen Testaments, by J.L. Hugl (4th edn, 1847). *TLAKZ* 26 (1847), pp. 1225ff.

Das Wesen des Protestantismus, aus den Quellen des Reformationszeitalters dargestellt. I. Die theologischen Fragen, by D. Schenkel. *TSK* (1848), pp. 141ff.

Sermons

Drey Predigten von Dr W.M.L de Wette (Berlin, 1821).

Predigt am XIII. Sonntage nach Trinitatis in der St Katharinen Kirche zu Braunschweig gehalten (Braunschweig, 1821).

Über das Gleichniss vom ungerechten Haushalter: Eine Predigt (Braunschweig, 1822).

Von der Prüfung der Geister: Predigt am heil. Pfingstfest in der St Elisabeth Kirche gehalten (Basel, 1822 [French translation by A. Vinet, *De l' épreuve des esprits* (Basel, 1822)]).

Von der wahren Verbindung der Christen mit ihrem Erlöser: Predigt am 5ten Sonntage nach Trinitatis in der St Theodors Kirche gehalten (Basel, 1822).

Über das fromme und gesegnete Verhalten des Christen in Ansehung der weltlichen Sorgen: Predigt am 5. Sonntage nach Trinitatis in der St Leonhards Kirche gehalten (Basel, 1823)

Über die Erweckung des Jünglings zu Nain: Predigt am 11. Sonntage nach Trinitatis in der St Elisabeth Kirche gehalten (Basel, 1823).

Über Petrus warnendes Beyspiel. Matth. 16, 13-24: Predigt am Sonntage Lätare in der Kirche zu St Theodor gehalten (Basel, 1824).

Predigten, theils auslegender, theils abhandelnder Art. Erste Sammlung (Basel, 1825). (Contains 10 sermons preached between October 1823 and October 1825).

'Predigt am siebenten Sonntage nach Trinitatis', in *Predigten über sämtliche Sonn- und Festtags-Evangelien des Jahres*, II (ed. D.E. Zimmermann; Darmstadt, 1827).

Predigten, theils auslegender, theils abhandelnder Art. Zweite Sammlung (Basel, 1827). (Contains 10 sermons preached between October 1825 and August 1827).

'Die tröstende und heiligende Kraft des christlichen Glaubens an die Unsterblichkeit', in *Bibliothek deutscher Canzelberedsamkeit*, X (Hildburghausen and New York, 1829), pp. 19ff. (See also *Predigten* [1825], No. 8).

'Die Liebe ist grösser als der Glaube und die Hoffnung, aber mit beiden stets nothwendig verbunden', in *Bibliothek deutscher Canzelberedsamkeit,* pp. 87ff. (See also *Predigten* [1825], No. 3).

'Zum Reformationsfeste am 31. October 1829', *Der Protestant, Zeitschrift für evangelisches Christenthum* (1829), pp. 713ff. (See also *Predigten* [1842], No. 1).

Zwei Predigten zu einem wohlthätigen Zwecke herausgegeben (Basel and Leipzig, 1829).

'Rede bei der Trauung eines Gottesgelehrten', *Zeitschrift für Predigerwissenschaften* 2.2 (1831), pp. 389ff. (Sermon at the wedding of K.R. Hagenbach and Rosina Geigy, 13 October 1829).

'Rede am Grabe eines der Theologie beflissenen Jünglings', *Zeitschrift für Predigerwissenschaften,* 2.2 (1831), pp. 403ff.

Wie die göttliche Weisheit Jesu Christi sich gerade darin bewährt, dass sein Reich nicht von dieser Welt ist: Predigt über Ev. Johannis 18, 36 gehalten in Mühlhausen am 14. Oktober 1832 (Mühlhausen, 1832).

Predigten, theils auslegender, theils abhandelnder Art. Dritte Sammlung (Basel, 1833). (Contains 10 sermons mainly from the period of the civil unrest in Basel, 1830–33).

'Christus ist mein Leben, und Sterben mein Gewinn', in *Ostergabe oder Jahrbuch häuslicher Andacht und frommer Betrachtung über Tod, Unsterblichkeit, ewiges Leben und Wiedersehen für das Jahr 1834* (ed. J.C.E. Lösch; Nürnberg, 1834), pp. 76-96.

Rede bei der Trauung seiner Tochter Anna mit Herrn Dr Heitz in Basel (Hamburg and Itzehoe, 1835).

'Lasset euer Licht leuchten. Predigt', in Zimmerman (ed.), *Die Sonntagsfeier, wöchentliche Blätter für Kanzelberedsamkeit und Erbauung,* II (ed. K. Zimmermann; Darmstadt and Leipzig, 1835), pp. 389ff.

'Das Auftreten Johannes des Täufers. Adventsbetrachtung', in Zimmerman (ed.), *Die Sonntagsfeier,* II, pp. 113ff, (See also *Predigten* [1842], No. 2).

Bibliothek deutscher Canzelberedsamkeit (Hildburghausen and New York, 9th edn, 1835). (Vol. XIX contains a sermon on Eph. 5.21 and vol. XX a sermon on Mt. 3.1-2, and Isa. 9.2. The sermons on Eph. 5.21 and Mt. 3.1 are published in *Predigten* [1833], Nos. 3 and 9, that on Isa. 9.3 in *Predigten* [1825], No. 6).

'Die evangelische Freiheit. Reformationspredigt über Gal. 5, 13-16, gehalten in Basel am 23. August 1835, dem Tage des Reformations-Jubiläums der Genfer Kirche', in *Musterpredigten der jetzt lebenden ausgezeichneteren Kanzelredner Deutschlands und anderer protestantischer Länder,* I (ed. H.A. Schott; Leipzig, 1836), pp. 79ff.

'Die freundliche Einladung Jesu', in Zimmerman (ed.), *Die Sonntagsfeier,* IV (1836), p. 197.

'Zur Weihnachts–Abendmahlsvorbereitung 1834 gehalten', in Zimmerman (ed.), *Die Sonntagsfeier,* III (1836), pp. 371ff.

'Christus vor Pilatus, oder die Gerechtigkeit in der Welt. Predigt über Matth. 27, 11-26', in Schott (ed.), *Musterpredigten,* II (1836), pp. 469ff.

Der christliche Glaube an die Unsterblichkeit. Osterpredigt. Ostergabe für das Jahr 1836 (Nürnberg, 1836), pp. 5-19.

'Rede, bei einer Haustaufe gehalten', in Zimmerman (ed.), *Die Sonntagsfeier*, IV (1836), p. 298.

'Das wahre christliche Streben nach Vollkommenheit. Predigt über Phil. 3, 12-14', in Zimmerman (ed.), *Die Sonntagsfeier*, V (1836), pp. 89ff.

'Das Heranwachsen Jesu vom Kinde zum Mann. Predigt am 22. Januar 1837 gehalten', in Zimmerman (ed.), *Die Sonntagsfeier*, VI (1837), pp. 381-95. (See *Predigten* [1842], No. 8 for a revised version).

'Erbauungsrede am zweiten Pfingstfeiertage, den 8. Juni 1835 zu Carlsbad gehalten', in Zimmerman (ed.), *Die Sonntagsfeier*, VII (1837), pp. 109-21.

Rede, bei der Trauung seines Sohnes gehalten (no place or date of publication given) (Ludwig W.M.L. de Wette was married to Amalie Jersing by de Wette on 26 June 1838 in the St Jakob Church in Basel).

'Taufrede über Matth. 19, 14', in *Magazin von Casual-besonders kleineren geistlichen Amstreden, als Abendmahls-, Beicht-, Confirmations-, Einführungs-, Einweihungs-, Grab-, Tauf-, Trau- und Verlobungsreden*, VI (Magdeburg, 1838).

'Die rechte Osterfreude. Predigt, gehalten Ostern 1838', in *Predigtsammlung schweizerischer evangelischer Geistlicher* (Zürich and Frauenfeld, 1839), pp. 101-10.

'Vom Gegensatze des Christenthums und der Welt. Predigt über Joh, 17, 14, gehalten im Betsaal des Bürgerspitals in Basel', in Zimmerman (ed.), *Die Sonntagsfeier*, IX (1839), pp. 281-96.

'Das fortgehende Werk der Kirchenverbesserung. Reformationspredigt über Eph. 4, 11-16, am Sonntage Trinitatis 1839 zu Basel gehalten' in Zimmerman (ed.), *Die Sonntagsfeier*, X (1839), pp. 385ff.

'Das verborgene Leben des Christen. Predigt über Col. 3, 1-4', in Zimmerman (ed.), *Die Sonntagsfeier*, XII (1840), pp. 633-44. (See also *Predigten* [1842], No. 3).

Rede bei der Beerdigung von Frau Wilh(elmine) Henr(iette) Elise Fischer, geb. Haupt am 14. Mai 1840 gehalten (Basel, 1840).

Die Allseitigkeit des christlichen Geistes. Predigt über 1. Cor. 3, 22f., gehalten in Mühlhausen am 24. Oktober 1841 (Mühlhausen, 1841). (See also Zimmerman (ed.), *Die Sonntagsfeier*, XVI [1842]), pp. 3ff..

Predigten, theils auslegender, theils abhandelnder Art. Vierte Sammlung (Basel, 1842) (Contains 12 sermons).

'Die Saat und Ernte des Menschen. Predigt über Gal. 6, 7-10 vom 23. Oktober 1842', in Handschin, *De Wette als Prediger*, pp. 127-34.

'Die Liebe Gottes und des Nächsten in ihrer nothwendigen Verbindung. Predigt über Matth. 22, 35-40', in Zimmerman (ed.), *Die Sonntagsfeier*, XVIII (1843), pp. 112ff.

Die Liebe als Merkmal des wahren Christenthums: Predigt zur Hochfeier der Versammlung des evangelischen Vereins der Gustav–Adolph–Stiftung in der deutsch-reformierten Kirche (von Frankfurt a.M.), am 24. September gehalten (Frankfurt, 1843).

Die Einheit der protestantischen Kirche: Reformationspredigt nebst einleitenden Bemerkungen über die kirchliche Gemeinschaft (Basel, 1843).

'Rede bei der Beerdigung von Emma Jung, 10 April 1844', in Handschin, *De Wette als Prediger*, pp. 143-46.

'Der Kampf Jesu in Gethsemane. Predigt über Matt. 26, 36-46, Gründonnerstag 1844', in Handschin, *De Wette als Prediger*, pp. 134-43.

'Christus der Weinstock. Predigt über Joh. 15, 1-6', in Zimmerman (ed.), *Die Sonntagsfeier*, XX (1844), pp. 177-86.

'Das Wort ward Fleisch. Predigt am Weihnachtsfeste 1843 gehalten', in Zimmerman (ed.), *Die Sonntagsfeier*, XXII (1845), pp. 3-13.

Die Wahrheit und das Leben: Predigt, gehalten am 9. Februar 1845 in der Kirche zu St Elisabeth in Basel (Basel, 1845).

'Die tröstende Kraft des christlichen Glaubens an die Unsterblichkeit', in *Encyclopädie der deutschen Nationalliteratur*, VII (1846), pp. 540ff. (See *Predigten* [1825], No. 8).

'Das Wort ward Fleisch. Predigt über Joh. 1, 14.16, Weihnachten 1846', in Handschin, *De Wette als Prediger*, pp. 147-53.

'Die Schuld des Irrthums. Predigt über Rom. 1, 18 vom 5. Sept. 1847', in Handschin, *De Wette als Prediger*, pp. 154-61.

Predigten, theils auslegender, theils abhandelnder Art. Fünfte Sammlung (Basel, 1849). The subtitle is: *Die Hauptstücke des christlichen Glaubens in einer Reihe von Predigten. Nach seinem Tode herausgegeben (von K.R. Hagenbach)*. This contains the series of 12 sermons, ten of which de Wette preached at the end of his life. See above pp. 262-63.

Undated Sermons

'Wir haben hier keine bleibende Statt, sondern die zukünftige suchen wir. Sylvesterpredigt über Hebr. 13, 14', (?1842–43). See Handschin, *De Wette als Prediger*, pp. 73 n. 239, 162-70.

'Das Kreuz Christi. Predigt über 1. Korinther 1, 23f.', (?1842–44). See Handschin, *De Wette als Prediger*, pp. 73 n. 240, 171-80.

'Die Zeit zwischen Ostern und Pfingsten oder die Empfänglichkeit für den heil. Geist. Predigt über Luk. 24, 49', (?1843–44). See Handschin, *De Wette als Prediger*, pp. 74 n. 241, 180-91.

'Das versöhnte Gemüth des Christen. Busstags-Predigt über Coloss. 3, 12-15', (?1842-44). See Handschin, *De Wette als Prediger*, pp. 74 n. 242, 192-203.

'Das Gericht Christi in seiner Milde und Gerechtigkeit. Predigt am 1. Advent über Matth. 25, 31-46', (?1842–44). See Handschin, *De Wette als Prediger*, pp. 74 n. 243, 203-13.

'Die Unentbehrlichkeit der Gemeinschaft mit Christus. Predigt über Joh. 15, 1-6', (1844), in Zimmerman (ed.), *Die Sonntagsfeier*, XX (1844), pp. 177-86.

'Die Ruhe des Volkes Gottes. Predigt über Hebr. 4, 9', (1845). See Handschin, *De Wette als Prediger*, pp. 213-21.

'Ein Aufblick zum Lichte der Erscheinung Jesu Christi aus einer trüben Zeit. Predigt über Jes. 9, 2', (26 December 1847). See Handschin, *De Wette als Prediger*, pp. 221-30.

'Die Gesinnung Jesu Christi. Predigt über Phil. 2, 5-11', (Early 1848). See Handschin, *De Wette als Prediger*, pp. 230-38.
'Was Christus für uns ist. Predigt über Gal. 2, 19f.'. See Handschin, *De Wette als Prediger*, pp. 238-46.
'Osterpredigt über Joh. 20, 19-21'. See Handschin, *De Wette als Prediger*, pp. 246-52.
'Selig sind die nicht sehen und doch glauben. Osterpredigt über Joh. 20, 24-29'. See Handschin, *De Wette als Prediger*, pp. 252-61.
'Christi Sieg über den Tod. Osterpredigt über 1. Cor. 15, 55.57'. See Handschin, *De Wette als Prediger*, pp. 261-69.
'Traurede über Luk. 10, 38-42'. See Handschin, *De Wette als Prediger*, pp. 270-78.
'Traurede über Phil. 4.4-7'. See Handschin, *De Wette als Prediger*, pp. 278-85.
'Ansprache bei der Beerdigung eines Jünglings'. See Handschin, *De Wette als Prediger*, pp. 285-89.

Prayers

'Gebet mit der Überschrift: "Vor der Predigt"', in Handschin, *De Wette als Prediger*, pp. 289-90.
'Gebet nach einem Gottesdienst im Auslande, anfangend mit den Worten: "Lasset uns abermals..." ', in Handschin, *De Wette als Prediger*, pp. 290-91.
'Gebet an Weihnachten, nach der Predigt gesprochen', in Handschin, *De Wette als Prediger*, pp. 291-92.
'Gebet an Ostern, vor der Predigt gesprochen, beginnend mit den Worten: "Gnade und Friede sei mit uns"', in Handschin, *De Wette als Prediger*, p. 293.
'Gebet an Ostern, vor der Predigt gesprochen, beginnend mit den Worten: "Dank sei Gott"', in Handschin, *De Wette als Prediger*, pp. 294-95.
'Gebet an Himmelfahrt, vor der Predigt gesprochen', in Handschin, *De Wette als Prediger*, pp. 295-96.
'Gebet an Pfingsten, vor der Predigt gesprochen', in Handschin, *De Wette als Prediger*, pp. 296-97.
'Gebet am Reformationsfeste', in Handschin, *De Wette als Prediger*, pp. 297-98.

Unpublished works

'Vorlesung über hebräisch-jüdische Archäologie', delivered in Berlin 1817–1818, Universitätsbibliothek Basel, De Wette Nachlass Section 1, 12.
'Die christliche Glaubenslehre in kurzer systematischer Zusammenstellung'. See Staehelin, *Dewettiana*, p. 21.
'Systematische Dogmatik', see Staehelin, *Dewettiana*, p. 21.
'Fragmentarische Gedanken über die Apokalypse', Universitätsbibliothek Basel, De Wette Nachlass Section 1, 6.
'Mich trieb's in ungewohnte Bahnen', poem composed on 28 December 1848 for Sophie Jung–Frey. Original with Prof. C.G. Jung, Küsnacht bei Zürich (see Staehelin, *Dewettiana*, p. 60).
'Was ist die Liebe denn?' poem. Original with Prof. C.G. Jung, (see Staehelin, *Dewettiana* p. 60).

'Introduction to Ecclesiastes', Latin lecture, Universitätsbibliothek Basel, De Wette Nachlass, Section 1, 7.

'Lectures on the Pentateuch, with first greeting of students in Basel', Universitätsbibliothek Basel, De Wette Nachlass, Section 1, 9.

'Latin address to students', Universitätsbibliothek Basel, De Wette Nachlass, Section 1, 10.

'Gedanken über das Unternehmen einer Lehranstalt für Kinder', 18 February 1826, Universitätsbibliothek Basel, De Wette Nachlass, Section 1, 12c.

LETTERS OF DE WETTE

The following is an attempt to list all the extant letters of de Wette known to me. It is probably not complete. See *Dewettiana* pp. 9-10 n. 3 for further details. This note also makes it clear that Wiegand must once have had access to many letters that are now no longer extant.

1. *Letters that exist in manuscript*

These are listed in accordance with Staehelin's classification in the De Wette Nachlass in the Universitätsbibliothek, Basel. Although these are mostly photo-copies, they are 98 per cent legible, and constitute the only collection of de Wette letters from many different sources, and thus the only resource for sustained research. For details of the location of the originals see *Dewettiana*. The originals of the many letters to Amalie von Voigt are now in the Staatsarchiv, Weimar. Where a letter is followed by an asterisk and a number, this refers to Staehelin's printed version in *Dewettiana*, e.g. *63 means p. 63 in *Dewettiana*. Where there is no such indication the letter remains unpublished. It should be noted that Staehelin hardly ever prints the whole of a letter. In the text of this book, I have indicated in the footnotes where I am citing from the unpublished portions of letters otherwise partly printed by Staehelin.

De Wette Nachlass. Universitätsbibliothek, Basel
Section 1
No. 13. Original letters to Ottilie Maria Hirzel (1792–1826) and her father Heinrich Hirzel (1766–1833).

1. 6 August 1823 (O.H.).
2. 15 August 1823 (O.H.).
3. 23 August 1823 (H.H.).
4. 7 October 1823 (H.H.).
5. 4 May 1824 (O.H.).
6. 7 May 1825 (O.H.).
7. 29 June 1825 (O.H.).
8. 28 October 1825 (O.H.).
9. 11 February 1826 (O.H.).
10. 16 February 1826 (O.H.).
11. 24 February 1826 (O.H.).
12. 22 March 1826 (O.H.).

No. 14. Original letter to Johann Joseph von Görries (1776–1848).
3 July 1844.

No. 15. Original letters to Friedrich Emanuel von Hurter (1787–1865).
1. 4 November 1836.
2. 22 March 1837.

No. 16. Original letter to Professor Alexander Schweizer (1808–88).
11 March 1843.

Section 2
A. To Karl August Böttiger (1760–1835).
1. 8 December 1798, *64.
2. 28 March 1800.
3. 5 January 1806, *64.
4. 3 February 1806.
5. 25 March 1807, *65.
6. 11 April 1808, *67.
7. 20 January 1815.
8. End of September 1825.
9. 20 September 1846, to Karl Wilhelm Böttiger (1790–1862).

B. To Jakob Friedrich Fries (1773–1843).
1. List of letters in the university library, Jena.
2. Undated, Staehelin suggests October 1822.
3. 4 June 1822, *120.
4. 21 September 1822, *122.
5. 14 November 1822.
6. 22 February 1823.
7. 28 September 1823.
8. 15 June 1824.
9. 5 February 1825.
10. 29 December 1825.
11. 28 March 1827.
12. 2 January 1828.
13. 2 August 1828.
14. 21 February 1829, *147.
15. 30 September 1829.
16. 7 March 1831, *152.
17. 30 March 1832.
18. 21 July 1837.
19. 10 June 1839.
20. 6 August 1839, *173.
21. 16 March 1841, *176.

22. 30 June 1842.
23. 8 August 1842, *177.

C. To Ludwig Friedrich von Froriep (1779–1847) (editor of *Weimarer Oppositionsblatt*).
1. 1 November 1819.
2. 10 November 1819.
3. 12 November 1819.
4. 19 November 1819.
5. 30 December 1819.
6. 14 January 1820.
7. 29 June 1821.
8. 23 September 1829.

Ca. To Wilhelm Gamper.
1. 5 February 1828.
2. 18 February 1823 (certificate of attendance at lectures).
3. 5 May 1826 (theological faculty certificate).

D. To Karl Rudolf Hagenbach (1801–74).
1. No date or place, Staehelin suggests 1829.
2. 28 July 1832.
3. 15 May 1835, *166.
4. March 1846. This 7-page letter from Rome was published in the *Kirchenblatt für die reformierte Schweiz*, 8-9 (1846), pp. 59ff.
5. 14 March 1846, *186.

E. To David Hess (1770–1843).
1. 21 June 1823.
2. 5 November 1827, *144.
3. 14 February 1832.

F. To Heinrich Hirzel (1766–1833).
1. 10 July 1820.
2. 15 July 1820.
3. 29 September–2 October 1820, *98.
3a. Postcard. 29 September 1820.
4. 2 June 1822, *119.
5. 2 July 1822, *121.
6. 17 July 1822, *121.
7. 31 October 1822, *124.
8. 4 January 1823, *125-26.
9. 25 January 1823.
10. 6 April 1823.

11. 24 April 1824, *135.
12. 29 October 1832, *157.
13. 19 November 1832, *157.
14. 29 January 1833, to Ludwig Hirzel (1801–41).
15. 23 April 1843, to Frau Hirzel.

G. To Carl Gustav Jung (1794–1864).
   1. No date.

H. To various members of the Kestner family.
   1. After 1831, to Charlotte Kestner (1788–1877).
   2. January 1832, to Johann Jakob Bischoff-Kestner.
   3. 11 August 1837, to Georg Kestner (1774–1867).
   4. 13 June 1845, to Charlotte Kestner.
   5. [?] Winter 1845–46, to August Kestner (1777–1853).
   6. 28 November 1845, to August Kestner.
   7. 18 January 1846, to August Kestner.
   8. 9 March 1846, to August Ketner, *186.
   9. 22 January 1847, to August Kestner.
   10. 22–23 July 1848, to Charlotte Kestner.

J. To Kanzler Friedrich von Müller (1779–1849).
   1. September 1822.
   2. 12 October 1822.
   3. 29 May 1824.
   4. 13 June 1825.
   5. 29 December 1825, *141-42.
   6. 26 October 1827.
   7. 18 August 1829.
   8. 29 March 1832, *154.
   9. 13 September 1836.
   10. 20 January 1844, *181–83.

K. To Karl Immanuel Nitzsch (1787–1868).
   1. 11 October 1815.
   2. 29 September 1816.
   3. 26 October 1817.
   4. 18 November 1817.
   5. 28 June 1818.

L. To Johann Caspar von Orelli (1787–1849).
   1. 15 July 1820.
   2. 2 July 1822.
   3. 26 December 1832.

M. To the Prussian Minister of Internal Affairs.
   1.   25 October 1811.
   2.   1 June 1816.

MM. To Karl Reimer.
   1.   25 November 1828
   2.   6 November 1844.

N. To Friedrich Schleiermacher (1768–1834) and Henriette Schleiermacher.
   1.   24 July 1810, *68. See also Dilthey, *Aus Schleiermachers Leben*, IV, p. 179.
   2.   7 November 1819, *91.
   3.   21 November 1819.
   4.   3 December 1819, *92.
   5.   Weimar, no date.
   6.   8 December 1819, *93.
   7.   18 February 1820, *93-94.
   8.   11 March 1820, *94.
   9.   23 May 1820, *95-96.
  10.   4 October 1820, *98.
  11.   30 December 1820, *100. See also Dilthey, *Aus Schleiermachers Leben*, IV, pp. 264-65.
  12.   20 February 1821.
  13.   18 May 1821, *101.
  14.   1 September 1821.
  15.   11–12 October 1821 (PS of 14 October), *107-108. See also Dilthey, *Aus Schleiermachers Leben*, IV, pp. 277-78.
  16.   29 December 1821 (H.S.), *109. See also Dilthey, *Aus Schleiermachers Leben*, IV, pp. 280-83.
  17.   29 December 1821 (F.S.), *109. See also Dilthey, *Aus Schleiermachers Leben*, IV, pp. 280-83.
  18.   28 September 1822, *122.
  19.   15 March 1823, *126.
  20.   11 June 1823 (H.S.), *132.
  21.   11 June 1823 (F.S.), *132. See also Dilthey, *Aus Schleiermachers Leben*, IV, pp. 312-13.
  22.   28 February 1824.
  23.   29 April 1824 (H.S.).
  24.   5 November 1830 (H.S.).

O. To Emma von Schwanenfeld.
   1.   27 January 1846.
   2.   4 February 1846.
   3.   17 October 1847.

P. To Alexander Schweizer (1808–88).
   1.   6 November 1834, *165.
   2.   20 May 1835.
   3.   7 June 1836.
   4.   30 June 1839, *173.
   5.   13 May 1840.
   6.   26 June 1840, *174.
   7.   1 August 1840.
   8.   2 July 1841.
   9.   8 January 1842.
  10.   21 March 1843.
  11.   1 July 1844.
  12.   7 December 1848.
  13.   No date.

Q. To Leonhard Usteri (1769–1853) and Leonhard Usteri (his son, 1799–1833).
   1.   2 May 1821 (father).
   2.   14 May 1821 (son).
   3.   11 May 1823 (son).
   4.   18 September 1824 (son).

R. To Alexandre Vinet (1797–1847).
   1.   23 April 1823.
   2.   15 September 1837.

S. To Amalie von Voigt (1778–1840).
a. 1820–21.
   1.   20 April 1820, *95.
   2.   25 May 1820.
   3.   18 April 1821.
   4.   11 September 1821.
   5.   17 September 1821, *105.

b. 1822–23.
   1.   26 April 1822, *117.
   2.   3 June 1822, *120.
   3.   15 July 1822.
   4.   15 September 1822, *122.
   5.   24 January 1823.
   6.   29 April 1823, *129.
   7.   Sonnet 'Die Schülerin', *130 n. 238.
   8.   12 August 1823.
   9.   21 September 1823, *133-34.

c. 1824–25.
  1. 16 January 1824; *134 says 14 January but the date is clearly 16 January and the postscript is dated 17 January.
  2. 28 February 1824, *174-75.
  3. 24 April 1824.
  4. 26 June 1824.
  5. 13 July 1824.
  6. 5 August 1824.
  7. 16 September 1824.
  8. 22 November 1824.
  9. 16 January–4 February 1825.
  10. 14 May 1825, *137-38.
  11. 11 June 1825.
  12. 31 August 1825.
  13. 14 September 1825.
  14. 22 October 1825.
  15. 28 December 1825.

d. 1826–27.
  1. Poem in handwriting of Anna Margaretha VonderMühll.
  2. 3 February 1826 (printed address spoken at the dedication of a house).
  3. 18 March 1826.
  4. 10 July 1826.
  5. 13 September 1826.
  6. 29 October 1826.
  7. 28 December 1826.
  8. 3 March 1827, *143.
  9. 4 May 1827.
  10. 26 August 1827.
  11. 17 September 1827.
  12. 26 October 1827.
  13. 26 December 1827.

e. 1828–30.
  1. 25 April 1828.
  2. 24 May 1828.
  3. 16 September 1828.
  4. 21 November 1828.
  5. 29 September 1829.
  6. 11 October 1829.
  7. 6 February 1830.
  8. 13 August 1830.

f. 1831–32.
1. 13 January 1831, *151.
2. 12 May 1831, *153.
3. 26 May 1831.
4. 28 August 1831.
5. 19 September 1831.
6. 15 December 1831.
7. 14 January 1832.
8. 20 March 1832.
9. 31 March 1832.
10. 15 July 1832. See Wiegand, *De Wette*, p. 70.
11. 6 September 1832, *156.
12. 29 December 1832, *158. See also Wiegand, *De Wette*, pp. 70-71.

g. 1833–37.
1. 28 February 1833.
2. 10 July 1834.
3. 15 September 1834, *164.
4. 11 October 1835, *166-67.
5. 22 February 1836.
6. 8 August 1836.
7. 24 October 1836.
8. 30 March 1837.

h. 1838–40.
1. 4 January 1838.
2. 15 April 1838.
3. 30 November 1838.
4. 29 May 1833 [*sic*].
5. No date.
6. 19 July 1839.
7. 16 October 1839.
8. 19 February 1840, *174.
9. 15 July 1840, *175.
10. 9 October 1840.

T. To various friends.
1. 11 September 1808, to Johannes von Müller (1752–1809).
2. 26 August 1811, to Johann Georg Zimmer (1777–1853).
3. 1 March 1819, addressee unknown (possibly Lücke).
4. 18 October 1822, to Ludwig Lucius, Buchhändler.
5. 22 November 1823, addressee unknown.
6. 17 April 1824, to Ludwig Tieck (1773–1853).
7. 14 October 1829, to Adam Walther Strobal.

8. 11 October 1835, to Heinrich Karl Abraham Eichstädt.
9. 26 July 1841, to a friend in Frankfurt (Kestner?).
10. 6 July 1846, to Jakob Christian Benjamin Mohr.
11. 13 June 1847, to an unknown 'verehrte Freundin'.
12. 1 May 1848, to Edouard Reuss.
13. 11 July 1848, addressee unknown.
14. 21 September 1848, to Gerald Meyer von Knonan.
15. No date, to Heinrichshofer (publisher in Magdeburg).

Nachlass Jung. Universitätsbibliothek, Basel. Section 14
To Sophie Frey (from letter 5 to Sophie Jung–Frey).
1. 15 August 1832.
2. 16 August [?1832].
3. 8 May 1848.
4. Autumn 1848.
5. 22 December 1848.
6. 20 January 1849.
7. 24 March 1849.
8. April 1849.
9. No date.
10. 1846, to C.G. Jung on his birthday.

Spittler Archiv. Staatsarchiv, Basel
Section 3
4 October 1820, to Anna Schlatter.

Section 4
Booklet of correspondence between de Wette and Spittler. Letters from de Wette to Spittler in this booklet.
4. 3 October 1825.
6. 12 November 1825.
8. 20 November 1825.

Additional letters.
December 1826.
5 June 1827.
27 October 1827.
15 October 1829.
13 January 1830.
4 February 1830.
17 March 1830.
21 May 1830.
24 May (no year).

20 October (no year).

9 December 1846.

Universitäts-Archiv. Staatsarchiv, Basel
Section I, 13: Professoren, Allgemeines
Letter from de Wette 29 (December?) 1823.

Erziehungsakten. Staatsarchiv, Basel
Section X, 9
Letters of de Wette.
  29 December 1823.
  28 June 1823.

Section Y, 15
 25b. 21 December 1822, to the Bürgermeister and chancellor.

4 letters to the Curatel.
 31. 2 July 1823.
 16b. 18 March 1824.
 19b. 12 October 1824.
 38. 13 December 1826.

Section Y, 7
  7 January 1830, to the Bürgermeister and Curatel.
  26 April 1830, to the chancellor of the university.
  15 November 1830, to the Erziehungsrat.

Voss and Ernestine III, 5, Boie–Voss–Nachlass. Schleswig-Holsteinische
Landesbibliothek
  31 March 1819, copy by Louise Voss (née Engler) of de Wette's letter to
  Frau Sand.

Manuscript Letters of de Wette in the Staatsbibliothek Preussischer Kulturbesitz,
(West-) Berlin
Signatur: Darmstaedter 2b 1840 (13) M.L. de Wette.
 1. 25 October 1811, to the Kultusministerium, Berlin.
 2. 1 June 1816, to the Kultusministerium, Berlin.
 3. 13 June 1847, to a 'verehrte Freundin' [see Nachlass T 11].
 4. 6 July 1846, to 'mein verehrter alter Freund'.
 5. 11 October 1835, to a 'hochzuverehrende Herr und Freund'.
 6. No date, to a 'verehrter Freund'.

Signatur: 141 (Adam) k. 49, W.M.L. de Wette.
 1. 19 March 1843, to Dr Tischendorf in Rome.

2. 6 November 1817, to a 'hochgeehrter Herr'.
3. 1 March 1838, to [Karl Wilhelm?] Böttiger.
4. 28 January 1823, to an unnamed correspondent.
5. 30 December 1815, to an unnamed correspondent.
6. 7 June 1812, to Frau Griesbach.
7. No date or correspondent given.
8. 31 August 1848, to M.L. Brönner.
9. No date or correspondent given.

Signatur: Auto I / 1158
  1 October 1821, to Ludwig Lucius

In the Nationale Forschungs- und Gedenkstätte Weimar
  1817, to Gottlob Schwabe.

Letters in the Possession of Professor C.G. Jung (or his family). See Staehelin,
Dewettiana, *pp. 43, 51, 62-63*
  6 letters to C.G. Jung, 2 dated 15 July 1829 and 30 July 1829.
  3 letters to C.G. Jung, 1 dated 18 August 1836.
  5 letters to C.G. Jung, 1 dated 16 June 1848, 1 dated 1 June 1849.
  8 letters to Sophie Jung-Frey.

2. Published Letters of de Wette

A. To Jakob Friedrich Fries.
a. In Henke, *Jakob Friedrich Fries*, pp. 344-64.
  1. 16 October 1810.
  2. 12 December 1810.
  3. 25 December 1810.
  4. 19 April 1811.
  5. 26 September 1811.
  6. 11 November 1811.
  7. 22 February 1812.
  8. 25 April 1812.
  9. 15 June 1812.
  10. 16 February 1813.
  11. 5 November 1813.
  12. 17 October 1814.
  13. 31 December 1814.
  14. 4 March 1815.
  15. 28 April 1815.
  16. 20 October 1815.
  17. End of March 1816.
  18. 3 April 1816.

18 February 1806, to Eberhardine's mother (pp. 19-20).

No date, to Reimer (p. 40).

9 April [?], no year, to the families Voigt and Günter (p. 43).

No date, to Heinrich Hirzel [?] (p. 45).

After 13 July 1820, to Günter (p. 46).

No date but presumably 1820, to Reimer (p. 48).

Before 9 February 1822 [?], to Reimer (p. 50).

9 February 1822, to Reimer (p. 50).

9 December 1820, to Reimer (p. 51).

20 August 1821, to Reimer (pp. 54-55).

Between 7 and 16 September 1821, to an unnamed correspondent in Weimar (p. 56).

12 February 1834, to Reimer (p. 58 n. 1).

12 October 1821, to Reimer (pp. 62-63).

31 January 1822, to Reimer (p. 63).

May 1822, to Reimer (p. 66).

24 January 1823, to a correspondent in Weimar (p. 68).

7 March 1831, to Reimer (p. 69).

15 July 1832, to Amalie von Voigt (see above) (p. 70).

29 December 1832, to Amalie von Voigt (see above) (pp. 70-71).

11 October 1835, to an unnamed correspondent (p. 71).

2 June, no year, to Heinrich Hirzel (pp. 79-80).

No date, to Reimer (p. 80).

September 1822, to an unnamed correspondent (p. 80).

24 September 1822, to Reimer (p. 80).

Christmas 1825, to an unnamed correspondent (p. 81).

8 February 1833, to Reimer, (p. 83).

June 1842, to an unnamed correspondent (p. 85).

Wiegand mentions 19 extensive letters about de Wette's visit to Rome (pp. 86-88).

1848, to an unnamed correspondent (p. 91).

D. To the church council of St Katherine Church, Braunschweig, in Venturini, *Beiträge*.

5 January 1821 [*sic*, but must be 1822] (pp. 60-62).

No date but several days after 29 December 1821 (pp. 138-139).

20 February 1822 (pp. 140-141).

7 March 1822 (p. 141).

E. In W.M.L. de Wette; *Aktensammlung über die Entlassung des Professors D. de Wette vom theologischen Lehramt zur Berlin* (Leipzig, 1820).

31 March 1819, to Frau Sand (pp. 2-6).

4 October 1819, to Berlin University Senate (pp. 12-14).

16 October 1819, to King Friedrich Wilhelm (pp. 16-20).

16 October 1819, to the Berlin Theological Faculty (pp. 20-34).

16 October 1819, to von Altenstein (pp. 35-36).

19 October 1819, to the Berlin University Senate (pp. 36-40).

28 October 1819, to von Altenstein (pp. 43-44).

18 November 1819, to von Altenstein (pp. 45-46).

3. Miscellaneous

To H.E.G. Paulus.

25 April 1805, in K.A. Reuchlin-Meldegg, *Heinrich Eberhard Gottlob Paulus und seiner Zeit* (Stuttgart, 1853), II, p. 270.

23 April 1839, in H.E.G. Paulus, *Skizzen aus meiner Bildungs- und Lebensgeschichte* (Heidelberg and Leipzig, 1839), pp. 183-84, and Staehelin, *Dewettiana*, pp. 171-73.

To Johann Georg Zimmer, in H.W.B. Zimmer (ed.), *Johann Georg Zimmer und die Romantiker: Ein Beitrag zur Geschichte der Romantik* (Frankfurt-am-Main, 1888).

16 February 1813 (p. 314).

22 June 1813 (pp. 314-15) (part in Staehelin, *Dewettiana*, p. 72).

12 December 1813 (pp. 315-16) (part in Staehelin, *Dewettiana*, p. 73).

28 April 1815 (p. 326).

5 September 1815 (p. 327).

10 February 1817 (pp. 335-36).

To Friedrich Wilken.

6 letters, in A. Stoll, *Der Geschichtsschreiber Friedrich Wilken* (Cassel, 1896), pp. 6ff.

To Heinrich Schmidt.

27 August 1846, in H. Schmidt, *Erinnerungen eines weimarischen Veteranen* (Leipzig, 1856), p. 45, and Staehelin, *Dewettiana*, p. 187.

To August Tweesten.

30 October 1826, in G. Heinrich, *August Tweesten nach Tagebüchern und Briefen* (Berlin, 1889), p. 395, and Staehelin, *Dewettiana*, pp. 142-43.

To Peter von Bohlen.

11 October 1835, in J. Voigt (ed.), *Autobiographie des ordent. Professor der orientalischen Sprachen und Literatur an der Universität zu Königsberg Dr Peter von Bohlen* (Königsberg, 1842), pp. 149-50.

SELECT BIBLIOGRAPHY

(A full bibliography of works about de Wette is in Handschin, pp. 331ff. Handschin also gives [pp. 330-31] a valuable list of reviews of de Wette's publications.)

Antiquar J. Meyri in Basel. Catalogue No. 40. Auction on 31 July 1850 of the libraries of de Wette and F. Hitzig.

Bachman, J., *Ernst Wilhelm Hengstenberg: Sein Leben und Wirken*, I (Gütersloh, 1879).

Beiser, F.C., *The Fate of Reason: German Philosophy from Kant to Fichte* (Cambridge, MA: Harvard University Press, 1987).

Bigler, R.M., *The Politics of German Protestantism: The Rise of the Protestant Church Elite in Prussia 1815–1848* (Berkeley: University of California Press, 1972).

Bornhausen, K., 'Wider den Neofriesianismus in der Theologie', *ZTK* 20 (1910), pp. 341-417.

Bornkamm, H., 'Die theologische Fakultät Heidelberg' in *Ruperto-Carola, Aus der Geschichte der Universität Heidelberg und ihrer Fakultäten* (Heidelberg, 1961).

Brosses, C. de, *Du culte des dieux fétisches: Ou parallele de l'ancienne religion de l'Egypt avec la religion de Nigritie* (Paris, 1760).

Brown, C., *Jesus in European Protestant Thought 1778–1860* (Studies in Historical Theology, 1; Durham, NC: Labryinth Press, 1985).

Constant y de Rebecque, B., *De la religion considerée dans sa source, ses formers et ses developpements* (6 vols.; Paris, 1824–31).

Creuzer, G.J., *Symbolik und Mythologie der alten Völker, besonders der Griechen* (4 vols.; Leipzig, 1810–12).

Crowther, P., *The Kantian Sublime: From Morality to Art* (Oxford: Clarendon Press, 1989).

Dibelius, O., *Das königliche Predigerseminar zu Wittenberg 1817–1917* (Berlin–Lichterfeld: Verlag von Edwin Runge, n. d. [presumably, 1917]).

Dilthey, W., *Leben Schleiermachers* (2 vols.; Berlin: de Gruyter, 1966–70).

—*Aus Schleiermachers Leben in Briefen*, V (Berlin, 2nd edn, 1860 [repr. Berlin: de Gruyter, 1974]).

Elliger, W., *150 Jahre theologische Fakultät Berlin* (Berlin: de Gruyter, 1960).

Euler, C., *Friedrich Ludwig Jahn: Sein Leben und Wirken* (Stuttgart, 1881).

Flanagan, S., *Hildegard of Bingen: A Visionary Life* (London: SPCK, 1989).

Foerster, E., *Die Entstehung der preussischen Landeskirche unter der Regierung König Friedrich Wilhelm des Dritten*, I (Tübingen: Mohr, 1905).

Franke, O., *Herder und das weimarische Gymnasium* (Hamburg, 1898).

Freiherr v. Reichlin-Meldegg, K.A., *Heinrich Eberhard Gottlob Paulus und seine Zeit* (Stuttgart, 1853).

Fries, H. (ed.), *Klassiker der Theologie. II. Von Richard Simon bis Dietrich Bonhoeffer* (Munich: Beck, 1983).

Bibliography 303

Fries, J.F., *Wissen, Glaube und Ahndung* (Jena, 1805 [new edn ed. L. Nelson; Göttingen: Vandenhoeck & Ruprecht, 1905 (with same pagination)]).

—*Dialogues on Morality and Religion* (ed. D.Z. Phillips; Oxford: Basil Blackwell, 1982).

—*Julius und Evagoras: Ein philosophischer Roman* (ed. W. Bousset; Göttingen: Vandenhoeck & Ruprecht, 1910).

—*Neue oder anthropologische Kritik der Vernunft* (Heidelberg, 1807; repr. of 2nd edn 1828, in *Sämtliche Schriften* [ed. G. König and L. Geldsetzer; Aalen: Scientia Verlag, 1967]).

—*Handbuch der praktischen Philosophie oder der philosophischen Zwecklehre*, I (Heidelberg, 1818; repr. in *Sämtliche Schriften*, X [1970]).

—Review of de Wette's *Über Religion und Theologie*, in *Heidelbergische Jahrbücher der Literatur* 19 (1816), pp. 369-87.

—*Von deutscher Philosophie Art und Kunst: Ein Votum für Friedrich Heinrich Jacobe gegen F.W. Schelling* (Heidelberg, 1812; repr. in *Sämtliche Schriften*, XXIV [1978]), pp. 623-728.

Gerlach, E.L. von, *Aufzeichnungen aus seinem Leben und Wirken* (Schwerin: F. Bahn, 1903).

Graf, F.W., *Kritik und Pseudo-Spekulation: David Friedrich Strauss als Dogmatiker im Kontext der positionellen Theologie seiner Zeit* (Münchener Monographien zu historischen und systematischen Theologie, 7; Munich: Chr. Kaiser Verlag, 1982).

Griesbach, J.J., 'Diss. qua Marci euangelium totum e Matth. et Lucae commentariis decerptum esse monstratur', in *Commentationes Theologicae* (ed. J.C. Velthusen; Leipzig, 1794).

Hagenbach, K.R., *Die theologische Schule Basels und ihre Lehrer von Stiftung der Hochschule 1460 bis zu de Wette's Tod 1849* (Basel, 1860).

—*Rede bei der Beerdigung des Herrn W.M.L. de Wette* (Basel, 1849).

—*Wilhelm Martin Leberecht de Wette: Eine akademische Gedächtnisrede mit Anmerkungen und Beilagen* (Leipzig, 1850).

Handschin, P., *Wilhelm Martin Leberecht de Wette als Prediger und Schriftsteller* (Basel: Helbing & Lichtenhahn, 1958).

Haym, R., *Die romantische Schule: Ein Beitrag zur Geschichte des deutschen Geistes* (Berlin, 1870 [repr., Darmstadt: Wissenschaftliche Buchgesellschaft, 1977]).

Heiderich, M.W., *The German Novel of 1800: A Study of Popular Prose Fiction* (Bern: Peter Lang, 1982).

Heltner, H., *Geschichte der deutschen Literatur im achtzehnten Jahrhundert* (Berlin: Aufbau Verlag, 1961).

Henke, E.L.T., 'Berliner Briefe von de Wette an Fries, von 1811 bis 1819', *Monatsblätter für innere Zeitgeschichte* 32 (1868), pp. 90-106.

—*Jakob Friedrich Fries, aus seinem handschriftlichen Nachlasse dargestellt* (Leipzig, 1867).

Hensel, W., *Preussische Bildnisse des 19. Jahrhunderts* (Berlin: Nationalgalerie, 1981).

Hirsch, E., *Geschichte der neuern evangelischen Theologie*, V (Gütersloh, 1964 [repr. Münster: Stenderhoff, 1984]).

Hupfeld, R., 'W.M. Leberecht de Wette und Hermann Hupfeld: Ein Briefwechsel aus theologisch und politisch bewegter Zeit', in *Neue Zeitschrift für systematische Theologie und Religionsphilosophie* 5 (1963), pp. 54-96.

Jacobi, J.L., *Erinnerungen an den Baron Ernst von Kottwitz* (Halle, 1882).

Jenny, E., 'Wie de Wette nach Basel kam', *Basler Jahrbuch* (1941).

Kant, I., *Der Streit der Fakultäten*, in *Kants Werke: Akademie Textausgabe*, VII (Berlin: Preussische Akademie der Wissenschaften, 1907 [repr. Berlin: de Gruyter, 1968]).

Keil, R., and R. Keil, *Die burschenschaftliche Wartburgfeste von 1817 und 1867* (Jena, 1868).

Keller, R.A., *Geschichte der Universität Heidelberg im ersten Jahrzehnt nach der Reorganisation durch Karl Friedrich 1803–1813* (Heidelberger Abhandlungen zur mittleren und neueren Geschichte, 40; Heidelberg: C. Winter, 1913).

Keyser, F. (ed.), *Reformations-Almanach für Luthers Verehrer auf das evangelische Jubeljahr 1817* (Erfurt, 1817).

Kiefer, R., *Die beiden Formen der Religion des Als-ob: Hauptsächlich dargestellt an de Wette und Overbeck* (Pädagogisches Magazin, Heft 1359; ed. H. Vachinger; Langensalza: H. Beyer & Sons, 1932).

Kitchen, M., *The Political Economy of Germany 1815–1914* (London: Croom Helm, 1978).

Kober, J., *Christian Friedrich Spittlers Leben* (Basel, 1887).

Lenz, M., 'Zur Entlassung de Wettes', in *Philotesia: Paul Kleinert zum LXX Geburtstag dargebracht* (ed. A. Harnack *et al.*; Berlin: Trowitzsch & Son, 1907).

—*Geschichte der Königliche Wilhelms-Universität zu Berlin*, I, II (Berlin: Buchhandlung des Waisenhauses, 1910–18).

Lindt, A., 'C.F. Spittler und W.M.L. de Wette: Zur Begegnung von Erweckungsfrömmigkeit und Universitätstheologie im Basel des 19. Jahrhunderts', in *Gottesreich und Menschenreich, Ernst Staehelin zum 80. Geburtstag* (Basel: Helbing & Lichtenhahn, 1969).

Lowth, R., *Praelectiones de sacra poesie hebraeorum* (trans. R. Gregory; London, 1787).

Lücke, F., 'Zur freundschaftlichen Erinnerung an D. Wilhelm Martin Leberecht de Wette', *TSK* (1850), pp. 497-535.

Lündtke, A., *Police and State in Prussia 1815–1850* (trans. from *'Gemeinwahl' Polizei und 'Festungspraxis': Staatliche Gewaltsamkeit und innere Verwaltung in Preussen 1815–1850* [Göttingen: Vandenhoeck & Ruprecht, 1982]; Cambridge: Cambridge University Press, 1989).

McClelland, C.E., *State, Society and University in Germany* 1700–1914 (Cambridge: Cambridge University Press, 1980).

Meiners, C., *Allgemeine kritische Geschichte der Religionen* (Hannover, 1806-1807).

Merx, A., 'Die morgenländischen Studien und Professoren an der Universität Heidelberg vor und besonders im 19. Jahrhundert', in *Heidelberger Professoren aus dem 19. Jahrhundert* (Heidelberg: C. Winter, 1903).

Mildenberger, F., *Geschichte der deutschen evangelischen Theologie in 19. und 20. Jahrhundert* (Stuttgart: Kohlhammer, 1981).

Müller, J.G., *Abriss meines Lebenslaufes* (Basel, 1875).

Nipperdey, T., *Deutsche Geschichte 1800–1866, Bürgerwelt und starker Staat* (Munich: Beck, 1987).

Otto, R., *Kantisch-Fries'sche Religionsphilosophie und ihre Anwendung auf die Theologie: Zur Einleitung in die Glaubenslehre für Studenten der Theologie* (Tübingen: Mohr, 1909).

—*The Philosophy of Religion* (trans. E.B. Dicker; London: Williams & Norgate, 1931).

—'Jakob Friedrich Fries' Religions-philosophie', *ZTK* 19 (1909), pp. 31-56, 108-61, 204-42.

Rogerson, J.W., *Myth in Old Testament Interpretation* (Berlin: de Gruyter, 1974).

—*Old Testament Criticism in the Nineteenth Century: England and Germany* (London: SPCK, 1984).

Rohls, J., *Profile des neuzeitlichen Protestantismus*, I (ed. F.W. Graf; Gütersloh: Gerd Mohn, 1990).

Roller, T., *Reimer und sein Kreis: Zur Geschichte des politischen Denkens in Deutschland um die Zeit der Befreiungskriege* (Berlin, 1924).

Sander, F., *D. Friedrich Lücke, Abt zu Bursfelde und Professor der Theologie in Göttingen (1791–1855)* (Hannover-Linden, 1891).

Schelling, F.W.J., 'Vorlesungen über die Methode des akademischen Studiums', in M. Schröter (ed.), *Schellings Werke*, III (Munich: Beck, 1927), pp. 229-374.

—'Philosophie der Kunst', Schröter (ed.) in *Schellings Werke*, III, pp. 375-507.

Schiller, F., *Über Kunst und Wirklichkeit: Schriften und Briefe zur Ästhetik* (Leipzig: Philipp Reclam, 1975).

Schleiden, K.A. (ed.), *Friedrich Gottlieb Klopstock, ausgewählte Werke* (Munich: Karl Hanser, 1962).

Schleiermacher, F.D.E., *Die Glaubenslehre* (Berlin, 1830).

Schmigalla, H. (ed.), '*Wir hatten gebauen ein stattliches Haus . . .* ': *Beiträge zur Geschichte der deutschen Burschenschaft 1815–1848/9* (Jena: Friedrich-Schiller-Universität, 1989).

Schoeps, H.J., *Aus den Jahren preussischer Not und Erneuerung: Tagebücher und Briefe der Gebrüder Gerlach und ihres Kreises 1805–20* (Berlin: Haude & Spenersche Verlagsbuchhandlung, 1963).

Schubert, G.H. von, *Der Erwerb aus einem vergangenem und die Erwartungen von einem zukünftigen Leben*, I (Erlangen, 1854).

Sheehan, J.J., *German History 1770–1866* (Oxford: Clarendon Press, 1989).

Smend, R., *Wilhelm Martin Leberecht de Wettes Arbeit am Alten und am Neuen Testament* (Basel: Helbing & Lichtenhahn, 1958).

—'Nachtrag zur Bibliographie de Wettes', *TZ* 23 (1967), pp. 206-208.

—'Wilhelm Martin Leberecht de Wette', in *Deutsche Alttestamentler in drei Jahrhunderten* (Göttingen: Vandenhoeck & Ruprecht, 1989).

—'Wilhelm Martin Leberecht de Wette (1780–1849)', in *Theologen des Protestantismus im 19. und 20. Jahnhundert*, I (ed. M. Greschat; Stuttgart: Kohlhammer, 1978).

Sonderman, E.F., *Karl August Böttiger, literarischer Journalist der Goethezeit in Weimar* (Mitteilungen zur Theatergeschichte der Goethezeit, 7; Bonn: Bouvier, 1983).

Staehelin, A., *Geschichte der Universität Basel 1818–1835* (Studien zur Geschichte der Wissenschaften in Basel, 7; Basel: Helbing & Lichtenhahn, 1959).

Staehelin, E., *Dewettiana: Forschungen und Texte zu Wilhelm Martin Leberecht de Wettes Leben und Werk* (Studien zur Geschichte der Wissenschaften in Basel, 2; Basel: Helbing & Lichtenhahn, 1956).

—'Kleine Dewettiana,' *TZ* (1957), pp. 33ff.

Stephan, H., *Geschichte der deutschen evangelischen Theologie seit dem deutschen Idealismus* (Berlin: Töpelmann, 2nd edn, 1960).

Stier, R., *Siebzig ausgewühlte Psalmen nach Ordnung und Zusammenhang ausgelegt* (Halle, 1834).

Strich, F., *Die Mythologie in der deutschen Literatur von Klopstock bis Wagner*, I (Halle: Niemeyer, 1910 [repr. Bern: Francke, 1970]).

Tieck, L., and J. Wackenroder, *Phantasien über die Kunst* (Hamburg, 1799).

Toland, J., *Christianity not Mysterious or a Treatise, Shewing that there is Nothing in the Gospel contrary to Reason* (London, 1696).

Tuckett, C., *The Revival of the Griesbach Hypothesis: An Analysis and Appraisal* (Cambridge: Cambridge University Press, 1983).

Venturini, K., *Beiträge zur neuesten Geschichte des Protestantismus in Deutschland. I. Des Doctor W.M.L. de Wette einstimmige und doch verworfene Wahl zum Prediger an der St Katerinen Kirche in Braunschweig* (Leipzig, 1822).

Vincent, J.M., *Leben und Werk des frühen Eduard Reuss* (Göttingen: Vandenhoeck & Ruprecht, 1990).

Vinet, A., *Oeuvres Ve serie—Letters*, I (ed. Pierre Bovet; Lausanne: Payot, 1947–49).

Weiss, G., 'Wilhelm Martin Leberecht de Wette', in *Die christliche Welt* (1911), pp. 266-71.

Weiss, J., *Life and Correspondence of Theodore Parker*, I (New York, 1864 [German trans. in A. Alther, *Theodor Parker in seinem Leben und Wirken* (St Gallen, 1895)]).

Wessell, L.P., Jr, *The Philosophical Background to Friedrich Schiller's Aesthetics of Living Form* (European University Studies, 578; Frankfurt: Peter Lang, 1982).

Wiegand, A., 'De Wette als Knabe und Jüngling in Ulla, Grosskromsdorf, Buttstädt und Weimar', *Kirchen und Schulblatt* 21 (1872), pp. 20-25.

—'De Wette in Heidelberg', *Kirchen und Schulblatt* 23 (1874), p. 82.

—'De Wette in Jena, 1799–1807', *Kirchen und Schulblatt* 24 (1875), pp. 311-14, 338-43, 355-9.

—*W.M.L. de Wette (1780–1849): Eine Säkularschrift* (Erfurt, 1879).

Zimm, A. (ed.), *Berlin (Ort)* (Ergänzungsheft 286 zu Petermanns geographischen Mitteilungen; Darmstadt: Wissenschaftliche Buchgesellschaft, 1990).

Zimmer, H.W.B. (ed.), *Johann Georg Zimmer und die Romantiker: Ein Beitrag zur Geschichte der Romantik* (Frankfurt, 1888).

INDEXES

INDEX OF BIBLICAL REFERENCES

OLD TESTAMENT

INDEX OF NAMES

Note: every effort has been made to trace the intials of modern authors and persons referred to, but in some cases the initials are not given in the sources, and the persons concerned are not dealt with in, for example, the *Allgemeine Deutsche Biographie*.

JOURNAL FOR THE STUDY OF THE OLD TESTAMENT

Supplement Series